THE REGIMENTAL COLORS

FROM DONIPHAN TO VERDUN

The Official History of the
140th Infantry

By
EVAN ALEXANDER EDWARDS
Regimental Chaplain *and*
Official Historian

The Naval & Military Press Ltd

Published by

The Naval & Military Press Ltd
Unit 5 Riverside, Brambleside
Bellbrook Industrial Estate
Uckfield, East Sussex
TN22 1QQ England

Tel: +44 (0)1825 749494

www.naval-military-press.com
www.nmarchive.com

In reprinting in facsimile from the original, any imperfections are inevitably reproduced and the quality may fall short of modern type and cartographic standards.

140TH GRAVES

Dedication

To
Those Good Comrades,
Loyal Friends and
Faithful Soldiers
The Men of the One Hundred and Fortieth
Who Sleep in France
"Heroes of the Wooden Cross"
this Book
is Dedicated

CONTENTS

			Page
Chap.	I.	THE THIRD AND SIXTH MISSOURI	9
Chap.	II.	CAMPAIGNING AT CAMP DONIPHAN	15
Chap.	III.	WITH THE BRITISH LION	21
Chap.	IV.	ALSATIAN DAYS	33
Chap.	V.	SWINGING INTO LINE FOR THE BIG DRIVE	48
Chap.	VI.	THE FIVE DAYS	57
Chap.	VII.	VERDUN	115
Chap.	VIII.	THE ARMISTICE, AND THE DAYS AFTER	123
Chap.	IX.	HOMEWARD BOUND	139
Chap.	X.	THE MEN BEHIND THE GUNS	147
		Divisional, Brigade and Regimental Commanders	148
		Roster of Officers 140th Infantry	149
		*Alphabetic Roster of Men, with Records	151
		*Alphabetic List of Losses, with Records	214
		National Guard Roster Third Missouri	237
		National Guard Roster Sixth Missouri	250
		List Distinguished Service Crosses and Citations	260

*According to Statistics of Personnel Section 140th Infantry.

ILLUSTRATIONS

The Regimental Colors - - - - - Frontispiece

	Page
Graves in the Battlefield	2
Chaplain Edwards	7
Colonel Albert Linxwiler	8
Brig. Gen. Chas. I. Martin	14
Lt. Wm. F. Ward, Lt. Frank Lott	17
Col. Wm. Newman	18
Maj. John W. Armour	24
Col. Bennett C. Clark	32
German Front Lines and German Trenches in Alsace	34
The Chaplain's Orchestra	47
Lt. Col. C. E. Delaplane	56
Lt. Col. Fred C. Lemmon	60
Capt. Rexroad, Lt. Holden, Capt. Kenady, Lt. Robertson	62
The Battlefield	66
Sgt. Raynor, Sgt. Tanner, Lt. Scott, Lt. Compton	70
Roy Roberts, Lt. Dwyer, Maj. Wm. A. Smith, Capt. Ray E. Seitz	72
Corp. Ritter, Pvt. Engberg, Sgt. Maj. Sayre	74
Capt. Rolla B. Holt	76
German Guns Captured by 140th	77
Two Views of Exermont	78
Maj. Murray Davis	80
Wayne R. Berry	82
Where the Line Held	84
Capt. John H. Pleasants, Maj. Ralph E. Truman	84
Capt. J. L. Milligan, Lt. Eustace Smith, Lt. Samuel T. Adams, Pvt. Stigall	86
Pvt. Fred Price and Pvt. Albert Bogen	88
Maj. E. W. Slusher, M. C.	94
Map of Route of Advance	100
Marching Up to Verdun	114
Maj. Gen. Traub Shaking Hands	118
Officers of First Battalion, 140th	122
Post Office Detail and Pont sur Meuse	124
Maj. Gen. Traub Reviewing 140th Inf.	128
Mess Line, and Some Friends from Missouri	130
Maj. Frank G. Ward and His Huskies	132
Wanderings of 140th Inf. in France	136
Lt. Col. Lemmon, Capt. Whitthorne, Sgt. Mace	138
The Band's Last Tune in France	138
Marching to the Nansemond, Homeward Bound, and Looking for Land	140
Officers of 140th Inf. Camp Stuart, Va.	144

(G. O. 11)
HEADQUARTERS SECOND ARMY,
AMERICAN EXPEDITIONARY FORCES,

GENERAL ORDERS March 7, 1919.
No. 11.

1. Upon the departure of the 35th Division from the Second Army for return to the United States, the Commanding General of the Army desires to congratulate the Division upon its services to its country in France. Organized and trained in the United States, it received a special training with the British Army in France beginning in June, 1918. In July it occupied the GERARDMER sector with the French and it executed various successful raids such as the HILSENFIRST and the MATTLE raids upon which it was highly complimented and received decorations from the French with whom it was serving. In the GERARDMER sector it covered and protected effectively a tremendous front.

In September the Division backed up the First American Army during its preparations in the ST. MIHIEL salient.

In the end of September the Division attacked as a part of the First Army in the great VERDUN-ARGONNE battle. It stormed and took VAUQUOIS Hill and Bois de ROSSIGNOL, two strong points of the German defensive line, and it afterward took the formidable positions near CHEPPY, VARRENNES, CHARPENTRY and BAULNY, and afterward MONTREBEAU woods and EXERMONT. It remained in the battle five days, executing five separate attacks and losing over six thousand officers and men. The Commanding General of the First Army commended the Division for its fighting spirit.

During the five days, battle the Division was opposed by some of the best divisions of the German Army, and from them captured over one thousand officers and men and large quantities of stores and material.

Relieved in the great battle of VERDUN-ARGONNE from the fighting line for rest, the Division after two weeks breathing spell was placed in the active SOMMEDIEUE sector southeast of VERDUN, where for three weeks it harried the enemy with patrols and raids and deeply penetrated his lines, unsettling his morale.

Relieved again about November 9th from the SOMMEDIEUE sector for rest it went into cantonment in preparation for early operations against the enemy in the vicinity of METZ. The Armistice of November 11th ended the war.

From the Armistice through a period of trying waiting to date the Division's interest in military duty has not flagged; its appearance, condition and state of readiness have steadily improved. Upon these the Commander-in-Chief of the American Expeditionary Forces has Congratulated the Division, and to his congratulation the Commanding General of the Second Army now wishes to add his congratulations and best wishes.

By command of Lieutenant General BULLARD:

STUART HEINTZELMAN,
Official: Chief of Staff.
ALLEN SMITH, JR.,
Adjutant General. Form 11-500
Printed by G-2 C. Second Army.

CHAPLAIN EVAN A. EDWARDS

COL. ALBERT LINXWILER
Who took the 140th over and brought it back.

CHAPTER I.

The Old Third and the Old Sixth

Take a map of the United States. Draw two lines cutting a wide strip down the center from North to South. This section will cover the territory whose drafted men showed the finest physical and mental standard. On either side East and West the percentage of drafted men passing the physical examination ranged from 50 to 65 percent. But in these Middle Western States the percentage ranged from 60 to 80, and in most cases well above 70 percent.

The broad stretches of country with men working in the open, and the small number of large cities may account in part for this, but it does not account for the spirit of the men. In the 140th Infantry there was a strength, a purpose, a power coming from the disciplined combination of a large number of strong men. A National Guard organization, part of it had gained some experience. But all of its men were eager to go to the defense of the National Honor, and when the supreme test came they fought and died wonderfully.

The reason is to be found in their ancestry and rearing. Their fathers were strong men; their mothers were brave women. Cities stand today where a generation ago there were open fields. It is but a short while since this was virgin country. The forbears of these men were pioneers. Strong and virile, generous and just, quick to defend their rights, eager to seize what they desired, their faults and virtues alike great. Conquering a new country, they grew apt in meeting emergencies, accustomed to bloodshed, fearless and determined. They were representatives of the Great American Spirit. And they bequeathed to their sons ruddy health, courage, strength, and a loyal love for the Nation.

When the time came these men proved worthy of their sires. The regiment was All-Missouri, but it had many Kansas men. Lt. Col. Lemmon, Captain Grigg, Captain Rexroad, Lt. Reid, Lt. Sullivan, Lt Eustace Smith, the Chaplain, and more than 400 others hailed from the Sunflower state.

I shall never forget my introduction to it. As Chaplain of the old First Kansas, I lost my place to make room for the new Chaplain of the 137th (formed of the 1st and 2nd Kansas). My Colonel, a splendid officer, Wilder Metcalf, was sent to Camp Beauregard with the rank of Brigadier General. He is a man of marked soldierly ability, and could have counted in France. When, on the first of October, I was transferred to the 140th it was not an unpleasant announcement. A good friend loaned me his horse to ride over and report. I confess I made a wide detour, dreading to meet the new Colonel and the officers. Only the Sixth was there, the Third arriving a few days later.

When I reported to Col. Linxwiler he welcomed me, and said "We have no Chaplain, and this regiment surely needs one." That evening there was a dinner for the officers of the Sixth—their last meeting as an organization, and I was given a hearty and friendly welcome. I slept that night a happier man than I had been for days, and that was the beginning of a pleasant association to last nearly two years. And as I came to know these men better, and to know the men of the Third, I grew more and more thankful that my lot had been thrown with them. It was not long until I came to know the manhood of the regiment—and was praying God to make me fit to go through it all with such real men.. Chaplain James Small of Kansas City had been Chaplain of the Third.

Through some error his papers did not go through, and he was not in Federal Service. But a very large number of the regiment were of his faith. He should have been Chaplain of the 140th, and I placed him to the front all I possibly could. He is a man of the finest type, with a fine spirit and a great big heart. Later he served with the 110th Sanitary Train. For ten months I was the only Chaplain the 140th had, but I always felt he would have made a better Chaplain for this splendid regiment than I.

THE THIRD MISSOURI INFANTRY

The Third Regiment was organized at Kansas City, Missouri, on April 3, 1886. The first commanding officer was Colonel Milton Moore, who was succeeded by Colonel L. E. Erwin on May 7, 1891. Colonel Erwin was succeeded by Colonel Nathan P. Simonds on July 12, 1893. Colonel Simonds was succeeded by Colonel George P. Gross on October 24, 1895. Colonel Gross commanded the Regiment during its federal service in the Spanish-American War. Upon the recognition of the Regiment after the Spanish-American War, Colonel Fred W. Fleming was made its regimental commander and served until January 12, 1901, when he was succeeded by Colonel Cusil Lechtman who succeeded by Colonel Fred A. Lamb on January 1, 1913. Colonel Philip J. Kealy was commissioned Colonel on June 29, 1916.

The Regiment volunteered for service under the call of the President on the declaration of war against Spain and was mustered into the federal service at Jefferson Barracks, May 14, 1898 as the

Third Missouri Volunteer Infantry. It moved to Camp Alger, Va., May 26, 1898 and remained there until August 23, when it moved to Camp Meade, Pa. It left Camp Meade September 6, 1898 and was mustered out of the federal service at Kansas City on November 7, 1898.

Under the President's order of June 16, 1916 the Regiment was mobilized at Camp Clark, Nevada, Mo., on June 23, 1916, and was mustered into federal service on July 7, 1916. It departed for border duty at Laredo, Texas, on July 8, 1916, arriving at Laredo July 10. It remained on duty in the Laredo district until September 2, 1916 when it returned to Camp Clark, Nevada, Mo., and was mustered out of the federal service September 26, 1916.

Under the call of the President the Regiment was mobilized at Kansas City, Missouri, on March 25, 1917 for the purpose of guarding bridges, terminals, etc., in Kansas City and vicinity. The third battalion under Major Francis D. Ross was sent to Camp Funston to guard buildings under construction at that point and received special commendation for its work. On October 13, 1917, the Regiment moved to Camp Doniphan, Oklahoma and was consolidated with the Sixth Missouri Infantry already on the ground into the 140th U. S. Infantry, Thirty-fifth Division. The Third was from Kansas City with the exception of Co. B, Boonville, and Co. H from Liberty.

THE SIXTH MISSOURI INFANTRY

This Regiment was organized June 27, 1898, by Brigadier-General Harvey C. Clark, at that time a Major in the Second Missouri Infantry. He became Lieutenant-Colonel of the Sixth Missouri Infantry on July 20, 1898, and served with the regiment during the time it was in the federal service. The regiment was mustered into the United States service at Jefferson Barracks, Missouri, July 20, 1898, and was mustered out May 10, 1899, at Savannah, Georgia. It served as a part of the Army of Occupation in Cuba.

Following the Spanish-American war a nucleus of the regiment was organized and designated the Sixth Separate Battalion, National Guard of Missouri. On January 23, 1908 the battalion was expanded into a complete regiment with Colonel Arthur L. Oliver of Caruthersville as its first regimental commander. On July 25, 1914, the regiment was disbanded.

On June 29, 1917 an executive order of the Governor of Missouri was issued authorizing the reorganization of the Sixth Regiment. Reorganization was completed on July 28, 1917 and the Regiment recognized by the War Department with Colonel Albert Linxwiler as the regimental commander. Under the draft of the President the regiment was mobilized at Camp Clark, Nevada, Missouri, On August 7, 1917 and immediately begun a course of intensive training. On September 26, 1917 it moved to Camp Doniphan, Oklahoma and was consolidated with the Third Missouri Infantry into the 140th U. S. Infantry, 35th Division, October, 1917.

To Major Warren L. Mabrey is due much of the credit for the organization of the sixth.

The following is a list of home stations of the companies composing this regiment:

Regimental Headquarters	Jefferson City, Mo.
Headquarters Company	Cape Girardeau, Mo.
Supply Company	Seymour, Missouri.
Machine Gun Co.	Carterville, Mo.
Company "A"	Lexington, Mo.
Company "B"	St. Joseph, Mo.
Company "C"	St. Joseph, Mo.
Company "D"	Sedalia, Mo.
Company "E"	Doniphan, Mo.
Company "F"	Willow Springs, Mo.
Company "G"	Richmond, Mo.
Company "H"	Dexter, Mo.
Company "I"	Kennett, Mo.
Company "K"	Sikeston, Mo.
Company "L"	Cape, Girardeau, Mo.
Company "M"	Poplar Bluffs, Mo.
Sanitary Detachment	West Plains, Mo.

The National Guard counted. It furnished seventeen combat divisions, and sent 382,000 men to France. In the Argonne-Meuse offensive there were five Regular Army divisions, composed largely of drafted men, eight National army Divisions, and eleven National Guard divisions. The National Guard divisions in many cases could have been sent to the field sooner by several months if they had not been compelled to wait for equipment.

There was fighting enough for all, and all deserve the highest praise. One needs only to think of the 89th Division to realize that the National Army was equal to all that could be demanded of it. One need only think of the gallant First and the steady Second to remember that the Regulars could always be counted on to the limit. But the National Guard furnished at the outset a half million fighting men who met every test and were of incalculable value. I have been with them on the field of battle and I have seen the Regulars on the same field. There was no task that could be set the men which they would not carry out. There is no fair criticism that can be passed upon them. They proved themselves soldiers, these National Guardsmen, of the finest type, and equal to the best the enemy could send against them. If it be claimed that they suffered because of incompetent leadership at times, that must be admitted as true. But they were largely officered by Regulars, who were selected for them.

No honest man can deny, in the light of their service, that a large citizen army, properly trained and equipped, and with limited federal control except in emergency, would prove the best supplement to a regular army of 300,000 men as General Pershing suggests, or even a smaller number.

We are told that no criticism should be offered on the Regular Army. That means that nothing is to be learned either by the war,

THE OLD THIRD AND THE OLD SIXTH

or the experience of the last thirty years. But surely we have not yet found perfection!

We are told that no word should be spoken that criticizes the individual Regular army officer. But the National Guard officer was criticized—stamped by an efficiency board as incompetent or not fully efficient, and the reasons named. Sometimes they were not even named.

The United States Army is our own army. We are proud of it, and give it all loyalty. Let no one think we do not love it because we do not wish it Prussianized. Let no one think we are criticizing it when we mark the few officers who deserve criticism. They were inferior not because they were Regulars but because they were inferior men, pushed into positions they were not competent to fill.

It was the First Division which relieved the Thirty-Fifth. On this event the historian of the First says:

"The courageous Thirty-Fifth Division, to whose relief we would go had fought fiercely for four days and nights. It advanced down the valley of the Aire river, captured Varennes, Cheppy, Very, Charpentry, Baulny, and the woods and the ridges south of Exermont. How nobly and savagely they fought we can testify, for as we marched over those positions we noted their deep trenches, machine gun nests and gun emplacements. The many dead from Kansas and Missouri who lay face forward as we stepped over the corpses spoke eloquently of the bravery and devotion of the Thirty-Fifth Division."

The two regiments, now one, were mustered into Federal Service in the 35th division. The process was short, a merciless Doctor gave one the typhoid shot in the arm, and one became a soldier in the great Army. The insignia of the division was a Santa Fe Cross within a circle. When the men went overseas, this sign was stenciled on trunks and baggage. When, later on in France, it became a shoulder insignia, curiously enough the breaks in the circle necessary for the stencil, became permanent in the cloth insignia, although obviously incorrect.

This, then, was the beginning of the 140th Infantry. Many of its men and officers had been given valuable training, and all had the old Missouri spirit. In the reorganization some good officers were lost, and in time the weaker ones were weeded out; but the regiment was singularly fortunate in having good men in the replacements sent in, and in the many excellent officers transferred to it.

The old Third and the old Sixth had served the State. They were ready and willing when called to serve the Nation.

The old Third and the old Sixth were to become a new One Hundred and Fortieth—they were to travel far and meet the hardest conditions of war. But the loyal spirit of these old regiments was so builded into the new that it could write splendid chapters in an honorable and glorious history.

BRIG. GEN. CHARLES I. MARTIN
Commanding 70th Brigade

CHAPTER II.

Campaigning at Camp Doniphan

The Thirty-Fifth Division was mobilized at Camp Doniphan, adjoining Fort Sill, Oklahoma. Nearby was the little town of Lawton, a discouraged and dying village, which was transformed into a busy little city by the trade of the neighboring troops.

Oklahoma has 70,000 square miles, of which 640 are water. But the water was a long way from Camp Doniphan. The climate is said to be of the "Continental type." It is! The "prevailing soil is a deep red loam largely made up of decomposed sandstone." At Doniphan it was of a dirty, grayish hue and largely made up of de composed sandstone—and everything else!

The Camp was situated in a large valley surrounded by hills, Signal Mountain being one of the most prominent. It is an excellent artillery range, but a poor place for an Infantry regiment.

The buildings were not completed, there was a poor supply of very poor water, and at first the men were crowded 10 in a tent, which was afterwards reduced to 8 and then to 6 or 7.

We began to drill and exercise at once and covered the whole territory of the Camp. And the ground was impartial. It covered us. One day it might blow over on the 137th, and they would be the favored ones. But the next day it would all blow back on us. It was a comfort to be assured that the bath houses would be completed in a few months.

The organization of the Division proceeded like magic. 10,000 Kansas men and 14,000 Missourians! On August 5th, 1919, they had been mustered into the Federal Service, and here for seven months they were to be hammered into a homogeneous whole. The Sixth Missouri had been so generous as to bring an extra Company—from Campbell—and a good outfit it was.

The new totals of organization called for so great a strength that the National Guard regiments doubled up, in this way losing half its officers. In this way we were to lose some fine men. Col. Kealy, Major Ross, Captain Imes, Captain Walter Williams and

Captain Barnes were some of the men lost by the Old Third who would unquestionably have made their marks with the outfit.

The Sixth lost Bain of Cape Girardeau, Thornburg, Malone of Sikeston, Braschler of Doniphan, Major Morgan and others who were officers of the finest type. If I may trust the judgment of the men and of other officers, if I may trust my own judgment, we lost at Doniphan some of our very best officers. Some of them remained in the Service and did splendid work at home. But I know them, and I know that all the time they were miserably unhappy because they could not go overseas.

Let us remember in writing the history of this army, those men who were wild to go overseas, but were compelled to remain at home. Their work here was necessary and helped win the war. They did their duty cheerfully. Their hearts were as big and true as yours. Their work was tiresome and difficult, with none of the excitement and the glory that lighted the horizon for the men overseas. All honor to "the man with Silver Chevron." He is a true American. We are proud of him, and we shall grow prouder as the real history of this war becomes better known.

But not all the officers were permitted to remain in the service. The men who were unfit were weeded out. And so with the officers. The standards for the men were clear. There were certain mental and physical standards, and the rulings seemed generally just.

With the officers, it was another matter. It seemed difficult to discover the standards. Major-General William M. Wright, a Regular Army officer, commanded the division. He was an officer of experience and commanded the confidence and loyalty of both officers and men. He cared far more for the men than for his personal reputation, and was fitted in every way to lead the Division into battle. If he could have remained with us in France, we might tell a different story of the Five Days.

He was soon sent to France on a tour of the trenches and to Brigadier-General Lucien G. Berry, who commanded the Artillery Brigade, was given the command of the division.

My one personal interview with General Berry left me with a very poor opinion of myself, and a very poor opinion of General Berry, so it can hardly be regarded as a success from any standpoint. He is the type of man who has learned everything, can instantly correctly judge any man, and never makes mistakes. I shall not mention many of the good men who were "ruled out," but there are four who are typical.

Brigadier-General H. C. Clark of Missouri had been of invaluable service to the National Guard. I heard many officers, including medical officers, speak of his case. All concurred in the statement that he was a soldier of the finest military ability, an inspiration to the men, and strong enough to go over. He was dropped in December.

Col. Hugh Means of the 130th Field Artillery lives in my town.

I have known him for years. There can be no question that he was in good health, and knew how to command men. He is a lawyer of unusual mental strength. But he could not go over.

Major Albert H. Krause was also dropped. He too lives in my own town, and has a fine record as a man and as a soldier.

Lt.-Col. Chas. S. Flanders, of the old First Kansas, had been a Captain in the Philippines in the famous 20th Kansas. His strength was iron. He was a soldier through and through. When they went up into Baulny the 137th could have had no better man with them than "Pop Flanders," but an efficiency board got him him just before we left for France.

These are but a few. They are men I know. My judgment is strengthened by my experience with men at war, and by the testimony of officers and men who knew them. There seems real reason to suppose that it was a disadvantage to be a Guardsman, and the conditions at Doniphan throw light on changes made at a most critical time. Were it not for these, one might be less disposed to look with suspicion on changes made in France—almost on the battlefield itself.

We lost some enlisted men by death at Doniphan, and Lt. Ward, a popular and capable officer, a competent, kindly man with many friends. In cases where the bodies had to be shipped, the band and firing squad were taken to the railroad station, and the men were given the the honors of a military burial.

Gradually the hospital was completed, and the men well cared for. Gradually the baths were completed and put to use—although some of the officers baths were only finished six months after we reached Doniphan, to be dismantled a few weeks later—and gradually the regiment developed into a husky, hardy, healthy and happy out-

LT. WM. F. WARD
Died at Doniphan

LT. FRANK LOTT
Band Master

COL. WILLIAM NEWMAN
U. S. Army

fit. Signal Mountain, Berry Pass and Rabbit Hill became home. The bayonet work of the outfit attracted general attention. Old divisions were forgotten, men became used to general discomfort,, and when one day the men returned from a hike singing for the first time, we felt at last that we had a real regiment

To one man the regiment owes a great deal. Col. Albert Linxwiler had been sent to the Brigade and Field Officers School at Fort Sam Houston, Texas, from which he graduated April 4th, 1918. During his absence, the Regiment was under the command of a Regular Army officer, Col. Wm. Newman of Nashville, Tennessee. Many an old soldier of the 140th will look on his portrait in this volume with pleasure. He is truly "an officer and a gentleman." A strict disciplinarian, he was just. Compelling hard work, he worked hard himself. To him is due much of the credit of whipping the regiment into shape. When he left it he left many friends and no enemies. In France his name was mentioned frequently, and always in a way that showed how the men honored him. "Daddy Newman" they called him—and a man who could win such a tribute from the 140th, in so short a time, had to be a real man and a real soldier. Many times in France I heard men say—and officers too—"If we only had Colonel Newman with us now!"

So the days went on—the men learned to throw grenades and to use the bayonet, to shoot the army rifle, and to dig trenches. Especially the latter. They dug trenches and dug more trenches.. They braided barbed wire by the rod. And then saw the artillery cheerfully blow up both wire and trenches in ten minutes. We even had a school in "Early English," and seventy-five men learned to read and write. One G. Co. man persistantly cut classes. A non-com was sent to bring him in, but failed to do so. I sought him out, and on his own confession that he could not write and could barely read, gave him a fifteen minutes talk on the value of an education. It was a fine talk. I waited for a reply—"Hell, Chaplain," he said, "I am going over there to shoot Germans, not to write letters to 'em!"

Each month rumors would come that we were to move. They needed a good division, and we were to move before Christmas. Then we had it straight—the 20th of January. Then the 22nd of February—always a few days off, and always "inside" information. We felt that we had learned our lesson. We were tired of Doniphan. We wanted to go.

One factor in enabling us to stand the weary grind was the 140th Infantry Band. Most of the Sixth bandsmen were taken from us, and the band was the Third Regiment Band, with a few from the Sixth (which had a good band) and six men were added in France.

Its concerts helped the weary days to pass. Early on the cold winter mornings its music as it marched up the regimental street helped us begin the day. In France it played at regimental parades, guard mounts and concerts. It gave the Chaplain splendid support, and was always ready to play at church parade. From all the bands of the Division, it was chosen to play when General Pershing reviewed the Thirty-Fifth Division.

Its members were trained as litter-bearers, but musicians were too valuable to lose. And the A. E. F. order prevented them from doing this work on the battlefield. John Shay of Booneville was the only member lost by death.

No one can conceive the value of this band to the morale of the regiment. It counted for much both at Doniphan and in France. The men were proud of it and appreciated it. It played so large a part that it seems worth while to give the Roster in full.

ROSTER 140TH INFANTRY BAND

2nd Lieut. Frank K. Lott Band Leader (See Illustration)

Sgt. John Crockett	{ Asst. Leader { solo cornet
Sgt. Bodo Kammann	asst. solo cornet
Walter Hunter	1st cornet
Charles Bowne	1st cornet
Herman Knabe	2nd cornet
Lawrence Parrish	3rd cornet
Harry Wheeler	solo clarinet
Ralph Weaver	1st clarinet
William Gormley	2nd clarinet
Ernest Gormley	2nd clarinet
L. Guillot	3rd clarinet
E. R. Holt	3rd clarinet
Roscoe Lenge	piccolo
Ted Wheeler	flute
Henry Prati	bassoon
Walter Kempe	baritone
Corp. Chas. Hall	baritone
Frank J. Burnell	1st trombone
Robert Vicksell	2nd trombone
Albert Buttz	3rd trombone
J. P. Ryan	tenor saxaphone
Carl Metz	1st horn
Chas. Keilhack	2nd horn
Boyce Lackaye	3rd horn
Corp. Harry Tibbs	4th horn
LeRoy Ballard	1st bass
Claud Sharp	2nd bass
Martin Breving	3rd bass
Sgt. Carl Holtzman	4th bass
Charles Wagner	drums
Corp. Dan Dedrick	drums
Corp. Herbert Johnson	bass drum

CHAPTER III.

With the British Lion

AT SEA AND ON LAND

The middle of April found us entraining for Camp Mills. After all our waiting, the move seemed to come suddenly, and we were hardly ready for it. In spite of all attempts at secrecy, the "home folks" found out when the men were coming through, and many good-byes were said in Kansas City. The trip was pleasant, and the men were comfortable, although a few complained of being crowded. They were not yet traveling in France.

After a week in the cold and mud of Camp Mills came the order to board the train at Mineola and it was a happy crowd that lifted their heavy packs into the cars. From Mineola we went by ferry to Hoboken, N. J., where we quietly marched up the gangway into the ships that were to be our home for two weeks. People in the busy street on the other side of the warehouse buildings did not know on that 24th of April that another Division was starting for France. On the 25th, as we dropped out past Sandy Hook, the men were all kept below, and to a watcher from the shore we might have seemed an innocent freighter. That is if anything could seem innocent which was painted with such odd hues and in such strange designs as our boat was.

We travelled in British ships. Of the more than two million men transported to France the British carried over one million. Of every hundred men forty-nine went in British bottoms, forty-five in American, three in Italian, two in French, and one in Russian under British control. That the losses were so small was largely due to the United States Navy. In 1917 when the submarine had almost won the war, and the Allies had reached the depths of discouragement, the Navy proved an invaluable help. And when one remembers that in addition to over two million men, nearly eight million tons of cargo reached France, the stupendous task of the Navy will be appreciated.

Our boat was the Australian freighter "Shropshire," nicknamed

"Slopjar" by the irreverent doughboy. She carried the 3d Bn., Supply, Sanitary and Regimental Headquarters while the 2nd Bn. was on the Aeneas, and the 3rd Bn. on the Adriatic. The Shropshire was a British ship. Indeed she was a British ship, and had been used for Australian soldiers as well as (according to rumor) a cattle ship on the previous voyage.

There is something of a romance about a ship. There is some thing wonderful about sailing for a distant haven. It was a red letter day, that day we really moved out on the waters. Long after the Big Drive a man said to me "Somehow I haven't thrilled much in France, and I never felt less like a soldier than when we came off the field. There were three great hours for me—hours when I felt a real soldier: one was when I stepped high out of 1113 Walnut street, (the Recruiting Station) in old K. C. One was when I kissed the folks goodbye and boarded the train for Doniphan; and the third was when the boat moved out for France!"

For most of the men this was their first introduction to the sea as well as to the British. They were delighted—for the first few days. They swarmed over the ship as soon as they were allowed on deck, and were curious about everything. They examined the wicked-looking little guns mounted forward and aft, and listened to the awful stories poured into their ears by the wicked-looking little gunners. They learned port and starboard, and to count time by bells. They came to realize the importance of the Ship's Captain, a mighty man who spent most of his time in his cabin or on the bridge, and might be approached only by the Colonel. They admired the First Mate, a fine upstanding Scot. And they thought a good top sergeant lost in the Yankee boatswain, a tall rawboned man with iron muscles.

If the Captain was difficult to approach, not so the crew. With them the doughboys quickly became great friends (except with the cooks) and listened with itching ears to the marvelous tales that only a sea dog can tell to a land lubber. The crew rose to the occasion, and satisfied the doughboys with horrible tales of submarine sinkings, of floating mines, of fearful storms, of battles at sea kept secret by cruel censors, of sea serpents and of German atrocities, until even the men from Poplar Bluffs could believe no more.

We began to study the British character, for we were to be with the British, as we discovered later, until June. One enlightening incident occurred the first day out. Some Red Cross goods had been placed in a room for later distribution among the men. This room was to be used as a barber shop. Upon being told that the goods would be removed at his convenience, the Ship's Steward said "That is very kind sir, and I am in a bit of an 'urry." On being pressed to name an exact period, he replied "When you are ready, Sir, but I really am in a bit of an 'urry." Supposing this meant hours, he was told the packages would be removed in two or three hours, whereupon he exclaimed "Oh, no Sir, TWO OR THREE DAYS will be time enough." And during our acquaintance with our British cousins, we never found them acquainted with the word "hurry."

The quarters for the officers were good. The service was good although some of the stewards had rather positive ideas on the subject of "bawths." The food was excellent, and every afternoon "tea" was served. The officers jested about "afternoon tea" but seemed to enjoy it—for a day or two.

We were told that a way had been found to increase the man-carrying capacity of American transports 50 per cent. The British seemed to have beaten that record. The men were crowded below decks in hammocks and rough bunks, with few conveniences. But they were ready for hardships and most of them made a jest of it. For food, I understand they were frequently given mutton. At least on more than one occasion men informed me that apparently it was mutton. It was not lamb. From the remarks of the men, I feel sure it was mutton!

For the first day we had a smooth sea and delightful weather. On the second day we were joined by the rest of our convoy, and became quite an imposing fleet. The sea remained smooth, and we tried a boat drill, which was not very successful. We were told that the journey was to be made along the most northern route and that we might pass ice bergs on the way.

On the third day the wind freshened and the waves were so high that the steamer began to roll. Several of the officers had been telling us what sailors they were, how to navigate a ship and from them we had received much valuable information about the sea.

Strange to say they were the first to be affected. They had little interest in lunch, and at dinner lost interest and principal as well.

Seasickness makes for democracy. It draws no distinction between officers and men, and the man never asks the rank of the man standing beside him at the rail. Although it was not yet really rough, some of the men had unhappy moments. One man lay helpless in his hammock, his sweetheart's picture in his hands; he was telling her how much he loved her, and that he was dying with her name upon his lips. One soldier, cheerful in adversity, said that he did not want to die because flowers for the funeral were so scarce. And a husky mule-skinner summed up the general feeling. A strong, fine man, he was able to eat only a little fruit during the whole trip. "When I get back to Old Missouri," he said, "When I get back to Old Missouri I am going to buy a team of good mules and a farm. I am never going to travel farther than the cross-roads store, and if there is a pond of water on that farm as big as this deck, I am going to dreen the blanked pond!"

On the fourth day the Overseas Literary Society was organized. Its articles of incorporation are given in full, as an illustration of the spirit of the outfit. The American sense of humor lightened the burdens every day we were in France. On the battle-field even, it

MAJOR JOHN W. ARMOUR
As Captain A Co., Explaining First Aid

flashed forth frequently. On the long marches, it shortened the miles. It was a great asset.

It may be well to say that rules were strictly obeyed. The ship was really as dry as Kansas, and no one lost over a million dollars gambling.

Articles of Incorporation of the Overseas Literary Society

WHEREAS, The President has seen fit to order us across the seas for service in foreign lands, and we are thereto proceeding thusly on the good ship Shropshire.

WHEREAS, We have it to our mutual advantage to form ourselves into a body to find amusement other than that mentioned below, and for our own protection and for the well-being of others concerned, and inasmuch as we have lost all our money and there is an excellent library on board, we hereby organize the OVERSEAS LITERARY SOCIETY, and in convention assembled, pass the following resolutions:

BE IT RESOLVED, That in our estimation the so-called games of "African Golf" and "Poker" are a degradation and a shame upon society and should be discouraged whenever we are not playing, and further,

BE IT RESOLVED, That inasmuch as it is not fitting that we encourage such games unless we can put the cash on the board, that we refrain from entering into or having anything to do with such degrading forms of amusement, and further,

BE IT RESOLVED, That we will endeavor to pass our valuable time in a more profitable manner in order that we may improve our minds and at the same time be an example to our erring brothers, and furthermore,

BE IT RESOLVED, That we appoint a committee to call upon the Commander of the boat to set aside a place in which the members of this society might engage in such games as "mumble peg," "hide and seek" and "Puss wants a corner," and furthermore,

BE IT RESOLVED, That we subscribe our names and agree to the following rules and regulations:

Rules and Regulations

1. That I will remain a member of this society as long as I am "broke."

2. That I will not desire to enter into any such games mentioned above unless I can find some poor sucker who will lend me a stake.

3. That I agree to spend one hour a day reading and improving my mind and the rest of the day depreciating and talking about the fellows who were unworthy of our esteem and lucky enough to win our money.

4. No new member will be admitted unless he can prove that he is absolutely "broke."

5. Meetings will be held three times a day (at meal time) to discuss ways and means of raising a "stake."

6. Any member violating any of the above rules will be subject to instant death or such other penalty as the court may decide.

7. Any person wishing to become eligible will interview Grant Davidson.

Officers

(Names omitted by request.)

President and Procurer of Liquid Refreshments.
Vice President and Bottle Dispenser.
Secretary and Lecturer on "Vice Conditions on Board."
Sergeant at Arms and Instruction on "The Easiest Way to Lose Your Money."
Treasurer and Keeper of the Cupboard Key
Lookout Boy and Secret Pass Word Giver
Messenger Boy and Liaison Officer."
Librarian and Chief Gab Purveyor.

The fifth, sixth and seventh days were rough. We received news by wireless every day, and the bulletins were read with avid interest. Each evening the band—or that part of it unaffected by mal-de-mer—played during dinner. The men became accustomed to the rough seas and watched the huge waves with delight. On the eighth day once more we struck calm weather. The men found their sea legs, and swarmed all over the decks, a fairly happy crowd. On each of the two Sundays, Church Parade was held, and a band concert given.

As we neared the coast of the north of Ireland, a number of submarine chasers dashed up, for all the world like a pack of hounds. They were a very welcome sight, as we realized that we were approaching the danger zone. The men watched their speedy evolutions and marvelled at them. Suddenly the ship was shaken by a tremendous explosion. The sensation was exactly as if the Shropshire had been struck a fearful blow below the water line. Almost everyone thought we had been torpedoed, and the the men rushed on deck, impelled not by fear but by curiosity, crying "Where is the sub?"

It turned out that depth bombs had been dropped on a submarine, or on a floating spar that was merely a bit of wreckage. Not until long afterwards was the truth discovered. Then in censoring the letters of the men, and reading letters of the officers that were published, it was learned that we had met and destroyed a whole fleet of submarines, the number variously estimated at from four to twelve.

Southward through the North Channel, along the Scottish coast, past the Isle of Man, we finally entered the mouth of the river Mersey and docked at Liverpool. England is a beautiful country, but it never looked more beautiful to anyone than it did to the One Hundred and Fortieth on that seventh of May. We disembarked in good order, and in an hour had moved out from the wharf. In that hour the Chaplain gathered the letters that had been written into a sack, and rushed into the Customs House, where he asked for the "Big Boss." He was shown into an office, where an elderly Englishman of rather distinguished appearance was in command. The situation was briefly explained to him. The letters had been censored, but as yet we had no censor stamp. They were important, and too heavy to carry on the march through town. He was very kind, and promptly cut the red tape, promising that they would start for the States on a boat leaving the next day.

We were met by an official, apparently a policeman of some kind. He looked like a Grand Duke turned undertaker, wore a black pill-box cap so very small it was held in place by an elastic, and a black robe or gown, perhaps a glorified cloak. He was mounted on a high stepping horse, and piloted us through the streets of Liverpool to the railway depot.

The streets were crowded with men, women and children, very different from the stolid English we had been led to expect. They commented on the large stature and fine teeth (of course the men were laughing) of these Westerners. They greeted us with the wildest enthusiasm. We were to meet nothing like it again until we marched in Cape Girardeau and Kansas City more than a year later. Every step of the march to the station was accompanied by cheers and applause so generous that we realized the tribute was really to the good old United States. The music of their cheers was good for homesick men, and the regiment marched like veterans.

At the railroad station we had our first glimpse of English rolling stock. The cars seemed tiny and odd, with their side doors, and little compartments like the stage coach of pioneer days. The engines seemed merely little switching engines of inadequate power. We had not yet seen the French trains and ridden in French box cars.

Our train was "Transport Number 563," and when we started, we changed our opinion of the little English train. There are no grade crossings in England, and we travelled at the top speed of the best American express. We made most of the trip to Southampton by day, and saw the country in Springtime at its best. We were impressed by the splendid buildings, in good condition despite the years of war. The farms were kept like lawns,, and we looked for hours on beautiful scenery such as can be found only where to the lavish gifts of Nature has been added a dozen centuries of loving care.

At almost every station we found a welcome as we rushed through. Banners with the inscription "With the best of luck" were displayed. Crowds of school children waved British and American flags, and our progress was like that of a victorious army returning from war rather than that of green troops going to the Front. But it did us no harm, for when we reached France we found rather a chilly reception in comparison, and it was not until after Chateau-Thierry that the French really warmed up to us.

Part of the regiment were sent to the rest camp in Winchester, saw the great Cathedral and marched up historic Morn Hill (re-christened "Mourn" by the doughboy). Headquarters, and the men brought over by the Shropshire were landed in Southampton after midnight, and a long march took us to the British rest camp. We had little rest, and on the evening of the eighth were found aboard a channel boat, the Archangel. She was fast and rather comfortable, at least compared with the boats furnished the remainder of the regiment. After dark, we started across the channel, accompanied by an aeroplane. Lights went out before supper was finished, and the men were cautioned to be quiet and not to smoke. The channel was not rough as we had feared it might be, and on Thursday, May 9th, 1918, just as coffee was being served, orders came to march down the gang-plank. We were on the wharves of Le Havre. At last we were in France. The harbor was crowded with ships flying flags of every nation save those with which we were at war. Camouflage of every color of the rainbow, laid on in the oddest patterns, covered these ships. As we marched out to British Rest Camp Number 1, we met a large Red Cross hospital train bringing in wounded. The sight sobered us, and increased our desire to get to the front.

We soon made ourselves at home in the camp, and were supposed to remain within its boundaries. But often the American soldier is not where he is supposed to be. It was our first opportunity to see France, and some of the 140th can give a very complete description of Le Havre.

While in this rest camp, a daring submarine entered the harbor and blew up a ship at anchor. Instantly there was wild confusion, destroyers chasing the submarine, and boats seeking a safer anchorage. The dangers we had passed through on the voyage over became very real to us. The submarine escaped.

Here we found a bar in the officers Y. M. C. A. club. That seemed strange after America, but one could get anything to drink, including the strongest potions.

Our rifles were taken from us, and we were given the British Enfields. Many of the men found it hard to see the rifles they had been taught to take care of piled up and left apparently to rust. Our barracks bags were turned in also, and some of them were pillaged even before we left the camp. Only about one hundred of them ever reached the regiment. Over 200,000 are piled up in the Lost Baggage Branch, Pier 2, Hoboken, N. J. No doubt many of ours are among them. But how they can ever be distributed no one can imagine.

Here too we were fitted with English gas masks, and given instruction in their use. At first a gas mask seemed a great nuisance, but in time we came to feel a very deep affection for tnem. The fitting was done by British non-coms. Their instructions were clear cut and clever.

There was one Scottish sergeant whose instructions were given in a humorous strain that reminded one of Harry Lauder. But one could not tell them anything and one could not argue with them. A British non-com does the accustomed thing. He does not think. He dreads anything strange or new. And his always unanswerable reply "It simply isn't done you know" reduces one to helplessness.

In two days our outfitting was completed. Our friends gave us their parting salutation the magic words we had seen and heard so often in England "With the best of luck." And on May the eleventh we boarded French trains for Eu. The French trains are smaller, dirtier and far more disreputable looking than the English. The box cars for the men were marked "Cheveaux 8, Hommes 40." This was a sign with which we were to become very familiar, and signified that the car had been used up to this time to carry eight horses or cattle, and that now it was supposed to furnish luxurious accommodation for forty men. In many of the cars evidence of previous service was still visible. The men were crowded uncomfortably, and had not sufficient room. Cars for the officers contained no conveniences of any kind. There were no lights anywhere and candles were forbidden.

Once started, we began to appreciate the British trains. A French military train only moves about ten kilometres an hour, frequently changing its mind and running backwards for a time. They measure the distance in kilometres, because a kilometre is a little over half a mile, and it sounds faster.

Two days later, May 13th, we detrained at Eu, and marched about ten miles to Gamasches where Regimental Headquarters was established. Monchaux, Longroy, Guerville and Chateau le Hays were also used for billeting the regiment.

The Division established headquarters in Eu. Whichever way you pronounce it is wrong. It contains the church of St. Laurent, a beautiful example of 12th century architecture. This is not a cathedral, but to the doughboys every large church was a cathedral.

There is also the chapel to the Jesuit college, in which are the tombs of Henry, third Duke of Guise and Katherine of Cleves, his wife. The town existed under the Romans, when it was called Augusta.

We were with the British for training purposes, and in case of need. At that time it looked as though we might really be needed. The guns could be heard, and at night the explosion of the bombs dropped on Abbeville. But we were in Normandy—Normandy in apple blossom time. The country was beautiful. A charming little river, the Bresle ran through Gamasches and on through Eu. Hills and valleys, fields and slopes were green with Springtime, while here and there a field of poppies would lend glowing color to the scene. Near the town was an old chateau where the second battalion was billeted. Surrounding the chateau was a pine forest, some of whose magnificent trees must have been over a century old. The Area Commandant was a British Colonel Lyons, and the town was shared with us by the British. Of course their billeting officers were thoroughly competent. A company of Argyle and Sutherland Highlanders were sent to us for training purposes, and the second battalion of the 17th Manchesters under Major Pomfrey, who had seen service in the Boer war. The Major seemed a strange soldier to the doughboys with his cane and monocle, and his quiet ways. However he soon won the respect of the men by his soldierly qualities and genuine manhood.

There was a good demonstration platoon, and our men gained much valuable information and training. Fine drill grounds were available, and when finally General Haig and General Williams inspected the regiment, they pronounced them fighting men—and fit.

British rations were issued to us. There were enough of them but they were not those things for which the American stomach yearned. The British have a weakness for tea and jam where the American calls for coffee and "ham and." The most bitter objections heard were offered to the British lime juice which was furnished as a ration. To travel five thousand miles and then be offered lime juice as a beverage seemed a hardship to some of the men.

Here we received a British Censor stamp, Number 6239, surmounted by the English crown. We hated to use it. We wanted a stamp with the American eagle rampant for American letters.

Our first mail reached us on May the 24th, a happy day in the regiment. It was our first mail from home, and came just a month after we left Camp Mills. The letters were read, and then re-read to be sure that nothing had been missed, and the whole regiment showed a better spirit.

At Longroy we had a little difficulty with the French. One of the husky members of the Supply company made off with a building, and was seen floating with it down the river. Lieutenant Kizer was diplomatic enough to arrange matters so that there was no charge and no trouble. But that was an unusual case.

At Monchaux the First Battalion had some trouble with American troops quartered near them. The difference grew until finally there was a pitched battle in which stones and other missiles were freely used, and the casualties were many. The "Fearless First" advanced in regular formation, and with file closers and excellent liaison, driving back the invaders in great confusion. Our British friends were delighted with the manner in which the situation was handled, and the men of the battalion were unpleasantly self-satisfied for some time.

It might be supposed that trouble would occur with the French because we could not understand their language. This did not prove to be the case. An American mule-skinner would pass a French teamster, and express his opinion The Frenchman would reply in kind.

Either opinion would incite a rabbit to red murder, but as neither understood the other, they would part friends. With the British—ah, that was different. The American understood the Englishman, in spite of his strange accent. The Englishman understood the American in spite of his strange oaths. And instead of parting friends, often some one had to part them!

The Englishman gives to a visitor a real hospitality. But while making you free of his quarters, he leaves you to entertain yourself. Sometimes, when one is kept uncomfortable by the well meant but constant efforts of an American host, it does not seem so inhospitable to be left alone.

And he speaks the plain truth. Crowd into an American motor car, already overcrowded, and to your statement (which is false) that you are sorry to cause any inconvenience, the reply will be made (equally false) that you cause no trouble, and it is a pleasure to have you. Crowd into an English motor-lorry, already full, and express your fear that you are crowding. Instantly the reply will come (true this time) that you certainly are crowding them but it cannot be helped and they will make the best of it.

Details of officers and men were sent up into the lines. Col. Linxwiler and some of the staff were with the Australians at Villers-Brettonneux The Australians made a great hit with us. They are not unlike Western Americans in appearance, and have that same free and offensive manner of which we are so proud. We knew that we would feel safe going into the line with them anywhere.

Our baggage detail rejoined us after a month's separation. The British were a good sort. They are soldiers. To those who say that England stood back, the million English dead return triumphant answer. We loved our British cousins, but it was getting to be the most difficult thing we did.

Our men had entertained visions of living in French houses, eating French cooking, and meeting beautiful French maidens; they were billeted in French stables, fed on British rations, and there wasn't a beautiful French woman in the whole town They had come to a far country to fight a dangerous foe, and were turned into a street cleaning department to clean up the refuse and dirt of a thousand years, which the French did not want cleaned up anyway.

We grew restless. We could see the light of burning buildings, and see the flashes of the Allies' anti-aircraft guns News came of German successes in May and the early part of June. The regiment was fit, well trained and well officered It had been built into a fine fighting machine, and now it wanted action.

Rumors grew. We were to be clothed in British uniform! We were to be brigaded with the British! At an opportune time orders came to move.

We were ready to leave Gamasches, but it was not easy. The French filed claims for damages. We began to learn the French idea of a claim for damages, and it was not complimentary to our intelligence It is not true we paid rent for the trenches. But we did pay heavily for almost everything else. Later I learned of a clever woman who collected damages for the same field, which was used as a drill ground, six times in as many weeks. The plain truth is that the French, like all the other foreign nations, regard us as easy marks. And we have done a good deal both as individuals and as a government, to justify that opinion.

One particularly valuable asset was a broken chair. Damages for it might be collected from every officer who was billeted in that house. In time we came to know that the Frenchman expected only about ten percent of the amount asked, and Uncle Sam lost a little less.

On the afternoon of June the sixth we moved out, carrying full packs. We were to leave the British behind! But en route we received our third rifle—the American Enfield this time. Never again did we carry such heavy packs. But we were happy. Now we were to see real war.

Dates are important here The men were paid on June the fifth, and we marched on June the sixth Any old soldier will grasp the significance of the dates. June the fifth was pay day. Pay day! And we moved out on June the sixth! It was a long hard march, that sixty miles to the rail road.

One thing is worthy of mention. The men had already overcome the "rookie" habit of falling out on the left during the rests on a march. The march discipline was good.

COL. BENNETT C. CLARK
Served as Lt. Col. 140th Inf.

CHAPTER IV.

Alsatian Days in Quiet Trenches

Our march through Clais to Critot was a strenuous one. All officers had been ordered to cut down to fifty pounds of baggage, and the men to discard all unnecessary articles from their packs, but we had not yet learned to cut down. Our baggage was too much for our transportation and the men's packs were heavily loaded. In 48 hours we marched nearly sixty miles under heavy packs. It was here one first began to realize the splendid temper of the regiment. Comparatively little equipment was thrown aside and few dropped out by the way. There had been a little celebration at Longroy the night before and one soldier was seen to start in such a condition that it was necessary for him to sight a tree and deliberately march towards that with clenched teeth, with perspiration streaming down his face. It seemed impossible that he could keep up but somehow he sweated the alcohol out of his system and finished strong at the end. We learned the value of men like Sergeant Johnson of the Medical Corps, who kept everyone in a good humor and was of the greatest help in keeping up the morale of the men. Few men dropped out. In fact C Company reported at the end of the march that they had not lost a man, but on the contrary had gained three. Upon investigation it was discovered that three men from the hospital had joined the company enroute. On June 8th the regiment landed at Critot, tired but cheering, and after another night spent on the bosom of mother earth made the second acquaintance with a French train.

These cars were smaller and dirtier and slower than the ones we had first seen, but we traveled through a beautiful country, through Rouen, the environs of Paris, the Champagne district, and June 12, after a long march reached Pouxeux. Parts of the regiment were at Aenemenil and Geromenil. The troops had suffered from lack of drinking water on the march. Indeed our entire stay in France the supply of drinking water was limited, as was the supply of wood. We were always thirsty and never warm. The French never drink water, and when

33

GERMAN FRONT LINES IN ALSACE

GERMAN TRENCHES FROM LOOKOUT POST
Vosges, Alsace

ALSATIAN DAYS IN QUIET TRENCHES

cold weather comes, simply add a few additional suits of clothes. During the eleven days training at Pouxeux the soldiers were getting better acquainted with the French. Contrary to the general opinion, the first thing a soldier does on getting to a new French town is not to seek vin rouge and vin blanc. He looks for eggs and potatoes and finds them. He finds them even when the officers cannot obtain them. We were received with kindly courtesy by the French and in our marches through the country gained an intimate acquaintance with the life and thought of the French peasant. His house is is built for two purposes—primarily to house his stock, and incidentally his family. Fertilizer means wealth when land has been farmed intensively for centuries and one would often be surprised to find an attractive room with splendid furniture and electric lights after passing through a stable in front of which there was an enormous pile of manure. This queer habit was sometimes the cause of misunderstanding. The French supposed that we were trying to rob them of their wealth when we were only following our habit of cleaning up the town. In most of the towns in Alsace are public watering places. Water flows down from the hills in a constant stream. There is a huge public trough divided into sections and from the first huge square tub water is taken for household purposes, from the second the cattle drink, the fourth is used for washing, and the third for rinsing clothes.

The men were interested in the French conservation of fuel. Contrary to our expectations we found plenty of trees and forests in France. There is probably no better wooded country in the world. Learning how the French love and replace their trees one can understand their hatred of the Germans for their wanton destruction. When a tree is felled the smaller branches are bound into fagots or bundles which sold before the war for about five cents and now sell for fifteen or twenty. A French woman will cook a meal on what would be used merely for kindling the American fire. We found the buck saw, but it is used in a new way. It is placed on the ground, the Frenchman bends over with the handle against his stomach, and the stick of wood is held in his hands and moved up and down as if he were grating nutmeg. Perhaps one should have said the French woman, for it is the woman who does most of the work in France and not the man. It was the usual thing to see in the field a lot of husky Missouri men helping the French women with their work. Perhaps, too a little homesick for the fair fields they had left behind.

In Pouxeux we were to receive assistance from the Regular Army. Col. P. A. Murphy was assigned to us on June 18th, and we lost Col. Linxwiler and Col. Clark.

Col Linxwiler had served nearly ten years in the Illinois National Guard, and nine years in the Missouri National Guard, serving in Cuba, and later on the Border. He remained with us until July 14th, when he became Corps Inspector of the Fifth Army Corps. He remained with the Fifth Army Corps in various capacities until November 12th, was assigned to duty as Liaison Officer with Headquarters of the Second British Army December 2nd, and was on duty in Duren and Cologne, Germany. On January 9th he was assigned to command the 158th Infantry, and February 15th transferred back to the 140th. February 20th he became Brigadier Commander of the 70th Brigade, and April 16th, 1919, again assumed command of the 140th, being mustered out on May the 14th, 1919. He was cited in orders G. O. 26 Fifth Army Corps Headquarters for faithful and conscientious devotion to duty during the St. Mihiel and the Meuse-Argonne offensives.

Colonel. Linxwiler was placed in a difficult position. In the formation of the 140th, Army Regulations had placed him in command. The commanding officer of the old Third, Colonel Philip Kealy, was a man of great executive ability with all the qualifications of a competent officer and extremely popular with his men. There is no question but that if he had gone to France and been given the opportunity he would have made a great record. And yet in time Colonel Linxwiler by his evident ability to handle men as well as the problems of war, and by strict discipline, made possible only by his disposition to be absolutely fair and just, had won the loyalty of the whole regiment. It was a cruel disappointment to him when he was relieved of command. For a month afterward, until July 14th, he remained with the regiment, attached. His attitude during this trying period won the admiration of all who observed him. Without the slightest apparent thought of himself he tried to help the new Commanding Officer and to encourage loyalty to him in the regiment. His work, cheerfulness, unselfishnesss and loyalty during this trying period showed his complete command of himself and his fitness to command others. There is no question but that if he and Lieutenant Colonel Clark could have led the regiment in the Argonne the losses would have been smaller, and the men better handled with possibly even greater gains of ground. Colonel Clark was thoroughly democratic in his sympathies, a good comrade with the officers, a brilliant and competent officers, who was always scrupulously jealous for the rights of the men. Those who knew him felt that he would have made any sacrifice to have remained with the troops and fought with them in the Argonne. The qualities these two men possess and the affection and loyalty held for them by the men made their absence a very great and real loss when the crucial time came. We lost our officers, but that spirit of Missouri manhood—fearless and aggressive, unable to retreat, counting honor dearer than life; that spirit which in older days had conquered the wilderness and builded a great and sovereign state; that spirit which in the sadness of Civil War had cheerfully given the very flower of its manhood; that spirit which in '98 had shown the ready response to the call of the Nation, thrilled in the breasts of the whole regiment. Neither the War Department nor the German army could take that away.

In Pouxeux we were issued helmets of steel, and an article officially designated as the "overseas cap." This cap is looked on by a soldier with the same aversion a dog bestows upon a tin can. One day a pro-German sympathizer became intoxicated. While in that condition he designated this monstrosity, and in some way it become adopted by the War Department. One can not describe it, but the more one thought of an overseas cap the better one loved the tin helmet! Spiral puttees were also issued, and the regiment was equipped with clothing and stores.

On June 23d we were transported in French motor lorries through the Bussang tunnel, crossing the Provincial Boundary line, into German-Alsace.

The 2nd Battalion went to Thiefosse, remaining two months.

The 3rd Battalion under Major Murray Davis and the Machine Gun Company under Lieut Billy Gordon entered Bitschweiler. They were assigned the next day to the section of trenches on this front line. They were the first of the 140th and among the first of the Division to go into the front line trenches. The remainder of the regiment, under Colonel Murphy was billeted in the delightful old town of Thann. The men were impressed by the fact that the school children carried gas masks. Old Thann, the older village, lies close by in utter desolation. Thann itself seems almost completely wrecked, great damage having been done by destructive artillery fire. The people speak German and a great many are evidently pro-German in their sympathies. There is a beautiful old church in Thann of the 14th century, which contains some paintings of great value and a very famous pipe organ. These works of art and the pipe organ were removed to the back area when the Boche advanced in 1914. The storks in Thann were an interesting sight. The stork is a symbol of Alsace, but the bird is almost extinct. In spite of the shelling, at eventide, perched on a chimney in Old Thann, a lonely stork could be seen outlined against the sky.

We began here to learn a lesson which became cleared throughout the war. The Boche are scientific artillerists; they registered on the fine old church, and dropped shells in the most frequented streets. It was here that "Shaky Pete," a useful and popular sergeant, succumbed to the fortunes of war. A cafe was shelled; proprietor and patrons quickly decamped. The flasks, bottles and casks were left unguarded. To "Shaky Pete" they seemed lonely. At any moment a shell might destroy them all, what a cruel waste! He entered to guard the property. A few hours later he approached the Chaplain. "Chaplain," he said, "I am going to be killed, I know I am going to die, but I'm going to die awfully happy."

We were in Thann but a week, camouflage and censorship hid our whereabouts from the folks at home and from the French and sometimes apparently from the high command. No one knew where we were except the Germans. We were withdrawn to prevent further shelling of the historic old town. Leaving there the 28th we marched back across the mountains to the splendid little manufacturing town of Saulxures. The men had a royal time and will always remember their week's stay. Some left warm friends, some left their bank rolls, some even left their watches and jewelry.

We reached Saulxures the 29th of June. It is a splendid little manufacturing town, the cleanest village we saw in France, the people were hospitable and kind, and the mayor anxious to do all he could for the American forces. The 2nd Battalion was in Thiefosse. Here we underwent a period of intensive training, in the working out of problems, to which the surrounding country was admirably adapted. The Moselotte, a beautiful little French river runs through the town. The Fourth of July was spent here. In the morning as the representative of the regiment, the Chaplain was invited to visit the French schools. All the children carried American flags, but the number of stars or the number of stripes was evidently regarded as immaterial. A handsome brown eyed boy presented a huge bouquet to the Chaplain for the Regiment and desperately delivered quite a long address, accompanied by gestures in which he had been carefully coached. He looked the Chaplain squarely in the eye and never forgot a word. Nor did the Chaplain understand a word. The Chaplain responded with an eloquent little address which had been written by Captain Beau, a French officer of the finest type, attached to the Regiment. The Chaplain had been carefully coached in the pronunciation but was utterly ignorant of the meaning of the words. It was an impressive incident.

In the afternoon the whole regiment and about 300 French people gathered to hear patriotic addresses by the Mayor of the town, Captain Beau, and Major Lemmon. A fine Band Concert was given and several boxing contests. An amusing incident occurred during Major Lemmon's address. The Major is well known as the most conscientious teetotaler of the regiment. At one point in his address he rose to the heights of impassioned oratory, his face was red, his gestures wildly emphatic. (The French made no gestures.) One of the school teachers, a very charming woman, turned to her companion and pityingly exclaimed "poor man boko zigzag."

The third boxing bout of six rounds had been a particularly vicious one between two evenly matched middleweights. Many blows had been struck that would have knocked an ordinary man senseless. After the contest the French Captain confided to an officer: "I was much worried at first until I saw that with those nice soft gloves they could not hurt each other."

Here the American doughboy displayed his versatility... He quickly made the acquaintance of French money and the French girl. An American dollar presented at the Y brought in exchange a handful of what looked like soap wrappers, and always seemed to possess about that value to the American soldier. The French franc was worth about 18 cents. A five franc note has a picture of a woman apparently about to throw a hand grenade. Upon closer inspection she is discovered to be sowing wheat. On our first pay day in France it took two men to carry the money, which filled a whole gunny sack.

ALSATIAN DAYS IN QUIET TRENCHES

The Y found us while were in Saulxures. Henry Allen came as Division Secretary, and made a splendid one. I do not think any other man could have obtained supplies as he did.

He came to know and love the men, and his interest later is readily understood. They were his men.

I have heard a husky Ozark mountaineer, who did not know he was addressing the future Governor or Kansas, and wouldn't have cared if he had known, say "Hello Fatty! When do you get some chocolate for us " And Henry Allen used half his French vocabulary in replying "Toot Sweet."

The American soldier loves children and made friends with them, even during our short stay in England. In France he was always surrounded by them, but his talents were particularly in evidence when dealing with the mademoiselles. The Missourian from the Ozarks, with but four words in French, and all of them incorrectly pronounced, could converse by the hour with a pretty French girl and each would understand the other perfectly.

When we first landed in Saulxures, tired from the long march over the mountain, and hungry as a matter of course, a husky doughboy from the First Battalion started out on the usual hunt after eggs. He pounded on the door of a house, which happened to be Colonel Murphy's billet. Colonel Murphy had made himself comfortable in a dressing gown, and tall, very slender, and new to the regiment, was taken for a Frenchman when he opened the door in person.

"Avez voo dezzuf?" queried the eager soldier. The answer may be imagined! Indeed those who know Colonel Murphy need not use their imagination—they know it. But it can not be printed.

The Colonel began an investigation into the lack of rations in the First Battalion.

While in Saulxures on July the 18th the Regimental Chaplain had his first burial service in France. Private Earl C. Gardner of the 130th Machine Gun Battalion had been killed at Theifosse. After great difficulty a Frenchman was found who could make a coffin... It was lined with soft white cloth purchased in a local shop. Men from the Supply Company worked willingly nearly all night painting it with a quick drying black. A plot of ground with additional room for many more graves was obtained in the walled cemetery. Private Gardner was buried beside the Priests of the old church; grave No. 6 from the great stone cross; grave No. 1, A. E. F. Proper identification was interred with the body and a large wooden cross painted white, with his name in clear black letters placed at the head of the grave. The grave was entered in the cemetery register, one report made to the French authorities, and report made to three different American sources, the Adjutant General, the Graves Registration Service and the Division Chaplain's Office. Those details are given to show how carefully each American soldier's name is marked and registered where possible.

In another aspect this grave is typical of the graves of all American soldiers buried in or near French towns. Some woman or girl from the church is appointed God-Mother to the grave and cares for it as if the person were a member of her own family. The God-Mother, a very charming French woman, her husband an officer in the French Army at once took charge of this grave. In the cemetery the St. Amarin, the Chaplain saw the grave of an American soldier who had been buried considerably over a year. It was beautifully tended, covered with growing shrubs, and fresh cut flowers had been placed upon it, either that morning or the day before. This is a beautiful custom and an evidence of the fine spirit of the French, as well as their sympathy for America. Whether we bring home the bodies of our fallen heroes or let them sleep in France seems as yet undecided. Of one thing I am sure that the graves of the American soldiers who sleep in France will never be forgotten or untended... They will always show the signs of kind remembrance and loving care.

Again time was beginning to drag. The men welcomed the order to move into the trenches, and on July the 20th with exultant hearts the regiment started its march back over the mountains into the front line trenches.

After a long march from Kruth, to which point we had been carried in trucks, we reached the top of a great mountain and took charge of a front of many kilometres in the Fecht sector. At last we were to look at the Germans through the sights of our rifles. While the trenches and dug-outs were old it was hard to realize that we were at last in the trenches. Beautiful little cottages were built on the slopes of the hills. Magnificent forests gave one the impression that we were in the mountains of Maine. Here and there people might be seen working in the fields. It was considered a quiet sector. It was used as a rest camp for both the French and Germans, but the occasional artillery duel or night raid took its toll and almost every day there was a burial in the French Military Cemetery a couple of hundred yards down the hill from headquarters.

We had been carefully censored and concealed since the day we left Camp Mills. Our marches were made at night. We never knew where we were. The morning after we took our position a sign was hung on the German wire reading "Welcome 35th Division, let's be friends." The Supply Company remained at Kruth doing splendid work. The First Battalion was held in reserve at Boussat nearly at the top of the mountain. All rations and wood were transported up the hill by a cable line which ended at Boussat. As we were brigaded with French troops the French wine ration was most important. It was interesting to watch this cable. One basket would carry up a cask of red wine, the next a bale of hay, the next a cask of wine, the next a box of rations, and then another cask, continuing in about the same proportion. The 1st Battalion remained at Boussat until August the 3rd when it took over the Collette Sector holding it effectively until August the 31st. The rats were numerous and at first the men found it difficult to sleep. Some of the men claimed to have rats with service stripes and wound chevrons. They gave them names and managed to find a good deal of amusement; the strength of the American Army is partly due to that spirit which can find fun in any situation and make a joke out of any difficulty. It was here that the boys invented the trench rat trap. A piece of bread would be placed on the end of a bayonet and the rifle held across the parapet. Pretty soon a rat would come along and nibble at the bait. A trigger pull and the rat was gone.

On the morning of July 31st the Germans attempted a raid, Combat Group 8, Point 400, Focheday. Our strength at that point was twenty-two men and one officer.

That night it was something like this in one place—Time 12:20. Violent artillery barrage from the Germans. There was a sentinel in the trench-lookout. There were 14 men resting but ready at call. There were 9 men back a little, in a place where, if a shell blocked the door, they would be shut in. It is 2 a. m. The Germans creep out in No Mans Land. They are well prepared. They carry some boxes of high explosives—two men to a box. It will blow a cement dugout to smithereens. They have the deadly flame throwers. And bombs of course. They are going to teach a lesson. They carry little flags with inscriptions. One in French "With great pleasure." Another in German "In honor of the German storm troops. There is a big hole in your line. Till we meet again." On a third "We fear no Americans nor French. Regards to your great Wilson." It is to be a fearful smash!

The lookout is cold and lonely. He is very lonely. And it is very dark. But he has hunted coons at night in old Missouri. His eyes are used to dark as no city boys can be. He sees a movement—looks intently and where you or I could see nothing, sees the enemy... "Come out boys, they're here" he shouts as he starts his gun going. Then action! Guns and guns and guns; back in the rear the artillery starts, the American to defend, the Germans to attack. In this little place in the line a few American boys simply licked the thunder out of a superior number of German trained troops! A lot of plunder is brought in, pistols, knives, grenades, explosives, and the little flags. The flags lie beside dead Germans. One is buried in our lines. A pitiful single slice of black hard inedible bread in his rations bag. An "unterofficer," with an ugly trench knife. But there is no hole in the line. The green boys have proved themselves real soldiers. A stretcher bearer is wounded, ties up his own wounds and for two hours works like a madman. More are killed than we know. The smell betrays them a day or two later to our patrol party out in the No Man's Land which we call over in France "The American's Land." Mark this! The first shell caved in the mouth of the dugout. No one was hurt, but the loyal 9 are caged. They listen in darkness with strained muscles, but they can not help the 14. No man could get through the barrier of debris and earth.

But the 14 had won out. The flurry is over. And after it is all over, the 14 find that the 9 are not there. They have won out alone. They have just realized that they had to win. And the whole 14 are still there! An unlucky number? For Fritz!

I reported the one German buried in our lines with sadness. After death one holds no malice. This poor "unterofficer," with brave hopes and sarcastic flags,—and bit of dirty bread! I shall never forget his name—Otto Hagedorn, 12 German Landwehr.

And the report goes in—for we do little but write reports. The report for this particular little bit of the line. "Enemy attacks but is repulsed with loss. Everything quiet." It is quiet out in the wires, where sleep the Germans whom no man dares bury. And I thrill with pride. For I know that my whole regiment is made up of the same sort of men as these 14 and they are the equal of the German "sturmers" or of any other troops. The officer and 22 men are cited in orders.

Our success in repelling this raid helped the confidence of our men a great deal. The trenches in some places hundreds of yards apart, at other parts came within less than 100 yards of each other. There was constant sniping, frequent use of grenades, artillery fire, and flying pigs. The men become accustomed to thinking for themselves, in emergencies, gained increased confidence in their officers, and the value of these days in the trenches was clearly seen in every hour of the great drive.

At 11:30 on the night of August 10th the enemy started a bombardment over the left flank of P. A. 9, which lasted for an hour. At 11:30 P. M. P. A. 9, called for our barrage and in 12 minutes after sending up six red rockets our artillery responded. Our machine guns at De Galbert and Petite Ferme opened fire on the first signal. All of our men were on post during the bombardment and ready for the enemy when the barrage lifted, but the counter barrage had been so effective that the enemy did not attempt to make an attack.

The Third Battalion with that dashing young officer, Major Murray Davis, had become seasoned veterans. The 2nd Battalion, under Major Warren Mabrey, occupied a dangerous sector and held it well, Major Mabrey combining that skillful handling of his men and careful thought for them which afterwards made his work so effective in the great drive. Major Fred Lemmon had come to know his battalion and they had come to know him, forming that splendid union which took such a leading part in the Meuse-Argonne offensive. About this time through some friction with the C... O... the regiment was deprived of the services of some of its best officers, whose help was much needed a month later.

THE FLAG IN NO MAN'S LAND

From Daily Report of 1st Battalion, 140th Inf., 11. Miscellaneous:

It is the ambition of G. C. I. Balmain to get hold of a small American Flag, which Company C will cause to float over the house in "No Man's Land." This particular point has formerly been considered the most dangerous on this Sector, from the standpoint of sniping and machine-gun fire. It has proved the most troublesome. However, by the continuous and courageous efforts of all men in this G. C., they have harassed the enemy by all sorts of fire, ruses and patrolling, night and day, and picked off snipers to the extent of having entirely broken down the morale of the enemy, and at the present time claim undisputed possession to this little section of "No Man's Land," to which they have given the name of "Yankee Land."

(GEORGE H. SIMPSON),
1st Lieut. 140th Inf.,
Adjutant.

To Major Lemmon, 1st Battalion, 140th Inf.

"I have advised the G. O. 70th Brigade that I will personally bear the expense and he has given instructions for the purchase of a Flag.

Signed (BOND.)

(The Flag was borrowed from Mail Orderly, 1st Battalion, Corporal James Kloster, by Capt. Rexroad.)

The following day arrangements were made to raise the Flag over the Old Stone House, known as Remi Farm, the house used by the snipers, giving so much trouble. Sergeant Joseph Winslow and Corporal Julius C. Hinkefent were detailed to do the job.

The following report from the Commander of G. C. I. Bis was forwarded the following morning:

"The Flag Flies. 'Twas a narrow escape. The boys just got on the top of the house, and they must have been heard, for Jerry rained machine gun bullets all around them. The flag went up just the same."

Signed (SGT. R. T. FLYNN.)
G. C. I Bis Commander.

The Flag stayed up until we were relieved by the French. As luck would have it, we were subject to an Artillery bombardment during the relief. On being notified of our relief by the French, it was necessary to remove the Flag and take it with us. Sgt. Joseph Winslow and Corporal Roy C. Strange were detailed to take the Flag down.

This task was much more difficult than that of putting it up, and they both received personal letters from the Division Commander, General Traub, dated Sept. 16, 1918, and indorsed by the intermediate Commanders. Sergeant Joseph Winslow also received another personal letter from General Martin.

A hundred yards down the mountain-side from Regimental P. C.

Larchey is a beautiful little French Military Cemetery. A hundred yards lower still is a lake reflecting the trees and shadows of the mountain-side.

In this cemetery we left the men who were killed while we were in the trenches, and the record is given to show how accurately the Government kept its papers. It may take a great while for clerks to sift out the facts from the great mass of documents, but there is no reason why we should not ultimately know the definite location of every American grave in France. Campbell, Long, Stone and Tucker were killed by the same shell, which exploded in the doorway of their dugout.

A sad and difficult duty devolving on the Chaplain was that of undertaker. The bodies of the dead were consigned to his care.

One day a man proudly showed him a photograph of his wife and two handsome children, which had just arrived in the mail from overseas. Two days later, it was a great shock to recognize this photograph in the pocket of one of the bodies brought for burial! The men were buried reverently, their bodies laid to rest with loving care. These were all buried in coffins, and there was a service even when the shells were dropping over. In fact Althenthal was killed by shrapnel on a spot over which a few minutes before had passed the funeral procession with the bodies of the men killed the previous day.

"GOD'S ACRE"

1. Harwood, Pvt. Normal S. Buried July 31, 1918. No. 223115. Co. B. 130 Machine Gun Battalion. Cemetery D Lindthal 300 yards South P. C. Reg. Larchey. Grave 2 from E. Line on N. Line. Name and disc on Cross, Bottle. Next E. Pvt. Richard Kepplin, Co. L 138th Infantry, A. E. F. No. 122.

2. Hagedorn, Underofficer Otto. 12 Co. 38 Landwehr. German. Buried 100 yards East trail P. A. Martin 100 feet South. Coordinates 451.59—127.88. On Sengern Map 5000.

3. Bridges, Pvt. Thomas W. No. 1460, 387 Co. D 140th Infantry. Buried Aug. 3rd N. E. Corner Cemetery D. Lindthal. Disc on Body and on Cross. Bottle. Next E. Norman S. Harwood No. 2231115.

4, Lewis, Pvt. Milton O., Co. G. No. 1461145. 140th Infantry. Buried August 7th, 1918. Cemetery D. Lindthal. 2nd Grave from N. Line. 4 from E. Disc on body and Cross.

5. Tucker, Pvt. Elmer. Hdq. Co. 140th Inf. No. 1459047. Buried August 11, 1918. Cemetery D. Lindthal Oberlauchen. 3rd from N. line. 5th from E. Just South. Milton Lewis. Cross both Discs.

6. Long, Henry J. Pvt. Hdq. Co. 140th Infantry No. 1458998.

ALSATIAN DAYS IN QUIET TRENCHES 45

Buried August 11th, 1918. Cemetery D. Lindthal, 3rd from E. 3rd from N. Just south of Captain Alexander M. Ellett, Co. I 139th Infantry. Disc with body.

8. Caton, H. P. Pvt. Co. B. 140th Infantry. No. 1459874. Buried August 14, 1918. Cemetery D. Lindthal. Disc. Cross. Next East Curtis Thackston. No. 1461449 2nd row N.

9. Thackston, Curtis, Pvt. Co. H. 140th Infantry, No. 1461449. Buried August 14, 1918. Cemetery D. Lindthal. Discs. 2nd from N. Just East Captain Alexander Ellett, I Co. 139th Inf.

10. Longan, Layton L. No. 1460424. Pvt. Co. D. 140th Infantry. Buried August 14, 1918. Cemetery D. Lindthal. Cross. Discs. Next E. E. Campbell, No. 1462357. 3rd from N.

1. Mitchell, Leslie L. Pvt. Co. D. 140th Infantry. Buried August 14, 1918. Cemetery D. Lindthal. Cross. Discs. 3rd Row from N. Next E. Layton Longan. No. 2222228.

12. Seely, Bert W. No. 2152677. Pvt. Co. 4. 140th Infantry. Buried August 14, 1918. Cemetery D Lindthal. 3rd Row from N. Next East of Pvt. Leslie Mitchell. No. 2222228. Cross. Discs.

13. Althenthal, Clarence. No. 1462126. Machine Gun Co. 140th Inf. Buried August 15, 1918. Cemetery D Lindthal. Discs. Cross. Just East of Elmer Tucker.

14. Breedlove, Elza, No. 2221999. Pvt. Co. G. 140th Inf. Buried August 16, 1918. Cemetery D Lindthal. Cross. Discs. Just East of Clarence Althenthal. Just South of Earl Campbell. No. 146237.

15. Button, Flynn F. No. 2222245. Pvt. Co. 140th Inf. Buried August 27, 1918. Cemetery D Lindthal. Tag with body. Bottle. Cross. Just E. James.

20. Tressell, Archie L. No. 2177657. Pvt. Co. C. 140th Inf. Buried August 31, 1918. Cemetery D. Lindtnal. 15 Amer. Grave in N. Row, West to East. Both tags.

21. Allen, Clay C. No. 1454406. Pvt. Co. A. 130th Machine Gun Battalion. Buried August 31, 1918. Cemetery D Lindthal. 16 Ame. Grave. N. Row. Cross. Discs.

22. Beaers, Raymond. No. 1454370. Pvt. Co. A. 130th Machine Gun Battalion. Buried August 31, 1918. Cemetery D Lindthal. Cross. Discs. 17th American N. Row.

17. Leahy, Dan J. No. 1459653. Pvt. Co. A. 140th Inf. Buried August 27, 1918. 2 Bottles. Cross. 4th from N. 2. E. Breedlove. Lindthal

18. Cullom, Geo. T. No. 1459560. Pvt. A. 140th. Buried August 27, 1918. Both tags. Cross. 4th from N. just E. Leahy.

19. James, Harold. No. 14566604. Pvt. Co. B. 130th Machine Gun Bn. Buried August 27, 1918. 4 N. E. Cullom.

We had lost many officers in the States. Majors Congdon, Constable and Ross. Constable and Ristine came over with other outfits, and wrote history. That grand old man, Archie Johnson M. C., had been taken away, a major. Captains Hardin, Barnes, Malone, Durnell, and others who have been mentioned. They were regarded as splendid officers. Lieutenants Bowman and Throckmorton, and Lieberman—good and efficient officers all. In France during July and August, and the first part of September we lost Grant Davidson, Henry E. Lewis, Edward P. Sammons, John R. Smiley, John P. Griebel, and Fred O.. Wickham among the Captains. These were all excellent efficient officers; some of them of exceptional ability. They were sadly missed when we went "over the top." Wickham had commanded I Company, and in the days at Doniphan had been seen more than once going into retirement with an unfortunate rookie, stripping off the insignia of rank as he walked. There were no court martials in his company, and the men were ready to follow him anywhere.

Among the Lieutenants we had removed were Wm. R. Stryker, a fine officer, Jerry F. Duggan, a born soldier, J. O. Ferguson, Wm. C. Gordon, H. P. Lawrence, Howard Frissell, Kiser and Hocker.

The removal of these officers, and others whose names the records fail to show, places the regiment at a real disadvantage. Men like Griebel could ill be spared. Not only as is it true that these men were for the most part competent oficers, who had the full loyalty of the men, but so many were removed that the 140th went into action on September 25th, sadly short of its full complement of officers, and unquestionably suffered because of that fact.

Two Chaplains joined us in the Vosges. Chaplain Oliver P. Buswell, Jr., a Presbyterian who was assigned to the second Battalion. Chaplain Buswell, a young man of twenty-three, was gifted with a magnificent physique, a splendid musical voice, brains and common sense. He won the hearts of the men at once, and his work was of the greatest value to the regiment. There was no more popular chaplain in the A. E. F. He was wounded in the Argonne, and cited in orders for bravery. He did not know the meaning of fear, and thought only of his men. From the 17th of August, when he joined the regiment, his presence and influence was of the greatest value. His genuine and simple Christian spirit won the respect and admiration of all who knew him. Always cheerful, never discouraging, he deserves with Chaplain Hart the credit for making real religion respected in the regim nt.

Chaplain Hart was the Knights of Columbus Chaplain, but we felt that he belonged to the regiment. He was an older man, and was indeed "Father Hart" to everyone. Protestants and Catholics alike loved him. Brave, kindly, gentle, there was not a man in the 140th who did not feel proud of him. Popular with the men, he was equally popular with the officers. Not that he cared for popularity;

ALSATIAN DAYS IN QUIET TRENCHES 47

his one desire was to be helpful to the men, and he never spared himself. Generous and unselfish, he would give anything he possessed to anyone who asked him. He too was cited in orders, but his finest citation comes from the men who pronounced him the most unselfish, big-hearted man they had ever met. So many requests have come for his address, that it seems wise to give it here. It is Lakeville, Minnesota. And we feel that Lakeville is a very fortunate town.

THE CHAPLAIN'S ORCHESTRA
These Men Gave Their Time at Church Parade for Eighteen Months.

CHAPTER V

Swinging Into Line for the Big Drive

A few days before we left the Vosges trenches, our artillery was brought up the steep mountain road—a killing pull on the horses. No doubt gun practice was needed, but we had found the utmost difficulty in getting a lightly loaded army wagon up the road. All our supplies came up the wire cable to Boussat. And we wondered how the horses would stand the heavy pull. After spending less than two weeks on the heights, they were brought down, and a long march across country followed. When they reached the Meuse-Argonne battlefield they had lost nearly a third of their horses.

The men of the 140th had grown accustomed to the hardships of of trench life. They had grown accustomed to the sound of the big guns, and they had seen death. The raids and scouting expeditions had helped them find themselves. Lt. George Smith with some men had been out in no man's land and when a barrage was fired by our own artillery. No one was hurt, but they were very angry about it, failing to appreciate the experience. In fact the whole regiment felt that it had enough preliminary experience and wanted a real fight. They were soon to find it!

The news came that they were to return to Saulxures, and it was welcome news. They had left many friends in this pleasant French village. They had left a good reputation and they liked the French. True they had found "profiteers" among the peasantry; but around the cantonments in the United States had been price-boosters besides whom the French were in the kindergarten class. Saulxures on the banks of the Pleasant Moselette was a good place in which to fight the war.

The Regimental Chaplain, during our previous visit, had been billeted with the Reicherts, who had a bicycle shop, and made post-card photographs of many of the men. On learning that the 140th was to return to Saulxures, they asked—having forgotten his name—for the "handsome Chaplain." This was not an accurate description of Chaplain Edwards; it was French politeness.

SWINGING INTO LINE FOR THE BIG DRIVE

Chaplain Buswell, twenty-three, with brown eyes and rosy cheeks, had joined us while in the trenches. The billeting officer sent him to the Reicherts, much to their surprise, and the Regimental Chaplain fared poorly indeed.

The First Battalion left August 31st, to be followed by the remainder of the regiment on September 2nd, being relieved by the French and a part of the Sixth Division Regulars. We marched cheerfully over the mountains to Saulxures, but our dreams of ease were soon shattered. Just after midnight on the morning of September 4th we were awakened by orders to move, and we entrained the same morning. The first train was bombed by a German aeroplane, and anti aircraft guns were mounted on all sections of the train. The Y. M. C. A. secretaries were ordered back by General Traub, but Bemish with the Second Battalion managed to get through. He went over the top with the boys, carrying a little cane. I have not seen him since, but he was a real man.

For some reason we never detrained at the nearest point to our objective, and on this occasion marched back about thirty kilometers of unnecessary hiking. Headquarters were at Chaligny Sur Mont and Chaligny Sur Val. Chaligny Sur Mont was larger with a 10th century church. Chaligny Sur Val was smaller and dirtier—which is saying a great deal.

After two miserable days, Col. Murphy moved us to Houdemont, a few miles from Nancy. In Nancy we found women running the street cars, and a fare of 20 centimes. Shades of Kansas City? On the 10th we marched out at dusk, retracing our steps past Chaligny, and reached Maron. On the 11th we marched into Foret-le-Haye, where we remained for a week. We were in reserve for the St. Mihiel drive, and eager to get into it, but remained in our pup tents, wet tired and disappointed.

We could hear the barrage, which started about midnight, and see the flashes in the sky of thousands of guns.

As we marched into the woods and the tired doughboys halted, one was heard to say, "Give me more room." When asked why, he replied "So I can get this darned billet off my back." And for a week our billets were what we carried with us.

While here, some negro troops were near us for a time. One of them was heard earnestly exhorting his friend, "Man, yo' sholy is got to watch these here white boys all the time. They jes nachelly steal everything you got!"

For several days before we moved up we had been trying to get clothing and supplies for the men—clothing and equipment which was sadly needed. Evidently the restlessness displayed on the battlefield was a characteristic of "higher ups." From place to place a lieutenant dashed, but "G-1" had always moved on. Finally, in desperation, this young lieutenant forged the august signature of "G-1". The requisition was honored, and the supplies obtained.

We had marched through the rain all night and were supposed

to be hidden from the Germans in the forest. The French troops marched cheerfully by day, but evidently their horizon blue uniforms were invisible to the Germans. They used lights whenever necessary, while we stumbled in the dark, and built fires to cook their food while we ate corned-willy cold. We were never able to fathom the secret of the low visibility of the French, but if this whole regiment does not turn out to be burglars it will not be because they lack experience in doing their work at night and creeping stealthily in and out of all sorts of places in utter silence and complete darkness. During the day the thunder of the guns on the St. Mihiel salient, Mont-Sec, was clearly audible, and the frequent heavy smoke clouds were evidence that the Boche was retiring leaving behind his usual trail of ruin and destruction. After a week of mud and misery on September the 18th the entire Division was moved by an almost endless truck train which was reached by the usual march by the usual longer route, through the usual mud; a French train, rented from the French. The men were so closely crowded that rest was impossible. Over the Nancy-Toul Bar-le-Duc road a distance of many kilometres to Triacourt where Division Headquarters were established. The 140th scattered in the village Eclair and the surrounding woods, mostly the surrounding woods. The nights of September 19th and 20th were spent here. The men were exhausted from the trip. Our regimental transport came overland; all the roads were overcrowded and congested. The American Army pay heavy rent for the use of French roads and repair them whenever damaged. Because of the overcrowded condition the transports did not reach us until the 22nd and 23rd. Rations were short. The men were tired, cold, wet, hungry and rations were very short. It is reported that the French entered heavy claims for food losses about this time. During the night, September 21st, the entire brigade marched northward, directly into the Argonne Forest, keeping carefully hidden from observation. The regiment halted at Camp General Marquette, about sixteen kilometres north of Eclair. By crowding troops into the wooden shacks poor accommodations were secured for nearly all. A few were still in shelter tents. There was plenty of rain and mud, but little water for drinking or bathing, in fact during our whole stay in France, including our return journey on board ship, the amount of water was limited and had to be carefully conserved. At Camp Marquette the men were partially dried out. All excessive equipment was collected, carefully tagged, and placed under guard. An extra issue was made of reserve rations and ammunition. Hand and rifle grenades were issued as the men marched out. The whole four days at Camp Marquette were occupied by hurried combat preliminaries. The men realized that at last they were to meet the acid test. Everywhere men could be seen reading over old letters from their sweethearts, mothers and wives. They wrote letters home, many being left in the Regimental Postoffice to be mailed only in case they did not return. A large mail arrived

SWINGING INTO LINE FOR THE BIG DRIVE

from the states just before we broke camp and greatly heartened the men. Colonel P. A. Murphy who had command of the regiment during its training in the Vosges was relieved from command in the Forest Le Haye. Major Fred L. Lemmon from the 1st Battalion took command for a few days and was relieved by Lieut. Col. C. E. Delaplane, recently a Major in the Ordnance Department with the Regular Army who was placed in command of an Infantry regiment, a full strength infantry regiment, two days before going into action.

The First American Army was a truly American Army. 138,000 French troops under American command, and 650,000 American soldiers were hurled against a front of 45 kilometers and took it. The 140th had held a sector of 35 kilometers in the Vosges. But this was a different matter. A little more than half as many troops were opposing us, but they were in strongly entrenched positions and had every advantage.

Chateau Thierry has its glory, the St. Mihiel drive was wonderful, but it is the Argonne-Meuse Battle which will form the story told the folks back home.

The Argonne-Meuse battle will live forever in the heart of America, for every state was there. There is no city, town or village or country cross-roads settlement but has its honored dead, or wounded hero. In every community men see a saddened widow, a sorrowful mother, a soldier maimed by honorable wounds or a man who on the anniversary of the 11 of November pins on his tunic a Distinguished Service Cross. It was our army, the army of all of us, that swept over the blood-soaked hills of France to victory.

From the Argonne forest to the sea, the British, French and Belgians flung our two million men against the enemy on a front of over 300 kilometers. On the Italian front the Italians were crushing the 63 divisions of Austria, and the the American army held 42 German divisions and compelled them to use reserves sadly needed elsewhere.

The German army was at the height of efficiency. Its morale was good. It's best divisions fought with great courage and tactical efficiency.

The troops opposed to the 35th were well clothed, well fed, and their blankets and equipment were of the best.

Our right flank was protected by the Meuse, while our left embraced the Argonne forest, whose ravines, hills and elaborate defenses screened by dense thickets had been generally considered impregnable. Our order of battle from right to left was the Third Corps from the Meuse to Malancourt, with the 33rd, 80th, and the 4th Divisions in line, and the 3rd Division as Corps reserve; the Fifth Corps from Malancourt to Vauquois, with the 70th, 37th, and 91st Divisions in line, and the 32nd Division in Corps reserve; and the First Corps from Vauquois to Vienne-le-Chateau, with the 35th, 25th and 77th Divisions in line and the 92nd in Corps reserve. The Army reserve consisted of the 1st, 29th and 82nd Divisions.

In 1917 the American Navy had turned the U-boat success into failure. We now know that the war would have ended by January, 1918, if the United States had not joined the Allies. And now the United States was to help strike the final and decisive blow for victory. It is the largest battle of American history. And its record is a proud one.

The troops were moved up as secretly as possible. A modern attack is a question of roads. The staffs figure what traffic each road will bear, place military police at the cross-roads, and then crowd on three times the travel the roads can accommodate. A study of the maps for this offensive will show that there were about one-fourth as many roads as necessary, and much of the criticism passed on this operation is due to the lack of roads.

The Germans knew we were to attack, but as late as September 22nd did not know whether the main attack was to be put on the Italian, French, British, or American front. And later they fully expected our advance to be made on Metz. We had nine divisions in line, and but three roads, one from Bethincourt to Montfaucon running diagonally across the direction of attack, and the territory of three divisions. The artillery, rolling kitchens, engineers supplies, etc., must have roads if they are to keep up with the infantry. They can not travel in mud. The Germans had three strong lines of defense, with several trenches to each one, the last line some distance back. When one remembers that we had to advance through woods and over hills, the progress is remarkable, and one looks with wonder at the traffic handled by the three roads.

Glory Enough For All

It is to be remembered that this is the history of one regiment. The 138th has a lasting monument of glory in Vauquois Hill. The 137th will never forget Baulny. The 139th wrote glorious history on every line of the battlefield. Rieger and Ristine are proud names. The 129th F. A. worked with the efficiency of a machine, and the 130th spared neither horses nor men. These, and the other units of the 35th fought as Kansas and Missouri men might be expected to fight, and gave new glory to the old Flag. The 140th is proud of them all, and feels it an honor to have fought with such men. It does not forget them; it never will forget them. And it asks the reader to remember that he is reading the history of but one regiment, and that we do not forget that others were with us every hour when needed most.

The 140th Under-officered

Brig. General. Charles I. Martin was regarded as a capable officer. Quiet and reserved, he is a man of force and power. He had been a captain in Funston's 20th Kansas, and his record was so good that he came home from the Philippines a major. He has been adjutant general of Kansas for some time. He knew the ground over which we were to fight accurately, having made perhaps the

SWINGING INTO LINE FOR THE BIG DRIVE

most thorough study of the terrain of any officer in the division. I have known him personally for years, and have heard a great many men and officers express frankly their good opinion of him. He knew the terrain, he knew the men, he is calm and does not lose his head, and he knows how to maintain perfect liaison. These qualities were conspicuously lacking in Col. Kirby Walker who replaced him as Brigade Commander of the 70th brigade on September 21st, four days before we went into battle. There were changes in the two brigades, but they did not affect the 140th. It was in the 70th all the time.

Col. Murphy was relieved Sept. 16th and Maj. Fred L. Lemmon commanded the 140th until Sept. 22nd, when Lt. Col. C. E. Deleplane was given command. Col. Delaplane had been attached to Brigade Headquarters for some occult reason, having as Major Delaplane been Division Ordnance officer since the Doniphan days. He was unacquainted with the officers and men, and was placed in a difficult position. In the days of peace he had commanded small units of men. He had made a good ordnance officer. But to be given 3500 men and ordered to fight them was a sudden shift and an unexpected task. He did the best he could. Companies F, H, I and L were without captains—a whole battalion—and went in under the command of lieutenants. Few of the other companies were fully officered. Lt. Ware of B. company who had been absent sick, reported on the 29th. The following is the list of officers who werewith the regiment in the drive:

Captains:
A—Armour, John W.
B—Wilson, Thomas J.
C—Rexroad, Guy C.
D—Campbell, Ralph W.
E—Smith, William A.
F—
G—Milligan, Jacob L.
H—
I—
K—Kenady, James C.
L—
M—McFadden, Shamus O.
Hq. Co.—Oliver, Alexander S.
M. G.—Osgood, Warren L.

Regt. Staff:
Lt. Col. Delaplane, C. E.
Capt. Seitz, Ray E.
Capt. Truman, Ralph E.
Capt. Redman, Julius A.
Chapl. Edwards, Evan A.
Chapl. Buswell, Oliver J.
Supply Co.:
Capt. Ward, Frank G.
Lieut. Reid, Marion C.
Lieut. Salisbury, Joseph H.
Sullivan, Clyde R.
1st Lieutenants:
Wise, Lloyd V.

Tharp, Lewis M.
James, William D.
Spicer, Morgan V.
(Lt. Ware reported fr. ab. sk Sept. 29)
Black, Henry E.
Adams, Samuel T.
Gardner, Albert S.
Scott, William E.
Robertson, David W.
Garner, Edward S.
Oliff, Julian S.
Brady, Robert K.
Farris, Cecil M.
Skelton, Claude M.
Holt, Rolla B.
Harrison, Pollard E.
Smith, Eustice
Slaughter, Stephen O.
Whitthorne, Harry S.
Gaines, Harry W.
Nottingham, William K.
Pleasants, John H.
Baxter, William J.
Stogsdill, Richard H.
Imes, Orie S.
Breckinridge, Archie
Bn. Staff:
Majors:
Lemmon, Fred L.
Maybrey, Warren L.
Davis, Murray.
1st Lt. Simpson, George H.
1st Lt. McGann, Henry K.
Stark, John V.
2nd Lt. Compton, Letcher C.

2nd Lt. Richter, Julius J.
2nd Lt. Han, Loyd R.
2nd Lieuts.
Otey, Basil R.
Sheahan, John J.
Kiddoo, Richard
Menges, Louis J.
Holden, George D.
Rosenfield, Milton O.
Smith, G. W.
Thomas, Roy E.
Hill, Clinton V.
Haberstroth, Roy E.
Baker, Roy D.
Munger, Earl L.
Barnert, Merle J.
Miller, Roy M.
Denham, Jesse H.
Stinson, Julian T.
Champion, Lloyd V.
Stephens, Reid
Buell, Fred W.
Keefner, Edward
Dwyer, Daniel M.
Jackson, Harvey
Gregg, Norris B.
Medical:
Major Slusher, Ernest
Capt. Broyles, Glen H.
Howell, John F.
1st Lt. Rothman, Henry
Biggs, James B.
Schlegelmilch, W. G.
Dental:
1st Lt. Reed, Willie C.
Cronkite, Walter L.

What Was the Matter With the Artillery?

There have been many questions asked about the artillery, and much blame has been laid upon it. There can be no question that we lacked sufficient guns. The gallant First Division relieved us, planning to advance seven kilometers at once. They could not do so. They were compelled to wait for several days until nearly 800 big guns were placed in support before they could advance. We were opposed by the best artillery the Boche had—and there are none better. We needed more guns. It took nearly a month to advance as far as the 35th did in five days.

The 130th, heavy, were delayed by blown-up bridges The men worked heroically. The regiment gave good support. The story has been told elsewhere, that they with the 128th, light, were in support most of the time. General Berry seemed unwilling to work in very close harmony with the Division Commander, but the men made good.

The 129th may be taken as an example. They participated in the opening barrage from 4:20 until 7:41 on the 26th. Under fire they took position on the 27th back of hill 221, and took part in the barrage as soon as orders reached them (the hour of advance was changed from 8:30 to 5:30). From that time the regiment—or one battalion not moving forward—was in position to fire whenever called on. The First Battalion moved into Charpentry at 10:30 a. m. Sept. 28th under fire, and remained there until October 3d. The Second Battalion was at Cheppy during this time.

Many reports of firing short occurred. On at least one occasion the 129th was requested to cease firing as it had been firing short, when it had not been firing at all.

German Guns On Our Left Flank

The Division advanced rapidly. The 28th was several kilometers back on our left. German batteries were located and fired upon west of Montblainville, southwest of Apremont, and west of the Aire. Unquestionably the Germans had a flanking fire from these points at times, on the 27th and 28th! As we were bearing slightly to the northwest, it seems probably that some of the fire reported as falling short from our own guns was in reality a flanking fire delivered by the enemy artillery. In every action of every army the infantry undoubtedly has suffered at times from its own artillery falling short. This can not be avoided and is recognized by army men. But it seems probable that these facts, together with the German battery reported by Ristine of the 139th, will account for many of the complaints of "short" firing when the true history of the engagement becomes known.

Another real difficulty lay in the lack of signal equipment. The artillery had been furnished with excellent wireless equipment—but none had been given the infantry, therefore it was useless. The telephone equipment was lacking, and the rocket-signals were of such a character as to be useless. The artillery—our own artillery—was

SWINGING INTO LINE FOR THE BIG DRIVE

ready to do its duty. It did a great deal, not only in furnishing barrages but in destroying ammunition dumps, trains, etc., behind the enemy lines. But it was hampered by lack of information, as it was compelled to depend entirely upon liason through runners, and the information furnished was not always correct. The runners displayed the greatest heroism. They were always ready, hesitated at no danger, and many of them gave their lives on the field.

On the 29th Major Miles ordered his battalion of the 129th to fire point-blank if necessary—they meant to stay with their guns until death! They are our kind of folks—the artillery. Let us be proud of them. They gave us loyal support, and we suffered together.

The 128th west of Very and the 130th F. A. at Varennes were doing their best. One who knows either outfit would be slow to feel they failed to do all that was possible.

As to our support in the air, one must tell a different story. Aeroplanes—American aeroplanes—there were none. The American planes had a "cocarde" or large circle of three rings; the center white, the next blue, and the outer red. But we became thoroughly familiar with the German plane—its appearance, and its behavior. Plenty of opportunity for observation was afforded us.

LT. COL. C. E. DELAPLANE
Who Led the 140th in the Argonne Drive

CHAPTER VI.

The Five Days

THE STORY OF A GREAT REGIMENT

From Camp Marquette the 140th marched into Aubreville. We left camp about 8 p. m., rifle ammunition and hand and rifle grenades were distributed as we marched out. It was a short two hours hike, but we were twice that long on the roads, which were blocked from time to time, and jammed with traffic all the way. We would pass the big guns, and hear the men softly swearing at the tired horses; then the guns would rumble past us, while our tired men waited impatiently.

For almost a month the regiment had been on the move, sleeping generally in the open, and undergoing every physical discomfort. We had lacked water, we had lacked opportunity for bathing and cleaning up, we were wet and cold and tired and dirty—but not discouraged.

As we tramped into Aubreville after midnight, I was thinking "It has been difficult, but we have fooled Fritz. He does not dream that we are near!" Just then—whang! a shrapnel burst in the very center of the road forty yards ahead. Its brilliant light made one think of fireworks, and its sound caused one to think of many things.

We marched through the ruins of the town, with several casualties in B Company, and the regiment rested on a protected hillside about four hundred yards beyond. I heard an indignant doughboy say "Protected hill-side hell! Protected by Providence."

The Lay of the Land

The map has proven so small that a brief description of the terrain may be in place. Starting from Vauquois Hill, and drawing a line slightly west of north, it is nearly three miles to Cheppy, nearly three miles from Cheppy to Charpentry, and nearly three miles from Charpentry to Exermont. Going northwest then, we find Cheppy, Charpentry and Exermont.

Very lay a little over a mile northeast of Cheppy or a little southeast of Charpentry. Baulny lay less than a mile northwest of Charpentry, and the line continued reached Apremont more than a mile further on.

Chaudron Farm lay nearly half way from Charpentry to Exermont, a little west of the line, and nearly a mile northeast of Baulny. These are merely rough approximations, but they may serve to outline the ground over which we fought.

On the wet grass under the trees we lay and tried to sleep. Some really did sleep for a time, but only for a time. About 2:30 the irregular fire of the artillery blended into a huge and deafening volume of sound. The barrage was on. Thousands of guns! Countless thousands of shells! There they go levelling barbed wire, obliterating trenches, smashing ammunition dumps, blocking dug-outs, a Niagara of flame, a river of iron flowing over the Boche trenches. One somehow sensed a magnificent power. It was our barrage, and it was magnificent. One will never forget it, but it cannot be described. A husky voice is heard "Some barrage!"; the answer "I'll tell the world!"

Then suddenly—quiet, a strange terrible silence. A grey, misty dawn. It is 5:30, the "zero hour." Light packs and ammunition bandoliers are adjusted, bayonets are fixed, and breakfastless, cold, stiff, but feeling suddenly young and strong and victorious the men stream "over the top." They were quiet, steady and determined. There was little evidence of excitement and none of fear. But continually one heard expressed the dread that the soldier might get lost or go the wrong way. In the haze of the smoke screen, and the clouds of the morning, this was but natural.

First Day, Thursday, September 26th

The 138th had preceded us into the line. Vauquois Hill is a huge fortress a hundred feet high and ten times as long, which dominates the country for miles around. The Germans had held it since 1914, it was thoroughly mined and completely fortified. Time after time the French had stormed it in vain. "Dead Man's Hill" they called it and vowed it could not be taken. It fell to the 138th in an hour, and as we followed them to clear up the ground, we were impressed by the trenches. We had never seen such solid, well built trenches. The machine gun emplacements were heavy and of solid concrete, while deep in the earth, many yards underground, were comfortable electric lighted dugouts with water and all the comforts of home.

We really moved out at 5:45 deployed in column of battalions in order, first, second and third, the Stokes mortars and one-pounders with the third, while Col. Delaplane and the Command Group went with the second. The battalions were in staggered platoon columns.

The foggy weather, smoke shells, and uneven ground caused some confusion and loss of contact between organizations, but after passing Vauquois Hill the different units established contact and were in their proper places.

The First, under Major Lemmon, gathered in A and C companies of the 137th in the woods south of Vauquois, and companies A, B and C 140th were sent around the right (eastern) end of the hill, while D with the two borrowed companies went directly over the hill. This battalion rendered assistance to the 69th brigade which was temporarily checked on our left. Prisoners were met going back—our first Germans, and they all seemed of a remarkably peaceful disposition.

Two American soldiers were seen advancing over Vauquois with a remarkable flag—the Stars and Stripes on one side and the French Tricolor on the other. They ambled joyfully along, apparently under their own orders, and were soon lost to view. The two splendid 137th companies moved up to join their regiment. The first kept in advance.

The second battalion under Mabrey followed in the rear of the 138th, and rendered assistance. There was little fighting, as our barrage had been most effective, but machine gun nests had to be cleaned out and dugouts mopped up. There were casualties from artillery and machine gun fire in this battalion, which halted at dusk north of Cheppy.

The third battalion under Davis marched in splendid order, and was in its proper place throughout the day. In the afternoon the direction was changed from nearly due North to northwest, passing to the right of the Varennes-Avocourt road through La Forge, Min, crossing the trench "Du Scorpion" and resting at night well northwest of Cheppy and just south of a line drawn from Very to Montblainville, fifty or sixty yards behind the 138th., which had suffered heavy losses. The third battalion was held as Divisional reserve remaining on the slope west of the little stream.

And so the day ended. It is not true as has been stated that we had no casualties. There were some, but they were few. In reserve, we had been spectators of a great battle. The Germans had been ordered to hold their position at any cost, and they were fighting desperately. In the morning we were to take the front line—and we were "ready to go."

The Second Day, Friday the 27th

In accordance with the plan elaborated by General Traub in consultation with General Berry, the 140th. moved up on a line with the 139th. This was the day of the famous "mixed orders." The first plan was to attack at 8:30 after a three hours' artillery fire. Apparently the final plan was to advance at 6:30, but the 140th received orders at 5:05 a. m. to advance at 5:30 after a five minutes barrage on machine gun nests. But the barrage failed to materialize. The first battalion on the left and the second on the right started their advance through the 138th., or what was left of that gallant

LT. COL. FRED L. LEMMON, D. S. C.
Wounded near Charpentry

regiment, for it had paid dearly for its successes of the day before. The third was in support. Our men tried to get through the heavy wire entanglements on hill 218, but were swept by a withering fire. Col. Walker kept calling for artillery support, but could obtain none. The enemy planes owned the air and gave the range to their artillery and our losses were heavy. We could not make any real gain. The corps howitzers were brought up and turned on the machine gun emplacements along the Very Charpentry road with little effect. Running to the east from Charpentry was a fine road lined with huge trees. All along the brow of this hill were machine gunners. Afterwards I got blankets for the wounded from these dead gunners, most of them killed near their guns. There were twenty or thirty there. In the afternoon the tanks came up. A gladsome sight they were, and manned by a fine lot of men. One red-headed Sergeant from Georgia had been in the St. Mihiel drive—a picnic to this he said. The 91st on our right was trying to move up. The second battalion gained a position north of the Very-Charpentry road, but lost 150 men and three officers killed and wounded. They started about 100 prisoners to the rear. None were reported as getting back, but it was learned that they reported to the headquarters of the 91st.

And so attack after attack failed. It seemed impossible to make a real advance. Finally, almost at dark, Col. Delaplane ordered an advance. There was no artillery, but a desperate resolve had settled on the men. The 140th. held up by a lot of Germans! It simply must not be. One man said quietly "just let me get two Boche first, and I'll take mine!" Some one said "This is Friday!" and Harry Kennedy replied "Friday is my lucky day." Poor brave Kennedy—loyal and plucky to the core. We left him on the field, and shall always be proud of him.

They were determined to go through. And they could not be stopped. The high explosives took their gruesome toll. The machine guns cut down the men in ranks. And the men went on. They dropped like leaves, and all hell seemed turned loose on them. And the men went on. They took Charpentry, they swept over the line of machine guns. And they captured a German battery. Its photograph appears in this volume, and is authentic, for it was made from a film in the camera of the officer commanding the battery.

Herld Smith of F Co. was mortally wounded rushing a machine gun nest. He calmly directed his platoon until death hushed his voice—thinking only of their work and his duty as a man. He was awarded the Distinguished Service Cross, but he is only an example of the kind of men we had. If there was one thing that stood out during these horrible days it was the efficiency of the non-com. He was not thinking about his own safety. His work and his men and all the time these men were performing prodigies of valor, and winning honor and glory for the service.

Major Lemmon was wounded severely in the side by a machine gun bullet as he passed to the northeast of Charpentry about 6:30 p. m.

He had been ill for a week with a severe attack of grippe and had a high temperature (we all had a high temperature about that time) and was an ill man before he was wounded. In spite of his wound he refused to go to the hospital, and fought his battalion for more than 24 hours, until he dropped from exhaustion and weakness caused by his wound. He received the D. S. C., but probably more than that he prizes the loyalty of his men.

CAPT. GUY C. REXROAD
Co. C. Twice Wounded

LT. GEO. D. HOLDEN
Died of Wounds

CAPT. J. C. KENADY
Co. K. Died of Wounds Received in Argonne

LT. DAVID M. ROBERTSON
Co. E. Killed in Action

THE FIVE DAYS

Rosenfield, a fine young lieutenant of D Co. was wounded. He was cheerful, and joked with the Chaplain as he was back on a stretcher. It was not a very good joke, but under the circumstances deserves admiration.

Captain Rexroad of C. Co., a quiet, brave officer, was wounded in the right arm by a machine gun bullet while at Charpentry. He remained with his company until the 29th, when he was severely wounded in the abdomen by a fragment of high explosive shell. He wanted to stay with his company, badly wounded as he was, but had to be removed from the field. Today he is well and strong again. Quiet and reserved, he was a strong, resourceful and capable officer, and made a splendid record.

K. Company with the third battalion was in support the 27th, yet it too suffered casualties. I had gone over the top with K company, but pressed on ahead where a chaplain was needed. In my notebook I recorded the wounded and their messages, the dead and their location.

Private Ford was the first man killed in K, and Captain Kenady, that gentle, brave, lovable soldier, knelt by the body and wept. Captain Kenady had made a record for splendid discipline. Even that strict Regular, Colonel Murphy, never found fault with him. He had no enemies, and many many friends. Terribly wounded, he too was to die later.

The Pioneer Platoon had men in the very front to cut wires and render various services. They helped as runners and as ammunition carriers. Out of two score men they lost eight. They had done a lot of hard and disagreeable work while in France, and now were at the front until the very last day.

The second battalion under Mabrey had a big part in wiping out the machine gunners to the right of Charpentry on the heights, just as the first battalion had a big part in taking Charpentry.

Major Mabrey was cool, steady, and thoughtful of his men. His officers said that he handled his men with great skill and splendid judgment on this day and throughout the drive, refusing to sacrifice them unnecessarily yet losing no opportunity to gain an advantage. "Like a veteran," said one of his men.

Pearl Chartier belongs to Co. H, and lives near the little town of Clyde, Kansas. When we ran into heavy wire entanglements near Charpentry he volunteered to go forward and cut the wires, and in the face of heavy machine gun and artillery fire cut a lane in the wires that the Second Battalion might move forward. There was not a chance in a thousand for him—but he got that lucky chance and came through the drive safely. He has the D. S. C., but will not talk about it. McCaferty of H and Haley of F were cited for cutting wire under similar conditions.

Bemish was a Y. M. C. A. Secretary All Y men had been ordered to leave the Division before we went up—Traub's order—and all the others had dropped out. But Bemish managed to sneak through. He carried a small cane, and seemed cool and collected through it all. I never saw him after we came out but bear witness to his love of the regiment and his courage.

Captain Edward Beau had joined us nearly three months before as French Liaison Officer. He had been with the Artillery, and had been twice wounded. Courteous, chivalrous, brave and brilliant, he represented the finest type of French Officer. I have seen him under difficult circumstances, always patient, untiring and cheerful. He won the respect and admiration of all the officers in the 140th., and was very popular with the men. He was gassed, and we did not see him again for weeks, but the regiment will always remember him.

Two other Frenchmen were with us, belonging to the Intelligence Department, and wearing on the collar of their uniforms the head of the Sphinx, first used as the insignia of this Department under the great Napoleon. Monsieur Chatot spoke English well and was familiar with Lowell, Longfellow, Whittier, Poe, Hawthorne and Cooper. He was lifted from the ground by the explosion of a shell, and we supposed him dead, but he turned up after the drive suffering only from gas and shock, and with the Croix de Guerre.

Monsieur Perronne had spent some years in the United States, and he too was with us through the hottest of the fight.

On the first morning the enemy had learned what it meant to fight in shell destroyed trenches, with defenses obliterated and annihilated, and against powerful artillery. And he had fallen back five kilometers. Today we had driven him back two and a half kilometers. And we had passed Charpentry!

We had passed Charpentry. Remember there was no barrage here to protect us and destroy the enemy. The Germans knew the ground over which they had retired to an inch. For four years it had been their home. Its hills and valleys, its roads and passages were to their artillery an open book.

We had neither artillery nor aeroplanes. They opposed us with both. We had to cross a broad flat plateau, go down a hill into a valley, and charge up a hill side in the face of a withering fire. For the advance we paid heavily. But the 140th advanced!

Not the Only Regiment

It must be remembered that this is the history of the 140th, and while its movements are given, it is all the while to be kept in mind that day by day there was more and more intermingling of commands, and that each of the other regiments was writing on the same page with us a history of courage, loyalty and glory.

Near Charpentry on this day I saw helmets bearing the device of the 139th, of the 138th, and a few of the 137th, which was in support of the 138th. But in Charpentry and to the west the loss fell heavily upon the 140th.

Newspaper writers tell of the piteous cries and dreadful groans of the wounded and dying on the field of battle. During the five days

THE FIVE DAYS

I talked with literally hundreds of wounded and dying and save in a few cases of shell shock, heard neither groans nor shrieks. A man would have a rough jest, a cheerful oath, a grateful word for cigarettes or beef juice, but no cry for pity. The grit and pluck displayed by the wounded men was almost superhuman. Missouri may well be proud of the men of the 140th. They fought like demons; they suffered like heroes; they died like men.

One man, badly wounded, lay in a dressing station and complained of the cold as he suffered from the chill which follows shock. I laid a trench-coat over him—it had a thick wool lining. I felt that it would be ruined, and I felt that I would never need it again for I was scared to death during the whole battle. When I found a blanket and returned with it later, he said that he was warm and added "See Chaplain, I have been careful to get no blood on your new coat!" And this coolness and self control characterized most of the wounded.

These men stood the test. In attack, in defense, in suffering, in death they were worthy to measure with the best. While somewhat disorganized, the morale of the regiment was strengthened by this day. We had taken the enemy's guns. We had wiped out his flock of machine gunners. We had shown how we could die. We had learned that we could count on each other to the limit. We had entered the battle-line a green regiment, and received our baptism of fire. Tonight we were veterans.

Darkness and chill fell on the dew drenched hills and valleys. The night blotted out the poor twisted, motionless bodies scattered over the muddy ground. It blotted out the patient figures of the wounded. It blotted out the shell holes in the battle torn earth. The shells continued to drop over, but irregularly, and they were not many. One could snatch a mouthful of bully-beef and hardtack. One could even sleep the sleep of exhaustion in fitful snatches.

In the dressing stations there was no rest nor slumber, and the stretcher bearers and ambulances were vainly striving to evacuate the wounded, but could not do three nights work in one. There were so many wounded! And the regiment grimly waited for the dawn.

The Third Day, Saturday, September 28th

The dawning of the third day found the 140th lying in fairly regular formation northeast of Baulny and north of Charpentry. It was cold, and a keen, biting fine rain drove in our faces.

We had swung to the left, or west, and the 91st was not quite up with us, while there was a wide space between them and our right. The 28th was held up, and had as yet failed to cross the Aire. Enemy batteries in Apremont were able to sweep our flank, and from the woods beyond, heavy artillery played upon us.

The 129th F. A. had moved its second battalion in front of Cheppy Friday afternoon, and the first battalion entered Charpentry under fire at 10:30 Saturday morning. The 128th was in position just west of Very, while the 155s of the 130th were in position at Varennes.

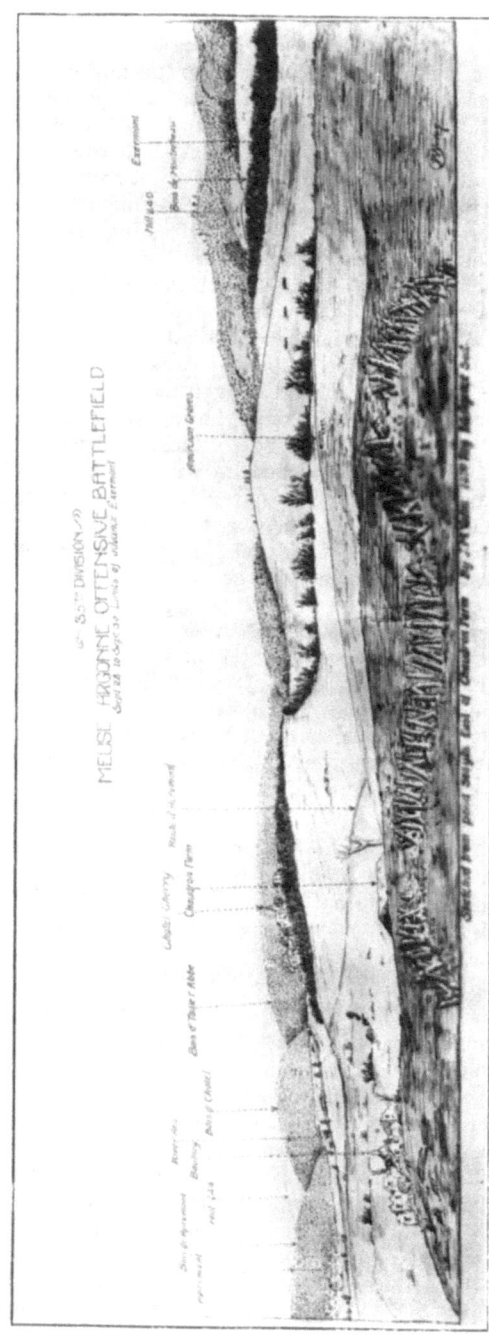

THE BATTLEFIELD
Looking N. E. from Point 300 Yards East of Chaudron Farm
Drawn by J. M. Yadon, 140 Int. Sec.

THE FIVE DAYS

They gave what support they could on this day. Our front had swung to the west so far that a flanking fire might easily seem to be short fire from our own guns.

The doughboy always "has it in" for the artillery, and naturally. I heard a trench-mortar Captain, winner of several decorations, give a vivid explanation of the work of the trench mortars. "They fire as fast as they can for three minutes, and then duck in a dugout, while the enemy shells hell out of the Infantry!" Our own trench mortars complained that in every position they sought they were urged to seek a better position somewhere else—just anywhere else.

After the battles in Artois the English had to separate the German prisoners, the infantry from the artillery, because of the bitter feeling between them. The infantry felt they had not had proper protection and that the artillery had failed them shamefully, and wanted to fight it out in the prison camp.

No one can tell how much was due to lack of ammunition, to lack of signal equipment, to lack of liaison. No one can tell just how much there was of shells falling short. But we do know that our artillery pulled their guns through hub-deep mud, used superhuman effort to get them up, and were ready to stay with us to the bitter end. They did far more than has been credited to them, and for any failure the blame lies elsewhere.

At half past three in the morning orders were received from the Brigade Adjutant to push forward with all speed and protect the right flank of the troops on our left, the 69th brigade which was to attack at 6:30. The tired men advanced, starting at 5:30 in the following order: Mabrey's battalion with a company from the 130 M. G. Bn., Murray Davis and the third battalion with another company from the 130 M. G. Bn., with the Headquarters Command Group with the second battalion. The first battalion was in the front lines, and late in the day Major Lemmon was sent back to the hospital, Captain Armour taking command of the battalion and Lt. Wise taking over A company.

At about eight the line was held up, the fire becoming so heavy that the men dug in and waited. At 8:20 a patrol of Cavalry reported, and about 9:45 the tanks came up, about twenty of them, and the attack was launched under terrific fire from the enemy. Through the draws, over the hillocks, through the dense brush and woods the men lost heavily. The regiment passed Chaudron Farm, reaching Montrebeau woods. There was little support from the Artillery, while the enemy planes were very active. It was a gruelling hour. The enemy artillery overwhelmed us with direct, indirect, and flanking fire. Planes with machine guns and bombs cut down on us from the sky. The losses were terrible, and when the regiment rested for the night in Montrebeau wood, with the second battalion in the hedge north of Chaudron Farm as reserve, it was badly cut to pieces. The third battalion had lost half its men. Murray Davis was wounded, but refused to pay any attention to it. Holt was terribly wounded, dying in a few hours. Harrison, Munger and Barnert of I company were casualties, Eustace Smith was in command of 1 and K comcompanies, plucky Captain Kenady having received his wounds. Stark and most of the battalion Headquarters were gone. M company had lost Captain McFadden, wounded—a strong, brave, splendid officer. Champion—the bravest of the brave—was killed. Nottingham, who had proved himself in Alsace, was wounded. Slaughter was terribly wounded, and Denham and Stinson, also of L company, were casualties. But in the driving rain, the men held firm.

As we pressed into Montrebeau Wood, the 138th closed up on our right. They are bonny fighters, those men of the 138th. In Doniphan days the names in front of the tents on "Officers' Row" read like a Berlin regiment. But the Germans never met more truly American soldiers nor heavier opposition.

The following messages are interesting:

From—RIO 140 Inf.
At—02.3-78.9 Foret d'Argonne, 1-80000.
Date—Sept. 28-18. Hour—2:30 p. m. No. 19. How sent—By runner.
To—Adj. 70th Brig.

Regt. halted by terrific artillery shelling and concentrated machine gun fire. See drawing showing approximately our front line. There may be a little change made during the night. We are flanked by artillery fire on every side but our rear. Our own artillery has given no support during the attack. Enemy planes very active during the day. One squadron of enemy planes over our position at 1 p. m. They turned their M. G.'s on the men causing some losses. 15 planes in the party. Also one enemy plane flew low over our troops all during the forenoon directing the fire of artillery. We have suffered heavy losses in killed and wounded. Men are now at dressing stations that were wounded yesterday. Numbers of men who are wounded have had no attention and are still lying on the ground where they fell. We are short of ammunition which is very badly needed in case of a counter-attack by the enemy. The Adjutant of the Regt. has been gassed and the C. O. has not been seen since the attack started. Runners unable to find any trace of him.

                                         Truman
                                         RIO.

From—RIO 140 Inf.
At—02.3-78.9, Forest d'Argonne, 1-20,000.
Date—Sept. 28. Hour—3 p. m. No. 20. How sent—By runner.
To—G-2, 35th Div.

Regt. halted by terrific artillery shelling and concentrated M. G. fire. See drawing forwarded by 70th Brig. We are flanked by artillery fire from every side but our rear. Our own artillery gave no support during the attack. Enemy planes over our lines during attack, flying low, directing artillery fire on our troops. At 1 p. m. 15 enemy planes flew over our lines firing on our troops with their M. G.'s, caus-

THE FIVE DAYS

ing losses. We have suffered heavy losseses in killed and wounded. Men are now in dressing stations that were wounded yesterday. Numbers of wounded men have not been carried off the field. We are short of ammunition which is very badly needed in case of a counter-attack by enemy. The Adjutant has been gassed and the C. O. has not been seen since the attack started. Runners unable to find any trace of him.

Truman

RIO

Clarence Dry, a Corporal in Co. I, had been promoted to Sergeant two weeks before. A machine gun nest, which could not be located, was taking heavy toll. Sergeant Dry volunteered to advance in the open to draw its fire. He walked coolly out, and was within fifty yards of the gun when he was killed. His platoon destroyed the enemy gunners, and the advance proceeded. Sergeant Dry was awarded the D. S. C.

Another non-com., Monte Coulter of B company was cut off with his squad in the rain and darkness of the early morning. Unable to fight their way through, they kept up a little battle of their own, and lay in shell holes until the regiment caught up with them late in the day. Coulter was later severely wounded, losing a leg. He was three times cited for bravery, and a year later married a fine Missouri girl who knew a real man.

In the afternoon about 5:30 the Colonel of the 363d found Traub, not the general, but the Chaplain's orderly, riding the Chaplain's horse, much farther front than he had any right to be.

The Colonel sent him back with a message to the artillery to lift their barrage. He rode back about seven kilometers, and delivered orders to cease firing until the new range was received. It was long after chow-time and to his indignation they refused to feed him. As he left, audibly and strenuously, expressing his indignation he passed a colored Major. "White boy, what's the trouble," the Major asked, and on being told took the messenger to the colored officers' mess and gave him a good feed.

Sergeant Rolf Raynor of K company was a typical "top-kick." He had received a slight wound in the left thigh late on the 26th., and had had a finger mutilated on the 27th. He began to feel safe from serious wounds, but about ten on Saturday morning he was badly wounded by shrapnel in the neck, left side, and left leg. With two ribs fractured, his "throat cut" and a bone in his leg fractured, he managed to hobble back to Major Slusher, and to this day swears the Major saved his life. I had heard nothing of him, and feared he was dead. To my delight, he was the first man I saw when the "home train" pulled into Kansas City.

Two other Sergeants of K company were killed, Ralph Tanner on Friday and William Bateman on Saturday. Bateman was clever, faithful and a good man. Tanner I knew the better of the two. An unusually fine character, he was patient, untiring, kindly, plucky, and did not know how to quit. What he was told to do, might be counted done.

Captain Redman was wounded and cited in orders for refusing to go back, and advancing. Captain Seitz was gassed and sent back, and his loss was felt by the regiment. He knew it and how to handle it.

As the Intelligence reports show, Colonel Delaplane became sep-

SGT. ROLF RAYNOR
Co. K. Wounded three times in the Argonne

RALPH PAINE TANNER
Sgt. Co. K. Killed in Action
Oct. 28th

LT. W. E. SCOTT
Killed in Argonne

LT. LETCHER C. COMPTON
Killed in Montrebeau Wood

arated from his regiment. He had received a shrapnel wound in the leg, but gave it no attention. He was not far away. At 6:45 p. m. he sent a message from Chaudron Road to Division Headquarters saying that he was separated from his command, had one company 129th M. G. Bn. and sixty riflemen with him, giving information about enemy fire, and asking for orders.

Slaughter of L company, an officer of unusual moral courage, was terribly wounded, but recovered. John Wilkinson of G. company, First Sergeant, was severely gassed, but refused time after time to be evacuated. He remained on duty for three days until we were relieved, and was unable to walk when he retired. For his courage and example he received the D. S. C.

It was on this day that our machine gun company lost heavily, going up in the face of heavy artillery and machine gun fire.

Osgood, its captain, was a remarkable man. There were few men in the A. E. F. who knew as much about machine guns as he did. With the company from its beginning, he was an ideal officer and a cool efficient fighter. Lt. Imes, a bright young officer, took command of the second and third platoons when their officers were wounded. Both he and Osgood should have been promoted under any intelligent system. Each night Imes could be seen going over the ground won that day, seeing that the wounded men were taken to the dressing station, and that the killed were buried. He possesses that great qualification for a good officer—he always looks out for his men. Lt. "Pat" Dwyer of Wichita, a plucky little officer, fought with the courage his name would suggest. Breckinridge was badly wounded but talked cheerfully with me in the dressing station, where McGann lay suffering with a lesser wound. Jackson kept up the credit of the company, and Norris Gregg, a quiet and resourceful young lieutenant from St. Louis, showed the greatest courage when the test came.

The machine gun company was on the job all the time, as its casualties show. It had a fine lot of men. Gunner Claude Payne is a type. His gun was well up on Saturday to repulse the counter attack from Montrebeau wood. At night instead of resting he dressed wounds and carried water to the suffering men. On the 29th when the regiment fell back, he assisted in carrying wounded, although burdened with his gun equipment, back from the Chaudron Farm dressing station. After miraculous escapes, he is still alive today.

Sgt. Leonard Hill took charge of his platoon and handled it with a big piece of shell in his leg until badly gassed.

Howard Beaumont of this company served as runner, going fearlessly through the worst barrages. After the gas officer became a casualty he assumed his duties, and later assisted in evacuating the wounded.

The regiment lay in a semicircular line, at evening, stretching west from the crest of the hill east of Montrebeau wood. There was more confusion, and considerable mixing of different units. The wounded who could walk were going back in little companies, and others were being gathered into dressing places, and bits of cover.

Lt. Holden of D company, wounded the day before, was carried back. He was cheerful and sure he would recover when I talked with him, giving me a message for his mother. But he had suffered twenty-four hours of exposure, and died a few days later.

PVT. RAY E. ROBERTS, Co. H
Killed in Action

LT. D. M. DWYER, M. G. Co.

MAJOR WM. A. SMITH
Captain Co. E

CAPT. RAY E. SEITZ
Adjutant. Gassed

Lt. Gardner of D company dreaded the sight of blood, and was regarded as rather mild. He had a terrible abdominal wound, and displayed the greatest fortitude and courage. Wounded the 29th, he was given shelter by a smashed tank, and taken back before the enemy captured the ground.

Chaplain Hart and I gathered a little company of wounded under the shelter of a hedge. Sergeant Snyder of F company and Reed of G were among them. We made them as comfortable as possible with blankets—obtained from dead machine-gunners—and shelter halves, putting dry socks on some of them. But the drizzle had become a heavy rain, and it was a miserable night.

I happened to have several hundred bouillon cubes, retained when I threw away my pack as too heavy. Four cubes to a canteen of water made a drink grateful to a wounded man after the fever had come on. Of course we had only cold water. Snyder was shot in the head. He took a drink, then pushed the canteen away and feebly asked "Is there plenty for the others?" One thought of Sir Philip Sidney. But men like him made up the 140th.

There were too few ambulances and not enough stretcher bearers. Some of the men lay forty-eight hours on the cold, muddy ground before being carried back.

This accounted for the deaths later of many wounded. Captain Kenady with a bullet through his lung lay unattended in a shell hole through the long night before being evacuated. His death was undoubtedly due to this.

Over the field the men of Major Slusher's detachment were living up to the best traditions of the American Army. Broyles, Howell, Rothman, Schlegelmilch, Biggs—all did what men could do and more. The Dentists could not be kept back and rendered what aid they could. And the men did what might be expected with such leaders. After we came out, and Slusher had won his D. S. C., Major Broyles wrote his report for the Sanitary Detachment. Usually these reports are long and full of detail. Major Broyles wrote simply, and truly, as follows:

"NOTHING SPECIAL TO REPORT. EVERY MAN DID HIS BEST."

McGaugh, Krenzer, Sydney Johnson, Mesara Howey, George, Krause, Lane, Lee, McDonald, Prater, Royle, Washington, Warren, Snyder, and Harry Davis, and the rest of the men in the Sanitary Detachment did heroic work. Nearly all of these men mentioned were wounded, and Sgt. Dillon was killed.

Private Engberg was wounded in the leg, and Ray Bryant and Leonard Walker were carrying him back. They had just crossed a ditch, and put the stretcher down to rest. As they straightened up, both were killed by the same shell, and Engberg was wounded again in the side and arm. Stretcher bearers were found, he was carried back, and while still in the hospital a year later, is well and cheerful as you may see from his picture.

Too much can not be said for these stretcher bearers. To work unarmed under fire, and know that the enemy was giving special attention to the wounded and those helping them, took nerve. Men worked until they were exhausted. There was no limit to their wil-

CORP. RAY W. RITTER
Co. B. Missing

PVT. R. O. ENGBERG
Twice Wounded, yet Alive

Over the Top with a Smile

SGT. MAJOR ROSWELL B. SAYRE
2d Bn. Killed in Action Sept. 28th

l'ngness but the fact that they were merely human. One of them, Paul Shool, met me with a man just wounded. He was badly shaken up, H. E., and I tried to reassure him by telling him that we would stay with him. He refused to be comforted. "I know you are here," he said, "but these Boche shells don't give a damn for chaplains!" When I proposed to go for stretcher bearers—he was a big, heavy chap—Shool said "No, you shall not go. It is too dangerous. The big ones are falling pretty fast, and I am going." And he did. He worked steadily until gassed, yet he was only one of the many who were doing their best to accomplish the impossible—for it would have taken ten times as many to handle the situation. These men deserve the highest praise, and to have been a stretcher-bearer in the 140th is a badge of honor.

Chaplain Buswell had gone with his battalion, cheerful and happy. He was wounded in the leg, and thoroughly angry because he had to go back. It undoubtedly saved his life, for had he remained, he would have been in the very front line the next day looking for trouble.

Big John Mace, Sergeant in H Co. won his D. S. C. on this day. He wore it on his unionalls on the trip home, but he had a right to wear it anywhere and any time. His battalion was held up by a machine gun nest. He volunteered to clean it up. He led a detachment, and was severely wounded, but kept going. The gunners were killed and the guns captured. Non-coms like this make a real regiment. And we had many of them.

Charles Coffin of L company was badly wounded in the chest. He recovered, came home, and married the fine girl who had waited for him.

Fred G. Smith of H company was the Chaplain's Assistant. He was an educated Baptist clergyman, and his one desire was to be of service. Before the regiment had a chaplain, he had led the men, and from the beginning gave himself unsparingly. He had been wounded in the leg, and I ordered him to remain in the dressing station, and go back, much against his will. But the men were suffering for water and he filled several canteens. As he was returning, Coffin called to him for a drink. While bending over the wounded soldier, Smith was instantly killed by a shell.

Fearless, patient, modest, unselfish and untiring, he was a good Christian, a good soldier and a good man. The 140th, and H company in particular will not soon forget "tall Fred Smith."

This night was the hardest of all. The many wounded who lay on the field, the miserable rainy weather, the news that we were to remain in (a rumor had passed current that we were to be relieved on Saturday night), the knowledge that we had lost nearly half the regiment—all these combined to discourage the weary men. They were hungry now, and tired, but not all in. A desire to make the enemy pay was in many hearts. I had heard much profanity. I had heard men swear to conceal their emotions. I had heard men

CAPT. ROLLA B. HOLT, CO. I.
Killed near Chaudron Farm

swear to keep from weeping. I had even heard men swear when they were really praying. But this night I heard many muttered curses of revenge, yet through the night with the wounded I was constantly greeted with a cheerful word. There was a great deal of silent suffering. But their heroism was wonderful.

I company was brought out of the drive by Sergeant Harry McFall of Kansas City. Captain Rolla B. Holt commanding I, was severely wounded Saturday evening, both thighs being badly crushed. Dr. Jones of the 138th dressed his wounds, but he died during the night or the next morning. His body was later found in an isolated spot, and he was buried after the First relieved us.

His death is evidence of his courage; the splendid work done by his company is evidence of his ability as an officer. He was equal to any emergency and I company banked on him, with loving loyalty. As one of them put it "We haven't a man in the company that wouldn't go through hell with him!" Lt. Geo. Smith was given command of what remained of I, and handled it like an old soldier.

The third battalion in its advance past Chaudron Farm to Montrebeau wood, between nine and one-thirty, had lost fifty per cent of its men, and a larger per cent of its officers. Not only was Kenady wounded, but Lt. Miller was also a casualty, leaving only Eustace Smith. Slaughter, Denham and Stinson were casualties from L company. Champion of M was dead, and McFadden and Nottingham wounded, leaving M without an officer. Murray Davis was wounded, and had four officers left for his four companies.

After dark the second battalion moved up to the crest of the hill on the edge of the woods, with the first and third holding the front line. We had won a little over a mile—a costly mile. And every yard of the way was spotted with crimson.

GERMAN GUNS CAPTURED BY 140TH
This Film in German Captain's Camera

TWO VIEWS OF EXERMONT
Top, Looking N. E.; lower N. W.

THE FIVE DAYS

THE FOURTH DAY. SUNDAY SEPT 29TH
EXERMONT

All night long they shelled us, and plenty of gas was sent over. Sunday morning we looked on a wet and gloomy world. It was St. Michael's Day, and I said the collect. In my book I read the Epistle "There was war in heaven"—Surely we needed succor here.

At 5:25 came orders from brigade to attack at 5:30. The order stated that the 138th would leapfrog us and lead the attack on Exermont. Orders were issued to form in column of battalions third, second, first, with staggered columns. While trying to get into formation peremptory orders were received from Col. Nuttman and Col. Hawkins to advance. Col. Walker was asked by Col. Delaplane if the 140th should go ahead, in view of the fact that the 138th was then moving up. He was ordered to advance at once. Before the third battalion had completed its formation, either Col. Nuttman or Col. Hawkins ordered Murray Davis to advance at once, which he did in column. The first battalion was ordered to bear to the west.

The higher commanders were in a state of confusion and excitement and to this cause was undoubtedly due much of the confusion of the troops. Here was the time when General Martin was sadly needed. He would have been thinking neither of himself nor of his reputation. Col. Delaplane said " I have less than 1200 men, but I am going ahead." And he went with the men, giving no heed to his wounded leg.

There was no friendly barrage, and the Boche gave us everything from the front. From Apremont on our left rear flank enemy guns were firing steadily. In the second battalion H and G were in front, each with less than a hundred men. But they deployed in thin lines, first and third platoons in the front wave, second and fourth platoons in support. At 500 yards they were held up by machine guns. In a little hut there two wounded men were found who had been twenty-four hours alone. Their wounds were dressed. Many third battalion men were passed, lying lifeless with gas masks on, a pitiful picture. They had given their full measure of devotion.

As the men swept down on Exermont they marched into a barrage of high explosives, shrapnel and gas, which was accompanied by the put-put-put of the Maxims and the vicious humming of bullets, a veritable inferno of fire.

About five hundred yards beyond Montrebeau wood the tanks gave up. Why, no one can tell, but they certainly failed to give the support the tanks had given earlier. Lt. Eustace Smith and Lt. "Duke" Sheahan, two red-headed fighters, were among the first in Exermont. Sheahan had crossed the little creek instead of going over the bridge, which probably saved his life, as the bridge was swept by fire. Dear old Sam Adams, Lieutenant of I but now with C, was killed in the main street, just behind Eustace Smith. He was loved by both officers and men, brave and big hearted as a lion, and deserved the Distinguished Service Cross awarded him.

MAJOR MURRAY DAVIS, D. S. C.
Killed near Exermont

Before nine o'clock the first men up had dug in at the edge of the cliff west of Exermont and were sending back messages asking for help. Simpson, Brady, Ferris, Gaines, and Captain Skelton of H were in the line about this time with small detachments. G company with Milligan were in the thick of it, and G company lost heavily that day. He was gassed, but refused to leave. His company went in with 224 men and came out with 90. Milligan wrote a great record that day.

Exermont was taken before nine, and by 9:30 the battalions, or what was left of them, were consolidated on a line about 300 yards beyond the town, and at the base of a cliff. Major Rieger with some of the 139th arrived about ten and extended the line to the east.

Gardner was wounded. Holden was wounded, to die later, and Compton was killed. Campbell alone was left in D. Compton had been killed by the road coming through the woods. He was one of the cleanest, finest young officers in the American Army. Campbell was cited in orders, so was Simpson, Milligan and Gaines. D company came out with 33 missing and 109 wounded and gassed.

What was left of A company got through Exermont, under Wise. Captain Armour took command of the first battalion on Saturday. He was cited in orders.

Lt. Rothman established a dressing station in Exermont and was later captured. He and Lt. Thomas of F company were the only officers captured by the Germans. Both of them, after many interesting experiences, were released, and came safely home. Rothman was cited.

Lt. Scott of E and Lt. Robertson of E were killed. Scott, cited for bravery, was a fine young officer from Kansas City. He had a wonderful faculty for keeping cheerful under all discouragements, and his courage was as fine as his spirit. No man had more friends, and none deserved them more. Until he was killed he gave an example of courage to his men. Robertson was a quiet, manly officer, who was promoted to a "First" and richly deserved it. Religious in character, he was possessed of a moral courage which kept him eager to fulfill his duty. Captain Smith of E was an excellent company commander, and these men had helped make E company into the splendid company which faced the enemy in the Argonne.

About ten o'clock, Major Murray Davis, already wounded, was killed in the angle between the hedge and the road a few hundred yards southeast of Exermont. Dumas, his orderly, was killed at the same time, and lies beside him. Major Davis wheeled, said that he was hit, and died instantly. Dumas asked if Major Davis was hurt, and died as the answer was given him. Only a few days before Major Davis had spoken of Dumas' faithfulness, the good care he gave him, and the many annoyances he saved him. It has been said that "no man is a hero to his own valet," but Dumas worshipped Murray Davis. He thought him the best officer and the best man in the regiment And he had reason for his good opinion. Major Davis

A DOUGHBOY WHO WAS IN EXERMONT

WAYNE R. BERRY, CO. B.
D. S. C.

THE FIVE DAYS

was a dashing officer, a splendid leader of men, and a real soldier. He had been wounded in the head on Saturday, but called it a trifle, and kept on with his men. Two days before the drive he had given nearly the whole day to men of the regiment who wished to make wills or settle business which should have been attended to long before. When I asked him for his help, reluctantly as I knew how busy he was at the time, he replied, "Chaplain, there is nothing I can do for any man in this regiment that I will not do gladly!" Not only did he cheerfully give his time to the men, but he never lost an opportunity to give them a word of good cheer and courage. We were billeted together at Camp Marquette, and had talked over a number of matters seriously. He had no fear of shell and felt that no bullet could harm him. But he dreaded gas, and gave great attention to his gas mask. With a brilliant mind, he had made an excellent Judge Advocate. I never knew a man with a keener sense of fairness and justice, and he was an admirable judge of men and character. His skill as an officer, his buoyant, virile spirit, and his care for his men made him typical of the best America had to offer. One of his men said to me "When Murray Davis got his, the third battalion lost heart. I tell you they don't make them any better!" The Distinguished Service Cross was awarded him.

Skelton says that Eustace Smith was in the line with the others in that party when he came up, and undoubtedly the officers named, and the men with them, were in the line beyond Exermont before nine in the morning. A lot of the evidence makes the hour from 8:30 to 8:45, but they were undoubtedly there by nine.

At 9:45 Col. Walker saw what might be called the third wave of the 140th held up by a heavy barrage. He did not know that one "wave" or really two "waves" had already swept through Exermont. He was apparently ignorant of a good many things which were happening on the battle-field, and so exhausted and nervous that his judgment was not very good even after the information was placed before him. About this time he sent a message to Division Headquarters which showed that he had confused the groups. One can not imagine General Martin confused, or making such a mistake. But this proves that the 140th was already there for none of its men got up later than this, and the dead in and around Exermont testify as to where a part of the regiment was on Sunday.

About ten Major Rieger came up with a detachment of the 139th. He was one of the finest men and best officers in the division, and he did his part nobly every day. All who know him admire and honor him. He has glory in plenty for his work in the drive, and would be the last man to desire anything not his due. When he reached the forward line, he found the 140th entrenched and fighting.

Lt. George W. Smith of E is a plucky, intelligent officer who was in Exermont in the hottest of the fighting and later helped to hold the men in line on Baulny ridge. About 1500 yards on our flank the enemy set up a battery of "whiz-bangs" and made it hot for us, but the men

WHERE THE LINE HELD

Officers Who Helped Hold the Line

CAPT. JOHN H. PLEASANTS   MAJOR RALPH E. TRUMAN
                                          R. I. O.

who were there wished to remain, especially as they realized what heavy toll would be taken in moving to the rear. But about one o'clock orders came from Col. Walker to retire.

GENERAL TRAUB ORDERS WOUNDED MEN INTO FRONT LINE

General Traub had asked a little earlier that the Division be withdrawn, and had sent orders for the troops to fall back. He had also sent orders to the rear that every able bodied man who was only slightly gassed or wounded should shoulder a gun and get into the line. Military Police were placed on the roads with instructions to stop all men passing back, and send them up. The "confusion" was not altogether in the front lines.

Col. Delaplane with about a hundred men and officers of the regiment had entrenched a little to the rear and right of Exermont, and were suffering with the rest. Waves of Boche came over from the East a little after noon, and we held on, but later in the day orders came to retire, and the men drifted slowly back. They were closely followed by the enemy, and there were many losses, and some thirty or forty men were taken prisoner.

The engineers had moved up and dug in on a line near Chaudron farm, under heavy fire. Captain "Tony" James whom I had often seen at K. U. was there, and ordered the men farther up on the ridge. The gallant engineers were a tonic. Somehow one felt that they were worth twice their numbers of average men. And the line held.

The orders had been given so carelessly, that the men knew for the most part only that they were to retire. Great firmness was necessary to prevent complete disorganization of the troops. Captain Truman, Captain Campbell, Lt. George Smith, Lieutenant Keefner and Lieutenant Han did heroic work in steadying the men. To them, and a number of non-coms is due in large degree the discipline maintained by the men. A few mistakes and the retirement would have degenerated into an utter rout. Too must can not be said for the engineers, and for the officers who steadied the line. On the right lay a portion of the 138th under Major Kalloch, and on the left we intermingled with the 137th, under Major O'Connor. All the units were mixed in with each other, until it was difficult to tell what the organizations were.

An order, or a false report, came down to retreat. Truman cried "For God's sake men, don't regard the order. If we retreat back over the hill, the day is lost." He gathered the shattered troops in the engineers' line, and stood like a rock calm and fearless in the storm of shells and bullets. Some of the men always called the line "Truman's Line" when they spoke of it. Truman was a staff officer, and could have gone back and spent the night in safety; instead he remained in the trench with the men. Too much praise can not be given him. He is Major Truman now.

CAPT. J. L. MILLIGAN
Twice Cited
He Fought Through Exermont

LT. EUSTACE SMITH
He Was in Exermont
Early

LT. SAMUEL T. ADAMS
Killed in Exermont

JOHN W. STIGALL, CO. K.
Killed near Exermont

Captain John Pleasants is another man who deserves the gratitude of the regiment. He was of material assistance in rallying the men. He seemed absolutely devoid of fear, and his personal courage and bravery stood out as unusual in a regiment which contained many brave men. There was no braver, truer man in the whole American army.

Chaplain Hart named men to take charge, and helped to steady the line. It was interesting to see him suddenly become Division headquarters. "You are a Captain" he would say to one doughboy. "You are a Lieutenant" to another "take charge of these men!" He also rallied a company of the 139th. He was a Knights of Columbus Chaplain, and not compelled to be with the regiment, yet he was always in the thickest of it, and ever with a cheery word. He was cited in orders, as were the other chaplains. The 140th is possibly the only regiment all of whose chaplains were given citations. After we came out Col. Delaplane, who is no lover of chaplains, said "We'l, Chaplain, I thought I had three chaplains, but I have not. I have three SOLDIERS!"

The line has been given as north of Chaudron Farm in every case where I have seen it mentioned, but our records and my recollection give it as just south of Chaudron farm. Certainly the wounded were carried back from Chaudron Farm. It is true that later a thin line was thrown forward north of Chaudron.

During Sunday we had better support from the artillery, and they put over six times as many shells as they had on Friday or Saturday. The first battalion of the 129th was in Charpentry, and worked their batteries like machine guns. Once a gun was hit, with casualties, but in an incredibly short time it was again firing. During the counter attack they sent over a wonderful barrage. When the men fell back in the afternoon, these batteries were ordered to prepare for a point blank fire, which meant they were to die with their guns if the enemy came through. About five there was a heavy counter attack from the Germans, but the line held. Stragglers began to come in. Men were stopped and sent up. Major Smith took about a hundred into line, men he gathered up who were ready to be led. Never were men found who were not willing to go where ordered. Many a man sent back as gassed got a little hot food and a cup of coffee, tore off his tag, grabbed a rifle, and came back to help his buddies. And the line held.

Wise, Spicer, Black, Tharpe and Keefner had been added to the wounded. There were few officers left. Nearly 1800 men and officers were casualties. And they hammered the "Engineer's Line." Big guns, little guns, trench-mortars, and whiz-bangs, machine-guns and gas—from front and flanks we caught the storm. And the line held.

The Division had spent its strength lavishly. It had been tried to the limit of human endurance. It was worn-out with fighting

PVT. FRED G. PRICE, CO. A, AND ALBERT L. BOGEN. CO. A
Both Wounded but Able to Feed Paul Sacker, German Prisoner
Cheppy. Sept. 29th, 1918

THE FIVE DAYS

exhausted from loss of sleep, parched for water, and starving for food. But the line held.

The 140th had won glory as it swept past Charpentry. It had shown strength as it doggedly won its way through Montrebeau wood. It had covered itself with new honors in its courageous dash through Exermont. But its hour of real glory, its magnificently splendid hour was when, decimated, exhausted, driven back, it took the line and stood firm.

That evening and the next morning wave after wave of Boche came over. Their artillery pounded us constantly. All the romance and glory was gone from battle. There among our dead, we grimly held the line. Write it on the monument some day to be erected to the heroic dead of the grand old 140th.

THE LINE HELD!

THE FIFTH DAY. MONDAY, SEPT. 30TH

Morning finally came. The men were wet to the skin, and their clothing was heavy with rain and mud, although the rain had ceased. No protection was afforded them but fox-holes, and it was found that the men had developed remarkable skill and speed in digging in since the Doniphan days.

The 91st had come up to Eclisfontaine, and the 28th, sturdy sons of Pennsylvania, had taken Apremont. We no longer suffered from that terrible flanking fire which had taken such heavy toll.

The enemy made two counter attacks in the morning, but the men had rallied to the line, and they were ineffective. The day passed uneventfully. Prisoners taken proved that the Germans were throwing fresh divisions into line.

In the afternoon word came that the First was to relieve us during the night, and a little later we were told that they were already moving into the reserve area.

The reports that had drifted back to Division and Corps Headquarters had been somewhat exaggerated. The Division had not been crushed, nor were all the men killed. But it was ready to welcome relief. The 140th came out with its regimental organization intact, the one regiment having the honor to be so recognized in the Divisional reports.

General Drum, Chief of Staff of the First Army, rightly said in his report. "Most of the straggling and confusion was caused by men getting lost and not having leaders." This was the belief of all who were really on the field. The men made good and the leaders were nearly all casualties.

I had made the acquaintance of a new man. He sometimes came from the city, but I call him "Bill Smith from the Cross Roads." He is the Average American. And he is a much finer character than we knew. Patient and cheerful in difficulty, loyal to his comrades and his flag, reckless and carefree, big in his sins but equally big in his virtues, afraid of nothing, generous to a fault, the best soldier in the world—but a citizen first of all—he is the safeguard of the Nation.

With him I marched over the long roads, with him I waited the weary days after the Armistice, with him I watched in the mountain trenches of Alsace, and with him I pressed forward over the bloody fields towards Exermont. And always I found him a real man. Bill Smith from the cross roads—he has saved the Republic and he will keep it safe.

C company kept four platoons intact the first four days. It suffered 162 casualties. Captain Rexroad was twice wounded. Lt Richard Kiddoo got machine gun bullets in both legs. Lt. Henry Black, a steady, good commander and a man with brains, lost one leg. Only two sergeants, Dedo and Mortarano, came out with the remnant of the company. Lt. Basil Otey, who had helped take Charpentry was also wounded.

M company lost all of its officers and 65 per cent of its men. Sergeant Lee King took comand of the company on the morning of the 28th, reorganized it, and brought it out.

Corporal Wayne Dunning had led his squad in attacking a German defense, and deserved a D. S. C. for his bravery. Another M company man, a cook named Clarence Crosley, crawled out into No Man's Land, risking his life to give aid to a wounded comrade.

Clarence Macom of M company, with two companions, was surrounded yet incapable of surrendering, they fought their way safely into our lines. Forty-five of our men and two officers were captured by the enemy. Clarence Gehig, Albert Stroble, Walter Stucker and Harvey Byrd died in German hospitals.

Sergeant Irving Smith, John Hummel and, George Kreger were among the captured who were returned. But Macom and his little party managed to fight their way back to the regiment.

Lieutenant Whitthorne of L company, a Captain now, organized a detachment, advanced 1200 yards in front of our lines, and brought back a score of wounded men, who would have fallen into enemy hands or died of exposure Later, although both wounded and gassed, he remained with his men until the regiment was relieved. He received the Distinguished Service Cross at St. Nazaire.

Captain D. H. Wilson of the 137th was in charge of the party taking back wounded from Chaudron Farm. Although the skirt of his raincoat was riddled by bullets, he was unharmed. Lt. Ralph Ware, who had been absent sick, and reported on the 29th, organized a detachment of men, largely from B company, and went to his assistance. He won a Captain's commission.

Sergeant Keys, who did such faithful work at Baulny, Sergeant Herbert Gray, Joseph Yadon and Corporal Victor Huerter of the Intelligence Department were all cited in orders. They were in the front lines the entire five days.

I company lost all its officers, and Sergeant McFall was in command at the end. Sergeant Stein, who was killed, was cited in orders. Trout, Rogers, Hill and Cooperider led their platoons with the greatest courage until wounded.

When the retirement of the division was ordered from Exermont, on the evening of September 29th, 1918, an interesting incident took place. A cook of compay C, in search for something to eat, discovered, near Charpentry, a German garden containing potatoes, carrots, green beans, and other vegetables. In the same area a kitchen containing two and one-half barrels of coffee and fully equipped with cooking utensils was located which the enemy in his rapid retreat was forced to leave undisturbed. Here a corporal was made to do manual labor; being close at hand he was put on "K. P." Within a short while hot coffee and "Slum" was served the half starved men at the front. The afternoon of the 30th of September, being discovered by Boche airplane, the kitchen was destroyed by enemy artillery, the kettles however were saved and moved under a near by hill where the good work continued until the company was relieved October 1, 1918.

As we went forward one company found a cow which had belonged to the Germans, living comfortably behind their lines. Some farmer boy milked her, and the cow was with us when we came out. Perhaps it was a sight of this innocent bovine which stirred the wrath of the Inspector who decided we bore marks of a National Guard Division.

Corporal Edgar H. Flanner was a soldier in whom I first became interested when he was in the hospital at Doniphan, suffering a severe attack of spinal meningitis. A quiet, modest man, and the best stenographer in the regiment, one hardly thought of him as a machine-gunner.

He led his squad through a number of barrages and was wounded in the head Sunday morning. A few minutes later a 5.9 shell exploded near him, knocking him down and wounding him severely. On being questioned, he admitted that he was hurt, but said "not seriously," and continued to push forward until too weak to stand. He was in the hospital nine weeks recovering from the wounds that he had insisted were not serious.

Private Leslie W. Hawks was severely wounded in the leg while crossing Hill 210 during that hot hour on the 28th. As a runner he had carried many messages through the intense artillery and machine-gun fire. He bandaged his own shattered leg, and then crawled from place to place dressing the wounds of other men. When urged to go to the dressing station, he replied that others were suffering more than he, and continued his search for the wounded, dragging his mangled limb after him. When I last heard of him he was still in the hospital.

Private Hugh G. White was a runner of the headquarters section, belonging to our Machine Gun Company. On Saturday he had responded to a call for volunteers to go to Very through a heavy and continued barrage. Throughout the night of the 28th, he was kept busy carrying messages. Liaison depended entirely upon runners and a great many of them were killed. Sunday morning, when the regiment pushed forward, White had just returned from Brigade Headquarters. He was heard to shout "I'll trade my pistol for your rifle," and was seen a few minutes later going against the enemy with the nearest company.

These men, and many others who showed similar bravery, should have been recognized. But if every man who showed unusual courage had been decorated, it would have made a brave show. The truth is that among so many cases of heroism it was difficult to select the cases deserving of honor, and Major Broyles summed up the history of the 140th during those five days in his simple, splendid report of his own men: "NOTHING SPECIAL TO REPORT. EVERY MAN DID HIS BEST."

The officers showed the same American spirit. There was Lt. Stephens, a scholarly young officer, who won the admiration of his men, and Buell who was brave to recklessness, and Captain Ware who, fresh from the hospital, pushed up to the front on the 29th, and Captain Gaines, who insisted on being relieved from the ammunition train and sent into the front lines. And Lieutenant Spicer who was wounded in the arm and side on that fateful Saturday.

One of his men wrote me "He led his platoon and kept them all together until he was wounded, and I consider him a very brave man."

The Supply Company had a picked lot of men. There had been days in the trenches when they had fed on canned meat and sent their portion of the fresh meat up to the men in the trenches.

The transport had spent over thirty consecutive days on the road. Captain Ward made his headquarters at Cheppy. Lieut. Gaines commanded the ammunition train, but turned it over to Reid Stephens and insisted on getting to the front line. The transport spent Thursday night at Neuvilly, and at five in the morning on Friday started for Cheppy. The bridge was blown up, and it was impossible to pull through the mud, so at 7 they started around Vauquois Hill. There was no feed for men or horses, and the going was very bad. When the crest of the hill in sight of Very was reached they halted. Horses and men were nearly exhausted. At four, orders came from G-1 to move on to Cheppy. After dark they pushed forward, not stopping at Cheppy, and reaching the valley south of Charpentry about half past eight.

On Saturday they could not find the C. O. of the regiment, and no one in Charpentry seemed able to give any definite information as to the location of the various units of the regiment, but towards evening they found M company and a part of the first battalion, and obtained their first rations.

On Sunday, the bloody 29th, Salisbury, Reid and Sullivan were

THE FIVE DAYS

determined to get the rations and ammunition wagons sent up to the men. All three were officers of courage and initiative. They started for Chaudron farm in the morning. The 91st was retiring. Beyond Charpentry, near the dressing station to the east, an aeroplane came over, and one cart was put out of commission. The direction was changed and they started towards Baulny.

As they entered Baulny they met a terrific barrage. Many were killed and wounded, but the transport escaped with little injury and none killed. Sullivan was badly gassed. The conditions were so bad that they returned to Charpentry and unloaded the rations there about the time that the front lines were falling back to Baulny Ridge and Chaudron Farm.

Sergeant Earl Chandler of Headquarters company with a detail from his company strengthened from the second and third battalions started getting rations up to the line back of Chaudron Farm. All night long they worked, and thought neither of themselves nor danger. Part of the renewed strength the line showed on Monday was due to the fact that the half-starved men had been given food.

The kitchens were started up on the afternoon of the 29th and evidently were mistaken for tanks by the enemy, as they came in for a very heavy shelling. It was here that Mitchell was killed. The artillery fire was so intense that they were compelled to turn back.

Throughout the battle the company was skillfully and courageously handled, and when it brought the rations out with us, spent a few days of great popularity.

General Pershing began his attack on September 26th. By the 27th his army had gained four miles, capturing 8000 prisoners and 700 cannon. By October 3rd they had captured the first two lines of defense and were attacking the third. On October 21 they took the fourth line, on November 5 they passed the Meuse, and on the 10th they entered Sedan and the road to Metz was open. The Germans were beaten. The great road from Lille to Metz which supplied all their extensive front was cut.

For the first time a German communique stated that their lines were broken and it was done by the AMERICAN ARMY!

An authority says of this battle:

"Resistance Never More Bitter"

The Argonne advance is by far the hardest job that has been assigned to the American soldier since he sailed from his faraway home. Never in this war has the American Army, or any part of it, made its way over a battlefield so difficult, struck at the German power in a point so vital or fought against a German resistance so desperate. Not at St. Mihiel, not on the Ourcq nor on the Vesle was the opposition so grim."

And the following from a great writer may be of interest to those who have just read how the men of the 140th fought and died.

I have talked with French soldiers who fought with the Americans.

MAJOR E. W. SLUSHER, M. C.
Who Won the D. S. C. in the Argonne

They are men of letters, careful observers, capable of expressing their impressions with exactitude.

They all admired the joy, the self-confidence, the good humor with which these sturdy lads, so recently arrived from America, advanced under fire. The Crusaders of Liberty attacked as tho they were invulnerable and when they fell never to rise again there was something about them that distinguished them from the other dying.

"I don't mean to say that they died in a different manner," said one of these writer-soldiers. "All soldiers die alike, and all the Allies fought for the same just cause. But in those American heroes there was a sort of amazement and shock at dying, as tho they felt it a great injustice, and this astonishment was reflected in their kindly, childlike eyes. Perhaps it was surprise at realizing that a citizen of a free country could die at the hands of a despotic monarchy's automaton soldier. Perhaps in his last gleams of consciousness he caught a glimpse of the absurdity of this old world in which the soldier of a republic that has no desire to conquer or enslave and aspires only to the establishment of peace, must lose his life to bring liberty to the very ones that kill him."

TUESDAY, OCTOBER FIRST

At three in the morning the First Division made the relief. During the relief we were shelled heavily and continuously, but fortunately escaped with but little loss. The regiment was reorganized and marched to a point south of Cheppy on the Vernays-La Forge road. Fires were started everywhere and the men were able to get warm for the first time in days. The kitchens were soon fired up, and the delightful aromas of cooking food and boiling coffee drifted over the fields.

Major Slusher was still with us. Taken to a hospital twice, gassed, he had each time returned to his work. For his courage there and at the Chaudron Farm dressing station he received the Distinguished Service Cross. He had always looked for the good points in his officers and developed them. He had a splendid attitude towards the men; with a strict discipline, he combined an interest and care that made for the effectiveness of the regiment. The 140th felt that he was just about all that a medical officer should be. Certainly he was always on the lookout to preserve the health of the regiment.

When he left us he had an admirable successor in Major Broyles. With the regiment during the trying times that came after the drive, he showed the same quiet ability and effective energy which had made him an ideal battalion officer.

Rothman was captured in Exermont, Howell and Schlegelmilch were worn out with their sleepless labors on the battlefield. Reed and Cronkite and the rest of the dental force went all through the battle. Biggs had worked steadily. A man whose wounds had been dressed but a moment before, was torn to pieces by a shell, and the medical orderly went to the rear with shell-shock. But Jimmy Biggs worked coolly and steadily on. In the battle and afterwards these officers and their faithful men gave their very best to the regiment. Major Broyles had said in his historic sentence, "Nothing special to report; every man did his best." To this the whole regiment would add "and no man could have done better."

There was little talking and that largely in disconnected sentences. One doughboy said "It will be a week before we can hit the line again." Another "I hope they send us over the same ground." And another "I want my next battle to be in old K. C." A few spoke of what they had seen, but none of what they had done.

They looked like tramps. Their faces were covered with a stubble of a week's growth, although some men had managed to shave almost every day, even under fire. The grime had worn into their skin, and they were unbelievably dirty. Their uniforms were soiled and torn, and they were mud to the top of their leggins. There had been a low concentration of gas everywhere, and their eyes were red-rimmed with gas and loss of sleep. But even the gas had not disturbed the cooties. After feeding, they dropped asleep on shelter halves or raincoats, and slept the sleep of utter exhaustion, their silent figures motionless as the dead.

More than half the regiment was missing. But worn out and dirty, there was a strange dignity and strength felt in the regiment. It had met the test. It had passed through fire and blood. Iron had entered its soul. Another action would find them a veteran body of troops, fit for any emergency.

The War Department figures give the following for the 140th: Killed, or died of wounds, 9 officers, 239 men; died of disease or other causes, 1 officer, 94 men; wounded severely, 7 officers and 485 men; wounded slightly, 46 officers, 802 men; wounded, degree unknown, 188 men; total wounded and dead, 63 officers, 1808 men; captured by the enemy, 2 officers and 45 men; total casualties, killed and wounded, not including death from disease, 62 officers, 1714 men; total losses 1823 officers and men.

The 140th Infantry had suffered terribly—but it was still a regiment.

EXPERIENCES OF A CAPTURED OFFICER OF THE 140TH INFANTRY

On the evening of the 27th of September, 1918, I was sent forward with the battalion by the senior battalion surgeon when the troops advanced under a heavy barrage after being held up all day by artillery and machine-gun fire. It was at 5:45 that we went over. The next few minutes, as I look back at them, are a hazy nightmare of shriek and explosion. The Germans had wasted no time and we were forced to advance through his counter-barrage—and it was a beauty. The only distinct recollection which I have is that of hearing a most terrific explosion directly behind me, imagining that the end of the world had come in one awful convulsion, and feeling a heavy jar on my right shoulder while I spun round like a top and then—I was on the ground with the battalion commander calling to me, "What's the matter, What's the matter?" I got up feeling rather shaky and replied that I wasn't quite sure but that I thought I was hit. My shoulder didn't seem to hurt much so we went on. I found afterward that my shelter-half had been cut to shreds by the shell and that a large piece had penetrated my pack-stop at the bottom layer. I hadn't even been scratched.

It was necessary for me to stop at about this time to dress some men who been hit by bits of shrapnel and high explosive shells. We stopped on the reserve slope of a flat-topped hill—the top of the rise being covered by a hedge fence. Jerry by this time had brought his Maxims into service and as I dressed the wounded I could see the hedge disappear in fragments as the machine-gun bullets cut their way through. The fire slackened after a while and it was possible to go forward again. The battalion had disappeared and it was only by the many wounded whom I dressed as I went forward, that I was able to trace them. That night the battalion or what was left of it slept on the field with a thin hedge between them and the Germans. The next two days were a solid round of advances by rushes, each advance marked by a thinning of the line and a number of green-brown patches on the newly taken ground. On the 29th of September we went over at 5:30 a. m. and walked into a most awful barrage of H. E. shrap, and gas which was penetrated by the rat-tat-tat of the Maxim and the vicious zip-zip of the bullets as they cut the grass at one's feet—or head. It was through this inferno that we swept down into Exermont.

I set up a dressing station in a trench just behind the town. There were a great many men in the trench when word came to fall back to prepared positions to meet an expected counter-attack. I could not obey this order as there were still some men to dress. They were just about done when a man staggered in saying the soldiers were falling in bunches at a certain large gap in the hedge which bordered the hill. I looked—and they certainly were. After dressing this last man I crawled up to where the men had fallen and, dragging them from in front of the gap, one after another, dressed them. Jerry seemed to think my brassard was a target. This wasn't the first time but somehow I noticed it more. While I was working there was an awful racket—and the lights went out. When I woke the first wave of Germans had gone over us evidently without molesting the wounded. I realized dimly that those grey figures were not Americans but was dazed for a few minutes—too much so to be sure of what was going on. When I really did realize that we were behind the German lines—well, it was a far from pleasant thought. There was nothing to do but dress the rest of the wounded which I proceeded to do—lying flat on my face as my every movement was a signal which brought down on me a hail storm of machine-gun bullets.

The second column or rather wave of Germans came at us with their bayonets. I told them that the men were all wounded. They wanted to know the nature of the wounds and, learning that one man had been shot across the abdomen, one Boche stuck an automatic pistol against him. He didn't shoot the man tho and the German noncom who came up told me that my men would be well cared for and asked me not to judge them all by the one who wished to shoot the wounded.

They went on and I continued my dressing, a third wave passing over while I worked. Laughing and saying I would be better off with them than with the Americans, they went on and, after finishing dressing the men, I decided to get through to our own lines if possible. When I got to my feet my ankle caved under me. I had been hit and since I had been working flat on my face, had not realized it until then. I crawled about two hundred yards and, looking toward the direction from which the Germans had come, saw a fourth wave coming over the top of the hill. Rolling into a fox-hole I remained hidden for about two hours. I was just getting ready to crawl out, having heard three waves go back towards Exermont, when somebody struck me forcibly in the back and in gutteral German commanded me to come out. I did.

I shan't forget the hike from the field back to the ambulance station if I live to be a thousand years old. The wound in my ankle was giving me fits and to help matters out I was carrying a wounded sergeant on my back. That hike was like a horrible dream and seemed unreal. I had never figured on the possibility of being made prisoner. It simply couldn't happen. The shells of our own artillery were falling mighty close around as we went toward the ambulance station but somehow it didn't seem to matter much whether we were hit or not and we rather hoped we would be. It was all a haze. At the ambulance station we stayed for about an hour or more. We had stopped at a field dressing station where the wounded were dressed and received a shot of A. T. S. but there I was too dazed to tell them that I had been hit. They discovered at the ambulance station, when they woke me to send me out that I had been wounded so they sent me to a hospital. I am not sure where this hospital was but I was told it was in Treves. The attendants tried to get my shoe off—once—but when it didn't come off easy they gave it up. It was four days, counting the first day, before I finally got to dress my ankle and, by that time the fleas had made a feeding ground of the wound. As a result the wound was badly inflamed and the ankle was much larger than natural. Luckily there was no infection and in about three weeks the injury was healed.

Of my trip from one town to another while being sent back to the rear there isn't much to tell except that we had nothing to eat and slept in pens that would be unsafe for a pig—they were too dirty. We had no beds and no covers. We were crowded together—wounded and all—in a small room with two French officers who were sick. One of them had pneumonia and the other had the influenza. The officer with the pneumonia died and they took the other man to the hospital. We didn't see him again.

The lack of food became unbearable. So much so that I stole a bucket of potatoes which the cook threw out as unfit for the German soldiers to eat (they were, too) and seven officers made a meal of them. That was the sixth day of my captivity and was the first meal I had had. Incidentally it was four days before I got another meal. This was at LeChesne—the potato meal I mean—and from here we went on foot to Amagne where we entrained for Karlsruhe, Baden. In Karlsruhe we first came in contact with the American Red Cross which worked thro the Spanish Ambassador—as smoooth a diplomat as ever lived—if diplomacy is the art of polished lying. From the Red Cross we received food and clothes and if necessary, money. From Karlsruhe we went to Villigen, Baden, where we stayed until after released after the signing of the Armistice, on November 29th, 1918—just two months to the day from the date of my capture.

During my stay in Germany I learned many things. First—that the German nation had been in favor of the war from the beginning. They had known its purpose and cost and had been prepared to pay. Their blind faith in the teaching that the Germans were Superhuman would have been amusing had it not been such a menace. The next fact that struck me was their admission that they had lost the war. I was asked how long the war would last and when I told them that it would last from five to seven months longer they laughed at me and said the whole thing would be over in six weeks—that there was to be a great revolution and the Emperor was to be deposed. The enlisted men as a whole and some of the line officers showed an absolute ignorance as to our purpose in the conflict and had only the vaguest idea of our strength. As a whole the enlisted men among the Germans treated us as well as they dared because they were punished for showing kindness to prisoners. The officers

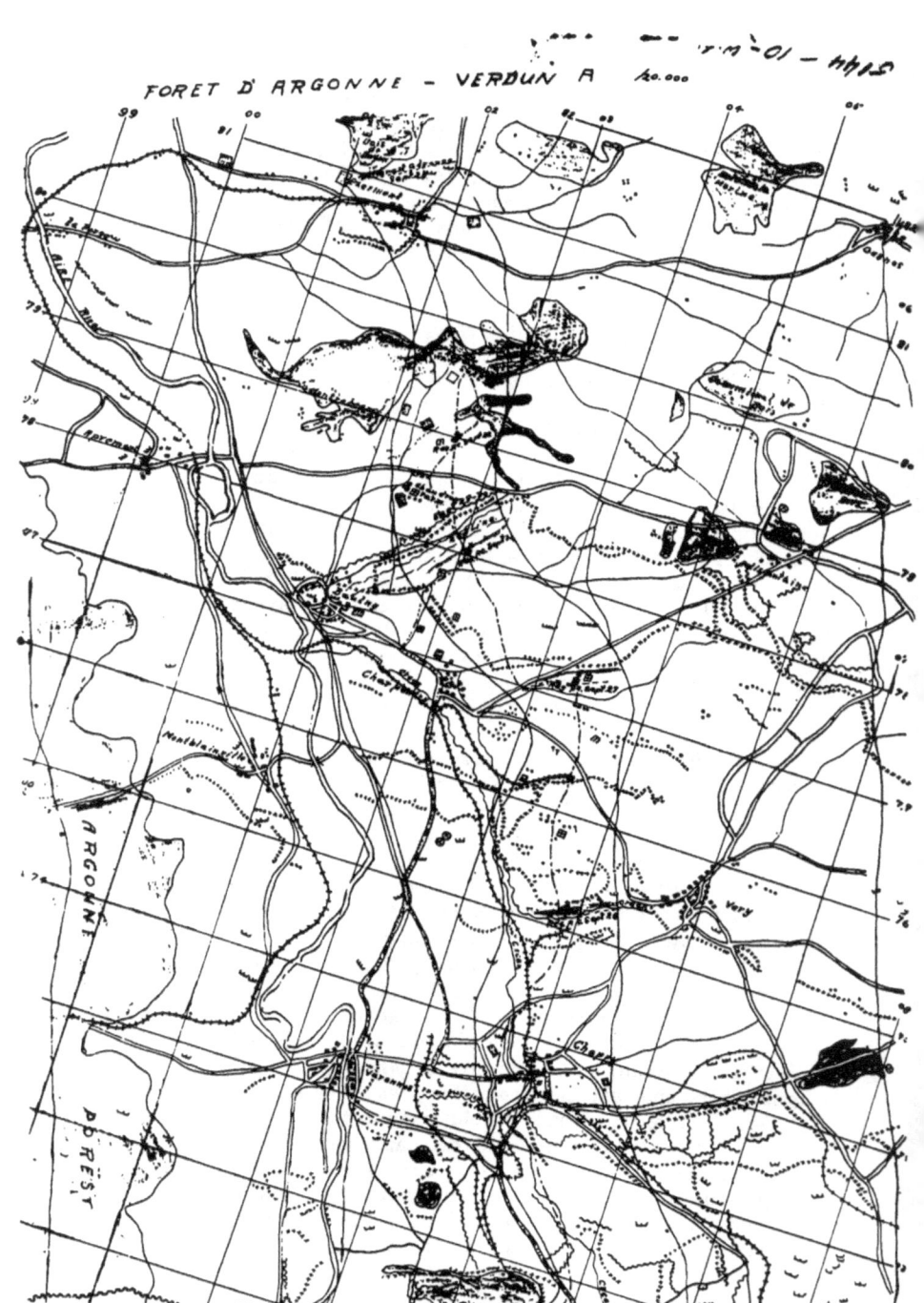

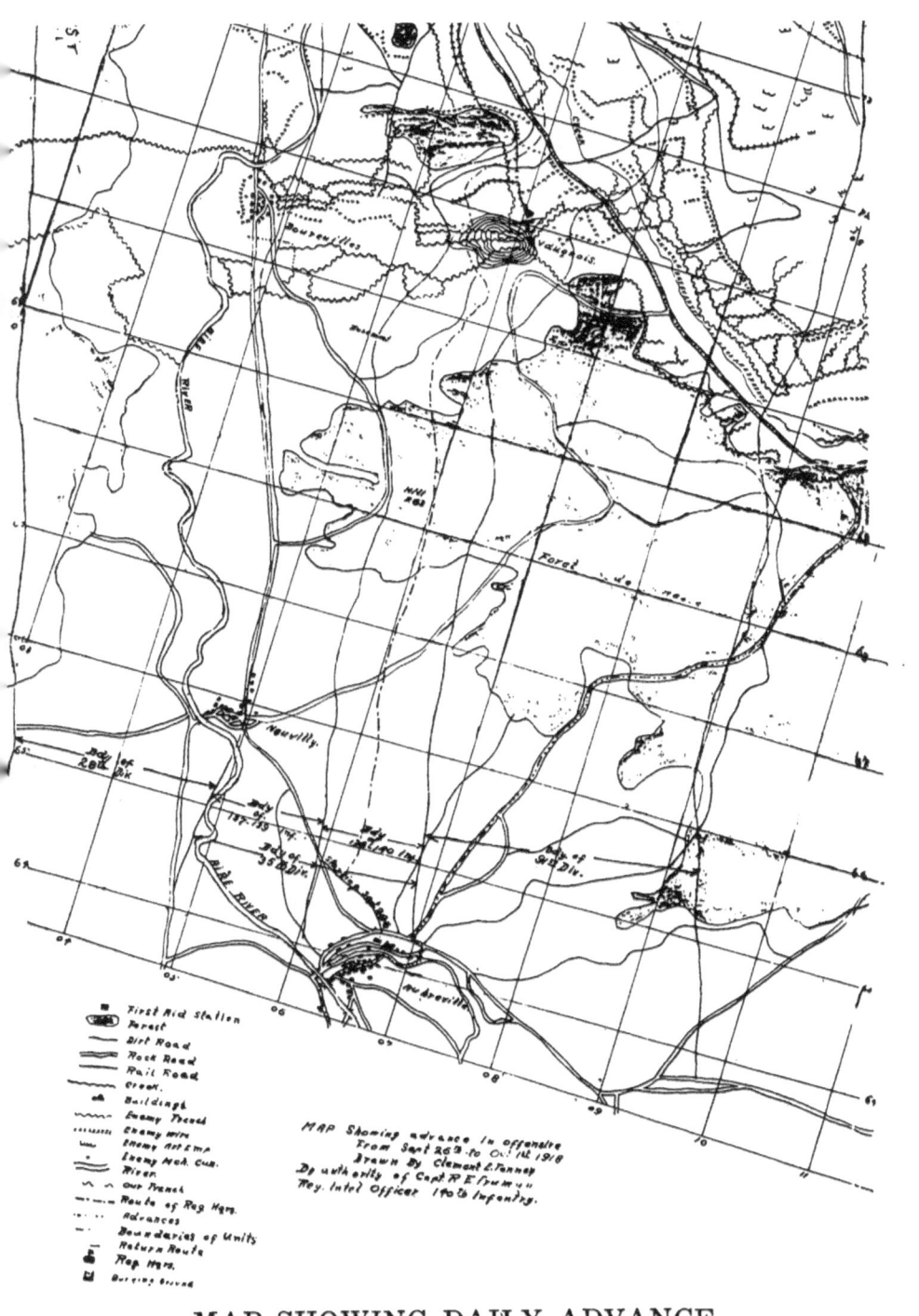

MAP SHOWING DAILY ADVANCE
From Aubreville to Exermont

as a class are brutal as one can imagine. I met only one officer who showed the least sign of humanity and he treated me really well—for a prisoner. So far as I could see there were no signs of starvation in Germany. The cry for food is only an attempt to win sympathy. The most amusing idea noted in the stay there was the constant hope, openly expressed, of emigrating to the United States after the war had ended. The facial expressions, on being told they were foolish to imagine that any nation would admit them, was a mixture of bewilderment and indignation. It was impossible for them to realize that their every action was not right and just. In their discussions with me they even attempted to deny facts which had previously been their boast. One even denied the work of Von Bernstorf and Dernberg. Lying reports as to the efficiency of the U-boat had been swallowed with the greatest delight and were recounted to me as absolute truth in an effort to convince me that the German nation was unbeatable and that further effort on the part of the Allies was fighting Providence. On the other hand there were many who realized that the reports emanating from the All-Highest were false, who knew themselves to be beaten and who said so without hesitancy. I must say that the news which we received of the war while we were prisoners, and we got papers each day, was far more reliable than Allied news received under similar conditions. Of course where the Allies stated that they had advanced their lines so many kilometres and taken certain towns, the German news stated that, in order to strengthen the lines they had retired to previously prepared positions; but on examining the map the reports coincided very well. The German is a child. He believes any thing that a superior may say even though he knows that it isn't true. It is a revival of the Old Roman—"Ipse dixit." They are slow in thinking. Their thoughts, so far as I could judge from those whom I met, were coarse and showed a low grade mentality. I met two men among the Germans who were not of this type. One was a young Lieutenant and the other a Colonel. They both seemed clean upstanding men. I didn't learn till later that they were as great liars as are bred in the universe. There were only two or three attempts made to question me and I developed a vast amount of ignorance on all essential points. I have heard many tales of cruelty toward prisoners at the hands of the Germans but can truthfully state that I never once saw a prisoner manhandled. We were starved and crowded into pens unfit for the vilest animal but this was to be expected. Sneers and gibes were plentiful but not once to my knowledge was a prisoner beaten. To sum up the whole thing; My treatment while a prisoner was not so bad as I should have expected from reports but it was bad enough.. The vaunted superior German mind is a myth—it does not exist.

THE STORY OF THE FIVE DAYS TOLD BY MESSAGES

Message No. 1

From—RIO 140th Inf.
At—N. Aubreville, 1 Kil.
Date—Sept. 26, 1918. Hour—5:30 A. M. No. 1. How sent—By runner.
To—Adj. 70th Brig.
Regt. started into action on time, 5:30 A. M.

TRUMAN,
RIO.

Message No. 2

From—RIO 140th Inf.
At—05.7-71.4, Vauquois, 1/10.000. (N. Vauquois Hill).
Date—Sept. 26th. Hour—6 A. M. No. 2. How sent—By runner.
To—Brig.-Adj. 70th Brig.
At—Mamelon Blanc, Hill, 267.

Regt. moving forward from the above point. No casualties reported. No opposition met with up to this hour.

TRUMAN,
RIO.

Message No. 3

From—RIO 140th Inf.
At—05.7-71.4, Vauquois, 1/10000. (N. Vauqois Hill).
Date—Sept. 26/18. Hour—10 A. M. No. 3. How sent—By runner.
To—Div. Intelligence Officer, 25th Div.

Regt. moving forward from the above point. No casualties reported up to this hour. We have met with no opposition so far.

TRUMAN,
RIO.

THE FIVE DAYS 103

Message No. 4

From—RIO 140th Inf.
At—05.9-71.7, Vauqois, 1/10.000. (1 Kil. N. Vauquois).
Date—Sept. 26th. Hour—1:10 P. M. No. 4. How sent—By runner.
To Brigade Adj. 70th Brig.

We are close behind 69th Brig. Strong machine gun N. E. of this point. Evacuated when we deployed to attack. Move north continued. No casualties reported. M. G. position was at 05.9-71.8.

TRUMAN,
RIO.

Message No. 5

From—RIO 140th Inf.
At—05.9-71.7, Vauquois, 1/10000. (1 Kil. N. Vauquois).
Date—Sept. 26. Hour—1:10 P. M. No. 5. How sent—By runner.
To—Division Intelligence Officer, 35th Div.

Have gained contact with 69th Brigade, are following closely. No casualties, reported to this hour in 140th Inf. Moving in N. W. direction from this point. 30 Boche surrendered to Lt. Otto Hine, 139 Inf. Lt. Hine reported to C. O. 140th Inf., having lost his way.

TRUMAN,
RIO.

Message No. 6

From—RIO 140th Inf.
At—04.8-75.1, Verdun A, 1/20000. (1 Kil. N. W. Cheppy).
Date—Sept. 26. Hour—6:30 P. M. No. 6. How sent—By runner.
To—Adj. 70th Brig.

Regimental P. C. temporarily established at the above point. 138 Inf. not to exceed 30 meters in advance of this Regt. Where will your next P. C. be established. No casualties up to this hour.

TRUMAN,
RIO.

Message No. 7

From—RIO 140th Inf.
At—04.8-75.1, Verdun A, 1/20000. (1 Kil. N. W. Cheppy).
Date—Sept. 26. Hour—6:30 P. M. No. 7. How sent—By runner.
To—G-2, 35th Div.

Regt. advancing in good order, keeping close contact with 138th Inf. No casualties reported up to this hour in this Regt. Temporary P. C. of Regt. established at the above point.

TRUMAN,
RIO.

Message No. 8

From—RIO 140th Inf.
At—04.8-75.1, Verdun A, 1/20000. (1 Kil. N. W. Cheppy).
Date—Sept. 27. Hour—7 A. M. No. 8. How sent—By runner.
To—Brig. Adj. 70th Brig.

140th Inf. began the advance at time set.

TRUMAN,
RIO.

Message No. 9

From—RIO 140th Inf.
At—04.8-75.1, Verdun A, 1/20000. (1 Kil. N. W. Cheppy).
Date—Sept. 27. Hour—7:00 A. M. No. 9. How sent—By runner.
To—G-2, 35th Division.

140th Inf. began the advance today at 6:30 A. M., passing through the 138th, now in support. No casualties on the 26th in the 140th Inr.

TRUMAN,
RIO.

Message No. 10

From—RIO 140th Inf.
At—300 yards north of P. C. of the 26th. (N. Cheppy on line Very).
Date—Sept. 27. Hour—9:30 A. M. No. 10. How sent—By Runner.
To—Brig. Adj. 70th Brig.

Both 140th and 139th Inf. held up by enemy M. G. fire. Troops cannot advance without artillery support. Tank commander has been notified. A few casualties in the 140th Inf. M. G. fire.

TRUMAN,
RIO.

Message No. 11.

From—RIO 140th Inf.
At—Point as given in last message.
Date—Sept. 27. Hour—10:30 A. M. No. 11. How sent—By Runner.
To—Brigade Adj. 70 Brigade.

Our line is still held up by M. G. fire. Three casualties in 1st Battalion Degree of wounds, slight. M. G.'s positively located at E 03.8-76.6. One at F 04.6-76.7. Very map. Enemy shelling hill north of Regt. P. C. possibly 50 H E in the last 45 minutes. (N. E. Charpentry and on Hill 210.)

TRUMAN,
RIO.

THE FIVE DAYS					105

Message No. 12.

From—RIO 140th Inf.
At—04.8-75.1, Verdun, A, 1/20,000.
Date—Sept. 27.   Hour 10:30 A. M. How sent—By Runner.
To—G-2, 35th Division.
    Our advance lines held up by M. G. fire from direction of 03.8-76.6 one at 04.6-76.6, Very map. The location given is correctly reported so my I. O. of the 1st Battalion reports. Enemy shelling hill north of Regt. P. C.—about 50 H E 105's in last 45 minutes. No casualties from shelling. Three casualties from M. G. fire in the 1st Battalion, 140th Inf. Will advance as soon as M. G. nests are cleaned out. (Machine guns due east Charpentry and on Hill 210.)
                                        TRUMAN,
                                            RIO.

Message No. 13.

From—RIO 140th Inf.
At—04.8-75.1, Verdun A, 1/20,000.
Date—Sept. 27.   Hour 12:20 P. M.   No. 13.   How sent—By Runner.
To—Adj. 70th Brig.
    Am sending to you for your information maps and tracings that will be of value to you. After they have answered your purpose forward to G-2, 35th. Heavy shelling of our troops all along our flanks.
                                        TRUMAN,
                                          RIO.

Message No. 14.

From—RIO 140th Inf.
At—05.8-75.1, Verdun A, 1/20,000.
Date—Sept. 27.   Hour 1:10 P. M.   No. 14.   How sent—By Runner.
To—Adj. 70th Brig.
    Am sending sketch of a point in front of our line. Three men killed by shell fire. Enemy still shelling our troops heavily and are not able to advance.
                                        TRUMAN,
                                          RIO.

Message No. 15.

From—RIO 140th Inf.
At—04.8-75.1, Verdun A, 1/20,000.
Date—Sept. 27.   Hour 1:10 P. M.   No. 15.   How sent—By Runner.
To—G-2, 35th Div.
    The attack began at 6 A. M. Our Regiment passed through the

138th Inf., and is now occupying a line running east and west, and south of Charpentry, about 1000 yards. Column halted by heavy machine gun fire from woods near Charpentry, and heavy artillery fire from the north of Charpentry. The right of our line is resting near the Charpentry-Very road. Tanks have been asked for to clear out machine gun nests. Advance will start as soon as they arrive.

TRUMAN,
RIO.

Message No. 16.

From—RIO 140th Inf.
At—04.76.1, Verdun A, 1/20,000. (3/4 Kil. S. E. Charpentry.)
Date—Sept. 27.   Hour—5 P. M.   No. 16.   How sent—By Runner.
To—G-2, 35th Div.

Boche are moving out of Charpentry in large bodies of what looks to be 75 or 80 men in each group. Also moving along road at point near 04.2-77.2, Verdun A, 1/20,000. Men moving along road can be seen carrying machine guns. Our lines have advanced slightly. See map of our lines at 3 P. M.

TRUMAN,
RIO.

Message No. 17.

From—RIO 140th Inf.
At—04.5-761, Verdun A, 1/20,000. (½ Kil. S. E. Charpentry).
Date—Sept. 27.   Hour 5:50 P. M.   No. 17.   How Sent—By Runner.
To—Adj. 70th Brig.

Letters taken from wounded Boche. 2nd. Bn. 140 has advanced one kilometer, with assistance of French tanks. Entire Regt. now advancing under barrage. Forward papers to G-2 35th Division.

TRUMAN,
RIO.

Message No. 18.

From—RIO 140th Inf.
At—02.9-78.7=L, Foret d'Argonne, 1/20,000. (1 Kil. due N. Charpentry.)
Date—Sept. 28.   Hour 7:30 A. M. No. 18.   How sent—By Runner.
To—Adj. 70th Brig.

Our lines held up by M. G. fire. 100 casualties in Regt. during past 24 hours. Our front lines are about 200 meters in advance of above point. Strong M. G. fire from our front. Also artillery

THE FIVE DAYS   107

fire but not doing any damage.   Enemy planes active.   Advance started at 5 A. M.

TRUMAN,
RIO.

Message No. 19.

At—02.9-78.7, Foret d' Argonne, 1/20,000. (1 Kil. due N. Charpentry.
Date—Sept. 28.   Hour 8:20 A. M. No. 19.   How sent—By Runner.
To—G-2, 35th Div.

Our troops started the advance at 5 A. M.   Have met with strong M. G. fire which is holding up the lines.   Line about 200 meters in advance of this point.   Tanks have arrived and are ready to go into action.   108 casualties in Regt. during the past 24 hours.

TRUMAN,
RIO.

Message No. 20.

From—RIO 140th Inf.
At—02.3-78.9, Foret d'Argonne, 1/20,000. (200 yards N. Chaudron Farm.)
Date—Sept. 28.   Hour 2:30 P. M. No. 20. How sent—By Runner.
To—Adj. 70th Brig.

Regt. halted by terrific artillery shelling and concentrated machine gun fire.   See drawing showing approximately our front line. There may be a little change made during the night.   We are flanked by artillery fire on every side but our rear.   Our own artillery has given no support during the attack.   Enemy planes very active, during the day.   One squadron of enemy planes over our position at 1 P. M.   They turned their M. G.'s on the men causing some losses. 15 planes in the party.   Also one enemy plane flew low over our troops all during the forenoon directing the fire of artillery.   We have suffered heavy losses in killed and wounded.   Men are now at dressing stations and are still lying on the ground where they fell. We are short of ammunition which is very badly needed in case of a counter-attack by the enemy.   The adjutant of the Regt. has been gassed and the C. O. has not been seen since the attack started.   Runners unable to find any trace of him.

TRUMAN,
RIO

Message No. 21

From—RIO 140th Inf.
At—02.3-78.9, Foret d'Argonne, 1/20000. (200 yards N. Chaudron Farm).

Date—Sept. 28. Hour—3 P. M. No. 21. How sent—By runner.
To—G-2, 35th Div.

Regt. halted by terrific artillery shelling and concentrated M. G. fire. See drawing forwarded by 70th Brig. We are flanked by artillery fire from every side but our rear. Our own artillery gave no support during the attack. Enemy planes over our lines during attack, flying low, directing artillery fire on our troops. At 1 P. M. 15 enemy planes flew over our lines firing on our troops with their M. G.'s causing losses. We have suffered heavy losses in killed and wounded. Men are now in dressing stations that were wounded yesterday. Numbers of wounded men have not been carried off the field. We are short of ammunition which is very badly needed in case of a counter attack by the enemy. The Adjutant has been gassed and the C. O. has not been seen since the attack started. Runners unable to find any trace of him.

TRUMAN,
RIO.

Message No. 22

From—RIO 140th Inf.
At—1 Kilometer north of 02.3-78.9. Foret d'Argonne, 1/20000). (¾ mile N. Chaudron Farm).
Date—Sept. 29. Hour—12:30 P. M. No. 22. How sent—By runner.
To—Adj. 70 Brig.

Our troops started the advance on time set. They had not the proper time to reorganize with the result that the organizations were split up and confused. Our artillery fell short in many cases causing losses to our troops. Enemy artillery very active as well as M. G. Numerous losses in the Regt. in killed and wounded. Our troops now occupy EXERMONT.

TRUMAN,
RIO.

Message No. 23

From—RIO 140th Inf.
At—1 Kilometer north of 02.3-78.9, Foret d'Argonne, 1/20000. (¾ mile N. Chaudron Farm).
Date—Sept. 29.—Hour—12:30 P. M. No. 23. How sent—By runner.
To—G-2, 35th Division.

Our troops now occupy Exermont. It was taken under a fierce artillery and M. G. fire. Our losses were heavy in killed and wounded. Our artillery gave little support and on several occasions fired short

THE FIVE DAYS 109

as much as 1 kilometer, causing losses to our troops. Weather very bad. Muddy ground.

TRUMAN,
RIO.

Message No. 24

From—RIO 140th Inf.
At—Trenches shown in sketch submitted. (Just south Chaudron Farm).
Date—Sept. 29. Hour—4:30 P. M. No. 24. How sent—By runner.
To—G-2, 35th Div.

Our troops started to fall back in accordance with orders received from the Brigade Commander to retire back to the position gradually, that was held last night. Instead of doing as ordered by the Officers and NCO's, they started to break and run, it almost turning into a stampede. Men of all regiments, Officers and NCO's were headed to the rear. It being a critical moment, I gathered a few of my NCO's and observers about me and stopped about 300. We are organized now in a line of trenches as shown by drawing. Everything is quiet at present with the exception of heavy shelling and machine gun fire during the day.

TRUMAN,
RIO.

Full report will be made as soon as time can be found to do so.

Message No. 25

From—RIO 140th Inf.
At—02.8-77.8, Foret d'Argonne, 1/20000, (Baulny Ridge, 200-300 S. Chaudron Farm).
Date—Sept. 30. Hour 9:15 A. M. No. 25. How sent—By runner.
To—Adj. 70th Brig.

The enemy is coming over in skirmish formation. Have reached hedge this side of MONTREBEAU woods. Unable to ascertain exact number. Our artillery and M. G. have opened fire. Our artillery falling short on our front and support line trenches. Barrage should be raised from 300 to 500 yards.

TRUMAN,
RIO.

Message No. 26

From—RIO 140th Inf.
At—02.8-77.8, Foret d'Argonne, 1/20000. (South Chaudron Farm).

Date—Sept. 30. Hour—9:15 A. M. No. 26. How sent—By runner.
To—G-2, 35th Div.

Enemy forming for an attack. Is coming over in wave formation. Have reached hedge this side of the MONTREBEAU woods. Unable to determine strength of enemy at this time. Our artillery and M. G. have opened fire.

TRUMAN,
RIO.

Message No. 27

From—RIO 140th Inf.
At—02.9-77.9, Foret d'Argonne, 1/20000. (Engineer's line.)
Date—Sept. 30, 1918. Hour 4 P. M. No. 27. How sent—by runner.
To—Brigade Adj. 70th Brig.

Enemy has been quiet during the day, since 9:15. All except heavy artillery fire at intervals during the day. Our troops are digging in and strengthening the line in every way possible, and we feel that we are able to hold the line in event the enemy should attack. Rations have been issued to the men in the lines and a good supply of ammunition carried up.

TRUMAN,
RIO.

Message No. 28

From—RIO 140th Inf.
At—02.9-77.9 Foret d'Argonne, 1/20000. (Engineer's line. S. Chaudron Farm.)
Date—Sept. 30, '18. Hour—4:30 P. M. No. 28. How sent—By runner.
To—G-2-35th Div.

Enemy did not attack. Was evidently driven away by our artilery and M. G. fire. Our troops are digging in as well as strengthening the line in every way possible, to hold it against an attack. We feel that the line can now be held in case he should attack. Rations have been issued to all troops. Also a plentiful supply of ammunition. A great deal of discomfort from the wet cold weather.

TRUMAN,
RIO.

Message No. 29

From—RIO 140th Inf.
At—06.2-72.9, Verdun 9, 1/20000. (1 Kilometer. S. E. Cheppy.)
Date—Oct. 1, '18. Hour—1:45 P. M. No. 29. How sent—By runner.
To—G-2, 35th Division.

The 140th Infantry was relieved in the line at 3 A. M., this date

THE FIVE DAYS 111

by the 18th and 28th Inf. Relief completed at 5:30 A. M. Regt. proceeded to march to camp at above given map reference. An unusually heavy shelling took place while the relief was being made. Also about 1000 gas shells were put over on our Regt. lines. This was followed by a barrage which lasted until our Regt. was out of the area. The probable cause of the gas shelling and unusual barrage at the hour it happened was on account of the incoming troops making such a great amount of noise. Am sending to you a map and photos taken from a German Captain killed by one of the Battalion Intelligence patrols.

TRUMAN,
RIO.

Message No. 30

From—RIO 140th Inf.
At—06.2-72.9, Verdun A, 1/20000. (1 Kilometer. S. E. Cheppy.)
Date—Oct. 1, '18. Hour—4 P. M. No. 30. How sent—By runner.
To—Adj. 70th Brig.
Location of Regt. P. C. 06.2-72.9, Verdun A, 1/20.

TRUMAN,
RIO
(Signed) DELAPLANE.

INTELLIGENCE SUMMARY, SEPT. 30, 1918
140th Infantry

From noon, Sept. 29, to noon, Sept. 30

I. GENERAL IMPRESSIONS OF THE DAY:
Enemy activity growing much stronger. Violent artillery action by enemy. Also machine gun activity to a great degree.

II. ENEMY FRONT LINE:
Enemy line extends at present from 01.2-79.0 to 01.4-29.9 and east to 02.8-79.4.

III. ENEMY ORDER OF BATTLE:
No additional identification.

IV. ENEMY ACTIVITY.
Infantry: Very active.
Machine Gun: Very active.
Trench Mortar: Nil.

V. ENEMY MOVEMENT:
Visibility: Poor.

VI. ENEMY AERONAUTICS:
Enemy planes very active, continually flying over our lines during

the entire day, firing at our troops with machine guns and directing artillery fire on our front lines.

VII. MISCELLANEOUS:

During the entire day our troops were continually pelted with fire of our own artillery as well as the fire of the enemy. The fire of our own guns was much more destructive to our troops than the fire of the boche. That condition still exists today. Our artillery laid down a heavy barrage on our front and rear lines at about 9:15 A. M. today. Repeated messengers and runners have been sent to notify the artillery that their range was short, I myself going to see the Major in command of one Battalion of artillery, and asked him to see that the word was passed to the other commanders. I also showed him where our lines are now located. Our aeroplanes have been of little use to us in combating enemy planes. So far as the good they have done in that respect we had just as well not had them. In the subject of reports will state that I have done the best that I possibly could do under the circumstances.

VIII. OUR OWN ACTIVITY:

The advance on EXERMONT was begun at 5:30 A. M., Sept. 29th, with two Battalions of the 140th Inf. in the line and one Battalion in support. The town of EXERMONT was taken before 9:15 A. M. and our troops passed through the town about 300 yards beyond. They were later compelled to retire on order from Brigade Commander, which stated that the 70th Brigade should withdraw gradually to the line held the night previous. The men, on the order to withdraw, began to retire gradually, passed the place designated, started on their way to CHARPENTRY, the organizations being mixed, most of the officers casualties and few non-commissioned officers left. Things began to look serious, and had it not been for the prompt action and force used by the few officers who could be gathered together and stop the rush, it is hard to tell what would have happened. As soon as they caught up with the men in front of the rush and stopped them we organized them in a line of trenches as shown in sketch submitted to you last night. We now have the situation well in hand and can withstand most any kind of an attack the enemy might put over, provided we can get the artillery to put the barrage on the boche and not on our own lines. I have sent five different message to the artillery this morning to lengthen their range, it being five separate occasions on which they have shelled our men. It is doing more to decrease the morale of our troops than if they knew the entire German army was attacking them. The situation is simply this: there is not a telephone in any organization I know of. There are no signal rockets left, no flares to shoot in the Very pistols. What signal lights were in the organization are either lost or broken, and we have practically no way of communicating with anyone except by runner. Our losses have been extremely heavy. Our regiment, the 140th Infantry, on going into action on the 29th, had, not to exceed 1000 men. The other

Regiments of the Division are in about the same shape as ours. We lost yesterday in officers killed and wounded: Major Murray Davis, Capt. Kenady and Lieut. Compton Bn. Intelligence Officer for the 1st Battalion, killed. Wounded: Capt. Redmond, Lt. Gardner, Lt. Wise, Lt. Spicer, Lt. Thorpe, Lt. Keefner. Degree of wounds not known.

R. E. TRUMAN,
Captain 140th Inf.
Regimental Intelligence Officer.

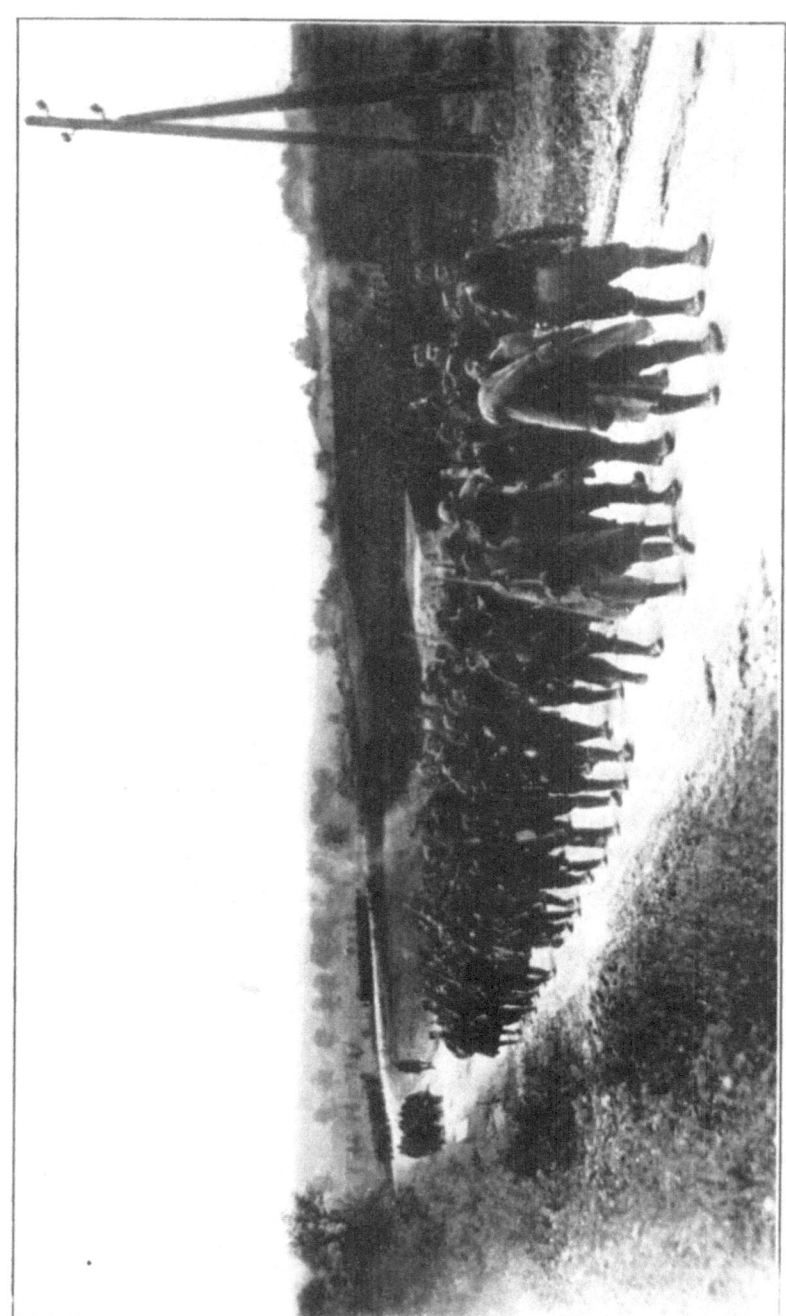

CO. H MARCHING UP TO VERDUN, OCTOBER 11TH, 1918
Note Spaces Between For Safety

CHAPTER VII

Verdun

We hiked, a long and miserable hike, to Camp Raton, spending the night of October 3d there, and reaching Marats-la-Grand on October 5th remained there just a week. The regimental Chaplain had shown the doughboy's fear of losing "The Regiment," and had gone A. W. O. L. from the hospital, reaching the command just before it left on October 12th. Ten days had made a wonderful change in the men. With rest and food and the elasticity of youth, they had already "come back."

On the march from the battle-field we were inspected. One of the chief duties of a soldier is to be inspected. Sometimes the sense of perspective seems to be lacking.

A dapper little Corps inspector looked us over. And he did not like our appearance. He sent up a sharp and bitter criticism, which was read by most of the officers in the regiment. Our shoes were worn and muddy and our clothing was torn and unpressed. Officers were too familiar with the men who had fought beside them in shell holes and up the hills against the enemy, in some cases saving their lives. And he wound up his criticism with this scathing sentence: "This Division bears all the earmarks of a National Guard Division, which indeed it is."

He had pierced our disguise, and discovered us! The gallant and steady old First Division had looked upon our dead and hailed us "comrades." The Germans had seen us drive back their seasoned troops kilometer after kilometer over bloody ground, and they thought that we were really soldiers. Why had we failed to make use of the barber shops and tailoring establishments scattered so thickly around Charpentry and Exermont! Why had we failed to ride in the limousines provided by a kindly government, and so remain unspotted by the mud! It was a fatal mistake. His eagle eye had discovered what we really were, merely National Guardsmen, and he did not like us. Neither did the Boches!

115

On October twelfth the first battalion reached the trenches in the Sommedieu sector, taking over the Eix sector, and Regimental Hqrs. reached Camp d'Escargot (Tavannes sector) on the fourteenth. Two battalions were in the line here, Eix and Damloup sector, and one in reserve at Camp St. Airy. Camp St. Airy was the muddiest hole we found overseas. The wagons frequently stalled in the axle-deep mud, the pup tents were pitched in the mud for a number of the men and the rain continued.

It was an old camp, and the rats and vermin were plentiful. The dugouts were old, and the men terribly crowded. In the front the trenches were old but in fair condition, and the enemy lines were some distance away.

The history of Verdun has been already written. It held a most important position, lying directly over against the fortress captured in 1870 by the Germans. And its glorious defense in this war is well known. We held a most important part of the line for nearly a month. Verdun has suffered terribly from bombardment, and the surrounding country was desolation itself. There seemed to be no living trees. Killed by shell or gas, their jagged branches and broken, ghastly trunks are monuments to the fearful warfare that raged among them. It is a picture of Death. The ground is pitted with countless shell holes, and the evidence of the thousands slain before its heights is everywhere seen. Nowhere in France did the 140th see such a picture of utter desolation and destruction. Yet, one day as I walked up to a listening post in an advanced position suddenly there was a familiar whir-r-r and a covey of plump partridges rose from the ground at my very feet.

Here we received a large number of replacements. We had begun to get new clothes and equipment at Marats-la-Grand, and now the regiment was regaining its strength in numbers.

They were a fine lot of men. From the days at Doniphan this regiment was fortunate in its replacements. All of the men who were sent to us averaged well, and soon became loyal to the traditions of the 140th.

But these men were, many of them, inexperienced, and one night we had a terrific gas barrage. Either because they were too slow in getting on their masks or because they removed them too soon, we had a large number of casualties.

Meanwhile the Germans were seeing the handwriting on the wall. They had lost, and they knew it. Aeroplanes began to drop leaflets in our trenches. Two are given here, but the originals were in English and French with important words and phrases in capital letters.

GERMANY ANSWERS PRESIDENT WILSON

The German Government, replying to the questions of the President of the United States of America declares:

The German government has accepted the terms laid down by the President in his address on the 8th January last, and in his subsequent addresses, as the basis of a lasting peace of justice. Its object in entering into discussions would be only to agree upon practical details of the application of those terms.

The German Government assumes that the Governments with which the Government of the United States is associated also stand on the ground of President Wilson's pronouncements.

The German Government, in agreeing with the Austro-Hungarian government, declares itself ready to comply with President Wilson's proposals for evacuation in order to bring about an armistice.

It leaves it to the President to effect the meeting of a mixed commission which would have to make the necessary arrangements for evacuation.

The present German Government, responsible for the peace step, has been formed by negotiations and in agreement with the great majority of the Reichstag."

The Imperial Chancellor, supported in each of his dealings by the will of this majority, speaks in the name of the German Government and of the German people.

Berlin, October 12th 1918.

(Signed) Solf,
Secretary of State for Foreign Affairs.

Why are we still fighting?

———o———

THE GERMAN PEOPLE OFFERS PEACE

The new German democratic government has this program:
"The will of the people is the highest law."
The German people wants quickly to end the slaughter.
The new German popular government therefore has offered an

Armistice

and has declared itself ready for

Peace

on the basis of justice and reconciliation of nations.

It is the will of the German people that it should live in peace with peoples, honestly and loyally.

What has the new German popular government done so far to put into practice the will of the people and to prove its good and upright intentions?

(a) The new German Government has appealed to President Wilson to bring about peace.

It has recognized and accepted all the principles which President Wilson proclaimed as a basis for a general lasting peace of justice among the nations.

(b) The new German Government has solemnly declared its readiness to evacuate Belgium and restore it.

(c) The new German Government is ready to come to an honest understanding with France about Alsace-Lorraine.

MAJOR GENERAL TRAUB SHAKING HANDS

Captain Grigg, Beau, Major Broyles, Truman, Lt. McGann, Lawrence, Bean, Chaplain Manning, Lt. Stephens. In rear, Col. Gray. Chaplain Buswell, extreme right

(d) The new German Government has restricted the U-boat war.
No passenger steamers not carrying troops or war material will be attacked in future.

(e) The new German Government has declared that it will withdraw all German troops back over the German frontier.

(f) The new German Government has asked the Allied Governments to name commissioners to agree upon the practical measures of evacuation of Belgium and France.

These are the deeds of the new German popular government. Can these be called mere words, or bluff, or propaganda?

Who is to blame, if an armistice is not called now?

Who is to blame if daily thousands of brave soldiers needlessly have to shed their blood and die?

Who is to blame, if the hitherto undestroyed towns and villages of France and Belgium sink in ashes

Who is to blame, if hundreds of thousands of unhappy women and children are driven from their homes to hunger and freeze?

The German people offers its hand for peace

On October 16th, Col Alonzo Gray, of the Regular Army, relieved Col. Delaplane as Commanding Officer. Col. Delaplane had won his way up from the ranks, and was thoroughly ingrained with the "regular" point of view. He led us in the Argonne, identified himself thoroughly with the regiment, and gave it the best that was in him. He would have given a good deal to have brought the men home.

Col. Gray was an older man, and familiar with the best traditions of the old army. He worked hard with the regiment, commanding it during a most trying period. He had a sense of humor, and possessed that rare quality of enjoying a joke even when he was the subject. He possessed another rare quality. He was almost the only regular officer we met overseas who could make a mistake about anything.

Under both of these officers the regiment exhibited splendid discipline, and did excellent work.

Beginning November 6th, we were relieved and moved out to Belrupt, Autrecourt, Pierrefitte, and reached the village Nigre the 10th.

The first battalion was at Fresnes, the second and third at Rupt. The march up was a gruelling one. Our Intelligence Officer was then a Captain, although afterwards he won a Major's leaves. He had auburn hair. There is a certain disposition popularly supposed to accompany this complexion. In this instance it did.

The officer had one pet aversion. He is strong in his likes and dislikes, but his strongest dislike is one of aviators. This attitude had been strengthened by our unfortunate lack of fliers in the Argonne.

He has also a remarkable gift of expression. He can put matters so that no one could mistake his meaning. Positively no one! His motorcycle broke down on this long hike. For an hour he had been working in the mud and rain, and his disposition had almost reached the breaking point. He wore a regulation helmet, and a rain coat which concealed his Captains bars.

Just at that inauspicious moment a limousine rolled by. In it a spick and span SECOND LIEUTENANT, Aviation, lolled on the cushions. The limousine slowed down; it stopped; it backed along the road until it stood opposite the damaged motorcycle and the already furious captain. The door opened and from the interior came these words, "My good man, don't you know enough to salute an officer?" Then ******.

The men faced the most trying conditions. It was cold with a damp chilly coldness unlike anything they had known. They lived in mud and ate in the rain and slept in old and worthless dugouts, or in pup tents. There was little variety in the food, and they suffered every physical discomfort. When one remembers how splendidly the regiment met these conditions, one has little patience with the complaints so readily made about trifles by the man who stayed at home.

Even here it was possible to obtain candy, tobacco and little luxuries for the men. Condensed milk was always a great favorite. It was interesting to see how boys from the farm, who a year ago would have scorned "canned cow" would eagerly drink a can of condensed milk. The supply was never equal to the demand.

Some times pay-days were far apart—or the men were not lucky—and the soldiers asked for credit. Thousands of francs stood in the regiment at times "Jaw-bone," expressive slang. There were times when $2,000 was owed by the men. It is a splendid tribute to the honesty of the 140th that $15.00 will cover the unpaid bills of the men who came home. They had their faults, but somehow one came to look for the good things in their character, and honesty was among them.

On the night of November 5th, just before we left the Verdun trenches, the First Bn. Scout Platoon, under Capt. Ralph Ware and Lt. Jacob Grondyke, and with Major Ralph E. Truman, R. I. O., made a patrolling expedition into No Man's Land and advanced almost to Etain, a distance of six or seven kilometers. They had several hairbreadth escapes, killed at least one of an enemy patrol, and brought back most valuable information. They passed through a series of interesting and dangerous adventures, and their work received the highest commendation. Upon their return, however, they simply reported that they had "established contact with the enemy."

At Village Nigre, Regimental Headquarters standing for the regiment, we were equipped with maps and necessary equipment, with the understanding that we were to take part in the drive on Metz in a few days. The new men were eager to be sent into the line, but the veterans were not so anxious to go. They were willing to advance if necessary, but they knew the real meaning of war.

It can not be doubted that in the drive on Metz the 140th, with its experienced officers and veteran soldiers would have made a great record.

French African troops had been quartered in Village Nigre. It was a very dirty and very miserable hole. Fresnes was so badly shot to pieces that there was not a whole building in the place, and Rupt was not much better. The days were rainy, the nights cold and fuel was scarce. But drill and inspections went on.

The men said "If this is resting, for Heaven's sake let us go out and fight!"

OFFICERS FIRST BATTALION 140TH, FRANCE

CHAPTER VIII

The Armistice and the Days After

No man dreamed that the end was near. On the Argonne battlefield the enemy had fought with no sign of weakness. At Verdun, except for the leaflets about peace—which we supposed were mere camouflage—the Germans were very active. The shells came over with far greater frequency than the peace pamphlets. We intended to be in Berlin by Christmas, and wanted to fight—or rather to go through with the job. Suddenly on Monday, November the eleventh, at eleven o'clock, came .

The Armistice. "Fini la guerre!"

Men took it quietly. Men like these learn to take everything quietly. Some were sorry—they wished to punish the Boche. One man said, "Now I'll eat mother's cooking again!" another "Now I'll see that girl of mine!" another, "Now we'll be home by Christmas!" Their thoughts were all turned toward home, but it was to be a long, long while after Christmas before they were to sight the shores of their homeland.

In the little French villages, in the trenches, or along the roads, wherever a Frenchman saw a doughboy, he would greet him with a joyous shout, and cry "Fini la guerre!" and if possible they would drop in somewhere to celebrate.

In Paris of course, all France celebrated. First the shops were closed. A little band of employees from one store would dance into an open store, sing a verse of the Marseillaise, and cry "Sortez, Sortez," whereupon the shop would begin to close, and the crowd go on with augmented numbers.

The Rue des Italiens and the Place de la Concorde were thronged with people instantly. The Place de la Opera was simply jammed, and one could not get through. With it all, the crowd was good-natured, and there was little drunkenness, although a great deal of exhilaration. From time to time a few French and American cornetists would climb on the pillars of the Grand Opera House, play the

POST OFFICE DETAIL, 140TH

PONT SUR MEUSE
Home of the First Battalion

Marseillaise and the Star Spangled Banner, and wave the two flags. Then the crowd would go wild.

Here would be seen a crowd of doughboys in a truck, and there a "class" of the next year, marching in sad disorder: the fathers, mothers and sweethearts of these boys, who in the Spring would have been in the trenches, marching arm in arm with them in delirious happiness. When one realized the heavy burden these boys would have to bear in rebuilding France, one wondered for the future.

Many were seen in the streets wearing mourning. They had personal sorrows, but they rejoiced for France! There is greater love of country in no land.

At night there was opera. The building was crowded. The curtain lifted, and on the stage was a machine gun camouflaged with red roses. In the rear of the stage was Clemenceau and a number of the Chamber of Deputies.

Marthe Cheval, draped in the Tri-color, sang the Marseillaise. The house went wild. Then a Frenchman waved the Stars and Stripes and sang the Star Spangled Banner. For ten minutes the house was filled with raving lunatics. Never was such cheering, and laughing, and weeping. We have taught a good many nations to sing the Star Spangled Banner. Then came God Save the King, the Brabanconne, and the orchestra played the National airs of all the Allied nations, graciously permitting the opera to begin about ten o'clock.

In the middle of the second act, eleven o'clock struck. That is closing time. The curtain dropped in the middle of a sentence, and the vast audience thronged homeward, the French perfectly satisfied.

Paris rejoiced. The captured guns were taken from their places of exhibition, girls rode upon them, and they were wheeled through the streets. "But they could have learned something about putting on a big noise from an American football game," said the doughboy.

When the Armistice was signed, the Germans had lost every commanding position north of Verdun, and had been driven out of the plains of the Woevre. They had no longer any natural defense, and but poor artificial ones. The main supply line of their Western Army was cut, and our troops were pressing them into the confusion of helpless retreat.

Much has been said of the wastefulness of life on the part of the American Army. We had in front of the American Army about 400,000 Germans, a fourth of their whole army. Of these we captured 16,000 or one in every 25. The total German casualties were about 100,000, while we lost (including the French fighting with us) about 122,000. When it is remembered that the enemy fought a defensive warfare, from strongly entrenched positions, and over familiar ground, these figures are remarkable.

Two million, eighty-four thousand soldiers were landed in France, and two out of three, a million four hundred thousand, saw front-line service. The time of greatest activity was the second week in October when twenty-nine divisions were in action over a hundred and one miles of front.

The average advance for each division was seventeen miles against desperate resistance. The prisoners captured totaled sixty-three thousand, while 4,400 Americans were captured by the enemy. In the total Meuse-Argonne offensive 1,200,000 Americans were engaged, and over 4,200,000 rounds fired by the artillery.

Boncourt and Pont sur Meuse

On the first of December the regiment moved about twenty kilometers to Boncourt and Pont-sur-Meuse, a few kilometers from St. Mihiel, and near Division Headquarters at Commercy. These were deserted little French towns, but while crowded and poor, gave us better billets than we usually had while in France.

Here we were given a period of intensive training. Men who had dug in more than once under fire, and sometimes with the lid to a mess-kit were taught to dig trenches. Men had bits of white cloth pinned on them and "simulated machine guns," while men who had taken machine gun nests without artillery support were taught how to attack machine guns by men who had never faced them. The various indoor sports went on, and golf (African) became popular with a small element.

The men made friends with the French. Of course their men were being demobilized, and the homes were needed for them. But the 140th could go back tomorrow to any French town it ever visited and find a warm and kindly welcome. Our men were well disciplined, and there were never any serious difficulties with the French.

A great deal of nonsense has been written about our relations with the French and British. Many a British soldier was heard to say "I wish I could enlist in the American Army!"

And those regiments who criticised the French most severely usually had given the French good reason to criticize them. Not only many a charming French girl, but many an old Frenchman or woman, and many a clever child misses the good old 140th. While sometimes we were overcharged, though never as badly as by the swine around our American camps, there were many cases where payment would be refused. The kind of men who come from old Missouri do not readily forget courtesies and kindnesses—they have many pleasant memories of the French.

Nothing more dreary, however, than the small French town can well be imagined. There are no newspapers, a town crier, with a drum, calling the news from the street corners. France has nothing like our popular magazines, there is no movie, there is nothing—nothing save the cafe. On the other hand, in the middle and better class French homes, there is a most beautiful life. It is often said that the French have no word for home. But "foyer" which might be translated hearthstone, takes its place: The children, parents, and grandparents: the family circle. Their unselfish care for each other, their pleasure in little things, and their unfailing courtesy in the home might well be adopted by Americans.

Christmas day came while we were here and the day was spent in examining the contents of our boxes—9x4 by 3 inches! But they brought a loving message from home. We furnished candles for the midnight Mass, the first in three years, and the good priest gave permission for us to have a Christmas tree for the children. These plans gave great pleasure to the soldiers, and it seemed both strange and touching to see these men who a few weeks before had been rough and dangerous soldiers, happy in the enjoyment of little children. And there are some children in France who will never forget one happy Christmas. Captain John Pleasants made a capital Santa Claus at Pont sur Meuse. He was a wonder in getting supplies and luxuries for his men. Everyone wanted to be in D company.

The Knights of Columbus furnished supplies to the chaplain with a lavish hand. Their courtesy and generosity was unfailing and will never be forgotten.

Col Gray was replaced by Lt. Col. Sidney D. Maize on January third. For a time Col. Paul Tucker commanded us, but managed to get back to his own regiment. Col. Maize was a "regular", and a good officer. He was replaced on Feb. 18th by Lt. Col. Smith A. Harris. Col. Harris really seemed to think the officers and men of the regiment had some intelligence, and some desire to do the right thing. He gave the regiment a chance, and it accomplished its work in a splendid manner, calling forth special commendation both at Le Mans and St. Nazaire.

The cold grew intense, but the maneuvers continued. Finally we sent nearly 200 men to the hospital in one week. Orders had come down to let the men get no wood, and later, to take the stoves out of their billets. General Thomas B. Dugan had taken charge of the 70th Brigade October 13th and of the 35th Division on December 29th, holding it until March 1st.

On his first tour of inspection, according to a story I frequently heard, and which Kenamore tells in his splendid history of the division, he called a Colonel to account for permitting his men to wear German souvenirs as equipment. They were wearing American trench knives, and the General did not know that they were regular issue!

Although he joined us twelve days after we came out, he was awarded the Distinguished Service Medal for his good work in handling the 70th brigade in the Argonne-Meuse offensive! At least the citation so read.

Major Broyles sent to him a statement of the growing hospital list, with a request that the men be permitted fires, or the maneuvers

GEN. TRAUB REVIEWING 140TH INFANTRY. COL. GREY AT RIGHT.
Rupt En Woevre, Nov. 18th, 1918

be conducted less frequently and the men be given a chance to rest and get dried out.

This brave General sat by his warm fire in comfortable quarters and dictated a snappy reply, ending with the words "The authorities prescribing these maneuvers doubtless felt that they were of PARAMOUNT IMPORTANCE TO THE HEALTH OF THE MEN" and men are buried in France—so officers assure me—who might have come home with us if we had been under a General with a heart.

On February 18th, Monday, the division was reviewed by General Pershing, accompanied by the Prince of Wales. It made a fine showing, although it marched and stood in mud and water. General Pershing went through the whole Division, and the Prince jumped ditches with him. Some excellent photographs were taken.

It was about 12:45 p. m. when the limousine containing General Pershing and staff reached the reviewing field. Leaving the limousine, the reviewing party changed to horses and came across the field, when the command "Present Arms!" was smartly snapped out to the 25,000 men. General Pershing personally inspected each platoon. To do this effectively it was necessary for him to walk 7½ miles in and out of the various ranks and lines. On the completion of the inspection, the Division was passed in review. Brigadier-General Dugan, accompanied by Lieutenant-Colonel A. F. McLean, acting Chief of Staff, headed the Division.

The 25,000 men marching at one time in the field was most impressive. At this time the sun began to peep over the hills beyond, and soon the ground glistened with its various puddles lit up by the first sunshine in four days.

All the officers were assembled and addressed by General Pershing, who complimented them on their showing in the Argonne Forest, where they took practically inaccessible positions.

The Prince of Wales highly complimented the Division, saying that he had watched this Division with great interest, as it was one of those to train with the English.

As the reviewing party were leaving the field, an amusing incident occurred. A guide taking them from the field toward the road where the limousines were parked endeavored to take a short cut and in so doing led them to a brook about four feet wide. General Pershing said, "looks as though we will have to jump." "All right, let's go," replied the Prince of Wales, and over he jumped, followed by General Pershing. An orderly, following miscalculated the jump and landed in the stream. He was fished out amid cheers.

During the winter we had two splendid Y. M. C. A. men with us, the Rev. A. Frank Johnson, of Erie, Kansas, and W. A. Rice, of Alton, Ill. Chester Freeman, K company, who lives in Tonganoxie, assisted Mr. Johnson until we were mustered out. These men were faithful and did splendid work.

Division players, and Y troupes began to give us entertainments The entertainments given by the men themselves were better, and

MESS LINE
The Out-Doors Dining Room

SOME FRIENDS FROM MISSOURI

THE ARMISTICE AND THE DAYS AFTER 131

they were of a higher class. Two Smith College girls, Miss Rose and Miss Brittingham were assigned to the regiment, and soon adopted it. They were very proud of the men, and were unusually fine young women. While the men had little use for the thousands of useless joy riders who swarmed into France on one pretext and another, they had the greatest admiration and respect for these young women, and others like them. These girls started doughnuts and chocolate for the afternoons, and helped in every possible way.

Our regiment was fortunate. Henry Allen as Division Secretary, had given us good care. He had been in Cheppy and Charpentry when the shells were coming over, and he was with us as we came out. The Y men sent to our regiment were uniformly unselfish, capable men of the highest type. And there were no finer women overseas than these two Smith College girls.

The men began to go on leave. Strange, fascinating names became realities to them. Nice and Monte Carlo were no longer mysteries. They had a good time, but they also accumulated a surprising amount of information.

In the regiment books and magazines were in constant demand, and in the regimental school nearly six hundred were enrolled. They met in cold barracks, and under difficulties, but they wanted to learn.

Here Captain Beau joined us for a time. He was sadly missed when he left. If he ever comes to America he will have a royal welcome. And Captain Grigg was given back to us by the brigade—one of the best adjutants overseas so the officers said. Stogsdill got his Captaincy, which he had long deserved. A manly, modest officer, representing the best in the American service. McFadden, Whitthorne, Wilson and Skelton returned bearing honorable wounds. Rothmann who had, while captured and wounded carried an American Sergeant on his back and probably saved his life. Brady, with his citation, and Chaplain Buswell, having forgotten all about his wound. These were all welcome and it began to seem like the old regiment.

Lt. Montgomery was town-major, and no better man could have been found for the work. In business life he ranks a Colonel. There were many cases of men like him, who had already proved their ability in civil life, who never had it admitted in the army.

The men had learned French money, weights, and liquid measures. They could never get used to the French way of washing clothes, paddling them on rock or board by the streamside and usually without soap. The chaplain had a laundry bill which Major Slusher insisted would require much explanation. It included "chaussettes and chemises;" Chausettes are only homely woolen socks, and chemises are army shirts—honestly.

Many of the chimneys had been arranged to discharge the smoke in the attics, whence it filtered through the red tiles, a camouflage to prevent an enemy aviator from knowing that the houses were inhabited. The towns were but a few kilometers behind the lines. The cold

CAP. WARD'S HUSKIES

MAJOR FRANK G. WARD
An Officer who Knew the Game and Played the Game

damp weather enabled the men to appreciate the reason for the feather mattress used as a coverlet on every French bed.

The men made many trips to the lines, which were easily marked by the skeletons, and brought home many souvenirs. One man in the Supply company found a watch which had lain in the pocket of a dead German for perhaps two years. It was a celluloid case, and on being wound ran with accuracy.

On the walls of the churches were funeral wreaths, made of beads. They were rather stiff and garish affairs representing flowers but there were so many of them that they gave one a shock. We pity Belgium, but it is France that has really suffered. America will not soon forget the price she paid.

In the church at Boncourt were a number of beautiful stained glass windows. Sandwiched in between St. Peter and St. Vincent—beautiful windows—was one of Corporal Thomasson who had been killed in Africa thirty years before. There he was in blue uniform, hair plastered over his forehead, the sort of picture one sees in cheap enlargements. At first he seemed strangely out of place, until one remembered that he had died for France—and the French love France.

Rumors kept spreading that we were to go home—the date was always given out by the K. Ps. The men were restless, and it was becoming more difficult to maintain discipline. The war was won, why were they keeping us? Yet the 140th has a right to be proud of the record it made during these trying days.

One husky G company man was heard turning the air blue with his complaints. They were feeding beans twice in one day! I had met him wounded on the field, going back to a dressing station. When asked about his condition he had replied "Fine, I'm really going back to get fed." Cheerful, plucky and ready with a joke. When reminded of it he replied "Well, ain't a soldier always got a right to kick about the chow." And these men who had suffered terribly without complaint, were nervous and restless—ready to find fault with everything. They were homesick, and did not care who knew it.

In this book many of the hardships suffered by the men overseas have been told, in order that the families of these men may know the full significence of their heroic service. It must not be thought that the men did not bear them cheerfully and bravely, although they were so very far from home.

THE 140TH INFANTRY ASKS NO SYMPATHY!

It is true that we lacked full aeroplane support, but perhaps the planes were more needed elsewhere. We only wished to be used where we could count most. It is true that a great many more guns, nearly 800 in all, were placed in support of the division that relieved us; we proved that we could advance if necessary, without much artillery support. We have no complaint to make. And these difficulties are only mentioned in order to explain why we did not accomplish even more than we did. As a B company private, who had been in a place where his company suffered heavy loss, put it "We hit a tough proposition; we made good: we got not kick coming."

The 140th Infantry Church

A religious census of the regiment proved interesting. The average figures were about the same in Camp Doniphan, and at Boncourt. There were about 11 per cent who were Roman Catholics, About 15 per cent were not members of any church, and had no religious preference. The Methodists had about 11 per cent, but a much smaller membership and a much larger preference than the Catholics. We had also Greek Catholics, Polish Catholics, Church of England and Church of Wales, Presbyterians, Lutherans, Episcopalians, Congregationalists, and the rest. There were no Christian Scientists—but 8 gave it preference. There were ten Jews, four Quakers, a few Latter Day Saints, Adventists and a few Mormons. One gave as his religion "Workman's Circle," there was one Armenian and one Fire Worshiper. But nearly or quite a third of those who were church members were Baptists and Disciples. These were classed together because they are Immersionists, and this is the reason a Baptist minister who could give valid immersion was selected as Chaplain's Assistant.

Just before we went up into the drive there were 60 awaiting Baptism. Part of them were baptised, but nearly three fourths, must be immersed. For two days we tried to dam up enough water at Camp Marquette for an immersion, but without success. Fred Smith assured these men that God would count them as baptized, and many of them never came back; they sleep today on the field of honor.

For months the Chaplain had been planning an Allied Church, and to the final plans the Catholic authorities gave their consent and an Allied organization was offered. It called out the church members of the regiment into definite mobilization, and gave them an objective; it gave the non-members something definite to join. And every member promised to report for duty to his home church on the first Sunday home.

The badge or token was a medal replica of the regimental insignia with a religious motto. It was worn around the neck with the scapular by the Catholics, and on the wrist like a wrist watch by the Protestants. With but a few hundred members, a splendid record was made in the drive. In the fatal five days the regiment lost over 50 per cent which was a fearful loss. But during the five days the 140th Infantry Church lost 90 per cent! A casualty list of nine out of ten is evidence of a devotion to duty and a courage which should forever silence those who say a religious man does not make a good soldier. Every officer belonging to this Allied Church was killed, wounded, gassed, or captured.

We did not try to push religion on anyone ,and our work was done unobtrusively. But a Lt. Colonel, a Major, several Captains and

THE ARMISTICE AND THE DAYS AFTER 135

a number of Lieutenants joined us, and when we sailed we counted over 1100 members, the largest religious organization in any A. E. F. regiment. It is true that at St. Nazaire we took in a considerable number and a few were from other organizations the 139th Inf., the 129th, M. G. Bn. and the 110 San. Train. We ran completely out of insignia, but anyone may now obtain one of the little war crosses by writing to the author of this book.

To Chaplain Buswell, Chaplain Hart, Chaplain Manning and Fred Smith belong most of the credit for the success of this organization. One likes to believe that it helped some in improving the discipline and strengthening the morale of the regiment, which undoubtedly all the way through made an unusually good record.

In the Le Mans area and at St. Nazaire the religious and morale directors sought out the chaplain and asked the secret of the 140th, saying that the regiment stood out clearly above the rest. The Ship's Chaplain on the Nansemond wrote that he had met many different organizations, but found none of them whose morale and attitude toward religion equalled the 140th.

On October 1st, 1917 the Regimental Chaplain was transferred from the 1st Kansas (formerly Funston's 20th Kansas) through the 137th to the 140th and remained with the latter regiment until it was mustered out. Transferred to a Missouri regiment, he was cut off from supplies. In the 137th he had unlimited financial backing; in the 140th he had none, and knew no one in Missouri to whom he could appeal. A "Y" secretary can put a ton of supplies aboard a train or transport; a chaplain not a pound. The former can call for a building, or take it from the chaplain, the latter can get it only by favor; the former can call for a detail, the latter finds it difficult to have his assistant —legally provided—assigned to him.

The regular Army Colonel regards the chaplain as useless, or a nuisance or both. This is not a criticism, as they may have been unfortunate in the chaplains they have known. It is a chaplain's duty to love his Commanding Officer, and I always did my duty, although at times it was a considerable strain upon my disposition. Our Commanding Officers gave too much of loyal effort, intelligent labor and hearty support to the regiment for me to remember anything about them except their good points, of which they had a great many.

The Battalion Commanders all gave the heartiest co-operation, as did the lower officers. But there is one man, who will not like this statement, to whom I owe especial gratitude. He gave me unlimited backing and but for him my supplies would have been exceedingly limited. But for this man most of what I did for the regiment—and it was little enough—would have been impossible.

He was always ready to back to the limit any move to get supplies, to make things easier for, or to improve conditions in the regiment.

He was said to have been the best Supply Officer in the Division. If he said that he knew a thing, he knew it. If he said he would

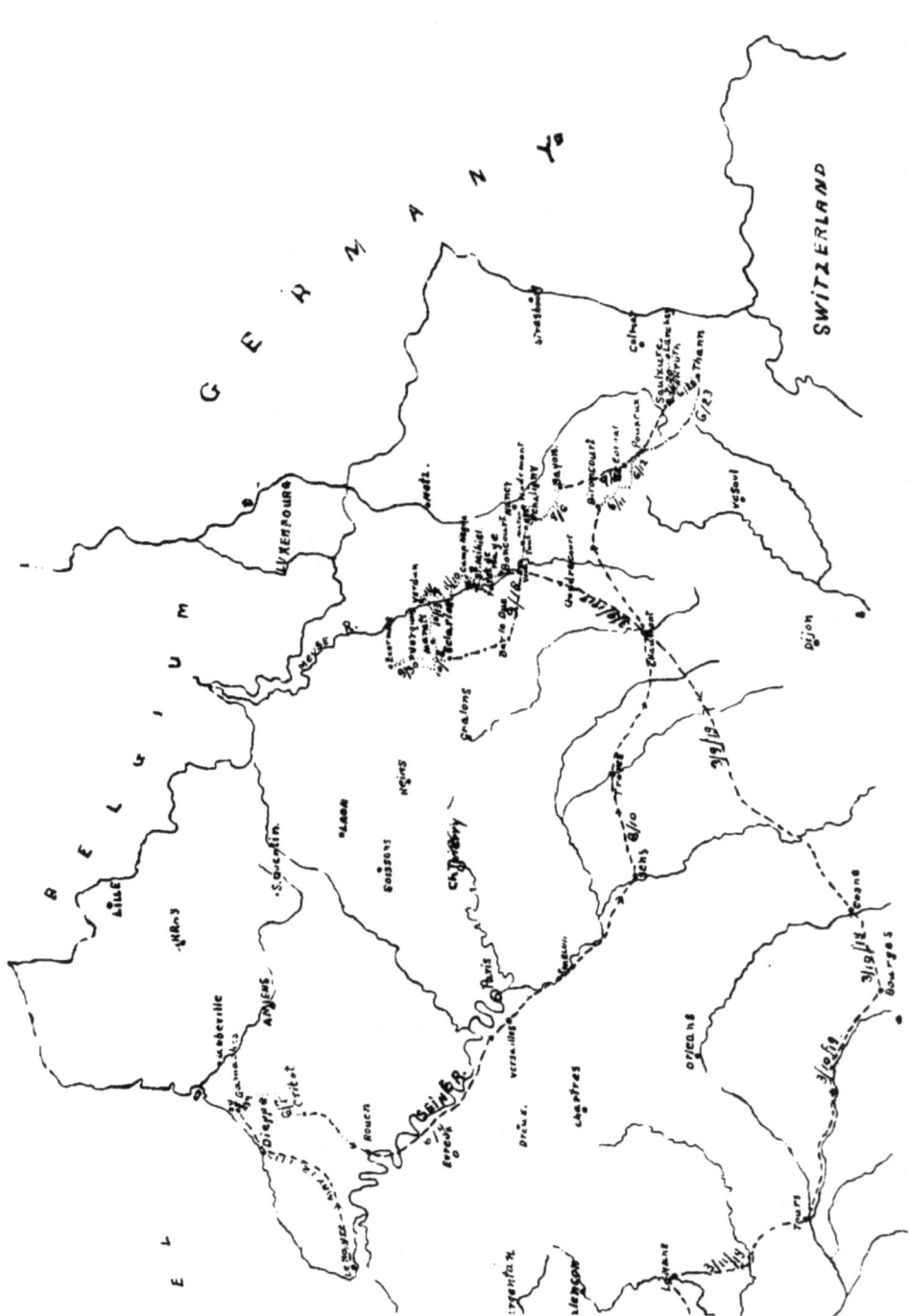

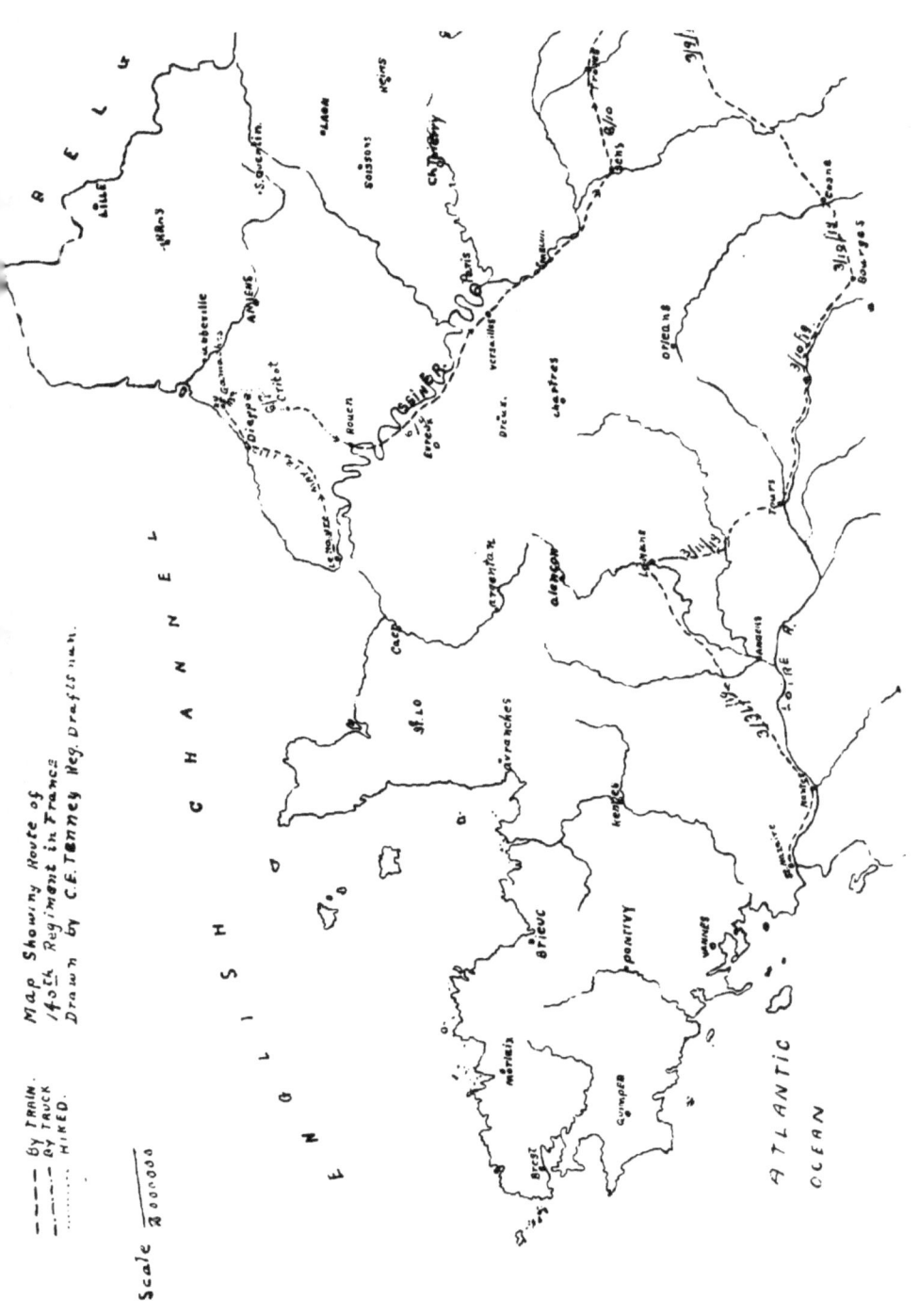

OUR TRAVELS IN FRANCE
By Rail, by Truck, and on Foot, with Dates

do a thing, he did it. As one of his men said: "He knows the game, he plays the game, and he is a square man."

His generous support was not given for personal reasons but because of his love for the regiment; he had been connected with the old Third for nearly twenty years. He is a Major now, but to me—and to the men—he will always be "Old Cap Ward!" To him the 140th owes a debt of gratitude. Taken from the Supply company he made a good line officer. He is a soldier all the way through. And when the returning regiment reached Kansas City, they were given such a welcome as the city had never seen, its great success being largely due to this same man.

Chaplain D. J. Manning, Catholic, had joined us as we came from the drive, losing his trunk in the woods. A fine, steady, faithful man, athletic and plucky, he took up Chaplain Hart's splendid work as few men could have done.

For three months we had dwelt in Boncourt and Pont sur Meuse. They were talking about the Spring ploughing back in Missouri. We wanted to start towards home.

LT. COL. LEMMON, CAPT. WHITTHORNE, SGT. MACE

THE LAST TIME THEY PLAYED IN FRANCE

CHAPTER IX

Homeward Bound

On the eighth of March we left Boncourt, and in three days were in the Le Mans area. Here we were placed in tents and were given a week on the rifle range. The kitchens were enormous, well arranged sheds, and the men were easily fed.

In this book will be found a map showing our travels in France, and indicating the kilometers traveled by truck, by train and on foot. It is the work of Captain Frederick R. Cogswell.

Later we moved over to the Belgian camp, where the men were housed in wooden barracks. There were good bathing facilities, there was little work, and the men had an opportunity to rest and get cleaned up. Major Hail, the Personnel Adjutant, here reaped the reward of his faithful and efficient service. Our paper work won the highest praise, and on the 29th just six months after we took Exermont, we began the movement from Montfort to St. Nazaire completing it in about three days.

It was in the Belgian Camp, on March 21st that we lost John Michal of the Supply company, by a sad accident. He was removing the detonator from the nose of a shell, in order to have a souvenir. He had done this many times before, and supposed there was no danger. In some way the detonator exploded, and he died in the hospital at two in the morning.

Headquarters entrained at 9 p. m. Sunday, March 29th, reaching St. Nazaire at eleven Monday morning, and by April 1st all of the regiment were in the port camp. It is said to be far superior to the camp at Brest, and certainly is deserving of the highest commendation. While here the regiment was drawn up in formation, and Lt. Col. Lemmon, Captain Whitthorne and Sergeant John Mace of H company received the Distinguished Service Cross. Their pleased expressions may be observed in the illustration.

The Colors had already been decorated and the ribbons clearly show the sectors in the illustration which is used as a frontispiece.

HOMEWARD BOUND

LOOKING FOR THE LAND

MARCHING TO THE NANSEMOND

The days passed uneventfully, with pleasant weather, and the men were given a final physical inspection. One of the examining physicians said that they had examined two hundred thousand men and that the 35th division were the finest, cleanest lot of men they had seen.

Here, as elsewhere, the good behavior and orderly discipline of the men was marked. The only happenings to mar these pleasant days was an explosion of a delouser which injured two of our men, and the sickness of Earl Charlesworth, who was left in the hospital with typhoid, of which he later died.

The rest, the sea air, the food and the amusements combined to put the men in good shape. It was a healthy, hearty, fine looking regiment which embarked on the Nansemond. The illustration shows some of the men on the way to the boat from camp—their last march.

On April 15th, we boarded the Nansemond. She had been a Hamburg-American freighter, the Pennsylvania, and was re-christened the Nansemond by Mrs. Woodrow Wilson when the United States took possesion. The men said that the same person who figured out that the French box cars had room for "40 hommes" had arranged the berthing space in the Nansemond. 70th Brigade Headquarters, all of the 140th Infantry and a part of the 139th together with a large company of sick casuals, were crowded aboard the ship. It was difficult to keep passage ways open, and the sentences "Move on there! You can't stand there" were constantly heard. But the men were happy, they were homeward bound, and they made the best of the situation.

The illustrations showed the crowded decks, and the men eagerly looking for the first sight of their own land—the land they had not seen for a year.

Bowman of the Y. M. C. A. and Secretary Johnson looked out for the comfort of the men. Charles L. Gulick, who had served as a Lieutenant of artillery in the 10th division, was the Red Cross representative and untiring in his efforts. Captain Isbell, Ship's Chaplain was constantly trying to serve the men. Chaplain Buswell had been taken out and sent to Toul a few days before we left. Chaplain Edwards spent the last of his funds in luxuries for the men.

Captain William Henry Allen of South Carolina and Lt. Commander Harrison E. Knauss of Pennsylvania, were in charge of the ship. They won the admiration of the 140th and were kind enough to praise the discipline and behavior of the men.

The Naval Officers observe a very strict discipline, they have a very heavy responsibility, and on the trip over kept rather to themselves in one corner of the big dining room, which was used in the evening by the officers as a gathering place.

One of the 140th officers had an alarm watch, which was the cause of considerable excitement on one evening. This watch gave a continuous alarm like an alarm clock, and while faint, the alarm was on the same note as the ship's bell whose continuous ringing was the alarm for fire.

This officer happened to show his watch to a passing Major, who questioned its utility. To prove its worth, the alarm was set off. Suddenly the ship was in great excitement. Captain Allen, Commander Knauss and the other ship's officers rushed out of the room, the bugles blew the fire call, and there was a rushing to and fro from the decks to the very lowest hold in the boat. No one thought of the watch, until half an hour later the breathless ship's officers returned stating that a false alarm of fire had been turned in and that a wooden box would be built around the ship's bell to prevent a recurrence. Only then was it realized that the French watch had been responsible.

While on the Nansemond every officer and man was asked to write out any information he could give, in view of the plan to write the history of the regiment. Not a score made any response, and the preparation of this book has been exceedingly difficult. The author has been compelled to rely largely on his personal experiences and observation, and many who deserved mention are omitted. The facts that are given can all be substantiated by more than one witness, and the lists are taken from the files of the regiment, reviewed with the greatest care. In the alphabetical list an attempt is made to give the disposition of every man who passed through the regiment, so far as the Personnel Section possessed the information. Due to the fact that a man was dropped after ten days in the hospital, and that the hospital usually made no returns to the regiment, some are listed as wounded who are really dead. The War Department has been unable to furnish a list of the dead, although the Adjutant General of Missouri has used every effort to obtain one. A careful reading of the history and examination of the lists will show that a great deal more time and labor has been given to this work than appears at the first glance.

The heroic deeds told of men and officers are given as typical. They were duplicated many times in the 140th.

The author is grateful to the many officers and men who have cheerfully rendered every assistance in their power. There are so many that it is impossible to mention them by name.

He regrets particularly that he was unable to obtain a photograph of Lieutenant Champion, whose brave and loyal service the regiment will never forget; and that he was unable to get a photograph of Major Mabrey, to whom the old Sixth owed so much, and whose splendid overseas record is a source of pride to the 140th. To Major Mabrey the formation of the Sixth was largely due. He gave unsparingly of time and money, and the 140th will always claim him although he came home with another regiment.

For the claim that this regiment was first in Exermont and last to leave there is overwhelming evidence, much of it in the form of signed documents, and no hesitation is felt in making the statement.

We landed at Newport News on Sunday, April the 28th, 1919. The Missouri and Kansas delegations met us in the harbor, and we docked to the music of cheers and the friendly whistles of the tugs. It was a happy crowd that marched out to the wooden barracks of Camp Stuart. The men could hardly realize that at last they were once more on American soil—home once more.

After a week of pleasant weather, we entrained for home—really home this time.

While on the Nansemond, Col. Linxwiler, who commanded the 70th brigade from February 20th to April 14th, when he took command of his regiment addressed the following letter to the men:

To The Enlisted Men, ("The Men Behind The Guns"), 140th Infantry:

As the time draws near for our separation from the service, I wish to express to the men of this organization my appreciation of the magnificent service rendered by them while in France. You can go to your homes realizing to the fullest extent that you have performed your duty well and faithfully, that you belonged to an organization of whose record you can be proud. Each of you assisted in making that record.

The most trying time of our service is approaching—that is the time between the date of embarkation and the date of muster out. We are returning to our home land and our friends. The days will seem long, but I wish to impress upon every man the fact that the quickest way out of the Service is to continue performing your duties in the same excellent manner that you have heretofore, helping in every way possible by your soldierly conduct to hasten the date of demobilization. I firmly believe that two weeks from the date we land will see us mustered out. Your service has been too honorable and the reputation of your organization too good to be marred by any act in the last few days of our service which might reflect discredit on you, your company, and your regiment, and for this reason I am writing this word of caution, believing as I do that the same spirit which has been manifest heretofore will carry you through to the date of demobilization and that no act of any man will be such as to bring discredit to himself, his comrades and the 140th Infantry.

If any man of the regiment has a legitimate reason and desires a discharge in the East, if he will make written application I assure you I will do all in my power to get it approved.

A. LINXWILER,
Colonel, 140th Infantry.

OFFICERS 140TH INFANTRY, CAMP STUART, VIRGINIA

Until the last minute when they were mustered out, the regiment was characterized by good behavior and soldierly discipline. They took advantage of none of the favors shown them, and remained a real regiment until disbanded. The regiment began well, it served well, and it ended well.

CAPE GIRARDEAU AND OLD K. C.

Our trains were delayed and we detrained in Cape Girardeau on the 9th, a day later than we were expected, finding mud and a light rain, but these could not dampen our spirits. We paraded in the town, and all Southern Missouri was there. Nothing like it had ever been seen before, and as the men swept through the crowded streets, flowers were strewn in the way. It was beautiful, but my heart went back to the men over whom the flowers would soon blossom in France. A royal welcome they gave us, these big-hearted whole-souled folks of Cape Girardeau, and the regiment will always remember them.

The next day, Saturday the 10th of May, we landed in Kansas City. Of the 1700 men who had been sent out in the old Third, there were but 600 with us when we returned. Their places had been filled by others.

As the first section pulled into the yards, the people were crowded in thousands around the tracks. The scene can not be described. Wives, sweethearts, friends, they were all there. They were so closely crowded that an accident seemed unavoidable, yet no one was injured. Although they had been waiting for hours, the huge crowd was happy and good natured. Some one recognized Colonel Linxwiler and started to cheer him. "Cheer the enlisted men," he shouted, "they are the best in the world!" And then I remembered when we entrained over a year ago at Mineola. All was hurry and confusion. An officer approached him and anxiously asked the location of the car for officers. "Blank the officers" said the Colonel. "What I want to know is that the men are taken care of!"

The men were bronzed, healthy and sturdy, and made a splendid appearance as they swung down the streets to the deafening cheers of the largest crowd Kansas City has ever seen. They tried to look like the veterans they were—soldiers grim and stern. But there was joy in their hearts, a lump in every throat. They were at last at—HOME!

The Ladies of the Auxiliary entertained them in Convention Hall, crowded to the roof. As each sturdy company marched across the floor a storm of cheers arose. It was a wonderful day, and the men thought it the best dinner they had ever eaten, but they did not really know what they were eating—they were home at last—HOME!

Jazz, the mascot of Doniphan days, had been brought in from the park and added his voice to the welcome. It all seemed a dream—the dust of Doniphan, the wide ocean, the little French villages, the long marches, the bloody field, the dead, surely it was all a dream. Here we were in Kansas City, home, HOME!

We reached Funston after midnight, and were compelled to leave the cars in which we had expected to spend the night. In two or three days the men had their pay, the $60 bonus, and were on their way home. By the 14th they were all mustered out. The 140th was but a memory.

The men of the 140th were scattered through every state in the Union. Volunteers, they were men who put these old United States first. Good soldiers once, they are good citizens now and, if the necessity comes, will again prove themselves good soldiers.

Many of them could not return to hear the acclaim of comrades and the praise of men. Heroes of the decoration of The Wooden Cross, they sleep in a distant land. The Nation honors them.

Some night when the rain is dashing against the windows, and we sit alone watching the fire—some night we shall see them all again—together we shall march over muddy, endless roads; together we shall wait and watch in the trenches; together we shall struggle forward against a storm of shot and shell over the bloody fields and valleys of the Argonne. The shadowy forms of our comrades will be with us—Davis and Scott and Kenady and Holden and Champion and Compton and Roberts and Stigall and Stein and Sam Adams and Tanner and Holt and Robertson and Dillon and Cooley and half a battalion more. Our hearts will thrill, and the tears will flood our eyes, and we shall whisper: "The old One Hundred and Fortieth. God bless them! There never was a finer Regiment!"

THE END

CHAPTER X

The Men Behind the Guns

Division, Brigade and Regimental Commanders

COMMANDING 35TH DIVISION

	From	To
Maj.-Gen. William M. Wright	Oct. 1, 1917	June 16, 1918
Brig.-Gen. Nathaniel F. McClure	June 16, 1918	July 20, 1918
Maj.-Gen. Peter E. Traub	July 20, 1918	Dec. 27, 1918
Brig.-Gen. Thomas Dugan	Dec. 29, 1918	March 1, 1919
Maj.-Gen. William M. Wright	March 1, 1919	May, 1919

70TH INFANTRY BRIGADE

	From	To
Brig.-Gen. Charles I Martin	Oct. 1, 1917	Sept. 21, 1918
Col. Kirby Walker	Sept. 21, 1918	Oct. 13, 1918
Brig.-Gen. Thomas B. Dugan	Oct. 13, 1918	Dec. 27, 1918
Col. Alonzo Gray	Dec. 27, 1918	Feb. 14, 1919
Col. Carl L. Ristine	Feb. 14, 1919	Feb. 20, 1919
Col. Albert Linxwiler	Feb. 20, 1919	April 14, 1919

Lt. Col. Paul Tucker was in command the first part of December, 1918.

Lt. Col. Roosevelt was assigned to the 140th, but never reached the regiment, being reassigned to his former regiment.

140TH INFANTRY

	From	To
Col. Albert Linxwiler	Oct. 1,1917	June 18, 1918
Col. Pierce A. Murphy	June 18, 1918	Sept. 16, 1918
Maj. Fred L. Lemmon	Sept. 16, 1918	Sept. 22, 1918
Lieut-Col. E. Delaplane	Sept. 22, 1918	Oct. 16, 1918
Col. Alonzo Gray	Oct. 16, 1918	Jan. 3, 1919
Lt.-Col. Sidney D. Maize	Jan. 3, 1919	Feb. 18,1919
Lt.-Col. Smith A. Harris	Feb. 18, 1919	Mar. 29, 1919
Lt.-Col. Fred L. Lemmon	March 29, 1919	April 14, 1919
Col. Albert Linxwiler	April 14, 1919	May 14, 1919

Col. William Newman was in command during a part of the training period at Camp Doniphan.

Roster of Officers, 140th Infantry

Colonel Albert Linxwiler
Lieutenant Colonel Fred L. Lemmon
Major William A. Smith
Major Ralph E. Truman
Major Frank G. Ward
Captain Robert K. Brady
Captain Frederick R. Cogswell
Captain Garry W. Gaines
Captain Frank H. Grigg
Captain Roy L. Hail
Captain Shamus O. McFadden
Captain Jacob L. Milligan
Captain Julian S. Oliff
Captain John H. Pleasants
Captain Merwin L. Pridle
Captain Guy C. Rexroad
Captain Joseph N. Salisbury
Captain Ray E. Seitz
Captain George H. Simpson
Captain Richard H. Stogsdill
Captain H. E. Sugden
Captain Harry S. Whitthorne
Captain Frank H. Terrell
Captain Thomas J. Wilson
Captain Eugene A. Wood
1st Lieut. Frederick M. Barnes
1st Lieut. Frank J. Barry
1st Lieut. Kendall T. Bates
1st Lieut. Fred W. Buell
1st Lieut. George W. Bruns
1st Lieut. Fitzhugh L. Conway
1st Lieut. David W. Craft
1st Lieut. E. M. Currie
1st Lieut. M. L. Dunn
1st Lieut. Lawrence Felker
1st Lieut. William L. W. Forsyth
1st Lieut. Miller C. Foster
1st Lieut. Frederick Gordon
1st Lieut. Charles W. Goyer
1st Lieut. Leon O. Graham
1st Lieut. Norris B. Gregg
1st Lieut. Myron Hill
1st Lieut. Richard R. Howard
1st Lieut. Ralph B. Huber
1st Lieut. Orie S. Imes
1st Lieut. Harold G. Ingraham
1st Lieut. Thomas E. Jahn
1st Lieut. William D. James
1st Lieut. Edwin H. Johnson
1st Lieut. Frank Kiser
1st Lieut. James H. Lanham
1st Lieut. Orion A. Mather
1st Lieut. Earl J. Means
1st Lieut. Louis J. Menges
1st Lieut. Robert Montgomery
1st Lieut. Virgil L. Myers
1st Lieut. Marion C. Ried
1st Lieut. John M. Robertson
1st Lieut. Noble B. Schumpert
1st Lieut. Leo Silverstein
1st Lieut. Eustace Smith
1st Lieut. Irvin B. Spangler
1st Lieut. Reid Stephens
1st Lieut. Julian T. Stinson
1st Lieut. Clyde R. Sullivan
1st Lieut. Noel P. Whitehead
2d Lieut. Raynor K. Anderson
2d Lieut. Roy D. Baker
2d Lieut. Merl J. Barnert
2d Lieut. James T. Carney
2d Lieut. Paul M. Clayworth
2d Lieut. Louis M. Dyou
2d Lieut. Orran F. Fadley
2d Lieut. Homer H. Hampton
2d Lieut. George P Harris
2d Lieut. Herman F. Huber
2d Lieut. Harold Y. Hughes
2d Lieut. Percy B. King
2d Lieut. Harry W. Lockridge
2d Lieut. Russell C. McBride
2d Lieut. Aura McCauley
2d Lieut. Lee C. McGee
2d Lieut. Roy K. McMillan
2d Lieut. Harold D. Miller
2d Lieut. Judson Mote
2d Lieut. Thomas J. Mountain
2d Lieut. John S. Muir
2d Lieut. Raymond L. Reils
2d Lieut. Earl L. Munger
2d Lieut. Basil R. Otey
2d Lieut. John H. Pike
2d Lieut. Carl L. Reed
2d Lieut. Robert F. Renard
2d Lieut. Julius J. Richter
2d Lieut. Arthur R. Ruplin
2d Lieut. George W. Smith

(Attached)
2d Lieut. Jefferson Sappington

ROSTER OF OFFICERS, 140TH INFANTRY—Continued

(Sanitary)

Major Glen H. Broyles
Captain Ralph G. Nelson
Captain Edward J. Howland

Capt. Henry L. Rothman
1st Lieut. Grover C. Rice
Capt. William C. Schlegelmilch

(Chaplains)

1st Lieut. Evan A. Edwards
1st Lieut. J. Oliver Buswell

1st Lieut. Daniel J. Manning

(Not now with 140th)

Colonel Alonzo Gray
Colonel Pierce A. Murphy
Lieut. Colonel G. E. Delaplane
Lieut. Colonel Bennett C. Clark
Lieut. Colonel S. H. Harris
Lieut. Colonel Sidney D. Maize
Major John W. Armour
Major Ralph W. Campbell
Major Samuel O. Clarke
Major Murray Davis
Major Nicholas F. Feury—M. C.
Major Warren L. Mabrey
Major Julius A. Redman
Major Ernest W. Slusher—M. C.
Major Randall Wilson
Captain Grant Davidson
Captain Cecil M. Farris
Captain John F. Howell
Captain James C. Kenady
Captain Henry E. Lewis
Captain Walter M. Mann
Captain Alexander S. Oliver
Captain Warren L. Osgood
Captain Wilas W. Pearson
Lieut. Colonel Edward C. Sammons
Captain Claude N. Skelton
Captain John R. Smiley
Captain William R. Stryker
Major Fred O. Wickham
1st Lieut. Samuel P. Adams
1st Lieut. William A. Alexander
1st Lieut. Rhodes F. Arnold
1st Lieut. Samuel D. Avery
1st Lieut. Arch M. Baird
1st Lieut. William J. Baxter
1st Lieut. Jule A. Bean
1st Lieut. Carl J. Bechtel
1st Lieut. J. E. Beardsley
1st Lieut. Samuel H. Biddlestone
1st Lieut. James B. Biggs
1st Lieut. Henry B. Black
1st Lieut. Harry W. Boardman
1st Lieut. Archie Breckenridge
1st Lieut. C. F. Burwash
1st Lieut. James V. Coffey

1st Lieut. Stephen W. Cook, Jr.
1st Lieut. Walter L. Cronkite
1st Lieut. John J. Dempsey
1st Lieut. Jerry F. Duggan
1st Lieut. Frank F. Farrar
1st Lieut. Joe O. Ferguson
1st Lieut. Robert E. Forrester
1st Lieut. Howard N. Frissell
1st Lieut. Edward S. Garner
1st Lieut. Albert S. Gardner
1st Lieut. Charles A. Grimes
1st Lieut. William C. Gordon
Captain John P. Griebel
1st Lieut. Jacob W. Grondyke
1st Lieut. Elmer C. Hanson
1st Lieut. Loyd R. Han
1st Lieut. Merwyn H. Hanson
1st Lieut. Clarence Harmon
1st Lieut. Pollard E. Harrison
1st Lieut. Samuel W. Henderson
1st Lieut. Clinton V. Hill
Captain Rolla B. Holt
1st Lieut. James E. Huffman
1st Lieut. Sylvester C. Judge
1st. Lieut. Fred Kase
1st Lieut. Hiram P. Lawrence
Captain Harvey N. Lewis
1st Lieut. Henry K. McGann
1st Lieut. Leicester P. Moise
1st Lieut. Malcom Newlan
1st Lieut. William K. Nottingham
1st Lieut. L. P. O'Connor
1st Lieut. Clyde J. Rasnic
1st Lieut. Willis C. Reed
1st Lieut. David W. Robertson
1st Lieut. Henry S. Rogers
1st Lieut. Arthur J. Ross
1st Lieut. William E. Scott
1st Lieut. John J. Sheehan
1st Lieut. Morgan V. Spicer
1st Lieut. Roy E. Stafford
1st Lieut. Whitney Starr
1st Lieut. John V. Stark
1st Lieut. William M. Stonestreet
1st Lieut. Louis M. Tharp
1st Lieut. Robert E. Utterback

THE MEN BEHIND THE GUNS 151

ROSTER OF OFFICERS, 140TH INFANTRY—Continued

Captain Ralph L. Ware
1st Lieut. Russel H. Ware
1st Lieut. Emmett E. Welch
1st Lieut. Fred C. Wilhelm
1st Lieut. Lloyd V. Wise
2d Lieut. Alfred D. Allen
2d Lieut. Edgar C. Bennett
2d Lieut. Fred A. Berghoff
2d Lieut. John P. Carritte
2d Lieut. Lloyd B. Champion
2d Lieut. Letcher C. Compton
2d Lieut. Frank M. Cox
2d Lieut. Jesse H. Denham
2d Lieut. Fred H. DeWitt
2d Lieut. Daniel M. Dwyer
2d Lieut. Fleming B. Fowler
2d Lieut. Ray E. Haberstroh
2d Lieut. Joseph M. Hayse
2d Lieut. Edgar B. Heylum

2d Lieut. George D. Holden
2d Lieut. Harvey Jackson
2d Lieut. Norman H. Imbush
2d Lieut. Edward W. Keefner
2d Lieut. Richard E. Kiddoo
2d Lient. Francis H. Little
2d Lieut. Roy M. Miller
2d Lieut. Clarence A. Nelis
2d Lieut. Ray G. Penrose
2d Lieut. Richard M. Phillips
2d Lieut. Irving M. Rediker
2d Lieut. Thomas R. Richards
2d Lieut. Donald A. Rogers
2d Lieut. Milton S. Rosenfield
2d Lieut. Clarence G. Smith
2d Lieut. Frank G. Steiner
2d Lieut. Roy E. Thomas
2d Lieut. Frank F. Tracy
2d Lieut. William W. Ward

Roster of 140th Infantry
(Alphabetically)
April 1, 1919

Abbott, Albert W.	Corp.	Co. G	
Abbott, Ollie E.	Pvt.	Co. F.	
Ables, Coleman H.	Pvt.	Co. G.	
Acree, Jim	Corp.	Co. C.	
Adair, Claud	Pvt.	Co. A.	
Adair, Robin	Pvt.	Co. D.	
Adamovich, Joseph S.	Bugler	Co. K.	
Adams, Andrew Jackson	Pvt.	Co. I.	
Adams, Charley R.	Pvt.	Hdqrs. Co.	
Adams, Frank V.	Pvt.	Co. A.	
Adams, George E.	Pvt.	Co. K.	
Adams, Hoyt	Pvt.	Co. F.	Wounded
Adams, John B.	Pvt.	Co. C.	
Adams, Vaughn K.	Pvt.	Co. E.	
Adkins, Mellville H.	Corp.	Hdqrs. Co.	
Adkisson, Bob	Pvt.	Co. K.	Wounded
Ahrens, Daniel	Sgt.	C. L.	
Ahrens, Walter Q.	Pvt.	M. G. Co.	
Akers, John D.	Mess Sgt.	M. G. Co.	
Alamdinger, Winfred F.	Pvt.	Co. E.	
Alberts, Samuel A.	Pvt.	Co. B.	
Albrecht, Arnold A.	Corp.	Co. D.	Gassed
Albright, Oscar R.	Mech.	Hdqrs. Co.	
Alcorn, George	Pvt.	M. G. Co.	
Alden, Rodney	Pvt.	Co. I	
Aldrich, Charles	Corp.	Co. B.	
Alexander, Robert J.	Pvt.	Co. A.	Wounded
Aleander, Albert G.	Pvt.	Co. B.	
Allee, Moses H.	Sup. Sgt.	Co. L.	

Allen, Garfield	Pvt.	Co. G.	
Allen, Howard E.	Corp.	Co. D.	Wounded
Allen, Lewdorth	Corp.	Co. H.	
Allen, Roscoe	Pvt.	Co. C.	
Allen, William	Pvt.	Co. G.	
Allman, Ora B.	Pvt.	Co. L.	
Allsman, Jerry	Pvt.	Co. M.	
Allstatt, Marion E.	Pvt.	Co. L.	Wounded
Alsup, Everett	Pvt.	Co. G. 140th Inf	Wounded
Althen, Charles W.	Corp.	Hq. Co.	
Ambrose, Joseph E.	Corp.	Co. I	
Amen, Nicholas C.	Pvt.	Co. D.	
Ames, Delle	Pvt.	Co. I.	Wounded
Amon, Nicholas C.	Pvt.	Co. D.	
Amos, James R.	Pvt.	Co. A.	
Amos, Virgil J.	Pvt.	Co. C.	
Anderson, Alfred C.	Pvt.	Co. D.	
Anderson, Chamblin	Sgt.	Co. F.	
Anderson, Charlie	Pvt.	Co. G.	Wounded
Anderson, Edger	Pvt.	Co. E.	
Anderson, Edward C.	Pvt.	M. G. Co.	
Anderson, Glenn	Corp.	Co. A.	
Anderson, Harold E.	Pvt.	M. G. Co.	
Anderson, Harry	Pvt.	Co. K.	
Anderson, Henry O.	Pvt.	Co. K.	
Anderson, James K.	Pvt.	Co. E.	
Anderson, John	Pvt.	Co. G.	
Anderson, Luther C.	Pvt.	Co. D.	
Anderson, Oscar W.	Pvt.	Co. E.	
Anderson, Pearl	Pvt.	Co. D.	
Anderson, Thomas A.	Cook	Co. F.	Gassed
Andis, Harry	Pvt.	Co. D.	
Andrews, Hadley J.	Pvt.	M. G. Co.	
Anes, William R.	Sgt.	Co. I.	Gassed
Angelo, Liverani	Cook	Co. M.	
Anglin, Ernest L.	Pvt.	Co. F.	
Annly, Robert	Pvt.	Co. B.	
Annon, Frank J.	Corp.	Co. K.	Gassed
Applegate, Wesley	Pvt.	Co. C.	
Appleton, George V.	Pvt.	Co. C.	
Arbuckle, Robert R.	Pvt.	Co. D.	
Archie, Donald F.	Pvt.	Co. F.	Gassed
Ardetto, Michele	Pvt.	Co. A.	
Arendell, Cecil B.	Pvt.	M. G. Co.	
Armer, Lewis	Pvt.	Co. F.	
Armour, Bud	Pvt.	Co. F.	
Armstrong, George R.	Pvt.	Co. G.	Wounded
Arnett, Harold J.	Pvt.	Co. K.	
Arnett, Wilson H.	Pvt.	Co. C.	
Arnold, Benjamin F.	Pvt.	Co. F.	
Arnold, Emole	Pvt.	Co. H.	
Arnold, George, Jr.	Pvt.	Co. E.	
Arnold, Harry P.	Pvt.	Co. A.	
Arnold, Terrell J.	Corp.	Co. E.	
Arnold, William L.	Mess. Sgt.	Co. M.	Wounded
Ashbaugh, Arthur A.	Corp.	Co. K.	Wounded
Ashcraft, Robert L.	Pvt.	Co. E.	
Ashley, Arlie	Pvt.	Co. B.	
Ashley, Leamon A.	Pvt.	Co. G.	
Ashmore, Artie L.	Corp.	Hg. Co.	
Ashton, Joseph R.	Pvt.	San. 140th. Inf	

THE MEN BEHIND THE GUNS 153

Atherton, Earl	Pvt.	Co. D.	
Atkins, Mellville H.	Corp.	Hdqrs Co.	
Atteberry, Cecil H.	Pvt.	Co. A.	Gassed
Auberger, George L.	Pvt.	Co. E.	
Aubley, Clifford F.	Pvt.	Co. D.	Wounded
Avery, Dean	Pvt.	Co. F.	
Awbrey, Arthur S.	Pvt.	Co. L.	
Azbill, Colman	Pvt.	Co. A.	
Babbitt, Charles H.	Pvt.	Co. H.	Wounded
Bachert, Francis X.	Pvt.	San. Det.	
Bachman, Lawrence J.	Pvt.	Co. G.	
Bacon, Amiel	Pvt.	San. Det.	
Bacon, Willie	Pvt.	Co. K.	
Bagby, Stephen Y.	Pvt.	Co. B.	Wounded
Bahgegian, Eddie	Cook	M. G. Co.	
Bailes, Cleveland A.	Pvt.	Co. G.	
Baley, Hobart	Pvt.	Hdqrs. Co.	
Bailey, Jefferson M.	Pvt.	Co. F.	
Bailey, Porter	Pvt.	Co. F.	
Bailey, Ralph D.	Corp.	Co. H.	
Bailey, Wallace L.	Pvt.	Co. B.	
Bailey, Walter H.	Pvt.	Hg. Co.	
Bair, Charles A.	Cook	Hdqrs. Co.	
Baker, Albert L.	Pvt.	Co. A.	
Baker, Clayton	Pvt.	Co. G.	Wounded
Baker, Eula U.	Pvt.	Co. H. 140th	
Baker, George G.	Pvt.	Co. M.	
Baker, Hugh E.	Pvt.	Co. A.	Wounded
Baker, Louis C.	Pvt.	Co. A.	
Baker, Sherman	Pvt.	Hdqrs. Co.	
Bakker, Lieuwe R.	Pvt.	Co. L.	
Ball, Harry N.	Pvt.	Co. H.	
Ball, Ira A.	Corp.	Co. I.	Wounded
Ball, Joseph	Pvt.	Co. M. 140th	
Ball, Otis	Pvt.	Co. L.	
Ballard, Calvin W.	Pvt.	Co. A.	
Ballard, LeRoy G.	Musician	Hdqrs. Co.	
Ballew, Marion C.	Pvt.	Co. E.	
Ballew, Walter R.	Corp.	Co. A.	
Bandy, Robert J.	Pvt.	Co. E. 140th	
Banister, Earl E.	Pvt.	Co. B.	
Barbarisi, Vincenzo	Pvt.	Co. E.	
Barber, Austin B.	Pvt.	Co. C.	
Barker, Jesse W.	Pvt.	M. G. Co.	
Barmann, Walter G.	Pvt.	Co. G. 140th Inf.	
Barnard, Raymond H.	Pvt.	M. G. Co.	
Barner, George William	Pvt.	Co. M 140th Inf.	
Barnes, Albert L.	Pvt.	Co. G.	
Barnes, Homer J.	Mechanic	C. K.	
Barnes, Isaac G.	Pvt.	Co. K.	
Barnes, Luther	Pvt.	Co. C.	
Barnes, Milburn	Pvt.	Co. G. 140th Inf.	Gassed
Barnes, Romie M.	Pvt.	M. G. Co.	Wounded
Barnett, George H.	Pvt.	Hg. Co.	
Barnett, Joseph	Mechanic	Co A.	Gassed and Wounded
Barnett, Lee D.	Pvt.	M. G. Co.	
Barnett, Robert L.	Corp.	Co. D.	
Barnett, Zack	Pvt.	Co. K.	
Barnhart, Merle	Pvt.	Co. M.	
Barnhill, Sidney A.	Pvt.	Co. K.	

Barrett, John T.	Pvt.	Co. E.	
Barringhaus, Frank	Pvt.	Co. I.	
Barron, Frederick C.	Pvt.	Co. D.	
Barry, Ivan	Pvt.	Co. A.	
Barry, Richard J.	Pvt.	Co. A.	
Bartel, Herman J.	Pvt.	Co. C.	
Bartlett, Adison A.	Pvt.	Co. E.	
Barton, Harvey L.	Pvt.	Co. M. 140th Inf.	
Basham, Elmer	Pvt.	Co. E.	
Bashara, Salem	Pvt.	Co. H.	
Bass, Acie	Pvt.	Co. D.	
Bates, Claude M.	Pvt.	Co. H.	
Bates, Don Arthur	Pvt.	San Det.	
Battles, Robert D.	Pvt.	Co. K.	Wounded
Bauer, Edwin	Pvt.	Co. M.	
Baughman, Albert	Pvt.	Co. A.	
Baum, George D.	Pvt.	Co. L.	
Baxter, William I.	Pvt.	Co. K.	
Bdysel, Al M.	Pvt.	Co. C.	
Beal, Arthur G.	Pvt.	Co. D.	
Bear Horse, John	Pvt.	Co. A.	
Bear, James A.	Pvt.	Co. A.	
Beard, Edgar A.	Pvt.	Co. F.	
Beard, Ernest L.	Pvt.	Co. B.	
Beard, Grover T.	Sgt.	So M.	Wounded
Beaumont, Howard B.	Sgt.	M. G. Co.	
Beaver, Oscar R.	Pvt.	Supply Co.	
Beavers, John M.	Pvt.	Co. C.	
Beavers, Roscoe	Pvt.	Co. B.	
Beck, Clyde O.	Horseshoer	Supply Co.	
Beck, James W.	Pvt.	Hdqrs. Co.	Wounded
Becker, Harry A.	Pvt.	Co. L.	
Becker, John S.	Pvt.	Co. E.	
Beckhusen, Gergard H.	Pvt.	Co. G.	
Beckman, Ralph P.	Corp.	Co. F.	
Beckman, Robert L.	Sgt.	Hdqrs. C.	
Becks, Ray L.	Pvt.	Co. H.	
Beecham, Clarence E.	Pvt.	Co. H.	
Bednarowicz, John F.	Pvt.	Co B	
Beery, Wilkerson C.	Pvt.	San. Det.	Wounded
Beil, Arthur	Pvt.	Co. C.	
Bell, Earl T.	Corp.	Co. C.	Wounded
Bell, George	Pvt.	Co. G.	
Bell, Guy E.	Pvt.	Co. F.	
Bell, John W.	Pvt.	Co. F.	Gassed
Belogh, Charley	Pvt.	Co. E.	
Belshe, Lawrence L.	Pvt.	Co. F.	
Belt, Alfred T.	Sgt.	Co. F.	
Benham, George S.	Sgt.	Co. G.	
Bennett, Clyde E.	Corp.	Co. A.	
Bennett, Horace L.	Pvt.	Co. I.	
Bennett, Joseph	Sgt.	Co. E.	
Bennett, Oda T.	Pvt.	Co. E.	
Benshoff, Winfred H.	Pvt.	San. Det.	
Benton, Joe	Corp.	Co. F.	
Berchette, William F.	Pvt.	San. Det.	
Berchette, Thomas N.	Pvt.	Co. I.	
Berding, Oliver S.	Pvt.	Co. L.	
Bergquist, Walter W.	Corp.	Co. L. 140th Inf.	Wounded
Bernhard, Fred C.	Sgt.	Co. I.	
Bernu, Alexander		Co. C.	

THE MEN BEHIND THE GUNS

Berry, Orion	Sgt.	Co. H.	Gassed
Berry, Wayne R.	Pvt.	Co. B.	Wounded
Bertholf, Mann V.	Pvt.	Co. G. 140th Inf.	
Best, Howard	Pvt.	Co. K.	
Best, John L.	Pvt.	Hdqrs. Co.	
Best, William	Pvt.	Co. I	Gassed
Bestenlehner, John J.	Pvt.	Co. D.	
Beto, Frank A.	Pvt.	Co. A.	
Bevans, George R.	Pvt.	Co. E.	
Bevard, George W.	Pvt.	Co. E.	
Biere, Theodore Fred	Pvt.	Hdqrs. Co.	
Bietz, Edward	Pvt.	Co. M.	
Bigos, Stanley A.	Pvt.	Co. B.	
Billington, Elmer H.	Pvt.	Co. F.	Gassed
Billington, Fred W.	Corp.	Hdqrs. Co.	
Biltz, Rolla	Pvt.	Co. B.	Gassed
Bingham, Frederick H.	Pvt.	Co. F.	
Binning, Charles L.	Pvt.	M. G. Co.	Wounded
Binns, Archie Z.	Wagoner	Supply Co.	
Binns, Eddie	Wagoner	Supply Co.	
Bione, John	Pvt.	Co. I.	
Bird, Claude Joe	Pvt.	Co. L.	
Bird, Hugh A.	Pvt.	Co. E.	
Bird, John B.	Sgt.	Hdqrs. Co.	
Bishop, Earn	Student Cook	M. G. Co.	
Bishop, Odie S.	Pvt.	Hdqrs. Co.	
Bittner, Emeran A.	Pvt.	Co. C.	
Bjertness, Ole	Pvt.	Co. D.	Wounded
Black, Elsworth H.	Wagoner	Supply Co.	
Black, Ermur	Pvt.	Co. I.	Gassed
Black, Herbert	Pvt.	Co. F.	
Black, Harley R.	Cook	Co. K.	
Blackburn, Marshall P.	Corp.	Co. A.	
Blackmore, Harry L.	Pvt.	Co. A.	
Blackwood, George W.	Pvt.	Co. G. 140th Inf.	
Blaich, Fred W.	Pvt.	Co. L. 140th Inf.	
Blair, Malcolm	Pvt.	Co. G.	
Blake, Charles R.	Pvt.	Hdqrs. Co.	
Blakey, Forest	Pvt.	Co. K.	
Blankenship, Cowen	Pvt.	Co. H. 140th	
Blankenship, Jess	Pvt.	Co. A.	
Blanton, Henry H.	Pvt.	M. G. Co.	
Blaylock, Orvil	Pvt.	Co. B.	
Blazier, Clarence	Pvt.	Co. M.	Wounded
Blecha, Albert	Pvt.	Co. C.	
Blevins, William Claude	Pvt.	Co. A.	
Blinco, Howard W.	Pvt.	Co. L.	
Blouch, Charles D.	Pvt.	San. Det.	
Bly, Joe D.	Pvt.	M. G. Co.	
Blythe, Aubrey A.	Pvt.	Co. A.	
Board, Curtis J.	Pvt.	Hdqrs. Co.	
Boatman, Clarence D.	Sgt.	Co. G.	
Boatwright, Walter Franklin	Corp.	Co. A.	Gassed
Boatwright, William H.	Pvt.	Co. H.	
Bobo, Sidy W.	Pvt.	Co. H.	Wounded
Bockhahn, Alfred	Pvt.	Co. M.	
Bodine, Martin	Pvt.	Co. L.	
Bodkin, Arthur J.	Pvt.	Co. C.	
Boeazier, Earl B.	Pvt.	Co. E.	
Bogen, Albert L.	Pvt.	Co. A.	Wounded
Boggs, Javan	Pvt.	Co. B.	
Boggs, Walter M.	Pvt.	Co. B.	
Bogh, Edward J.	Pvt.	Co. G. 140th Inf.	

Bogue, Charles A.	Pvt.	Co. D.	
Bogue, Henry L.	Pvt.	Co. H.	
Bohn, William H.	Pvt.	San. Det.	
Boll, Joseph	Pvt.	Co. M.	
Bollinger, George H.	Pvt.	Co. G.	
Bolly, Fred	Pvt.	Co. M.	
Bolstad, Clarence G.	Pvt.	Co. M.	
Bolte, August G. M.	Pvt.	Hdqrs. Co.	
Boltz, Thomas	Pvt.	Co. B.	
Bomeke, Frank C.	Pvt.	Co. D.	
Bonasera, Emilo	Pvt.	Co. I.	
Bone, Daniel O.	Pvt.	Co. E.	
Boner, Edward	Pvt.	Co. I.	
Bonham, Joseph L.	Cook	Co. H.	Gassed
Boock, Alfred E.	Pvt.	Co. M.	
Booher, Benjamine F.	Pvt.	Hdqrs. Co.	
Booker, William H.	Pvt.	Co. F.	
Borca, John	Pvt.	Co. I.	
Bortz, Benjamin	Pvt.	Co. C.	
Bosse, John F.	Pvt.	Co. E.	
Bostordo, Tom	Pvt.	Co. H.	
Boswell, James R.	Pvt.	Co. A.	
Boteman, Clarence D.	Corp.	Co. G.	
Boulware, Sidney F.	Mess Sgt.	Co. D.	Wounded
Bourbina, Alfred	Pvt.	Co. A.	
Bowden, Charlie	Pvt.	Co. H.	
Bowden, James	Pvt.	Co. B.	Killed
Bowen, Alvin	Pvt.	Co. B.	Wounded
Bowen, Charles D.	Pvt.	Co. B.	Wounded
Bowers, Joseph M.	Sgt.	Co. H.	Wounded
Bowman, James	Pvt.	Co. A.	
Bowman, Roscoe F.	Corp.	Co. G.	
Bowman, Thomas F.	Pvt.	Co. E.	
Bowman, William L.	Pvt.	Co. A.	
Bowne, Charles G.	Musician	Hdqrs. Co.	
Bowr, Ralph M.	Pvt.	Hdqrs. Co.	
Boxx, Walter W.	Pvt.	Co. E.	Wounded
Boyce, Herbert	Pvt.	Co. K.	Gassed
Boyd, Ezra	Pvt.	Co. F.	Gassed
Boyd, Floyd	Pvt.	Co. D.	
Boyd, Harry W.	Pvt.	Co. H.	
Boyd, Isaac	Pvt.	Co. F.	
Boykin, Walter J.	Pvt.	Co. H.	
Boys, Ralph R.	Pvt.	Co. K.	Wounded
Brace, Leonard L.	Pvt.	Co. D.	
Bradley, George S.	Pvt.	Hdqrs. Co.	
Bradley, Glenn V.	Pvt.	Co. C.	
Bradley, Joseph W.	Pvt.	Co. H.	
Bradshaw, Fred L.	Pvt.	Co. D.	
Bradshaw, Walter	Corp.	Co. F.	
Brady, Elvis W.	Pvt.	Co. G.	
Brady, Harrison W.	Corp.	Co. G. 140th Inf.	
Brady, Stanley	Pvt.	Co. A.	
Brandenburg, Fritz J.	Pvt.	Co. A.	
Brandt, Fredrick	Pvt.	Co. K.	
Brandt, Martin O.	Pvt.	Co. L.	
Brandt, Paul W.	Pvt.	Co. M.	
Brannan, Norbert E.	Pvt.	Co. A.	
Brannon, William R.	Pvt.	Co. K.	
Brant, Frank	Pvt.	Co. L.	
Brant, Gilp	Regtl.Sgt.Maj.	Co. C.	
Brantler, Claude L.	Sgt.	Co. F.	
Brantley, Felix	Pvt.	Hdqrs. Co.	
Brasfield, Caleb R.	Pvt.	Co. H.	

THE MEN BEHIND THE GUNS 157

Bratcher, Bernie	Pvt.	Co. F.	
Bratcher, Lee Roy	Corp.	Co. H.	Wounded
Brattensborg, Albert	Pvt.	Co. C.	
Brawner, Clark E.	Sgt.	Co. F.	
Breakey, John E.	Pvt.	Co. A.	Gassed
Breckenridge, Dewey J.	Sgt.	Co. F.	
Brenden, Oliver	Bugler	Co. A.	
Brents, Henry D.	Corp.	Co. K.	Wounded
Brennan, Robert E.	Pvt.	Co. A.	
Bresnahan, James J.	Pvt.	Co. E.	Wounded
Brenning, Winfield H.	Mechanic	M. G. Co.	
Brevig, Martin L.	Musician	Co. F.	
Brewer, Crawford W.	Pvt.	Co. H.	
Brewster, Willie E.	Sgt.	Hdqrs. Co.	Wounded
Bridge, Louis L.	Corp.	Co. F.	
Bridges, Dorsie O.	Pvt.	Co. H.	
Bridges, Edwin	Pvt.	Co. B.	Wounded
Briggs, Franklin O.	Cook	Supply Co.	
Brigham, Robert	Corp.	Co. C.	
Bright, Joseph J.	Pvt.	Co. F.	
Brink, Frank M.	Pvt.	Co. B.	
Briody, George W.	Sgt.	Supply Co.	
Briscoe, Delo M.	Corp.	Co. F.	Wounded
Britt, Ruffin P.	Pvt.	Co. E.	
Britton, Harry	Pvt.	Co. B.	
Brizzi, Ovidio	Pvt.	Co. E.	
Brock, William D.	Pvt.	Co. G.	
Brocker, George H.	Pvt.	Co. C.	Wounded
Brockman, Guthrie	Corp.	Co. G.	
Brodrick, Waldo O.	Pvt.	Hdqrs. Co.	
Brogdon, Nathan T.	Mechanic	Supply Co.	
Broker, William F.	Pvt.	Hdqrs. Co.	
Brook, Irving B.	Pvt.	M. G. Co.	
Brookbank, Charles E.	Pvt.	Co. B.	
Brookins, Lonnie C.	Pvt.	Co. F.	
Brooks, Charles E.	Corp.	Co. D.	
Brooks, Chester C.	Corp.	Co. D.	
Brousseau, Royal A.	Pvt.	Co. L.	
Brower, Fred	Pvt.	Co. I.	
Brown, Albert A.	Pvt.	Co. H.	
Brown, Alfee T.	Pvt.	Co. F.	
Brown, Bert	Pvt.	Co. B.	
Brown, Charles E.	Pvt.	Co. I.	
Brown, Charlie W.	Pvt.	Co. H.	
Brown, Clarence W.	Pvt.	Co. I.	
Brown, Clyde M.	Corp.	Co. I.	Gassed
Brown, Earl T.	Wagoner	Supply Co.	
Brown, Edward C.	Cook	Co. G.	Gassed
Brown, Floyd O.	Corp.	Co. H.	Wounded
Brown, Fred S.	Pvt.	Co. C.	
Brown, Gene M.	Pvt.	Co. B.	
Brown, George F.	Pvt.	Co. A.	
Brown, Gerald B.	Corp.	Co. G.	Wounded
Brown, James C.	Pvt.	Co. I.	Wounded
Brown, John L.	Pvt.	Co. L.	
Brown, Orville A.	Pvt.	Hdqrs. Co.	
Brown, Paul	Pvt.	Co. F.	
Brown, Ray N.	Pvt.	Co. K.	
Brown, Raymond	Pvt.	Co. M.	
Brown, Robert A.	Corp.	Co. I.	
Brown, Waverly N.	Pvt.	Co. K.	
Brown, William E.	Pvt.	Co. I. 140th	
Brown, William E.	Sgt.	Co. G.	
Browning, Claud	Pvt.	Co. K.	

Browning, John W. T.	Pvt.	Co. H.	
Browning, Merle R.	Pvt.	Co. F.	
Browning, Rollie C.	Corp.	Co. I.	
Bruce, Charles F.	Pvt.	Co. G.	
Brumbaugh, John W.	Corp.	Co. E.	
Brumbaugh, Michael	Pvt.	Co. B.	
Brumitt, Carl	Sgt.	Co. I.	Gassed
Brummett, Elvis	Corp.	M. G. Co.	
Brunner, Charles L.	Pvt.	Co. C.	
Bryan, Charles V	Pvt.	San. Det.	
Bryan, Herbert L.	Pvt.	Co. A.	Wounded
Bryan, Harry M.	Bugler	Co. M.	
Bryant, Bunyan	Pvt.	Co. H.	
Bryant, Clyde C.	Pvt.	Co. A.	
Bryant, Ray	Pvt.	Co. K.	Killed
Bryant, Richard S.	Pvt.	Co. M.	
Bryant, Ellis E.	Pvt.	Co. D.	Wounded
Bryant, James O.	Pvt.	Co. I.	
Bryce, James	Corp.	Co. G.	
Buhlic, Steve	Pvt.	Co. E.	
Buch, William A.	Pvt.	Co. B.	
Buchan, William	Pvt.	Co. K.	
Buchanan, Everett G.	Pvt.	Hdqrs. Co.	
Buckingham, Allie	Pvt.	Co. D.	Wounded
Bucklin, Julian Allen	Pvt.	Co. L.	
Buckner, Ivory C.	Pvt.	Co. C.	
Buell, Ralph B.	Sup. Sgt.	Co. E.	
Buescher, Arthur F.	Pvt.	Co. A.	
Buescher, Elmer	Pvt.	Co. B.	
Buford, William	Corp.	Co. M.	
Bullard, James A.	Pvt.	Co. G. 140th Inf.	
Bullock, Callus	Pvt.	Co. B.	
Bundren, James	Pvt.	Co. L.	
Burchette, William F.	Pvt.	San. Det.	
Burditt, Sam	Pvt.	Co. G. 140th Inf.	
Bureman, Oscar T.	Pvt.	Co. K.	
Burger, William	Pvt.	Co. I.	
Burgess, Frank	Corp.	Co. B.	
Burgess, Harry S.	Corp.	Co. A.	
Buri, Fred E.	Pvt.	Supply Co.	
Burke, John F.	Pvt.	Co. I.	
Burke, Cornelius Leo	Pvt.	Co. M. 140th Inf.	Wounded
Burkett, Elbert H.	Pvt.	Co. C.	
Buri, Fred E.	Pvt.	Co. A.	
Burnell, Frank J.	Musician	Hdqrs. Co.	
Burnett, Fred	Pvt.	Co. D.	
Burnett, Ralph E.	Pvt.	Co. C.	
Burns, Neil	Pvt.	Co. K.	
Burrow, Arthur P.	Sgt.	Co. H.	
Burtch, Barton H.	Pvt.	Co. A.	
Busackino, Martin P.	Pvt.	Co. I.	
Busch, William A.	Pvt.	Co. B.	
Butcher, George	Pvt.	Co. F.	
Butler, Frank A.	Corp.	Co. F.	
Butterfield, Howard	Pvt.	Co. K.	
Buttz, Albert D.	Musician	Co. F.	
Byler, Roy F.	Pvt.	Co. F.	Wounded
Byrd, Alvin B.	Pvt.	Hdqrs. Co.	
Byrd, Claud H.	Pvt.	Co. I.	
Byrd, Harvey K.	Pvt.	Co. A.	Killed
Byrne, George T.	Corp.	Co. K.	
Cagle, James C.	Sgt.	Co. I.	Gassed
Cain, Clarence L.	Corp.	Co. C.	

THE MEN BEHIND THE GUNS 159

Caldwell, Luther R.	Pvt.	Co. H.	
Caldwell, Otis W.	Corp.	Co. I.	
Calfee, John C.	Corp.	Co. F.	
Calhoun, Raymond L.	Corp.	Co. M.	
Callaway, James Frank	Pvt.	Co. A.	
Callen, Ollie Bucker	Pvt.	Co. A.	
Callenback, Henry A.	Pvt.	Co. F.	
Calvert, James W.	Pvt.	Co. M.	Wounded
Campbell, James W.	Cook	Co. A.	Wounded
Campbell, John N.	Pvt.	Co. K.	
Campbell, John R.	Pvt.	Co. F.	
Campbell, William	Corp.	Co. L.	
Canady, Max	Pvt.	Co. D.	
Cantlica, Carmelo	Pvt.	Co. B.	
Capehart, Charles Wm.	Pvt.	Co. A.	Wounded and Gassed
Caputo, James	Pvt.	M. G. Co.	
Caraker, Horace	Pvt.	Co. L.	
Caraway, Lewis George	Pvt.	Co. L.	
Carey, Dady M.	Corp.	Co. A.	
Carey, Ira N.	Corp.	Co. H.	
Carey, James	Corp.	Hdqrs. Co.	Wounded
Carey, Walter O.	Pvt.	Hdqrs. Co.	
Carfrae, Robert W.	Sgt.	M. G. Co.	
Carl, Luther	Cook	Co. K.	
Carlisle, Joseph	Pvt.	Co. I.	
Carlisle, Walter	Pvt.	Co. C.	
Carlisle, Walter L.	Pvt.	Co. B.	
Carloch, Horace L.	Pvt.	Hdqrs. Co.	
Carlock, Leroy G.	Corp.	Hdqrs. Co.	
Carlson, Aaron	Corp.	Co. A.	Wounded
Carlson, Charles N.	Pvt.	Co. K.	
Carlson, Edgar G.	Corp.	Co. C.	
Carlson, Gilbert T.	Pvt.	Co. M.	
Carlton, Ora	Pvt.	Co. H.	
Carmack, Louis	Pvt.	Co. I.	Gassed
Carney, Philip L.	Pvt.	Co. G.	
Carpenter, Dave	Corp.	Co. M.	
Carpenter, Jesse R.	Corp.	Co. H.	
Carpenter, Oliver P.	Pvt.	Co. D.	Wounded
Carr, Charles L.	Pvt.	San. Det.	
Carr, Louis T.	Pvt.	Co. C.	
Carr, Merl C.	Pvt.	Co. D.	
Carr, Noflet B.	Corp.	Co. L.	
Carrick, Raymond	Pvt.	Ord.	
Carroll, George W.	Corp.	Co. A.	Wounded
Carroll, Sam	Pvt.	Co. K.	
Carstens, Nicholas K.	Bugler	Co. C.	
Carter, Archie C.	Pvt.	Co. D.	
Carter, Cully C.	Corp.	Co. F.	
Carter, Harvey L.	Pvt.	Co. F.	
Carter, Garrett W.	Wagoner	Supply Co.	
Carter, John A.	Horseshoer	Supply Co.	
Carter, Thomas M.	Pvt.	Co. C.	
Cartwright, Walter F.	Pvt.	Co. E.	
Carty, Abi H.	Pvt.	Co. K.	
Carver, Ruben Bert	Pvt.	Co. A.	
Cary, Frank	Pvt.	Co. I.	
Cash, Frank W.	Corp.	Co. B.	
Cashman, John J.	Pvt.	Co. G.	Gassed
Cason, Orvil L.	Pvt.	Co. D.	
Cassity, Ora Bryan	Pvt.	Co. A.	
Cates, James L.	Pvt.	Co. M.	Wounded
Cates, Jesse L.	Mechanic	Co. G.	Gassed

Catlette, Roy P.	Pvt.	Co. H.	
Caulder, John H.	Pvt.	Hdqrs. Co.	
Caulk, Ross B.	Cook	Supply Co.	
Cauthon, John	Cook	Co. B.	
Cerruti, Gugliemo	Pvt.	Co. I.	
Cerveny, George	Pvt.	Co. A.	
Chaffin, Benjamin L.	Pvt.	Co. H.	
Chaffin, John B.	Pvt.	Co. H.	Wounded
Chamberlain, Harry	Pvt.	San. Det.	
Chamberlain, Roy	Pvt.	Co. F.	Gassed
Chamberlin, Jesse F.	Pvt.	Co. C.	
Chambers, Dan J.	Pvt.	Co. A.	
Chamblin, Lee S	Cook	Hdqrs. Co.	Wounded
Chamblin, Robert L.	Sgt.	Co. F.	Wounded
Chance, Jim	Corp.	Co. I.	
Chancellor, John E.	Pvt.	Co. K.	
Chandler, Earl M.	Cook	Hdqrs. Co.	
Chandler, Robert B.	Pvt.	Co. M.	
Chandler, Samuel G.	Pvt.	Co. I.	
Chandler, William D.	Pvt.	Co. C.	
Channell, Sam L.	Pvt.	Co. F.	
Chapman, Frank P.	Pvt.	Co. M. 140th Inf.	
Chappius, Pierre S.	Pvt.	Co. L.	Wounded
Charchula, Kazimerz	Pvt.	Co. I.	
Charles, John W.	Pvt.	Co. G.	
Charles, Ralph E.	Corp.	Co. K.	
Charlesworth, Earl A.	Corp.	Co. B.	Died B. H.
Charlton, Rowland H.	Pvt.	Co. F.	Gassed
Chartier, Pearl D.	Pvt.	Co. H.	
Chase, David	Corp.	Co. B.	
Chasteen, Otto	Pvt.	Co. H.	
Chatman, Richard C.	Pvt.	Co. H.	
Chauncey, William R.	Pvt.	Co. F.	
Chellis, Willard D.	Pvt.	Co. D.	
Chestnut, Earl	Pvt.	Co. B.	Gassed
Chestnut, Robert L.	Pvt.	Co. H.	
Chilson, Clifford C.	Pvt.	Co. C.	
Chilton, Paul J.	Pvt.	Co. B.	
Chiluski, Henry J.	Pvt.	Co. A.	
Chipman, Woddie	Pvt.	Co. F.	
Chlopek, Ladislaus F.	Corp.	Co. I. 140th Inf.	
Chmielewski, Frank J.	Pvt.	Co. I.	
Chorette, Edward	Corp.	Co. F.	
Chormanski, Stanley	Pvt.	Co. E.	
Chrisco, Herbert P.	Pvt.	Co. F.	
Christman, William H.	Pvt.	Co. C.	
Christopher, Frank G.	Pvt.	Co. F.	
Cisneros, Felix	Mechanic	Co. E.	Wounded
Cisnerous, Louis	Corp.	Co. E.	
Claborn, Walter Hampton	Pvt.	Co. A.	
Clacby, Earl D.	Pvt.	Co. A.	
Clanton, Jesse C.	Pvt.	Co. A.	
Clapper, Lucious L.	Pvt.	Co. C.	
Clarke, Charles F.	Pvt.	Co. K.	
Clark, Columbus B.	Pvt.	Co. M.	
Clark, Irvin R.	Pvt.	Co. I.	
Clark, James E.	Pvt.	Co. D.	
Clark, John	Corp.	Hdqrs. Co.	
Clark, Mertie	Corp.	Co. M.	Wounded
Clark, Ralph William	Pvt.	Co. M. 140th Inf.	
Clark, Ray	Pvt.	Co. B.	
Clark, Walter L.	Sgt. Bugler	Hdqrs. Co.	Wounded
Clark, William J.	Pvt.	Co. K.	
Clarke, Harvey H.	Pvt.	Co. H.	

THE MEN BEHIND THE GUNS 161

Clarke, Jesse C.	Sgt.	Co. A.	Wounded
Clauser, William	Pvt.	Co. I.	
Clawson, Charmie E.	Cook	Co. H.	
Clay, Robert A.	Pvt.	Hdqrs. Co.	Gassed
Claxton, Howard N.	Wagoner	Supply Co.	
Claypole, William F.	Pvt.	M. G. Co.	
Cleary, Clarence F.	Corp.	Co. M.	
Cleary, Grover C.	Sgt.	Co. A.	
Clements, Floyd	Pvt.	Co. I.	
Clemings, Claude F.	Pvt.	Co. E.	
Clemmons, Ralph L.	Sgt.	Co. A.	
Clevy, Clarence T.	Corp.	Co. M.	Wounded
Clifford, Courtney T.	Corp.	Co. L.	Wounded
Clinkinbeard, Fletcher	Pvt.	Co. A.	
Clinkinbeard, Smith	Pvt.	Co. A.	
Clippard, Ersul D.	Pvt.	Co. A.	
Cloud, Austin W.	Pvt.	Ord. Dept.	
Clounts, Jake E.	Pvt.	Co. F.	Wounded
Clouse, Oscar C.	Pvt.	Co. C.	
Clowers, Clifton T.	Pvt.	Co. I.	
Clubb, John	Pvt.	Co. I.	Wounded
Clubb, Grover	Pvt.	Co. I.	
Clymer, Harry E.	Pvt.	Co. G.	
Cobb, Luther W.	Pvt.	M. G. Co.	
Coberly, John A.	Pvt.	Co. K.	
Coberly, Leonard	Sgt.	Co. G.	
Cochran, Herbert W.	Pvt.	Co. C.	
Cochrane, Clarence E.	Pvt.	Co. C.	
Cochran, Joe	Pvt.	Co. E.	
Coday, Walter C.	Sgt.	Supply Co.	
Coen, James R.	Corp.	Co. E.	
Coen, Ray C.	Pvt.	Co. C.	
Coffee, Archie T.	Pvt.	San. Det.	
Coffman, Harrison A.	Pvt.	Co. C.	Wounded
Cole, Clarence	Pvt.	Co. B.	
Coleman, Frederick	Pvt.	Co. C.	
Collier, Pearcey	Pvt.	Co. M.	
Collins, Edward H.	Mechanic	Co. A.	Wounded
Collins, Raleigh R. M.	Pvt.	Hdqrs. Co.	
Colliton, Patrick J.	Pvt.	Co. B.	
Columbia, Harmon	Pvt.	Co. H.	
Colville, James M.	Sgt.	Co. D.	
Colville, Tecumseh P.	Pvt.	Co. D.	Wounded
Colvin, Ed.	Pvt.	Co. A.	
Combs, Alford Washington	Pvt.	Co. A.	
Comegys, Samuel H.	Pvt.	Co. B.	Wounded
Comer, James E.	Corp.	Co. K.	
Comer, William	Pvt.	Co. I 14th Inf.	
Compton, Charles R.	Pvt.	Co. D.	
Conley, Dugan	Pvt.	Co. B.	Wounded
Conlon, Hugh Edward	Pvt.	Co. L.	
Conlon, Luke J.	Wagoner	Co. D	Wounded
Conn, David W.	Pvt.	Co. C.	
Connor, James H.	Pvt.	Co. K.	
Connor, Floyd W.	Pvt.	Co. K.	
Connor, Lloyd W.	Pvt.	Co. K.	
Connor, Roy	Pvt.	Co. C.	Wounded
Cook, Al J.	Pvt.	M. G. Co.	Wounded
Cook, Myrel J.	Corp.	Co. G.	
Cooke, Rodger	Pvt.	San. Det.	
Cooley, Clarence Emery	Pvt.	Co. M.	Wounded
Cooley, Harry	Corp.	Co. K.	
Cooley, McCabe	Pvt.	M. G. Co.	
Cooley, William W.	Corp.	Co. C.	

Coon, William	Bugler	Co. D.	
Coonoe, Leo R.	Corp.	Co. M.	Wounded
Cooper, Columbus B.	Pvt.	Co. B.	
Cooper, Ernest E.	Pvt.	Co. K.	
Cooper, William E.	Corp.	Co. A.	
Cooperider, Nathan L.	Sgt.	Co. I.	Wounded
Copas, Leslie A.	Pvt.	Co. L.	
Copeland, Ben H.	Pvt.	Co. B.	
Copeland, John L.	Pvt.	Co. D.	
Copeland, Ross	Wagoner	Co. G.	
Corbin, Robert D.	Pvt.	Supply Co.	
Corn, Howard M.	Pvt.	Co. A.	
Cosby, Albert	Pvt.	Co. A.	
Costello, Gerald J.	Pvt.	Co. A.	
Cotrell, Iden	Pvt.	Co. B.	
Coughlan, John	Pvt.	Co. L.	
Coulter, Harry R.	Pvt.	Co. C.	
Coulter, Monte C.	Corp.	Co. B.	Wounded
Court, Arthur C.	Pvt.	Co. G.	
Cousins, Sidney A.	Sgt.	Co. A.	
Cowan, Floyd L.	Pvt.	Co. F.	
Cowell, Clarence G.	Pvt.	Co. H.	
Cown, Roy	Pvt.	Co. M.	
Cox, Earnest O.	Corp.	Co. F.	Wounded
Cox, Frank	Pvt.	Co. B.	
Cox, James K.	Corp.	Co. I.	
Cox, John M.	Pvt.	Hdqrs. Co.	
Cox, Richard	Corp.	Co. F.	
Cox, Willie G.	Pvt.	Co. A.	
Cozine, Roy	Pvt.	Co. B.	Wounded
Cracker, Horace	Pvt.	Co. L.	
Crafton, John W.	Pvt.	Co. M.	
Craig, Henry J.	Pvt.	Co. C.	Wounded
Craig, Henry	Pvt.	Co. B.	
Craig, James R.	Corp.	Co. C.	
Craig, Rufus C.	Pvt.	Co. B.	
Craig, William G.	Wagoner	Supply Co.	
Crain, William J.	Pvt.	Co. F.	
Cramer, Wyatt	Cook	Hdqrs. Co.	Wounded
Crandell, Earl	Pvt.	Co. B.	Wounded
Cranford, Fred	Pvt.	Co. I.	
Craven, Herman	Sgt.	Co. K.	
Crawford, Clarence E.	Corp.	Co. F.	
Crawford, Henry L.	Pvt.	Co. F.	
Crawford, Marimon	Pvt.	Co. K.	
Cregar, James	Pvt.	Co. D.	
Crews, Arthur	Pvt.	Co. C.	
Crider, Albert T.	Pvt.	San. Det.	
Crider, Alva	Pvt.	Co. D.	
Crim, Arthur	Pvt.	Co. I.	Gassed
Crisco, Herbert	Pvt.	Co. F.	
Crittendon. Calvin G.	Pvt.	Co. I.	
Crocket. William A.	Pvt.	Hqrs. Co.	
Crockett, Claud	Pvt.	Co. C.	
Crockett, John	Band Sgt.	Hdqrs. Co.	
Crook, Jesse C.	Pvt.	Co. H.	
Cropp, Ezra	Pvt.	Co. K.	
Crosby, Mason H.	Pvt.	Co. K.	
Crose, Albert	Corp.	Co. B.	
Crosley. Clarence J.	Cook	Co. M.	
Cross, Harry M.	Pvt.	Co. A.	
Crossetti, Tom	Pvt.	Co. H.	
Crossley, Ernest	Pvt.	Co. F.	Gassed
Crossley, Earnest	Pvt.	Co. F.	

THE MEN BEHIND THE GUNS

Crosswhite, Merideth Elmer	Pvt.	Hdqrs. Co.	
Crow, Herbert	Pvt.	Co. H.	
Croy, Albert	Pvt.	Co. B.	
Cruciani, Ulisse	Pvt.	Co. G.	
Csikos, George	Pvt.	Co. D.	
Cudd, Willie	Pvt.	Co. M.	
Culley, Stewart	Pvt.	Co. A.	
Cullumber, William R.	Pvt.	Co. B.	
Culver, Fordys	Pvt.	M. G. Co.	
Cummings, Joe	Pvt.	Co. C.	
Cummins, Raymond W.	Corp.	Co. H.	
Cundiff, Chester A.	Sgt.	Co. E.	
Cunningham, Clyde C.	Sgt.	Co. A.	
Cunningham, Earl	Sgt.	Co. K.	
Cunningham, George W.	Pvt.	M. G. Co.	
Cunningham, Henry D.	Corp.	Co. D.	Wounded
Cunningham, Hugh R.	Corp.	Co. F.	
Cunningham, John O.	Pvt.	Co. A.	Wounded
Curry, Earl	Pvt.	Co. A.	
Curry, Homer	Pvt.	Co. A.	Wounded
Curtin, Arthur	Pvt.	M. G. Co.	
Curtis, Clark	Pvt.	Co. E.	Wounded
Cuzzort, Harry D.	Pvt.	Hdqrs. Co.	
Czak, Joseph	Pvt.	Co. E.	
Dabney, Frank W.	Corp.	Co. D.	Wounded, Died
Daggett, William H.	Corp.	Co. F.	
Dalanzo, Frank	Pvt.	Co. E.	
Dale, Virgil	Pvt.	Co. G. 140th Inf.	
Dallenbach, William E.	Pvt.	Co. A.	
Damico, Edward O.	Reg. Sup. Sgt.	Supply Co.	
Dana, Herbert C.	Corp.	M. G. Co.	
Daniels, Almon T.	Pvt.	Co. G.	Wounded
Daniels, Charley A.	Wagoner	Supply Co.	
Daniels, Elmer A.	Pvt.	Co. G.	
Darby, Fred W.	Corp.	Co. M.	Wounded
Darddea, Pasquale	Pvt.	Co. D.	
Darrah, Forest	Pvt.	Co. A.	
Daub, Harry J.	Pvt.	Hdqrs. Co.	Gassed slightly
Daum, Henry	Pvt.	Co. D.	
David, Cecil R.	Pvt.	M. G. Co.	
Davidson, Bert	Pvt.	Hdqrs. Co.	
Davidson, Burle H.	Pvt.	Co. B.	
Davis, Amos	Pvt.	Co. H.	
Davis, Carl H.	Pvt.	Co. I.	
Davis, Claude J.	Pvt.	Co. H.	
Davis, Earl D.	Pvt.	Co. M.	
Davis, Evan	Pvt	Co. B.	
Davis, Everett	Pvt.	Co. H.	
Davis, Golden R.	Pvt.	Hdqrs. Co.	
Davis, Harry	Pvt.	Co. E.	Dead, Wounds
Davis, Jesse H.	Pvt.	Hdqrs. Co.	
Davis, Joe, Jr.	Pvt.	Co. A.	
Davis, John C.	Corp.	Co. I.	
Davis, John O.	Pvt.	Co. H.	Gassed
Davis, Junious C.	Mess Sgt.	Co. B.	
Davis, Leo T.	Pvt.	Co. L.	
Davis, Levi A.	Pvt.	Supply Co.	
Davis, Monroe W.	Pvt.	Co. G.	
Davis, Noah	Pvt.	Hdqrs. Co.	
Davis, Otto J.	Pvt.	Co. L.	
Davis, Paris	Pvt.	Co. I.	
Davis, Ressie H.	Wagoner	Supply Co.	
Davis, Robert	Sgt.	Co. E.	

Davis, Robert L.	Pvt.	Co. C.	
Davis, Swiff S.	Pvt.	Co. I.	
Davis, William J.	Pvt.	M. G. Co.	Wounded
Davis, William R.	Wagoner	Supply Co.	
Davis, William T.	Corp.	Co. B.	
Dawson, Harold L.	Sgt.	Co. E.	
Day, Cecil L.	Sgt.	Co. H.	
Day, Charley	Pvt.	Co. M.	
Day, Edward	Pvt.	Supply Co.	
Day, Emery D.	Pvt.	Co. C.	
Day, John R.	Pvt.	Co. B.	
Day, Melvin	Wagoner	Supply Co.	
Deal, Albert	Pvt.	Co. B.	
Dean, Albert R.	Pvt.	Supply Co.	Died of Wounds
Dean, Frank M.	Corp.	Co. I.	
Dean, John B.	Pvt.	Co. B.	
Dean, Marquess	Sgt.	Hdqrs. Co.	
Deaton, Andrew H.	Mechanic	Co. G.	
DeCamp, James W.	Pvt.	Co. D.	
Dechaume, George T.	Pvt.	Co. M.	
Dedrick, Daniel D.	Band Corp.	Hdqrs. Co.	
Deen, Cleao C.	Corp.	Co. H.	
Deer, John	Pvt.	Co. D.	
Deery, Leonard	Pvt.	Co. B.	
Degraffenreid, Joe	Sgt.	Co. L.	
DeGasero, Anerigo	Pvt.	Co. B.	
Degregoria, Nicolo	Pvt.	Co. K.	
DeGrot, Fred E.	Mess Sgt.	Co. C.	
DeLahunt, John L.	Sgt.	Hdqrs. Co.	
DeLoach, William C.	Pvt.	Co. F.	
Demarais, James	Pvt.	Co. D.	
Denam, Harvey	Corp.	Co. I.	Gassed
Denelsbeck, David	Corp.	Co. L.	
Denny, William W.	Wagoner	Supply Co.	
Dennis, Bert	Pvt.	Co. B.	
Dennis, Charles J.	Corp.	Co. G.	Wounded
Dennis, Otto	Corp.	Co. I.	
Dennis, Waldo C.	Corp.	Co. M.	
Denny, Leonard W.	Pvt.	Co. G.	
Denton, Alcie	Pvt.	Co. I.	
Derby, John F.	Pvt.	Co. K.	
Dermody, James	Pvt.	Co. D.	
Derry, Leonard	Pvt.	Co. B.	
Desebeo, Mike	Pvt.	Co. D.	Wounded
Desich, Emery	Pvt.	Co. E.	
Detweiler, Ira	Sgt.	Co. C.	Wounded
DeVane, Boyd B.	Mechanic	Co. I.	
Devito, James	Mechanic	Co. E.	
Dew, Henry Vernon	Pvt.	Hdqrs. Co.	
Deweese, Frank E.	Corp.	Co. F.	
DeWitt, Armond A.	Sgt.	Co. F.	
Deyer, George D.	Corp.	Co. C.	
DeYoung, John W.	Corp.	Co. H.	Wounded
Dice, John O.	Pvt.	Co. G.	
Dicinceio, Santo	Pvt.	Co. I.	
Dickens, William L.	Pvt.	Co. M.	
Dickerson, William E.	Pvt.	Co. I.	
Dickerson, Arthur L.	Wagoner	Supply Co.	
Dickey, Fee	Pvt.	Co. K.	
Dickey, Ward S.	Sgt.	Co. G.	Gassed
Dickison, William A.	Sgt.	Supply Co.	
Dicks, Jesse W.	Pvt.	Co. I.	Wounded
Dielman, Glen F.	Pvt.	Co. C.	
Digiralamo, Peter	Pvt.	Hdqrs. Co.	

THE MEN BEHIND THE GUNS 165

Dilliard, Murta G.	Pvt.	Co. G.	
Dillingham, Heston	Pvt.	Co. B.	
Dillingham, James	Corp.	Co. L.	Wounded
Dillon, Clarence	Wagoner	Co. K.	
Dimmitt, Cecil E.	Corp.	Co. A.	Wounded
Dimon, Louis	Pvt.	Co. D.	Wounded
Dischinger, Carl F.	Pvt.	Hdqrs. Co.	
Disheaux, Ray	Pvt.	Co. L.	
Dishion, Percie	Corp.	Co. B.	Wounded
Dissler, William A.	Pvt.	Co. L.	
Dittemore, Aubrey C.	Pvt.	Co. B.	
Dittus, Albert H.	Pvt.	Co. B.	
Divine, William	Pvt.	Co. B.	Shell shocked
Dixon, Arlin K.	Cook	M. G.	
Dixon, Leonard L.	Corp.	Hdqrs. Co.	
Dixon, Ton R.	Pvt.	Co. I.	
Dobbs, Roy	Pvt.	Co. G.	
Dodd, Carl W.	Student Cook	Co. F.	
Dodd, Frank	Pvt.	Co. H.	
Dodson, Chris E.	Pvt.	Co. C.	
Dodson, Homer E.	Pvt.	Co. K.	
Dolan, Joseph T.	Pvt.	Co. C.	
Doles, Henry F.	Pvt.	Co. B.	
Doll, Joseph H.	Pvt.	Co. E.	
Dollard, David B.	Sgt.	Co. G.	
Donaldson, Ernest H.	Pvt.	Co. I.	
Donati, Albert	Pvt.	Co. C.	
Donhost, Otto	Pvt.	Co. D.	
Donley, Wilbur	Pvt.	Co. B.	
Donnelly, James	Pvt.	Co. E.	
Donnelly, James O.	Pvt.	Co. A.	Wounded
Donnelly, Roy V.	Pvt.	Cos. M. G.	
Dooley, Jake	Pvt.	Co. K.	Gassed
Dorflinger, John M.	Pvt.	Hdqrs. Co.	
Dorland, Leland R.	Pvt.	Hdqrs. Co.	
Dorminy, Drew C.	Pvt.	Co. K.	
Dotty, Tony	Pvt.	Co. F.	
Douglas, John H.	Corp.	Co. A.	
Douglas, Norman H.	Cook	Co. A.	
Dousett, George W.	Pvt.	Co. G.	
Douthat, Richard H.	Pvt.	Co. C.	
Douthitt, Lee A.	Pvt.	Co. H.	
Dove, Fred E.	Pvt.	Co. F.	
Dowd, Lee M.	Corp.	Co. D.	
Dowdette, George	Pvt.	Co. G.	
Dowler, Harold C.	Sgt.	San. Det.	
Downey, Carl B.	Pvt.	Co. A.	
Downing, Elmer C.	Pvt.	Hqrs. Co.	Gassed
Downing, Richard B.	Pvt.	Co. D.	Killed
Doyle, Thomas C.	Pvt.	Co. H.	
Dreeben, Harry	Mess Sgt.	Co. L.	
Dreese, Bernard	Pvt.	Co. M.	
Dresser, Richard	Corp.	Co. F.	Gassed
Driskell, Robert H.	Pvt.	Co. H.	Wounded
Dryman, Floyd	Sgt.	Co. F.	Wounded
Duce, Frank L.	Corp.	Co. F.	
Duckworth, Joe L.	Pvt.	Co. K.	
Duckworth, Joseph W.	Pvt.	Co. F.	
Dudzie, Joseph	Pvt.	Co. E.	
Duggan, Albert G.	Pvt.	Co. L.	
Duggan, Ivan A.	Pvt.	Ord. Dept.	
Duke, Arlie M.	Pvt.	Co. I.	
Duke, Melvin N.	Pvt.	Co. I.	
Dukes, LeRoy A.	Pvt.	Co. C.	Wounded

Duncan, Everett H.	Pvt.	Co. K.	
Duncan, James N.	Pvt.	Co. E.	
Duncan, Jess O.	Pvt.	Co. E.	Wounded
Duncan, Roscoe B.	Pvt.	Co. H.	
Duncan, Walter W.	Pvt.	Co. M.	
Dunham, Cecil R.	Sgt.	M. G. Co.	
Dunivan, Cecil	Pvt.	Co. I.	
Dunlap, David D.	Pvt.	Co. G.	
Dunn, Michael	Corp.	Co. E.	Wounded
Dunning, James M.	Pvt.	Co. H.	Gassed
Dunning, Wayne	Corp.	Co. M.	Wounded
Durbin, Ray E.	Pvt.	Co. A.	
Durel, Caron	Pvt.	Co. E.	Wounded
Durham, Ira C.	Pvt.	Co. I.	
Durish, Will	Pvt.	Co. B.	
Durkin, Joseph W.	Pvt.	Co. B.	Wounded
Dye, Milton E.	Wagoner	Co. L.	
Easom, Lee	Pvt.	Co. H.	
Eastburn, Leon P.	Pvt.	Co. K.	
Eatman, John	Corp.	Co. I.	Gassed
Eaton, James B.	Pvt.	Co. G.	
Eaton, Richard	Pvt.	Co. L.	
Eaves, James R.	Pvt.	Co. K.	Wounded
Ebeling, Louis J.	Pvt.	Co. L.	Wounded
Ebert, Benjamin	Pvt.	Co. K.	Wounded
Eckland, George A.	Sup. Sgt.	Co. C.	
Eddleman, Walter C.	Corp.	Co. B.	Gassed
Edgar, Sam W.	Pvt.	M. G. Co.	
Edge, Dee	Pvt.	Co. F.	Wounded
Edmundson, John P.	Pvt.	Co. A.	
Edwards, Charles	Pvt.	Co. E.	
Edwards, George H.	Pvt.	Co. D.	
Edwards, Herman	Pvt.	Co. I.	
Edwards, James	Pvt.	Co. F.	
Edwards, Ralph F.	Pvt.	Co. G	Wounded
Egelston, Fred M.	Pvt.	Co. E.	
Eggen, Henry Joseph	Pvt.	Co. F.	
Ehler, William R.	Pvt.	San. Det.	
Eichelberger, Harvey L.	Corp.	Co. E.	
Eidson, Robert V.	Sgt.	Co. H	Wounded
Eikmeyer, Arthur	Pvt.	Co. K.	
Eklund, Carl V.	Pvt.	Co. B.	
Eklund, Olaf V.	Pvt.	Co. B.	
Ekstam, Carl H.	Pvt.	Co. D.	
Elbs, George J.	Sgt.	Co. L.	
Elder, Roy	Pvt.	Co. I.	
Ellerman, John H.	Pvt.	Co. E.	
Elleson, Carl E.	Pvt.	Co. E.	
Ellfeldt, Ralph J.	Corp.	Co. D.	
Ellington, Louis	Pvt.	Co. K.	
Elliot, James D.	Pvt.	Co. M.	
Elliott, Asa	Pvt.	Co. G.	
Elliott, Dolph P.	Pvt.	Co. I.	Gassed
Elliott, Edgar G.	Corp.	Co. H.	
Elliott, Harry E.	Pvt.	Co. G.	
Elliott, John G.	Pvt.	Co. D.	
Elliott, Lonnie	Pvt.	Co. F.	
Elliott, Ralph J.	Pvt.	Co. D.	
Ellis, John E.	Pvt.	Co. K.	
Ellis, Miller J.	Pvt.	Co. I.	
Ellis, Walter	Pvt.	Co. B.	
Elrod, Calvin	Pvt.	Co. H.	
Elsbernd, Edwin	Pvt.	Co. A.	
Elson, Fred R.	Corp.	Co. C.	

Embree, Charles D.	Pvt.	Co. K.	
Emerson, Jesse P.	Pvt.	Co. F.	Wounded
Emery, Omry	Pvt.	Co. A.	Wounded
Emory, Roy	Pvt.	Co. I.	
Endicott, Adrian E.	Pvt.	Co. C.	
Endres, Edward M.	Pvt.	Co. I.	
Engle, Thomas F.	Pvt.	Co. I.	Wounded
Engle, King Alfred	Pvt.	Co. M.	
English, Burnham T.	Pvt.	Co. B.	
English, Havis B.	Pvt.	Co. H.	
Enochson, James A.	Pvt.	Co. B.	
Enos, Laran D.	Corp.	Co. D.	
Ensminger, Archie P.	Pvt.	Co. M.	
Erevig, Martin L.	Pvt.	Co. F.	
Erhardt, Charles C.	Pvt.	Co. E.	
Ermovick, Michael	Corp.	Co. I.	
Ervin, Lawrence	Pvt.	Co. B.	Gassed
Erwin, William E.	Sgt.	Co. M.	
Eskridge, Edd J.	Pvt.	Co. I.	
Estes, Charlie	Pvt.	Co. L.	
Etzker, Richard J.	Sgt.	Co. F.	
Evans, Cecil D.	Corp.	Hdqrs. Co.	
Evans, Earl F.	Pvt.	Hdqrs. Co.	
Evans, Frank A.	Pvt.	Hdqrs. Co.	
Evans, Frank R.	Pvt.	Co. A.	
Evans, Fred	Pvt.	Co. M.	
Evans, Frederick S.	Pvt.	Co. I.	
Evans, Tubert	Pvt.	Co. C.	
Everett, Hally L.	Pvt.	Co. E.	
Evers, John F.	Pvt.	Co. B.	
Evinger, Clem	Pvt.	Co. C.	
Ewing, John T.	Pvt.	Co. D.	
Fader, William W.	Pvt.	Co. A.	
Fagon, Raymond C.	Pvt.	Co. B.	
Fahey, William J.	Pvt.	Co. I.	
Fairbanks, Louis	Pvt.	Hdqrs. Co.	
Fairbetter, Barney G.	Pvt.	Co. H.	Wounded
Fairchild, Milon	Corp.	Co. H.	Wounded
Falac, Alex	Pvt.	Co. K.	
Falkner, Charles C.	Pvt.	Co. D.	Wounded
Farar, Dave Walter	Pvt.	Co. L.	
Faris, Henry W.	Pvt.	Co. B.	
Farkas, Adam	Corp.	Co. B.	Wounded
Farley, Clarence E.	Pvt.	Hdqrs. Co.	
Farmer, Noel E.	Pvt.	Co. I.	
Farr, Fred A.	Pvt.	Co. F.	
Farrar, Robert M.	Sgt.	Co. H.	Wounded
Farrell, John J.	Pvt.	Co. B.	
Farris, Harold F.	Corp.	Co. I.	Wounded
Farris, Robert	Pvt.	Co. K.	
Farris, Samuel	Pvt.	Co. M.	
Farver, Lawrence	Pvt.	Co. B.	
Faulk, Clarence N.	Pvt.	Co. F.	
Featherston, Joseph B.	Pvt.	Co. I.	Wounded
Feilding, Albert C.	Pvt.	Co. K.	
Feiner, Walter J.	Pvt.	Co. K.	
Feisler, Joe F.	Pvt.	Co. K.	
Felin, Henry E.	Corp.	Ord. Dept.	
Feller, Harry J.	Pvt.	Co. K.	
Fenical, Jewell	Corp.	Co. B.	
Fenn, Herbert K.	Corp.	Co. I.	
Fennell, Walter R.	Pvt.	Co. K.	Wounded
Fenster, Emil A.	Pvt.	Co. D.	
Fenstermaker, Wm. H.	Pvt.	San. Det.	

Fergeson, Harry	Pvt.	Hdqrs. Co.	
Fergerson, Willie L.	Sgt.	Co. I.	
Ferguson, George E.	Horseshoer	Supply Co.	
Ferguson, Joseph D.	Pvt.	Hdqrs. Co.	Gassed
Ferrell, Clifford E.	Wagoner	Supply Co.	
Ferry, Harrison H.	Pvt.	Co. E.	
Fetheroff, Jacob	Pvt.	Co. C.	
Fetters, Theodore R.	Pvt.	Co. C.	
Feuge, Louis C.	Pvt.	Co. I.	
Few, Walter W.	Pvt.	Co. E.	
Fielding, Albert C.	Pvt.	Co. K.	
Fielding, Ed. H.	Sgt.	Co. G.	
Fields, George W.	Pvt.	Co. M.	
Fields, Louis	Pvt.	Co. F.	
Fields, Rufus A.	Cook	Co. H.	
Finley, Harry M.	Pvt.	Co. A.	
Fisher, Dean H.	Pvt.	Co. K.	Wounded
Fischer, Florence L.	Pvt.	Co. B.	
Fisher, Gurie W.	Pvt.	Co. D.	
Fischer, James M.	Pvt.	San. Det.	
Fischer, Joseph J.	Pvt.	Co. C.	
Fisher, Leonard	Pvt.	Co. A.	
Fisher, Orlin E.	Pvt.	Co. C.	Wounded
Fisher, Roy E.	Pvt.	Supply Co.	
Fisher, Rubin R.	Pvt.	Co. A.	
Fisher, Ruben Roy	Pvt.	Co. A.	
Fitts, Dawdell B.	Pvt.	Co. H.	
Fitzer, William R.	Pvt.	Co. B.	
Fitzgibbons, Joseph E.	Pvt.	Co. K.	
Fitzmaurice, Robert E.	Corp.	Co. M.	Wounded
Fitzpatrick, James Joseph	Pvt.	Co. M.	Wounded
Fitzpatrick, Clifford E.	Pvt.	Co. E.	
Flanagan, Van	Pvt.	Co. D.	Gassed
Flanders, Louis H.	Pvt.	Co. G.	Wounded
Flanner, Edgar H.	Corp.	M. G. Co.	Wounded
Fleak, Roy E.	Pvt.	Co. G.	
Fleshman, Alva L.	Mechanic	Co. I.	
Fletcher, Edward S.	Corp.	Co. F.	Gassed
Fletcher, William H.	Pvt.	Co. D.	
Flora, Norman E.	Pvt.	Co. I.	
Florence, Joe R.	Pvt.	Co. I.	
Flowers, Grover C.	Wagoner	Supply Co.	
Flowers, John I.	Pvt.	Co. D.	
Floyd, John W.	Pvt.	Co. F.	
Floyd, Robert M.	Pvt.	Co. C.	
Flucky, Lester	Pvt.	Co. D.	
Flynn, Richard T.	Sgt.	Co. C.	Gassed
Fogbe, Conrad A.	Pvt.	Co. K.	
Fogg, Oscar	Pvt.	Hdqrs. Co.	
Foley, Luther B.	Pvt.	Co. H.	
Foley, Roy P.	Pvt.	Co. H.	
Folta, Francis J.	Pvt.	Co. A.	
Foppe, Harry J.	Pvt.	Co. L.	
Forbes, Lewis S.	Pvt.	Co. K.	
Ford, Alvin H.	Pvt.	Co. M.	
Foreman, Garland A.	Pvt.	Co. K.	
Foreman, Glenn J.	Corp.	Co. H.	
Forinash, Harry Tony	Pvt.	Hdqrs. Co.	
Forkner, Artie C.	Sgt.	Co. C.	
Fornes, Benjamine B.	Pvt.	Co. L.	
Forshee, Charles D.	Pvt.	Co. D.	
Foster, Arthur B.	Pvt.	Co. A.	
Foster, Frank	Corp.	Co. G.	Wounded
Foster, Robert	Corp.	Co. E.	

THE MEN BEHIND THE GUNS 169

Foster, Roy	Pvt.	Co. D.	
Foust, Melvil	Corp.	Co. A.	
Fouts, Fred	Pvt.	Co. B.	Wounded
Fowler, Edwin D.	Pvt.	Co. A.	
Fowler, Howard C.	Pvt.	Co. M.	
Fowler, Jesse	Pvt.	Co. M.	Wounded
Fox, Cornelious N.	Pvt.	Co. E.	
Frabetto, Alfonso	Pvt.	Co. H.	
Frank, Napolean R.	Pvt.	Co. F.	
Franklin, Arthur	Pvt.	Co. K.	
Franklin, Clinton	Pvt.	Co. K.	
Franklin, Joseph D.	Corp.	Co. D.	
Frantz, Ralph R.	Pvt.	San. Det.	
Frasher, Dennis	Pvt.	Co. I.	
Frazier, Charles D.	Sgt.	Co. M.	
Frazier, Enos	Pvt.	Co. L.	
Frazier, John W.	Sgt.	Co. A.	
Frederick, David C.	Pvt.	Co. I.	Wounded
Frederickson, Walter P.	Pvt.	Co. M.	
Freed, Herman F.	Pvt.	Co. K.	
Freed, Joe I.	Pvt.	Co. A.	
Freels, Arthur	Pvt.	Co. K.	
Freeman, Chester A.	Corp.	Co. K.	
Freeman, Ernest V.	Pvt.	Co. D.	
Freeman, John	Pvt.	Co. K.	
French, Lester	Pvt.	Co. K.	
Frey, William S.	Pvt.	Co. C.	
Fries, Louis	Corp.	Co. L.	
Friesz, Charles R.	Mechanic	Co. G.	Gassed
Fritz, William A.	Pvt.	Co. M.	
Frizzell, Byron H.	Pvt.	Co. E.	
Frost, Harry L.	Corp.	M. G. Co.	
Fry, Elzy A.	Pvt.	Co. M.	
Fry, Francis W.	Pvt.	Co. B.	
Fuhrer, Roy	Pvt.	Co. B.	
Fuhs, Fred A.	Pvt.	Co. L.	
Fulford, Clayton C.	Pvt.	Co. B.	
Fulks, Ira	Pvt.	Co. B.	
Fuller, Ben	Pvt.	Co. E.	
Fultner, Philip	Pvt.	M. G. Co.	
Fulton, John C.	Sgt.	M. G. Co.	Wounded
Fuqua, Samuel O.	Mechanic	Co. M.	Wounded
Fuson, John O.	Corp.	Hdqrs. Co.	Wounded
Fuson, Harry J.	Corp.	Hdqrs. Co.	Gassed
Fuson, Olen Sterling	Pvt.	Co. A.	
Fyan, William H.	Pvt.	Ord. Dept.	
Gabriel, Clarence O.	Pvt.	M. G. Co.	Wounded
Gabriel, Jacob	Pvt.	Co. B.	
Gabriel, William	Pvt.	Co. I.	
Gaffney, William P.	Corp.	Co. M.	
Gail, Augustus	Pvt.	Co. I.	Gassed
Galazin, Joseph	Pvt.	Co. A.	
Gallagher, John	Pvt.	Co. K.	
Gallagher, John P.	Pvt.	Hdqrs. Co.	Wounded
Gandy, Ed	Pvt.	Co. I.	
Gappa, Ignitius	Pvt.	Co. K.	
Gardner, Carl A.	Pvt.	Co. A.	
Gardner, Harry	Pvt.	Co. F.	
Gardner, Richard O.	Reg. Sup. Sgt.	M. G. Co.	
Gardner, William D.	Pvt.	Co. M.	
Garfield, William	Corp.	Co. A.	Wounded
Gargist, Patsy	Pvt.	Co. E.	
Garrett, Charles	Pvt.	Co. B.	
Garrison, Edward	Sgt.	Co. B.	

Name	Rank	Unit	Status
Garthwait, Roy C.	Cook	Co. I.	
Gartman, Robert H.	Pvt.	Hdqrs. Co.	
Gary, Ovey	Pvt.	Co. K.	
Gaspers, John T.	Pvt.	Co. D.	
Gaston, Richard M.	Pvt.	Hdqrs. Co.	
Gately, Stephen	Pvt.	Co. D.	
Gattis, Laymonn	Pvt.	Co. B.	
Gattorn, George J.	Pvt.	Co. G.	
Gault, John M.	Corp.	Hdqrs. Co.	
Gaultney, Izra	Pvt.	Co. I.	Gassed
Gautreaux, Adam W.	Pvt.	Co. K.	
Gawlak, Joseph	Corp.	Co. H.	Wounded
Gay, Merrol K.	Pvt.	Co. C.	Wounded
Gee, Leslie	Pvt.	Co. M.	Wounded
Gehig, Clarence D.	Sgt.	Co. A.	Died Ger. Hosp.
Geiser, Fred C.	Pvt.	Co. K.	Wounded
Geisner, Leo	Cook	Co. L.	Gassed
Gellman, Sam	Pvt.	Co. M.	
Gentry, Ben	Cook	Co. B.	Wounded
Gentzell, Robert	Pvt.	Co. B.	
Gentzell, Robert	Pvt.	Co. B.	
George, Hollis A.	Pvt.	San. Det.	Wounded
George, Pleamon A.	Wagoner	Supply Co.	
Geraughty, James	Pvt.	Co. A.	Wounded
Gerber, Harry	Pvt.	Co. C.	
Gerdeman, Robert	Pvt.	Co. I.	
Gerecke, Alvin	Pvt.	Co. L.	Wounded
Gerlach, Francis J.	Pvt.	Co. G.	
German, Walter	Corp.	Co. E.	
Giamorone, Frank	Pvt.	Co. H.	
Giammarino, Mike	Pvt.	Co. I.	
Giauge, Beecher	Pvt.	Co. E.	
Gibbons, Austin	Pvt.	Co. I.	
Gibbs, Clarbourne R.	Corp.	Co. L.	Wounded
Gibbs, Edward	Corp.	Co. M.	
Gibson, Albert G.	Pvt.	Co. F.	Wounded
Gibson, Charles L.	Pvt.	Hdqrs. Co.	
Gibson, Charles R.	Corp.	Co. E.	
Gibson, Homer	Corp.	Co. E.	
Gibson, Jake	Pvt.	Co. B.	
Gieber, Leo	Pvt.	Co. L.	Wounded
Giffin, John W.	Pvt.	Co. D.	
Gilbert, Wilbert H.	Pvt.	Hdqrs. Co.	
Gilbreath, Cloral L.	Pvt.	Co. D.	
Gilbreath, Thomas L.	Pvt.	Co. C.	
Gildea, Francis	Sgt.	Co. M.	Wounded
Gililland, Waldon Tilroy	Pvt.	Co. A.	Wounded
Gill, Elmer E.	Pvt.	Co. E.	Wounded
Gill, Elmer	Cook	Co. K.	Wounded
Gill, Richard	Pvt.	Co. A.	
Gillespie, Joseph J.	Pvt.	Co. D.	
Gillespie, Ola W.	Pvt.	Co. M.	
Gillespie, William R.	Pvt.	Hdqrs. Co.	
Gillibert, Louis C.	Pvt.	Co. A.	
Gillin, Miles	Pvt.	Hdqrs. Co.	Wounded
Gillmore, Orris	Pvt.	Co. A.	
Gilmerr, Clyde A.	Pvt.	Co. C.	
Gipson, Floyd	Pvt.	Co. B.	
Gipson, Russell R.	Pvt.	Co. K.	
Gire, Carl	Pvt.	Co. F.	
Givens, Allen	Corp.	Co. M.	Wounded
Glass, James W.	Pvt.	Co. D.	
Glass, Walter	Pvt.	Co. L.	Wounded
Gleason, Leo F.	Corp.	Co. F.	

THE MEN BEHIND THE GUNS 171

Glover, Edward E.	Corp.	Co. E.	
Glover, James A.	Pvt.	Co. C.	
Gnibar, Leo M.	Pvt.	Co. E.	
Gobovic, Wade	Pvt.	Co. G.	
Goddard, Lloyd	Corp.	Co. I.	
Godding, Jack	Pvt.	Co. B.	
Goetting, Phillip O.	Pvt.	Co. E.	
Goff, John E.	Pvt.	Co. H.	
Gold, Louis V.	Pvt.	Co. M.	
Goldsberry, William O.	Corp.	M. G. Co.	
Goldschmidt, Edwin B.	Pvt.	Co. L.	
Goldweitz, Samuel	Pvt.	Hdqrs. Co.	
Golladay, Roscoe H.	Sgt.	Co. A.	
Gomel, Frank L.	Wagoner	Co. C.	
Gooch, Lee	Pvt.	Co. G.	Wounded
Goodin, Sidney	Pvt.	Co. K.	
Goodin, William A. J.	Pvt.	Hdqrs. Co.	
Goodman, Lewis O.	Pvt.	Co. C.	
Goodwin, Stanley	Pvt.	Co. M.	
Goosey, Merl J.	Pvt.	Co. B.	
Gordon, George H.	Pvt.	M. G. Co.	Wounded
Gordon, James W.	Corp.	Co. D.	
Gordon, John R.	Pvt.	Co. I.	
Gordon, William L.	Pvt.	Co. F.	
Gore, Fred	Pvt.	Co. K.	
Gore, Ilda	Pvt.	Co. B.	
Gorham, Stanford B.	Corp.	Co. G.	
Gorman, Patrick F.	Pvt.	Co. K.	
Gormly, Charles E.	Musician	Hdqrs. Co.	
Gormly, Willison W.	Musician	Hdqrs. Co.	
Gossett, Carl G.	Pvt.	Co. F.	
Gossin, George D.	Pvt.	Co. C.	
Goxham, Sanford B.	Pvt.	Co. G.	
Grabowski, Leopold	Pvt.	Co. C.	
Grace, William A.	Pvt.	Co. I.	
Graham, Albert H.	Cook	Co. C.	
Graham, Newburn L.	Pvt.	Co. G.	
Graham, William B.	Pvt.	Hdqrs. Co.	
Grains, Russell	Pvt.	Co. I.	
Granzella, Viver	Cook	Co. M.	Wounded
Grassi, Loreto	Pvt.	Co. B.	
Grauerholz, William C.	Pvt.	Co. M.	Wounded
Graves, Elvis M.	Pvt.	Co. E.	
Graves, Fred D.	Pvt.	Hdqrs. Co.	
Graves, Harry N.	Pvt.	Co. B.	
Graves, Russell	Pvt.	Co. I.	
Graves, Wesley	Cook	Co. I.	Gassed
Gray, Arthur A.	Corp.	Co. E.	
Gray, Bub	Corp.	Co. H.	
Gray, Clarence	Pvt.	Co. I.	
Gray, Herbert C.	Sgt.	Hdqrs. Co.	
Gray, Leslie O.	Pvt.	Co. F.	
Gray, Ralph	Pvt.	Co. G.	
Greathouse, Ivory	Sgt.	Co. C.	Wounded
Greek, Frank	Pvt.	Co. E.	
Green, Benjamin	Pvt.	Co. L.	
Green, Earl H.	Pvt.	M. G. Co.	
Green, Edward E.	Pvt.	M. G. Co.	
Green, Frank	Corp.	Co. C.	
Green, Harry	Pvt.	Co. C.	
Greene, James	Pvt.	Co. D.	Wounded
Green, John	Pvt.	Co. M.	Wounded
Green, Joseph W.	Pvt.	Co. I.	
Green, Martin L.	Pvt.	Co. F.	

Green, Thomas	Pvt.	Co. A.	
Greenberg, Benjamine	Pvt.	Co. D.	
Greene, Patrick J.	Corp.	Co. B.	
Greenfield, Edward D.	Pvt.	M. G. Co.	
Greenlee, Arnold	Cook	Co. K.	
Greenup, Earnest F.	Pvt.	Co. E.	
Greenwaldt, Fred	Pvt.	Co. B.	
Greer, Sebert	Sgt.	Co. M.	Wounded
Gregg, Walter S.	Corp.	Hdqrs. Co.	Wounded
Gregory, Edward L.	Pvt.	Co. D.	
Gregory, George T.	Pvt.	Co. F.	
Gregory, Jeff C.	Pvt.	Co. K.	
Gregory, Joseph H.	Pvt.	Co. M.	
Gregory, William J.	Pvt.	M. G. Co.	
Gregory, William S.	Sgt.	Co. L.	Wounded
Greten, Henry F.	Pvt.	Co. H.	
Gretz, Charles	Pvt.	Co. B.	
Greuell, Richard F.	Pvt.	Co. D.	
Griffin, Herlie	Pvt.	Co. D.	Gassed
Griffin, Orville T.	Pvt.	Co. I.	
Griffith, Earl	Pvt.	Co. B.	
Griffith, Lester O.	Corp.	Co. B.	
Griffith, Robert E. L.	Pvt.	Co. I.	
Griffiths, David H.	Pvt.	Co. A.	
Griffiths, Wilbur E.	Pvt.	Co. C.	
Grigg, Steven	Corp.	Co. F.	
Grigsby, John H. C.	Pvt.	Co. L.	
Grimes, William F.	Pvt.	Co. F.	
Grimmett, Alfred B.	Pvt.	San. Det.	
Griner, Forest P.	Pvt.	Co. G.	
Griner, John H.	Pvt.	M. G. Co.	Wounded
Grissom, Charles W.	Pvt.	Co. D.	
Grissom, Joe	Pvt.	Co. I.	Wounded
Grist, James	Pvt.	Co. A.	
Groce, Dallas	Pvt.	Hdqrs. Co.	
Groce, Lawrence E.	Pvt.	San. Det.	
Grohowski, Stanley	Pvt.	Co. L.	
Gromek, John	Pvt.	Co. I.	
Gromer, Ernest S.	Pvt.	Co. H.	
Gronlund, Emil J.	Pvt.	Co. A.	
Grose, Albert	Pvt.	M. G. Co.	
Gross, Fred J.	Pvt.	Hdqrs. Co.	
Grow, Lionel A.	Pvt.	Co. A.	
Grozinger, Otto	Pvt.	Co. F.	
Guetermann, Peter B.	Pvt.	Co. F.	
Guibor, Leo M.	Corp.	Co. E.	
Guillon, Joe J.	Pvt.	Co. I.	
Guillot, Leo, Jr.	Musician	Hdqrs. Co.	
Gumm, Alva G.	Pvt.	Co. I.	Wounded
Gunderson, Albert L.	Pvt.	Co. A.	
Gunderson, Gustave	Pvt.	Co. A.	
Gunderson, Lawrence	Pvt.	Co. D.	
Gupton, Carl W.	Corp.	Co. D.	
Gurley, Jim	Corp.	Hdqrs. Co.	
Gurney, Frank S.	Pvt.	Co. F.	Wounded
Gustav, Joseph	Pvt.	Co. C.	
Guthrie, Willie H.	Pvt.	Hdqrs. Co.	
Guy, Ode C.	Pvt.	Co. G.	
Gwartney, James C.	Pvt.	Co. K.	
Gwinn, Clayton N.	Pvt.	M. G. Co.	
Hadley, Lonnie D.	Pvt.	Co. H.	
Hadley, Walter D.	Horseshoer	Supply Co.	
Haeberle, Harry	Sgt. Maj.	Co. B.	
Haekker, Karl P.	Pvt.	Co. A.	

THE MEN BEHIND THE GUNS 173

Hagan, Fendal A.	Sgt.	Co. F.	Gassed
Hagberg, Carl A.	Pvt.	Co. A.	
Hagen, Carl O.	Pvt.	Co. D.	
Hagenstein, Adolph A.	Pvt.	Co. G.	
Hagerman, Edward D.	Pvt.	Hdqrs. Co.	
Hann, Andrew	Pvt.	Co. B.	Gassed
Hailey, Joseph T.	Wagoner	Supply Co.	
Haine, Clyde E.	Pvt.	Co. L.	
Hainline, Wallace N.	Pvt.	Co. C.	Wounded
Hakes, Harry	Pvt.	Co. K.	Wounded
Hale, James W.	Pvt.	Co. K.	Wounded
Haley, William J.	Pvt.	Co. F.	
Hall, Cecil L.	Pvt.	Hdqrs. Co.	
Hall, Charley L.	Pvt.	Hdqrs. Co.	
Hall, Edwin	Pvt.	Co. A.	
Hall, Ernest H.	Pvt.	Co. G.	Wounded
Hall, Frank	Pvt.	Co. A.	
Hall, Hugh	Pvt.	M. G. Co.	
Hall, John A., Jr.	Pvt.	Co. K.	
Hall, John H.	Pvt.	Co. K.	
Hall, Lee	Pvt.	Co. A.	
Hall, Lester C.	Corp.	Co. G.	
Hall, Robert S.	Sgt.	Co. L	Wounded
Halm, Wilbur G.	Pvt.	Co. B.	
Halter, Albert	Cook	Co. L.	
Ham, Walter W.	Pvt.	Co. F.	
Hambidge, John W.	Pvt.	Co. A.	
Hames, Samuel	Corp.	Hdqrs. Co.	
Hamil, William F.	Pvt.	Co. G.	
Hamilton, David A.	Sgt.	Ord. Dept.	
Hamm, George C.	Horseshoer	Supply Co.	
Hamm, William M.	Pvt.	Co. D.	
Hammer, Karl F.	Sgt.	Co. A.	
Hammer, Morris	Pvt.	Co. H.	
Hammondtree, Ovid	Pvt.	Co. F.	
Hamner, Roy	Pvt.	Co. K.	
Hampshire, Horatio	Pvt.	Co. B.	
Hampton, Homer	Pvt.	Co. K.	
Hampton, Luther	Pvt.	Co. D.	Wounded
Hampton, William	Pvt.	Co. B.	
Hanak, Anton	Pvt.	Co. A.	
Hancock, Aaron S.	Corp.	Co. E.	
Handy, Roy	Wagoner	Supply Co.	
Haney, Lee	Pvt.	Co. K.	
Hanks, Ackland	Sgt.	Co. I.	
Hanks, Harry	Corp.	Co. K.	
Hanna, Joe E.	Pvt.	Co. I.	
Hannah, Charley	Pvt.	Co. G.	Wounded
Hannon, Noah B.	Pvt.	Co. F.	Gassed
Hansen, Billy	Pvt.	M. G. Co.	
Hansen, Edward J.	Pvt.	Co. D.	
Hansen, Elmer	Pvt.	Co. M.	
Hansen, John	Pvt.	Co. E.	
Hanson, Arent H.	Pvt.	Co. A.	
Hanson, Ernest E.	Pvt.	M. G. Co.	
Hanson, John	Pvt.	Co. E.	
Hanyan, William A.	Sgt.	Co. F.	Gassed
Harberts, John	Pvt.	Co. C.	
Harbottle, Thomas	Pvt.	Co. H.	
Hardin, Jesse J.	Pvt.	Co. E.	
Hardman, Charles H.	Pvt.	Co. B.	Wounded
Hardy, Harold	Corp.	Co. A.	
Hardy, Dewey H.	Pvt.	Hdqrs. Co.	
Harfst, Eilert E. L.	Pvt.	M. G. Co.	

Harlan, Harry L.	Pvt.	Co. G.	
Harlan, Vern	Pvt.	M. G. Co.	
Harman, Ernest P.	Sgt.	Co. D.	
Harmon, Lindsey	Pvt.	Co. A.	
Harmon, Roscoe	Pvt.	Co. E.	
Harney, Joseph F.	Pvt.	Co. A.	
Haroldson, John	Pvt.	Co. E.	
Harper, Cecil B.	Pvt.	Co. F.	
Harrell, Walter	Pvt.	Co. K.	
Harrington, Charles T.	Pvt.	Co. M.	
Harrington, David	Pvt.	Co. B.	
Harris, Arthur	Corp.	Hdqrs. Co.	
Harris, George S.	Pvt.	Co. K.	
Harris, George W.	Pvt.	Co. H.	Wounded
Harris, James A.	Mechanic	Co. E.	
Harris, James R.	Pvt.	Hdqrs. Co.	Gassed
Harris, Jesse T.	Corp.	Co. H.	
Harris, Lawrence L.	Corp.	Co. F.	Wounded
Harris, Samuel D.	Pvt.	M. G. Co.	
Harrison, Arthur W.	Sgt.	Hdqrs. Co.	
Harrison, E.	Pvt.	Co. F.	
Harrison, Harry C.	Pvt.	Co. M.	
Harrison, John H.	Pvt.	Co. B.	Gassed
Harrison, Jess	Pvt.	Co. I.	
Harrison, Robert	Pvt.	Co. B.	
Harry, Wilbert C.	Pvt.	Co. E.	
Harshman, Gilbert J.	Pvt.	Co. D.	
Hart, Eugene M.	Pvt.	Co. G.	
Hart, John C.	Pvt.	Co. I.	
Hart, Sam B.	Corp.	Co. F.	
Hartge, Paul	Sup. Sgt.	Hdqrs. Co.	Wounded
Hartley, Clinton N.	Sgt.	Co. H.	
Hartman, Fred William	Pvt.	Co. L.	
Hartman, John D.	Pvt.	M. G. Co.	
Hartnup, Herbert W.	Pvt.	Co. C.	
Hartshorn, Denzil D.	Pvt.	Co. M.	
Hartsoe, Otho	Pvt.	Co. I.	
Hartson, James	Pvt.	Co. C.	
Harwood, Morris S.	Pvt.	Hdqrs. Co.	
Hasford, Guy F.	Pvt.	Co. M.	
Hassler, James	Sgt.	Co. L.	
Haston, Samuel O.	Pvt.	Co. H.	
Hatcher, Charles L.	Pvt.	Co. M.	
Hatfield, Robert A.	Sgt.	M. G. Co.	
Hathcoat, James R.	Corp.	Co. K.	
Hatten, Ralph	Pvt.	Co. A.	
Hauber, Joseph M.	Pvt.	Hdqrs. Co.	
Haughen, Artie	Pvt.	Hdqrs. Co.	
Haugen, Oscar M.	Pvt.	Co. A.	
Haught, Ellis	Pvt.	Co. K.	
Hausman, Milton H.	Pvt.	Co. A.	
Haver, Oliver O.	Pvt.	Co. L.	
Hawk, William C.	Pvt.	Co. K.	
Hawke, William A.	Corp.	Co. C.	
Hawkins, William	Pvt.	M. G. Co.	
Hawkins, LeRoy D.	Corp.	Co. H.	
Hawks, Leslie W.	Pvt.	M. G. Co.	Wounded
Hawley, Isaac	Pvt.	Co. B.	
Haxton, Ellis C.	Wagoner	Supply Co.	
Hay, Thomas	Corp.	Co. L.	
Haycraft, Phillip E.	Duty Sgt.	Co. F.	
Hayes, George E.	Pvt.	Hdqrs. Co.	
Hayes, Guy C.	Pvt.	Co. I.	Wounded
Hayes, John E.	Corp.	Co. L.	

THE MEN BEHIND THE GUNS 175

Hayes, Ruthford B.	Pvt.	Hdqrs. Co.	
Hayes, William A.	Pvt.	Co. D.	Wounded
Haynes, Russell	Pvt.	Co. E.	
Hays, James	Pvt.	Co. M.	
Hays, John W.	Pvt.	Co. M.	
Hays, Oben E.	Pvt.	Co. A.	
Hayse, Claud	Pvt.	Co. M.	Killed in Action
Hayward, Orville C.	Pvt.	M. G. Co.	
Hazen, Raymond	Pvt.	Co. K.	
Hazlip, Robert	Pvt.	Co. H.	Wounded
Head, Noel P.	Bugler	Co. F.	
Heavenhill, Clint G.	Sgt.	Co. H.	
Heffner, Cecil E.	Pvt.	Co. I.	
Hegerman, Fred F.	Pvt.	Co. G.	
Heidepriem, Harman F.	Pvt.	Co. L.	
Heimer, Charles W.	Pvt.	Co. D.	
Heineman, Alfred D.	Pvt.	Co. I.	
Heinzman, Merrel	Pvt.	Hdqrs. Co.	
Heisay, Irvin A.	Pvt.	Co. G.	Wounded
Hellums, Lawrence L.	Corp.	Co. L.	Wounded
Helmers, Claus	Pvt.	Co. B.	
Helmick, Andrew J.	Sgt.	Co. L.	
Helton, Charles	Pvt.	Hdqrs. Co.	
Helzer, Charles L.	Wagoner	Supply Co.	
Henderson, Floyd H.	Corp.	Co. G.	
Henderson, George H.	Wagoner	Supply Co.	
Henderson, James C.	Pvt.	Co. F.	
Henderson, Joseph M.	Pvt.	Co. M.	Wounded
Henderson, Ray	Pvt.	Hdqrs. Co.	
Hendricks, Clyde C.	Pvt.	Co. C.	Wounded
Hendrix, Jesse F.	Pvt.	Co. H.	
Hengel, Carl J.	Pvt.	Co. F.	
Henke, Richard L.	Pvt.	Co. A.	
Henkel, William J.	Pvt.	Co. M.	
Henley, Archie	Pvt.	Co. L.	
Henley, Dutton	Pvt.	Co. I.	
Henley, Otis	Pvt.	Co. K.	
Henris, Frank	Pvt.	Co. E.	
Henry, Charles L.	Pvt.	San. Det.	
Henry, Edgar H.	Pvt.	M. G. Co.	
Hensley, Acie W.	Pvt.	Co. D.	Wounded
Hensley, George C.	Pvt.	Hdqrs. Co.	
Hensley, Jack	Bugler	Co. I.	
Henslin, John E.	Pvt.	Co. I.	
Hepker, Howard	Pvt.	Co. G.	
Herndon, Charles W.	Corp.	Co. I.	
Herndon, Joseph F.	Musician	Co. F.	Wounded
Hervey, Edward	Pvt.	Co. L.	
Hesketh, Edmund G.	Pvt.	Co. C.	
Hess, Ernest W.	Pvt.	Hdqrs. Co.	
Heuer, Bertram F.	Bugler	M. G. Co.	
Heuitt, Henry C.	Corp.	Hdqrs. Co.	
Heurter, Francis E.	Pvt.	Co. G.	
Heurter, Victor J.	Pvt.	Co. G.	
Hewett, Burton E.	Corp.	Co. L.	
Hey, Edwin D.	Pvt.	Co. L.	
Heyeisen, Frank	Pvt.	Co. B.	Gassed
Hickcox, Thomas	Corp.	Co. B.	
Hicks, Albert T.	Corp.	Co. G.	
Hicks, Henry P.	Pvt.	Co. K.	
Hicks, Spencer E.	Pvt.	Co. H.	
Hicks, Tillman	Pvt.	Co. G.	
Hicks, William A.	Pvt.	Hdqrs. Co.	
Hicks, Will G.	Pvt.	Co. D.	Wounded

Higbea, George R.	Pvt.	Co. L.	
Higdon, John L.	Pvt.	Co. G.	Wounded
Higginbotham, Earl	Pvt.	Co. M.	
Higginbotham, Herman H.	Pvt.	Co. F.	Wounded
Higginbottom, Martin	Pvt.	Co. E.	
Hightower, Sherman V.	Pvt.	Co. I.	
Hill, Bob	Pvt.	Co. F.	
Hill, Earl M.	Pvt.	Co. L.	
Hill, Elmer E.	Corp.	Co. E.	
Hill, Freddie R.	Pvt.	Co. F.	
Hill, Harry	Sgt.	Co. H.	
Hill, Ivor E.	Pvt.	Hdqrs. Co.	
Hill, Oscar E.	Wagoner	Supply Co.	
Hill, Roy A.	Pvt.	Co. K.	
Hill, Leonard E.	Sgt.	M. G. Co.	
Hilliard, Charles McK.	Pvt.	Co. F.	
Hilton, Theodore	Pvt.	Co. H.	
Hinds, Ernest	Pvt.	Co. I.	
Hinkefent, Julius C.	Sgt.	Co. C.	
Hinkle, George E.	Pvt.	Co. K.	
Hinkle, Gilbert H.	Pvt.	Co. L.	
Hladek, Tony E.	Pvt.	Co. G.	
Hoard, Edgar F.	Pvt.	M. G. Co.	
Hoffman, Christ	Pvt.	Co. D.	
Hoffmann, Joe	Pvt.	Co. C.	
Hogan, Lineas G.	Pvt.	Co. G.	Gassed
Hogan, Willis W.	Pvt.	Co. G.	
Hoggard, Odra B.	Bugler	Co. I.	Gassed
Hogue, Samuel V.	Wagoner	Supply Co.	
Hogue, Thomas	Pvt.	Co. D.	
Holcomb, John A.	Sgt.	Co. G.	Wounded
Holdass, Alfred J.	Pvt.	Co. I.	
Holdass, John R.	Pvt.	Co. I.	
Holdeman, Perry S.	Pvt.	Hdqrs. Co.	
Holden, George E.	Mechanic	Co. F.	
Holl, Steve	Corp.	Co. I.	
Holland, Enos R.	Pvt.	Co. I.	
Holland, John J.	Pvt.	Co. H.	
Holland, Walter E.	Pvt.	Co. H.	
Hollenbeck, Harry M.	Pvt.	M. G. Co.	
Holley, Everett	Pvt.	Co. E.	
Hollingsworth, Jay G.	Pvt.	Co. A.	Wounded
Hollis, Ivy	Pvt.	Co. I.	
Holloway, James A.	Pvt.	M. G. Co.	
Hoare, Frank R.	Pvt.	M. G. Co.	
Hobert, Richard A.	Pvt.	M. G. Co.	
Hodgin, Robert H.	Pvt.	Co. I.	
Hodgson, Elway B.	Pvt.	Co. K.	
Hoff, Calvin	Pvt.	Co. I.	Gassed
Hoffman, Carl A.	Pvt.	Co. M.	
Hodges, McDuffie	Pvt.	Co. M.	Wounded
Hinkle, Lyman J.	Pvt.	Co. B.	Wounded
Hinkle, Roy S.	Pvt.	Co. C.	Wounded
Hinote, Hugh R.	Pvt.	Co. F.	
Hintz, Anthony F.	Pvt.	Hdqrs. Co.	
Hinzman, Harry	Corp.	M. G. Co.	
Hirsch, Mathias J.	Pvt.	Co. C.	
Hirshfield, Harry C.	Pvt.	Co. G.	Gassed
Hixon, Edward	Corp.	Hdqrs. Co.	
Holloway, Oscar H.	Pvt.	Co. K.	
Holloway, William J.	Pvt.	Hdqrs. Co.	
Holmes, Ernest	Pvt.	Co. I.	
Holmes, Robert	Pvt.	Co. D.	Wounded
Holmes, Thomas E.	Mess Sgt.	Co. D.	

THE MEN BEHIND THE GUNS 177

Holschuh, Adam W.	Pvt.	Co. A.	
Holt, Earl R.	Musician	Hdqrs. Co.	
Holt, Obra V.	Sgt.	Co. E.	
Holte, Wilbur S.	Pvt.	Co. K.	Wounded
Holtz, Henry T.	Pvt.	Co. I.	
Holtzman, Carl	Band Sgt.	Hdqrs. Co.	
Homme, Knut	Pvt.	Co. F.	
Hoover, Frank D.	Stable Sgt.	Supply Co.	
Hoover, Frank	Pvt.	Co. K.	
Hope, Anderson	Sgt.	Co. E.	
Hope, Charley	Corp.	Co. E.	
Hopkins, Elza	Corp.	Co. H.	
Hopkins, James S.	Pvt.	Co. E.	
Hopkins, Paul F.	Pvt.	Co. M.	Wounded
Hoppas, Charles T.	Pvt.	Co. L.	
Hopper, Ray	Corp.	Co. L.	Wounded
Horine, Sidney F.	Corp.	M. G. Co.	
Horn, Edmond M.	Pvt.	Co. D.	Wounded
Horne, John, Jr.	Pvt.	Hdqrs. Co.	
Horn, George H.	Pvt.	Hdqrs. Co.	
Horner, Bertram C.	Pvt.	Co. D.	
Horner, Ralph A.	Pvt.	Co. C.	
Horton, Jackson	Wagoner	Co. H.	
Hosea, James F.	Pvt.	Co. H.	
Hosking, Frederick	Pvt.	M. G. Co.	
Hoskins, Lonnie C.	Pvt.	Co. B.	Wounded
Hoskinson, Leonard	Pvt.	Co. L.	
Hosler, Harvey H.	Pvt.	Hdqrs. Co.	
Houchin, William T.	Wagoner	Supply Co.	
Houge, Julies	Pvt.	Co. H.	
Houghtaling, Forest M.	Pvt.	M. G. Co.	
Houston, Richard Y.	Cook	Hdqrs. Co.	
Hovey, James A.	Mechanic	Co. B.	Wounded
Howard, Armour J.	Pvt.	Co. L.	
Howard, Elley L.	Pvt.	Co. F.	
Howard, Frederick M.	Corp.	Co. C.	
Howard, George C.	Wagoner	Co. D.	
Howard, George D.	Pvt.	Co. L.	
Howard, Orvel	Pvt.	M. G. Co.	
Howe, Ward W.	Pvt.	M. G. Co.	
Howell, Homer	Pvt.	Co. H.	
Howell, George W.	Mechanic	Co. C.	
Howk, Howard B.	Wagoner	Co. D.	
Hoxy, Russell T.	Corp.	Co. C.	Gassed
Hruska, Theodore	Pvt.	Co. G.	
Hubbard, Fred	Corp.	Co. L.	
Huber, Charles H.	Sgt.	Co. B.	
Hubert, Ira L.	Pvt.	Co. D.	
Hucht, Harry	Pvt.	Co. A.	
Huddleston, Jacob	Pvt.	Co. K.	
Hudgepeth, John H.	Pvt.	Co. F.	
Hudson, William H.	Pvt.	Co. F.	
Huerter, Victor J.	Sgt.	Hdqrs. Co.	
Huerter, Albert V.	Corp.	Co. H.	
Huff, Alonzo	Pvt.	Co. L.	
Hughes, Benjamin F.	Pvt.	Co. A.	Wounded
Hughes, Clinton H.	Pvt.	Co. H.	
Hughes, Forest Wilton	Cook	Co. I.	
Hughes, John W.	Pvt.	Co. M.	
Hughes, Milton E.	Pvt.	Co. C.	
Hughes, Phillip H.	Pvt.	Co. F.	
Hughes, Thomas U.	Corp.	Co. B.	
Hughey, Edward L.	Pvt.	Supply Co.	
Hulbert, Ralph D.	Corp.	Co. L.	Wounded

Name	Rank	Unit	Status
Hummel, John H.	Pvt.	Co. K.	
Humphrey, Harry G.	Pvt.	Co. K.	
Hundahl, Ernest	Pvt.	M. G. Co.	
Hunley, Elmer O.	Pvt.	Co. D.	
Hunold, Joseph H.	Pvt.	Co. D.	
Hunsaker, Jake I.	Pvt.	Co. D.	
Hunt, Lester E.	Pvt.	Co. D.	Wounded
Hunt, Ralph M.	Pvt.	Co. E.	
Hunter, Alec	Cook	Co. K.	
Hunter, H. Ward	Corp.	Co. A.	
Hunter, Walter E.	Pvt.	Hdqrs. Co.	
Huppert, Elwin	Pvt.	Co. K.	Wounded
Hurckes, Francis John	Corp	Co. B.	
Hurley, Carl J.	Pvt.	Co. E.	
Huron, Arthur	Pvt.	Co. I.	
Hurst, Floyd J.	Pvt.	Co. H.	
Hurst, William A.	Corp.	Co. H.	Wounded
Husband, Leslie	Corp.	Co. I.	
Husken, Carl E.	Pvt.	Co. E.	
Hutchins, Earl E.	Pvt.	Co. D.	
Hutchison, Hubert L.	Corp.	Co. G.	
Hutchinson, William S.	Pvt.	Co. G.	
Hutton, Harry C.	Pvt.	Hdqrs. Co.	
Hyatt, John B.	Sgt.	Hdqrs. Co.	
Hyde, George W.	Pvt.	Co. K.	Wounded
Hyde, James M.	Corp.	Co. K.	
Hyer, Charles	Pvt.	Supply Co.	
Hynes, George I.	Sgt.	Co. I.	
Hynes, Phillip J.	Pvt.	Co. H.	
Hyzy, Michal	Pvt.	Co. H.	
Idelman, Abraham W.	Pvt.	Co. C.	
Igelkjon, Christ J.	Cook	Co. B.	Gassed
Iles, Claude	Pvt.	Co. D.	
Imes, George D.	Corp.	M. G. Co.	
Inches, Clyde	Pvt.	M. G. Co.	
Ingebretson, Oscar J.	Mechanic	Co. L.	
Inger, Earl L.	Sgt.	Co. C.	Wounded
Inghram, Frank	Pvt.	Co. K.	
Ingles, Robert	Pvt.	Co. E.	
Ingold, Marion T.	Sgt.	San. Det.	
Ingram, Claud	Pvt.	Co. G.	Wounded
Instead, Louis	Pvt.	Co. C.	
Iverson, Hans Christian	Pvt.	Co. I.	
Ivey, John L.	Pvt.	Co. M.	
Jablonowski, Albin A.	Pvt.	Co. K.	
Jacks, John W.	Pvt.	Supply Co.	
Jackson, Harvey	Sgt.	M. G. Co.	
Jackson, Isaac	Pvt.	Co. I.	Gassed
Jackson, Marcus B.	Pvt.	Co. K.	
Jackson, Tipton	Pvt.	Co. F.	
Jackson, Watson	Cook	Co. I.	
Jackson, William S.	Corp.	Co. G.	
Jacobs, Angus L.	Pvt.	Co. K.	
Jacobs, Floyd S.	Pvt.	Co. D.	
Jacobs, Hawley	Sgt.	Hdqrs. Co.	
Jacobson, John M.	Sgt.	Co. I.	
Jagelky, Conrad J.	Pvt.	M. G. Co.	
Jahn, August C.	Pvt.	Co. G.	
James, Albert R.	Pvt.	Co. G.	Wounded
James, Andrew J.	Pvt.	M. G. Co.	
James, Charles L.	Pvt.	Co. H.	Gassed
Jameson, Luther Y.	Pvt.	M. G. Co.	
Jay, James E.	Pvt.	M. G. Co.	
Jay, William C.	Corp.	Co. C.	

THE MEN BEHIND THE GUNS 179

Jeans, Chester D.	Pvt.	San. Det.	
Jeffers, Leon	Pvt.	Co. K.	
Jenkins, Charles A.	Pvt.	Co. C.	
Jenkins, Clarence J.	Pvt.	Co. A.	
Jenkins, Herbert J.	Pvt.	Co. D.	
Jenkins, William N.	Pvt.	Co. K.	
Jennings, Corwin B.	Pvt.	Co. M.	
Jennings, James H.	Pvt.	Co. A.	
Jeno, Hiram	Pvt.	Hdqrs. Co.	
Jensen, Peter	Pvt.	Hdqrs. Co.	
Jentho, Carl J.	Pvt.	Co. K.	
Jester, Albert	Pvt.	Hdqrs. Co.	
Jett, Dolpha	Pvt.	Co. M.	Wounded
Jett, Everett	Pvt.	Co. H.	Gassed
Jindela, Joseph	Pvt.	Co. I.	
Jocoy, Charles W.	Pvt.	Co. D.	Wounded
Johns, Clarence L.	Sgt.	Co. C.	
Johns, John O.	Pvt.	Co. B.	Wounded
Johns, William M.	Pvt.	Co. H.	
Johnson, Albert John	Pvt.	Co. M.	Wounded
Johnson, Albert R.	Pvt.	Co. H.	
Johnson, Albin W.	Pvt.	Co. K.	
Johnson, August E.	Pvt.	Co. H.	
Johnson, Burt W.	Pvt.	Co. K.	
Johnson, Clifford L.	Pvt.	Co. K.	Wounded
Johnson, C. P.	Pvt.	Hdqrs. Co.	
Johnson, Doc	Pvt.	Co. D.	Wounded
Johnson, Earnest A.	Pvt.	Hdqrs. Co.	
Johnson, Elmer M.	Pvt.	Co. F.	
Johnson, Harrison	Pvt.	Co. K.	
Johnson, Harry H.	Sgt.	Co. C.	
Johnson, Harry L.	Wagoner	Supply Co.	
Johnson, Henry	Mechanic	Co. E.	
Johnson, Henry F.	Pvt.	Co. A.	
Johnson, Henry W.	Pvt.	Co. D.	
Johnson, James O.	Pvt.	Co. I.	
Johnson, John N.	Pvt.	Co. F.	
Johnson, Kent D.	Pvt.	Co. H.	
Johnson, Marion F.	Wagoner	Supply Co.	
Johnson, Mike C.	Pvt.	Co. K.	
Johnson, Oscar O.	Pvt.	Co. I.	Gassed
Johnson, Raymond	Pvt.	Co. B.	
Johnson, Sydney J.	Sgt.	San. Det.	
Johnson, William	Pvt.	Co. D.	Wounded
Johnson, William J.	Pvt.	M. G. Co.	
Johnston, Dewey	Cook	Co. I.	Wounded
Johnston, Harvey T.	Sgt.	Co. I.	
Johnston, Herbert E.	Pvt.	Co. D.	
Johnston, Herbert J.	Band Corp.	Hdqrs. Co.	
Johnston, John H.	Pvt.	Hdqrs. Co.	
Johnston, Vier R.	Pvt.	Co. L.	
Jones, Albert	Pvt.	Co. L.	Wounded
Jones, Albert C.	Sgt.	Co. I.	
Jones, Bishop M.	Pvt.	Co. F.	
Jones, Charles A.	Cook	Co. B.	Wounded
Jones, Claude	Pvt.	Co. B.	
Jones, Claude	Pvt.	Co. L.	
Jones, Earl	Corp.	Co. L.	Wounded
Jones, Everett N.	Pvt.	Co. C.	
Jones, Fred A.	Sgt.	Co. I.	Wounded
Jones, Fred H.	Pvt.	Co. H.	Wounded
Jones, George W.	Mess Sgt.	Co. K.	
Jones, Gerald J.	Pvt.	M. G. Co.	Wounded
Jones, Harry S.	Pvt.	Co. G.	Gassed

Jones, James A.	Pvt.	Co. H.	Wounded
Jones, James P.	Corp.	Co. L.	
Jones, Jesse	Pvt.	Co. F.	
Jones, Jim	Pvt.	Co. K.	
Jones, John	Pvt.	Co. F.	
Jones, John R.	Pvt.	Co. H.	Wounded
Jones, Joseph D.	Pvt.	Co. M.	
Jones, Lawrence O.	Pvt.	Co. G.	
Jones, Lee O.	Pvt.	Co. I.	
Jones, Leonidas J.	Corp.	Co. L.	
Jones, Oscar	Sgt.	Co. B.	
Jones, Robert L.	Pvt.	M. G. Co.	
Jones, Sam	Pvt.	M. G. Co.	
Jones, Stanley	Corp.	Co. H.	Gassed
Jones, Wallace	Pvt.	Co. K.	
Jones, William B.	Wagoner	Supply Co.	
Jordan, R. C.	Pvt.	Co. F.	
Jordan, William H.	Pvt.	Co. K.	
Jorgenson, Gilmer	Pvt.	Co. G.	
Jorgensen, Otto	Pvt.	Co. L.	Wounded
Joseph, Oliver	Sgt.	Hdqrs. Co.	
Joyner, Herbert L.	Pvt.	Co. I.	
Judd, Seth Vernon	Pvt.	Co. M.	Wounded
Judy, Harry A.	Pvt.	Co. B.	
Julian, Elbert R.	Pvt.	Co. H.	
Julian, John T.	Corp.	Co. H.	
Julian, Wesley H.	Wagoner	Supply Co.	
Justinger, Joe F.	Pvt.	Co. C.	
Kabler, Ira C.	Pvt.	Co. E.	
Kale, David E.	Pvt.	Co. G.	Wounded
Kammamm, Bodo A.	Band Sgt.	Hdqrs. Co.	
Kane, Richard H.	Pvt.	Co. E.	
Kapsiotis, John	Pvt.	Co. G.	
Karas, Nick L.	Pvt.	Co. C.	
Karns, Clyde	Pvt.	Co. K.	
Kasl, Louis	Pvt.	Co. K.	
Kates, Miles	Pvt.	Co. D.	
Katlowski, Stanley	Pvt.	Co. I.	
Kaufman, William C.	Pvt.	Co. F.	Wounded
Kearbey, Robert A.	Corp.	Co. M.	
Keaton, James S.	Pvt.	Hdqrs. Co.	Gassed
Kee, Edd	Pvt.	Co. I.	
Kee, Lonnie	Corp.	Co. I.	Gassed
Kee, Thomas	Pvt.	Co. E.	
Keel, George M.	Pvt.	Co. F.	
Keen, Dennis H.	Pvt.	Supply Co.	
Keene, John W.	Pvt.	Co. B.	Wounded
Keeney, Perry L.	Corp.	Co. B.	
Kehew, George H.	Pvt.	M. G. Co.	
Keifer, Clarence A.	Sgt.	M. G. Co.	
Kielhack, Charles J.	Musician	Hdqrs. Co.	
Keith, Hudson A.	Sgt.	Co. E.	
Keith, Lloyd B.	Pvt.	Co. D.	
Keith, Sherman E.	Pvt.	Co. K.	
Kell, James O.	Pvt.	Supply Co.	
Keller, Adolph Albert	Corp.	Co. L.	
Keller, Martin	Wagoner	Supply Co.	
Kelley, James A.	Pvt.	Hdqrs. Co.	
Kellums, John	Corp.	Co. M.	Wounded
Kellums, Nottley	Corp.	Co. M.	
Kelly, Earl H.	Corp.	Co. C.	Wounded
Kelly, Francis P.	Pvt.	Co. H.	
Kelly, John F.	Pvt.	Co. I.	
Kelly, Ray R.	Pvt.	M. G. Co.	

THE MEN BEHIND THE GUNS 181

Kelly, Thomas B.	Pvt.	Co. L.	
Kelsey, LeClaire H.	Pvt.	Co. G.	
Kelton, Leonard	Pvt.	Co. G.	
Kemp, Colonel S.	Pvt.	Hdqrs. Co.	
Kemp, Don	Pvt.	Co. D.	
Kempe, Walter F.	Musician	Hdqrs. Co.	
Kendrick, Dean S.	Pvt.	M. G. Co.	
Kendricks, Timothy P.	Pvt.	Supply Co.	
Kenedy, John M.	Pvt.	Co. L.	
Kennedy, Frank P.	Pvt.	M. G. Co.	
Jennedy, John R.	Pvt.	Co. I.	Wounded
Kennedy, John	Pvt.	Co. G.	Wounded
Kennedy, John W.	Pvt.	Hdqrs. Co.	Wounded
Kennedy, Joseph L.	Sgt.	Co. H.	
Kennedy, Miller R.	Pvt.	Hdqrs. Co.	
Kennedy, John	Pvt.	Co. K.	Wounded
Keown, Fred	Pvt.	Hdqrs. Co.	
Kennon, Jesse E.	Pvt.	Co. E.	
Kern, Ora O.	Sgt.	Co. M.	
Kersey, Bronnie	Sgt.	Co. I.	
Kertz, Martin M.	Pvt.	Co. E.	
Kessler, Sylvester O.	Pvt.	Co. G.	Gassed
Ketchum, James K.	Corp.	Co. I.	
Kettleson, Thomas	Pvt.	Co. K.	
Key, Adrian A.	Pvt.	Co. F.	
Keys, Burson	Bugler	Co. I.	
Keys, John W.	Sgt.	Hdqrs. Co.	
Kienzel, John W.	Pvt.	Co. C.	
Kight, John R.	Pvt.	Co. C.	
Kilgore, Crane	Pvt.	Co. K.	
Kilgore, Hazel A.	Pvt.	Co. K.	Wounded
Kilgore, Thomas F.	Pvt.	Co. K.	
Kilgore, William	Pvt.	Co. B.	
Killer, Harry	Pvt.	M. G. Co.	
Killian, Charles	Corp.	Co. I.	
Killian, Theo.	Pvt.	Co. M.	
Killion, Maynard L.	Pvt.	M. G. Co.	
Killmer, William A.	Pvt.	Co. G.	
Killough, Josephus	Pvt.	Co. L.	Wounded
Kimbrell, Walter	Pvt.	Co. I.	
Kindell, Ollie B.	Pvt.	Co. E.	
Kindig, Frank R.	Pvt.	Hdqrs. Co.	
Kindred, Shannon	Pvt.	Co. L.	
King, Albert	Pvt.	Co. I.	
King, Cecil F.	Cook	Co. C.	
King, Edward	Pvt.	Co. I.	Gassed
King, Edward	Pvt.	Hdqrs. Co.	
King, Emmett C.	Pvt.	Co. F.	
King, James A.	Corp.	Co. H.	
King, James T.	Pvt.	Co. G.	
King, Kirk	Pvt.	Co. B.	
King, Lee	Sgt.	Co. M.	
King, Robert H.	Pvt.	Co. C.	
King, Roy	Pvt.	Co. L.	
King, William	Pvt.	Co. B.	
King, William E.	Pvt.	Hdqrs. Co.	
King, William F.	Pvt.	Co. L.	
King, William T.	Pvt.	Co. B.	
Kinney, John	Corp.	Co. K.	Wounded
Kiper, Richard G.	Sgt.	Co. D.	
Kirby, Charles D.	Pvt.	Co. H.	
Kirchhoff, Carle	Pvt.	San. Det.	
Kirchner, Alfred L.	Pvt.	Co. L.	Wounded
Kirchner, Paul J.	Pvt.	Co. F.	Wounded

Kirk, Clifford	Pvt.	Hdqrs. Co.	
Kirkley, Arthur	Pvt.	Co. B.	
Kirkpatrick, Roy	Pvt.	Hdqrs. Co.	
Kirkwood, Leo O.	Corp.	Co. K.	
Kitchell, Ralph J.	Pvt.	Co. E.	Wounded
Kizer, Newton T.	Pvt.	Co. K.	
Kleasner, Eugene	Pvt.	Co. B.	
Klein, George	Pvt.	Co. B.	
Klein, Harold R.	Corp.	M. G. Co.	
Klein, Tony	Corp.	Co. B.	
Klingel, Charles	Pvt.	Co. L.	
Kmak, Wojcieck	Pvt.	M. G. Co.	
Knake, Herman H.	Musician	Hdqrs. Co.	
Knauer, Earl J.	Pvt.	M. G. Co.	
Kneer, William C.	Sgt.	Co. C.	Wounded
Knight, Cecil	Corp.	Co. I.	
Knight, Clyde P.	Pvt.	Co. D.	
Knight, Jesse	Pvt.	Co. H.	
Knott, Charles W.	Pvt.	Co. A.	
Knott, William R.	Pvt.	Co. F.	
Knox, Lloyd V.	Corp.	Co. D.	
Knoy, Frank L.	Pvt.	Co. K.	
Knutson, Theodore	Pvt.	Co. K.	
Koch, Raymond	Pvt.	Co. L.	
Koefneer, Edward W.	Sgt.	Co. G.	
Kohler, Bion	Pvt.	Co. D.	
Kohring, Mansfield	Corp.	Co. I.	
Kollsmith, Earl O.	Pvt.	Co. B.	
Kossey, Richard H.	Pvt.	Co. G.	
Kovalick, Mike	Pvt.	Co. M.	
Kraft, Leo E.	Pvt.	Co. D.	
Kramer, Jacob	Pvt.	Co. A.	Wounded
Kramer, Lawrence	Pvt.	Co. M.	
Krank, Joe	Pvt.	Co. F.	
Kraske, August	Pvt.	Co. I.	
Krateville, Milo	Corp.	Co. M.	Wounded
Krause, Martin J.	Pvt.	San. Det.	
Kreeger, James L.	Pvt.	Co. B.	
Kreinbring, George H.	Pvt.	Co. G.	
Krenzer, William L.	Pvt.	San. Det.	
Krepik, Pete	Pvt.	Co. K.	
Kriebs, Alfred F.	Pvt.	Co. K.	Wounded
Krier, Charley J.	Pvt.	Hdqrs. Co.	
Krisle, William L.	Pvt.	Co. B.	
Kroencke, Emil L.	Pvt.	Co. A.	
Krog, Oscar F.	Pvt.	Co. H.	
Krohn, Henry	Pvt.	Co. K.	
Kroir, Paul	Pvt.	Co. D.	
Krotta, Walter	Pvt.	M. G. Co.	
Krum, Albert	Pvt.	Co. E.	
Kubas, Adam	Pvt.	M. G. Co.	
Kubersky, Alter	Pvt.	Co. I.	
Kubicki, Felix C.	Sgt.	Co. E.	
Kubik, Wesley	Pvt.	Co. G.	
Kuchnowski, John J.	Pvt.	Co. M.	
Kugler, Albert C.	Pvt.	Co. B.	
Kuhn, Alvin H.	Corp.	Co. C.	
Kuhn, Earl T.	Pvt.	Co. L.	Wounded
Kuhns, Ivan Clarence.	Sgt.	Supply Co.	
Kulcak, Johnie H.	Pvt.	Co. A.	
Kullman, Arthur A.	Pvt.	M. G. Co.	
Kumpf, Carl M.	Pvt.	Co. L.	
Kunicki, Adam	Pvt.	Co. H.	
Kuns, Sven W.	Pvt.	Co. E.	

THE MEN BEHIND THE GUNS 183

Kunz, Frederick G.	Pvt.	M. G. Co.	
Kupinski, Albert	Pvt.	Co. K.	
Kupka, Edward R.	Pvt.	M. G. Co.	
Kupski, John	Pvt.	Co. M.	
Kurzhals, Otto H.	Pvt.	Co. L.	
Kutter, Harry	Pvt.	Co. G.	
LaChapelle, George	Pvt.	Co. I.	
Lachner, William G.	Sgt.	Co. B.	Wounded
Lackender, Jesse J.	Pvt.	M. G. Co.	
Lackey, Boyce T.	Musician	Hdqrs. Co.	
Lacy, George T.	Sgt.	Co. B.	
Lacy, Iley L.	Pvt.	Co. K.	
Laird, Edward	Corp.	Co. I.	
Laird, Otto Lawrence	Pvt.	Co. L.	Wounded
Lamb, Charles R.	Pvt.	Hdqrs. Co.	
Lamb, John A.	Pvt.	Co. D.	
Lambert, Albert	Pvt.	Co. C.	
Lambert, Jesse	Mechanic	Co. L.	
Lamberty, Charles F.	Pvt.	M. G. Co.	
Lambright, Eldridge M.	Pvt.	Co. G.	
Lamm, Gordon G.	Corp.	Co. D.	Wounded
Lancaster, Ernest	Pvt.	Co. K.	
Lanciotti, Agostine	Pvt.	Co. C.	
Lane, Clark	Pvt.	San. Det.	Wounded
Lane, Richard T.	Sgt.	Co. D.	
Langford, James C.	Pvt.	Co. K.	
Langhans, George	Cook	Co. B.	Gassed
Langley, Charles	Pvt.	Co. M.	
Lape, Walter B.	Pvt.	Co. I.	Gassed
Lardis, Steve	Pvt.	Co. D.	
Lardner, Michaell J.	Pvt.	Hdqrs. Co.	
Larrabee, Vernice	Mechanic	Co. G.	
Larson, Arthur C.	Pvt.	Co. K.	
Larson, Edwin L.	Pvt.	Co. D.	Wounded
Larson, Elmer J.	Corp.	Co. F.	
Larson, Gustaf A.	Pvt.	Co. D.	
Larson, John M.	Pvt.	Co. K.	
Larson, Ole	Pvt.	Co. K.	
Larson, Theodore G.	Pvt.	Co. K.	
Lasater, Thomas J.	Corp.	Co. H.	
Lashier, Roe F.	Pvt.	M. G. Co.	
Laster, James R.	Corp.	Co. K.	
Laudermilk, Freeman	Pvt.	Co. E.	Wounded
Laudermilk, Raymond	Pvt.	Co. E.	
Lauritzen, Hans M.	Corp.	Co. A.	
Lawhon, Calvin M.	Corp.	Co. E.	
Lawhon, Frank	Corp.	Co. E.	
Lawhorn, Robert A.	Pvt.	Co. K.	Wounded
Lawler, Thomas J.	Pvt.	Co. I.	
Lawrence, Marion K.	Pvt.	Co. H.	
Laws, Orvil G.	Pvt.	Co. F.	
Lawson, Edmund R.	Pvt.	Co. D.	
Lawson, John Shults	Reg. Sgt. Maj.	Co. M.	
Layfield, Harry M.	Pvt.	Co. E.	
Leaf, Murvall J.	Corp.	Co. E.	
Lear, Albert	Pvt.	Co. B.	
Learned, George H.	Pvt.	Co. G.	
Leasko, John R.	Pvt.	Co. M.	
Leckey, Robert J.	Corp.	Co. C.	
Ledford, Thomas C.	Pvt.	Co. G.	
Lee, Charles E.	Pvt.	Co. M.	Killed in Action
Lee, John	Pvt.	Co. M.	
Lee, John C.	Pvt.	San. Det.	Wounded
Lee, Richard F.	Pvt.	Co. M.	Wounded

Lee, Sellie	Pvt.	Co. I.	
Lee, Thomas	Pvt.	Co. K.	
Lee, William R.	Mechanic	Co. L.	
Lefker, George J.	Pvt.	Co. A.	
Leftwich, James W.	Pvt.	Co. D.	Gassed
Legg, Arthur P.	Pvt.	Co. A.	Wounded
Leggett, Irvin F.	Pvt.	Co. K.	
Lehtola, Oscar	Corp.	Co. B.	
Leibundguth, Charles	Pvt.	M. G. Co.	
Leider, Leo	Pvt.	Co. L.	
Leigh, Harry W.	Pvt.	Co. D.	
Leighton, William Frank	Pvt.	Co. L.	Wounded
Leighty, Edward	Pvt.	Hdqrs. Co.	
Lemarr, James E.	Pvt.	Co. D.	
Lembeck, William H.	Corp.	Co. F.	
Lemley, John C.	Pvt.	M. G. Co.	
Lemley, Richard S.	Pvt.	M. G. Co.	
Lemley, Walter A.	Pvt.	M. G. Co.	
Lemon, Roy	Sgt.	Co. G.	Gassed
Lenge, Roscoe E.	Musician	Hdqrs. Co.	
Lenihan, Raymond D.	Pvt.	Co. M.	
Lennon, Otto	Corp.	Co. K.	Wounded
Lenz, Henry F.	Pvt.	Hdqrs. Co.	Gassed
Leonard, John	Corp.	Co. L.	
Leonardo, John	Pvt.	Co. A.	
Lepage, Clarence P.	Pvt.	Co. D.	
Lerche, John M.	Sgt.	Co. A.	
Lerdel, Ole S.	Pvt.	Co. D.	
Leroy, Frank	Pvt.	Co. B.	
LeRoux, John M.	Pvt.	Co. E.	
Lester, Willis F.	Pvt.	M. G. Co.	
Lewellyn, William W.	Pvt.	Co. G.	
Lewis, Charles E.	Pvt.	Co. M.	
Lewis, Charles W.	Pvt.	Co. A.	
Lewis, Elmer B.	Pvt.	Co. K.	
Lewis, Frank E.	Bugler	Co. D.	
Lewis, Fred	Pvt.	Co. B.	Wounded
Lewis, Hiram N.	Pvt.	Co. E.	
Lewis, Ira E.	Sup. Sgt.	Co. M.	
Lewis, Miller	Pvt.	Co. I.	Gassed
Lewis, Rees L.	Cook	Co. C.	
Lewis, Samuel V.	Pvt.	Co. D.	
Lewis, Wilburn T.	Pvt.	Co. E.	
Lewis, William C.	Pvt.	Co. K.	
Lewis, William O.	Pvt.	Co. D.	
Lewis, William V.	Pvt.	Co. F.	
Leysath, Lewis J.	Pvt.	Co. K.	
Liantanio, Nicola	Pvt.	Co. I.	
Liebst, Kaspar M.	Sup. Sgt.	Co. M.	
Lien, Chris	Pvt.	Co. K.	
Lienhart, Herman	Pvt.	Hdqrs. Co.	
Ligon, Bart	Pvt.	Co. G.	
Ligon, Millard G.	Wagoner	Supply Co.	
Lime, Hurless F.	Pvt.	Co. M.	
Linaman, John H.	Pvt.	Co. A.	
Lind, Edwin J.	Pvt.	Co. B.	Gassed
Lindeman, Albert	Pvt.	Co. K.	Wounded
Linder, William C.	Pvt.	Co. B.	
Lindhe, George C.	Sgt.	Co. K.	
Lindholm, Elmer C.	Pvt.	Co. C.	
Lindlow, Charles D.	Pvt.	Co. K.	
Lindsay, Ben B.	Pvt.	Co. F.	Gassed
Lindsay, Lee	Corp.	Co. H.	Gassed
Lindsay, Mont O.	Pvt.	Co. H.	

THE MEN BEHIND THE GUNS 185

Lindsay, Roy W.	Pvt.	Supply Co.	
Lindsey, Ross	Pvt.	Co. K.	Wounded
Lindenberger, Anton P.	Pvt.	Co. F.	
Lingol, Walter S.	Pvt.	Co. F.	
Link, Alexander G.	Pvt.	Co. C.	
Link, Arthur L.	Mechanic	Co. A.	Wounded
Linkanas, John	Pvt.	Hdqrs. Co.	
Linn, Phillip O.	Pvt.	Co. D.	Wounded
Linville, Floyd F.	Pvt.	Co. G.	
Lipshitz, Albert	Pvt.	Hdqrs. Co.	
Lisenbee, Clifford L.	Pvt.	Co. I.	
Lisenbee, Larnie L.	Pvt.	Co. L.	
Little, Ray	Pvt.	M. G. Co.	
Littler, Virgil W.	Pvt.	Co. E.	
Littleton, Charles L.	Pvt.	Co. I.	
Littman, Meyer	Pvt.	Hdqrs. Co.	
Litts, Benjamin F.	Pvt.	Co. G.	
Lizza, Felice	Pvt.	Co. I.	
Lloyd, John C.	Pvt.	Hdqrs. Co.	
Lloyd, James J.	Pvt.	Co. G.	Wounded
Loch, William A.	Pvt.	Supply Co.	
Lochner, Frank Grahin	Pvt.	Co. L.	
Lockmiller, Elmer L.	Pvt.	Co. D.	Wounded
Lockard, Ernest M.	Pvt.	Co. G.	
Lofstead, Martin	Pvt.	Co. B.	Wounded
Lofties, Earl	Pvt.	Co. L.	
Loftin, Henry G.	Pvt.	M. G. Co.	
Lofton, Elmer W.	Pvt.	Co. D.	Wounded
Loftus, William A.	Pvt.	Co. M.	
Logan, John A.	Corp.	Co. K.	Gassed
Logan, Jesse G.	Pvt.	Co. K.	Wounded
Logan, John P.	Sgt.	Co. B.	Wounded
Logan, John W.	Pvt.	Co. E.	
Logerman, Johnnie Wm.	Pvt.	Hdqrs. Co.	
Lohse, Edgar	Sgt.	Co. B.	
Lokey, Courtney	Pvt.	Co. E.	
Lollis, Oscar	Sgt.	Co. B.	
Lollis, Perry	Pvt.	Hdqrs. Co.	
Lombardy, Louis	Pvt.	Co. E.	
Long, Harry C.	Pvt.	Co. C.	
Lonsdale, William E.	Sup. Sgt.	Supply Co.	
Lonsdalen, Peter	Pvt.	Co. C.	
Lonzo, Bradley	Pvt.	Co. G.	
Looper, William G.	Pvt.	Co. F.	
Lopez, Eleuterio	Corp.	Co. G.	
Lopez, Geheiben	Pvt.	Co. H.	
Lopez, Toney	Pvt.	Co. I.	
Lopshire, Thomas	Pvt.	Co. K.	
Lossons, Frank R.	Pvt.	Co. L.	
Lott, Frank K.	Band Leader	Hdqrs. Co.	
Lotza, Joseph J.	Pvt.	Co. C.	Wounded
Louck, Ernest L.	Mechanic	M. G. Co.	
Lovejoy, Albert B.	Pvt.	Co. E.	
Lovelace, Courtlan F.	Pvt.	Hdqrs. Co.	
Lovett, Delbert D.	Sgt.	Co. C.	
Lowe, James H.	Sgt.	Hdqrs. Co.	
Lowe, John C.	Pvt.	Co. K.	Wounded
Lowe, Oscar R.	Pvt.	Co. E. Sup. Co.	
Lowery, William P.	Pvt.	Co. H.	
Lownsdale, Edgar	Pvt.	Supply Co.	
Lowry, Leonidas	Pvt.	M. G. Co.	
Loyd, Claudy O.	Corp.	Co. M.	
Lubbening, Fred	Pvt.	Co. I.	
Luczkrowsky, Wladyslaw	Pvt.	Co. D.	

Ludwig, Carl W.	Pvt.	San. Det.	
Lue, Frank L.	Pvt.	Co. I.	Wounded
Lueck, Albert E.	Pvt.	Co. K.	
Luellen, Frank M.	Pvt.	Co. G.	
Luken, Edward R.	Pvt.	Co. D.	
Lukowski, Frank	Pvt.	Co. H.	
Lumpkin, John W.	Pvt.	Co. K.	
Lusk, James C.	Corp.	Co. A.	
Lutchansky, William	Pvt.	Co. I.	
Lutkiewicz, John	Pvt.	Co. M.	
Lutz, Albert B.	Pvt.	San. Det.	
Lutz, Herman G.	Pvt.	San. Det.	
Lynch, Thomas	Pvt.	Co. K.	Wounded
Lynd, Ralph R.	Pvt.	Co. L.	
Lynn, Cornelius	Pvt.	Co. K.	
Lyon, Lewis B.	Pvt.	M. G. Co.	
Lyons, Paul O.	Pvt.	Co. D.	Wounded
Lyons, Michael	Pvt.	Co. B.	
Lytle, Glen E.	Pvt.	Co. A.	
McAnally, John F.	Pvt.	Co. I.	Gassed
McAvoy, John J.	Pvt.	Co. D.	
McBee, John N.	Pvt.	Co. G.	
McBrayer, Arthur	Pvt.	Hdqrs. Co.	
McBride, James H.	Pvt.	Co. F.	
McCall, John L.	Pvt.	Co. A.	
McCallister, Harry	Pvt.	Co. H.	Wounded
McCann, John L.	Pvt.	Co. E.	Wounded
McCarthy, Louis	Cook	Co. I.	Gassed
McCartt, Albert	Pvt.	Co. I.	
McCarty, William A.	Pvt.	Co. L.	
McCauley, Doctor Barney	Corp.	Co. I.	Wounded
McCaulla, Willis B.	Pvt.	Co. C.	
McClaren, Chas.	Pvt.	Co. M.	Wounded
McClellan, Ralph E.	Pvt.	Co. F.	
McClendon, William C.	Pvt.	M. G. Co.	
McCloskey, Thomas F.	Pvt.	Co. M.	
McCluney, Jesse F.	Pvt.	Co. F.	
McClure, Clyde H.	Pvt.	M. G. Co.	
McClure, Clyde E.	Pvt.	Co. A.	
McClure, Hubert	Pvt.	Co. L.	
McClure, Marvin	Pvt.	Co. M.	
McClure, Moody	Corp.	Co. I.	
McCole, Peter F.	Pvt.	Co. B.	
McCollum, Ben	Pvt.	Co. I.	Gassed
McCollum, Bert J.	Mess Sgt.	M. G. Co.	
McConkey, Lawrence B.	Pvt.	Co. K.	
McCormack, Otis E.	Pvt.	Hdqrs. Co.	
McCormick, Jim H.	Pvt.	Co. K.	
McCormick, Marshall	Pvt.	Co. K.	Wounded
McCormick, Myron M.	Corp.	Co. A.	
McCown, Edwin P.	Pvt.	M. G. Co.	
McCoy, Charles T.	Pvt.	Co. B.	
McCoy, Gilbert G.	Wagoner	Co. C.	
McCoy, Guy	Pvt.	M. G. Co.	
McCoy, Jess	Pvt.	M. G. Co.	
McCullough, Edward A.	Pvt.	Co. L.	
McCune, Fay J.	Pvt.	Co. G.	
McDaniel, James E.	Sgt.	San. Det.	
McDearmon, Thomas G.	Pvt.	Co. E.	
McDonald, Charles P.	Pvt.	M. G. Co.	
McDonald, George H.	Pvt.	Co. L.	
McDonald, Theodore	Pvt.	San. Det.	Wounded
McDonald, William J.	Sgt.	Co. A.	
McDonough, Felix	Pvt.	Co. C.	

THE MEN BEHIND THE GUNS

McDowell, Benjamine	Pvt.	Co. H.	
McDowell, William J.	Corp.	Co. E.	
McDuffie, John R.	Pvt.	Co. F.	
McElyea, Davis G.	Pvt.	Co. G.	
McFadden, Clarence	Pvt.	Co. A.	
McFadden, John H.	Pvt.	Co. M.	Wounded
McFall, Dave	Corp.	Co. C.	
McFarland, Lantie V.	Pvt.	Co. L.	
McGarry, Willie C.	Pvt.	Co. A.	
McGeary, Pete M.	Corp.	Co. D.	
McGehee, Cecil	Pvt.	Co. H.	
McGehee, Gilbert	Pvt.	Co. H.	
McGinnis, Claude W.	Pvt.	Co. L.	Gassed
McGinty, Charles	Pvt.	M. G. Co.	
McGlinn, Edward J.	Pvt.	Co. B.	
McGovern, Martin T.	Pvt.	Co. L.	
McGowan, Jasper C.	Pvt.	Co. F.	
McGraugh, Hugh	Pvt.	San. Det.	
McGregor, Jess W.	Pvt.	Co. B.	
McGrew, Charles Bert	Pvt.	Co. L.	Gassed
McGuire, Arnold R.	Sgt.	M. G. Co.	
McGuire, Richard	Pvt.	Co. M.	Wounded
McGuire, Robert E.	Pvt.	Co. L.	
McHarness, David E.	Cook	Co. D.	
McIntosh, Walter	Pvt.	Co. I.	
McJunkin, Charles	Pvt.	Co. D.	
McKee, Arnold C.	Pvt.	Co. A.	
McKee, George T.	Pvt.	M. G. Co.	
McKee, Samuel	Corp.	Co. I.	Wounded
McKeehan, John E.	Mess Sgt.	Supply Co.	
McKenna, Frank	Pvt.	Co. L.	
McKenzie, Leo L.	Pvt.	Co. A.	
McKeon, Thomas A.	Corp.	Co. D.	
McKeown, Owen Joseph	Corp.	Co. L.	
McKinley, James	Pvt.	Co. G.	
McKinley, Noah F.	Corp.	Co. D.	
McKinley, Reuben F.	Pvt.	M. G. Co.	
McKinley, Robert H.	Pvt.	Co. B.	Wounded
McKinney, Noah	Corp.	Co. E.	
McKinzie, Albert	Sgt.	Co. K.	
McKinzie, Leo Leonard	Pvt.	Co. A.	
McLaughlin, Charles R.	Pvt.	Co. L.	Gassed
McLaughlin, Donald H.	Pvt.	M. G. Co.	
McLaughlin, James E.	Pvt.	Co. M.	
McLayd, Lawrence E.	Pvt.	Hdqrs. Co.	
McMahen, Thomas H.	Pvt.	Co. F.	
McMahon, Joseph B.	Corp.	Co. F.	Gassed
McMillen, Clifford E.	Pvt.	Co. E.	
McMullen, John K.	Pvt.	M. G. Co.	
McMullon, John H.	Pvt.	Co. B.	Gassed
McNabb, Leon	Pvt.	Co. G.	
McNamee, Eugene J.	Pvt.	Co. G.	
McPherson, Lewis	Pvt.	Co. I.	
McQuone, Clark J.	Pvt.	Co. G.	
McRoberts, Emmett F.	Sgt.	Co. B.	Killed
McSwain, George M.	Pvt.	Hdqrs. Co.	
McWilliams, Louis F.	Pvt.	Co. E.	
Maberry, Olivert	Corp.	Co. E.	
Macatis, William	Pvt.	Co. I.	
Mace, John H.	Sup. Sgt.	Co. H.	Wounded
Mackay, Caleb	Wagoner	Supply Co.	
Macom, Clarence	Pvt.	Co. M.	
Maddox, Edgar D.	Pvt.	Co. G.	
Madsen, Frank	Pvt.	Co. M.	

Madsen, John C.	Sgt.	Co. D.	
Magdalena, Julius J.	Pvt.	Co. I.	Gassed
Mager, Walter C.	Pvt.	Co. B.	
Magrini, Armando	Pvt.	Co. G.	
Maham, Ray	Corp.	Co. C.	
Mahaney, Ernest C.	Pvt.	Co. A.	
Maher, James A.	Pvt.	Co. L.	
Mahieu, Arthur Philip	Pvt.	Co. L.	
Main, Harold H.	Pvt.	Co. F.	
Major, Duncan A.	Pvt.	M. G. Co.	
Males, Earl	Pvt.	San. Det.	Wounded
Maley, Samuel T.	Pvt.	Co. B.	Gassed
Mallard, Lonzo F.	Corp.	Co. I.	Gassed
Malone, Thomas	Pvt.	Supply Co.	
Maloney, John H.	Pvt.	Co. L.	
Malott, John	Pvt.	Co. B.	Wounded
Malott, Sylvanus	Pvt.	Co. B.	Wounded
Maloy, James	Pvt.	Co. D.	
Mandgold, Thomas	Corp.	Co. I.	Gassed
Maness, Henry M.	Corp.	Co. D.	Wounded, Died
Mangone, Pietro	Pvt.	Co. E.	
Mann, Fred G.	Pvt.	Co. A.	
Mann, George J.	Pvt.	Co. H.	
Mann, Howard H.	Pvt.	Co. C.	
Manners, Henry H.	Pvt.	Co. F.	
Manning, Charley F.	Pvt.	Supply Co.	
Manning, James	Pvt.	Co. L.	
Manning, William H.	Sup. Sgt.	Co. F.	Gassed
Mansuzak, Joe	Pvt.	Co. M.	
Maples, John F.	Corp.	Co. G.	Wounded
Marcellus, Mahlon G.	Sgt.	Co. F.	Gassed
March, John	Pvt.	San. Det.	
March, Thomas B.	Pvt.	Co. D.	
Marchant, Henry C.	Pvt.	Co. I.	
Marcum, Willie	Pvt.	Co. D.	
Maritata, Paola	Pvt.	Co. E.	
Markerson, Henry L.	Pvt.	Co. D.	
Marlen, John C.	Pvt.	Co. C.	
Marlin, Ellsworth L.	Pvt.	Co. A.	
Maroni, Ralphello	Pvt.	Co. K.	
Marono, Onopio	Pvt.	Co. M.	
Marousek, Frank J.	Pvt.	Co. L.	
Marsh, Ralph J.	Pvt.	Co. A.	
Marshall, Edward	Pvt.	Hdqrs. Co.	
Marshall, Herman H. P.	Pvt.	Hdqrs. Co.	
Martgan, Tad L.	Pvt.	M. G. Co.	
Martin, Alva E.	Pvt.	Co. I.	
Martin, Alva T.	Pvt.	Co. L.	
Martin, Benjamin A.	Pvt.	Co. H.	
Martin, Connie O.	Pvt.	Co. H.	
Martin, Henry J.	Bugler	Co. G.	
Martin, John J.	Pvt.	Co. L.	
Martin, Lee W.	Pvt.	M. G. Co.	Wounded
Martin, Luke	Pvt.	Co. D.	
Martin, Marshall	Pvt.	Co. I.	
Martin, Nick	Pvt.	Co. E.	
Martin, Orin A.	Sup. Sgt.	Co. D.	
Martin, Samuel E.	Corp.	Co. G.	
Martin, Theodore	Pvt.	Co. A.	
Martin, Thomas J.	Corp.	Co. E.	
Martin, William E.	Corp.	Co. D.	
Martinez, Silviano	Pvt.	Co. I.	
Mash, Archie C.	Pvt.	Co. I.	
Mason, Henry	Pvt.	Co. B.	

Mason, Jeptha H.	Pvt.	Co. D.	
Massey, John B.	Pvt.	Co. B.	
Massey, Tom	Pvt.	Co. K.	
Massey, William H.	Pvt.	Co. I.	
Masters, Jacob	Pvt.	Co. I.	Wounded
Matesich, Charles	Pvt.	Co. I.	
Matheny, Gardiner	Pvt.	Co. H.	
Mathews, Clarence J.	Corp.	Co. M.	Wounded
Mathews, Walter I.	Pvt.	Co. D.	Wounded
Mathis, James E.	Pvt.	Co. I.	
Matney, George	Pvt.	Co. E.	
Matson, Joe F.	Sgt.	Co. C.	Wounded
Mauk, Charley	Wagoner	Supply Co.	
Mauk, Claude	Wagoner	Supply Co.	
Mauk, Hiram	Wagoner	Supply Co.	
Mavis, William A.	Pvt.	Co. C.	Wounded
Maxwell, Roy E.	Pvt.	Hdqrs. Co.	
Mayabb, John R.	Pvt.	Co. D.	
Mayberry, Claude	Pvt.	Co. M.	Wounded
Mayberry, Robert	Pvt.	Co. H.	
Mayer, Frank T.	Pvt.	Co. L.	
Mays, Frank P.	Pvt.	Co. K.	
Maze, Luther C.	Pvt.	Co. A.	
Mead, Harvey	Pvt.	M. G. Co.	
Meade, Merril B.	Pvt.	Co. B.	
Meadows, John T.	Pvt.	Co. M.	
Meagher, Leo J.	Cook	Co. D.	Gassed
Meagher, Vincent M.	Sgt.	M. G. Co.	
Means, John C.	Pvt.	Co. F.	
Means, Oscar B.	Pvt.	Co. F.	
Meede, Alva	Pvt.	Co. I.	
Meeks, Cletis	Pvt.	Co. H.	
Mehlhaff, John J.	Pvt.	Co. L.	Wounded
Meistrell, John Henry	Pvt.	Co. M.	
Mellert, Willard	Pvt.	Co. A.	
Melnik, Frank	Pvt.	Co. B.	
Melton, Charles	Pvt.	Supply Co.	
Melton, Ira	Corp.	Hdqrs. Co.	
Melton, Jesse	Wagoner	Supply Co.	
Melvin, Harry L.	Pvt.	Co. A.	
Menconi, Abel	Pvt.	Co. G.	
Mercer, Claude S.	Pvt.	Co. I.	Wounded
Mercer, Wesley	Bugler	Co. K.	
Merchant, Myron	Pvt.	Co. B.	
Merendoni, Silvio	Pvt.	Co. G.	
Merriweather, George E.	Sgt.	Hdqrs. Co.	
Mersch, Charles R.	Pvt.	Co. K.	
Mesara, Thomas W.	Pvt.	San. Det.	Wounded
Mesaros, Frank	Corp.	Co. E.	
Messenger, Webb	Corp.	Co. B.	Wounded
Messer, Elmer	Pvt.	Co. B.	
Messmer, Albert	Pvt.	Co. L.	
Messner, John	Pvt.	Co. C.	
Metz, Adolph	Pvt.	Co. C.	
Metz, Carl M.	Musician	Hdqrs. Co.	
Meyer, Abraham	Pvt.	M. G. Co.	
Meyer, Henry	Wagoner	Co. L.	
Meyers, Clarence	Pvt.	Co. L.	
Michael, James	Corp.	Co. G.	Gassed
Michaelson, Bennie T.	Pvt.	Co. C.	
Micholski, Joe	Pvt.	Co. E.	
Mick, Arthur J.	Pvt.	Co. C.	
Mickles, Mike	Pvt.	Co. I.	
Michon, George V.	Pvt.	Co. G.	

Middleton, Charles K.	Pvt.	Co. G.	Gassed
Mikieta, Peter	Pvt.	Co. M.	
Mikley, William	Pvt.	Co. D.	
Mikula, Joseph L.	Pvt.	Co. D.	
Milam, Otis E.	Pvt.	Co. K.	Gassed
Milam, Plesa	Pvt.	Co. L.	
Miler, Isaac Roy	Pvt.	Co. L.	
Miles, George T.	Corp.	Co. B.	
Miles, Marshall L.	Pvt.	Co. G.	
Miller, Amon E.	Corp.	Hdqrs. Co.	
Miller, Carl A.	Corp.	Co. B.	Wounded
Miller, Charles	Corp.	Co. M.	Wounded
Miller, Clinton	Corp.	Co. B.	Wounded
Miller, Clyde E.	Pvt.	Co. F.	Gassed
Miller, Emil J.	Pvt.	Co. A.	
Miller, Frank B.	Pvt.	Co. A.	
Miller, George D.	Pvt.	Hdqrs. Co.	
Miller, Herbert F.	Pvt.	M. G. Co.	
Miller, James Thadeus	Pvt.	Co. A.	
Miller, Joseph W.	Pvt.	Co. B.	Gassed
Miller, Leo L.	Pvt.	Co. M.	
Miller, Lewis	Corp.	Co. E.	
Miller, Lewis R.	Pvt.	Co. C.	
Miller, Robert	Corp.	Co. B.	Gassed
Miller, Rufus	Corp.	Co. H.	
Miller, Steve	Pvt.	Co. D.	
Milliken, Ralph R.	Pvt.	Co. A.	
Mills, Charlie	Corp.	Co. M.	
Mills, Fred J.	Pvt.	Co. C.	
Mills, Jesse R.	Pvt.	Co. E.	
Mills, Walter W.	Saddler	M. G. Co.	
Mills, William L.	Pvt.	Co. I.	Gassed
Millsap, William O.	Pvt.	Co. E.	
Milner, Bernice	Corp.	Co. H.	
Mingus, Ephriam L.	Pvt.	Ord. Dept.	
Mingus, Lester	Pvt.	Ord. Dept.	
Minker, Edward	Corp.	Co. C.	
Mires, Louis T.	Pvt.	Co. F.	
Mirrell, Peter V.	Pvt.	Co. L.	
Mirth, Andrew W.	Pvt.	Co. G.	
Miscncik, John	Pvt.	Co. C.	
Mishler, Lonzo L.	Pvt.	Co. M.	
Misun, John	Pvt.	Co. E.	
Mitchell, Clarence V.	Pvt.	Co. G.	
Mitchell, Jake G.	Pvt.	Co. I.	Wounded
Mitchell, John K.	Corp.	Co. C.	Wounded
Mitchmore, John L.	Cook	Co. I.	
Mobberly, James F.	Pvt.	Co. A.	
Moberly, William H.	Pvt.	Co. D.	Wounded
Mock, Carl W.	Pvt.	Co. B.	
Mock, Joseph W.	Pvt.	Co. B.	
Mode, William J.	Sup. Sgt.	Co. K.	
Modglin, Lyndolph	Pvt.	Co. K.	Wounded
Moeckel, Fred P.	Pvt.	Co. D.	Wounded
Moehenbrink, Carl Henry	Pvt.	Co. M.	
Moffitt, Henry	Pvt.	Co. F.	
Moilnen, John C.	Pvt.	Co. C.	
Mojzis, Frank J.	Pvt.	Co. K.	
Moldahl, Ole	Pvt.	Co. I.	Wounded
Monroe, Harrold R.	Pvt.	Co. C.	Wounded
Monroe, Herschel	Pvt.	Co. K.	
Montague, Benjamin F.	Pvt.	Co. M.	Wounded
Montcalm, Ravel S.	Corp.	Co. A.	
Montgomery, Clarence J.	Pvt.	M. G. Co.	

THE MEN BEHIND THE GUNS

Montgomery, Elisha A.	Pvt.	M. G. Co.	Wounded
Montineo, Flameno	Pvt.	Co. I.	
Moody, Dave M.	Pvt.	Co. D.	
Moody, Harry L.	Corp.	Co. F.	
Moon, William W.	Pvt.	Co. E.	
Moon, Charles H.	Cook	Co. E.	
Moore, Calvin	Sgt.	Co. B.	
Moore, Clay	Pvt.	Co. H.	
Moore, Earl	Pvt.	Co. G.	
Moore, Edward A.	Pvt.	Co. G.	
Moore, James A.	Sgt.	Co. E.	
Moore, James B.	Pvt.	Co. I.	
Moore, Kemper	Corp.	Co. B.	
Moore, LeRoy	Pvt.	Co. B.	Wounded
Moore, Pearl	Pvt.	Co. I.	
Moore, Robert A.	Pvt.	M. G. Co.	Wounded
Moore, Roy D.	Pvt.	Co. H.	Wounded
Moore, Samuel J.	Pvt.	Co. C.	
Moore, Scott H.	Pvt.	Co. G.	
Moore, Tad	Pvt.	Co. L.	
Moore, William A.	Pvt.	Co. K.	
Moorman, Russell S.	Corp.	Co. D.	Gassed
Moos, Gottlieb	Pvt.	Co. L.	
Morehead, Charles A.	Pvt.	Co. G.	Gassed
Morehouse, Robert E.	Pvt.	Co. M.	
Morgan, Albert	Pvt.	Co. I.	
Morgan, Fred K.	Pvt.	Co. L.	
Moriarity, Donald F.	Pvt.	San. Det.	
Moriarty, Will T.	Pvt.	Co. I.	
Morolf, Louie	Pvt.	Co. L.	
Morrell, Elbert	Pvt.	Co. L.	
Morris, Arthur	Pvt.	Co. C.	Wounded
Morris, Glen B.	Corp.	Co. C.	
Morris, Roscoe L.	Pvt.	Ord. Dept.	
Morris, William C.	Corp.	Co. H.	
Morse, Harry	Corp.	Co. I.	Wounded
Morse, Ira L.	Sgt.	Co. A.	Wounded
Morse, Lee	Pvt.	Co. G.	
Morton, Virgil Franklin	Pvt.	Hdqrs. Co.	
Morterano, Frank	Sgt.	Co. C.	
Mossman, Eugene L.	Pvt.	Co. M.	Wounded
Mott, Marvin	Pvt.	Co. L.	
Mounce, Charles S.	Pvt.	Co. E.	
Mount, Eugene V.	Cook	Co. C.	
Mount, Ross	Pvt.	Co. G.	
Moxon, Theo. R.	Pvt.	Co. A.	
Moyer, Allen B.	Pvt.	Co. G.	
Mueller, Louis	Pvt.	Co. L.	
Mueller, Ralph E.	Pvt.	San. Det.	
Mullikin, Elmer	Corp.	Co. G.	Gassed
Mullineaux, Joseph A.	Sgt.	Co. D.	
Mullins, Clarence	Pvt.	Co. I.	
Mullins, Kelly	Corp.	Co. I.	
Muncy, Claude L.	Pvt.	Co. B.	
Munden, Louis E.	Corp.	Co. B.	Killed
Mundorf, Quincy E.	Pvt.	Co. C.	
Munger, Earl L.	Sgt.	Co. G.	
Munsill, Alexander P.	Pvt.	Co. E.	
Muntz, Louis A.	Pvt.	Co. G.	
Murphy, Fred	Bugler	Co. L.	
Murphy, John J.	Sgt.	Hdqrs. Co.	
Murphy, Riley W.	Corp.	Co. B.	
Murphy, William J.	Pvt.	Co. G.	
Murray, George	Pvt.	Co. E.	

Murray, John R.	Corp.	Co. B.	
Murray, L. C.	Corp.	Co. K.	
Murrell, Mc F.	Corp.	Co. F.	
Musick, John, Jr.	Pvt.	Co. L.	
Mussatto, Joseph A.	Pvt.	Co. A.	
Muxlow, Glenn D.	Pvt.	Co. F.	
Myers, Albert	Pvt.	Co. B.	Gassed
Myers, Henry L.	Pvt.	Co. G.	
Myers, Jesse	Pvt.	Co. L.	
Myers, John P.	Pvt.	Co. L.	
Myers, Joseph A.	Pvt.	Hdqrs. Co.	
Myers, Roy J.	Sgt.	Co. F.	
Myers, Worthy C.	Pvt.	Co. G.	
Myhran, Gustave E.	Pvt.	Co. M.	
Myhre, Olaf E.	Pvt.	Co. M.	
Mystowski, Stanislaw	Pvt.	Co. E.	
Nachbor, Walter G.	Corp.	Co. I.	Gassed
Nacsa, Louis	Sgt.	Co. E.	
Nall, Roly P.	Pvt.	Co. L.	
Nance, Obb E.	Pvt.	Co. C.	
Narlsun, Casper	Pvt.	Co. E.	
Nash, Charles S.	Pvt.	Co. K.	
Naska, Levi	Pvt.	Co. E.	
Neal, Arthur C.	Pvt.	Co. G.	
Neal, Roma P.	Pvt.	Co. E.	
Neale, Marshall D.	Wagoner	Supply Co.	
Neale, Virgil C.	Pvt.	Hdqrs. Co.	
Needles, Clifford C.	Pvt.	Co. F.	
Needles, Ralph E.	Corp.	Co. G.	
Neff, Jesse	Pvt.	Hdqrs. Co.	
Neff, Leol M.	Pvt.	Hdqrs. Co.	
Neff, Louis	Pvt.	Co. B.	
Neher, Ludwig	Pvt.	Co. M.	Wounded
Neighbors, William E.	Cook	Co. H.	
Neilson, Herman	Pvt.	Co. L.	
Nelson, Adler	Pvt.	Co. H.	
Nelson, Allen L.	Pvt.	Co. C.	
Nelson, Charles W.	Pvt.	Co. M.	Wounded
Nelson, Charles P.	Pvt.	Co. H.	
Nelson, Edwin O.	Pvt.	Co. H.	
Nelson, Frank C.	Pvt.	M. G. Co.	Wounded
Nelson, Gus	Pvt.	San. Det.	
Nelson, Henry A.	Pvt.	Co. M.	Wounded
Nelson, John B.	Pvt.	Co. B.	
Nelson, Morris	Pvt.	Co. F.	
Nelson, Oscar W.	Pvt.	Co. M.	
Nelson, Sture	Pvt.	Co. M.	
Nerlien, Oscar A.	Pvt.	Co. M.	Wounded
Neves, Albert L.	Pvt.	M. G. Co.	
Nevins, William J.	Sgt.	Co. L.	
Newby, Milton	Mechanic	Co. L.	
Newell, Frank A.	Pvt.	Co. C.	
Newell, Jerimiah	Pvt.	Co. M.	
Newlin, Lyle E.	Cook	Co. L.	
Newman, Floyd	Pvt.	Co. L.	
Newman, Willie A.	Pvt.	Co. M.	
Newton, Joseph R.	Corp	Co. D.	
Nichol, Arthur P.	Corp	Co. L.	
Nichols, Audie E.	Pvt.	Co. G.	
Nichols, Ronald Edward	Pvt.	Hdqrs. Co.	
Nicholson, Ernest	Mechanic	M. G. Co.	
Nickel, Adam	Corp.	Co. L.	
Nickelson, Marcus C.	Pvt.	Co. E.	
Niehaus, Joseph W.	Pvt.	Co. D.	

THE MEN BEHIND THE GUNS 193

Nieman, Samuel	Pvt.	Co. D.	
Niemet, Lawrence J.	Pvt.	Co. I.	
Nienow, Walter T.	Pvt.	Co. B.	Wounded
Niess, Herman	Pvt.	Co. F.	
Niewiedomski, Stephen	Pvt.	Co. I.	
Niles, LeRoy	Corp	Co. A.	Wounded
Niszczak, Stanley W.	Pvt.	Co. G.	
Nitchals, Harry E.	Bugler	Co. E.	
Nitx, August	Pvt.	Co. B.	
Nixon, Bearl	Pvt.	Co. C.	
Nixon, Frederick H.	Pvt.	Co. B.	
Noblitt, Thomas E.	Corp	Co. F.	Wounded
Noe, Erie	Pvt.	Co. I.	Gassed
Noffzinger, Ernest E.	Cook	Co. G.	
Noke, Oscar	Pvt.	Co. C.	
Nolan, Walter J.	Pvt.	Co. M.	
Nooe, Willie M.	Sgt.	Co. A.	
Norby, John J.	Pvt.	Co. E.	
Norby, George P.	Pvt.	Co. F.	Gassed
Norman, Elmer M.	Pvt.	Co. L.	Wounded
Norris, Cecil L.	Corp	Co. F.	
Norris, Fred	Pvt.	Co. L.	
Norris, Otis G.	Pvt.	Co. A.	
Norris, Wallace	Pvt.	Co. K.	
Norris, William	Pvt.	Co. M.	Wounded
North, Ralph O.	Pvt.	Co. C.	
North, William G.	Pvt.	Co. H.	
Northcott, Joe	Pvt.	Co. G.	
Norville, Ollie	Pvt.	Co. I.	
Norwood, Joe F.	Corp.	Co. C.	
Notbohm, Fredrick J.	Pvt.	Co. G.	
Novak, Joseph	Pvt.	Co. K.	
Nylund, Fred	Pvt.	Co. D.	
Oakley, Thomas L.	Pvt.	Co. I.	
Oaks, Charles E.	Pvt.	Co. I.	
O'Brien, Martin J.	Pvt.	Co. M.	Wounded
O'Connell, Denis M.	Corp.	Co. M.	
O'Connor, James A.	Pvt.	Co. B.	
O'Connor, Richard J.	Sgt.	Co. C.	
O'Connor, William D.	Mechanic	Co. F.	
O'Day, William J.	Pvt.	Co. L.	
O'Dell, Raymond	Corp.	Co. K.	
O'Dell, William T.	Pvt.	Co. C.	Gassed
Odland, Ben C.	Pvt.	Co. M.	
Odom, Walter E.	Corp.	Hdqrs. Co.	
Oesterreich, Milton E.	Corp.	Co. L.	
Ogelvie, George	Pvt.	Co. H.	
O'Hara, Sidney	Pvt.	M. G. Co.	
Oldham, Earom T.	Wagoner	Supply Co.	
Olive, John W.	Pvt.	Co. F.	
Oliver, Benjamin F.	Pvt.	Co. D.	
Oliver, Carl E.	Pvt.	Co. M.	
Oliver, Clarence P.	Sgt.	Co. H.	Wounded
Oliver, Clifford C.	Pvt.	Co. B.	
Oliver, Henry K.	Cook	Co. A.	Wounded
Oliver, Kamp	Sgt.	Co. L.	
Olney, Howard R.	Mess Sgt.	Co. A.	
Olsen, Benjamine	Wagoner	Supply Co.	
Olson, Arthur G.	Pvt.	Co. M.	
Olson, Carl F.	Pvt.	Co. D.	Wounded
Olson, Elmer Gustaf	Pvt.	Co. I.	Wounded
Olson, Oliver E.	Pvt.	Co. G.	
Olszweski, Joseph	Pvt.	Hdqrs. Co.	
O'Mara, James A.	Pvt.	Co. E.	

O'Neal, Gordon	Pvt.	Co. K.	
Oneal, Henry I.	Pvt.	Co. L.	
O'Neal, William A.	Mechanic	Co. G.	Gassed
O'Neil, Jesse	Mechanic	Co. M.	
O'Neill, Clinton	Pvt.	Co. E.	
O'Reilly, Peter	Pvt.	Co. A.	
Ormsbee, Earl D.	Pvt.	Co. M.	Wounded
O'Rourke, Walter R.	Sgt.	Co. A.	
Orr, James R.	Wagoner	Co. F.	
Orseth, James R. A.	Pvt.	Co. M.	
Ortell, Earl	Sgt.	Co. K.	
Orton, Theodore R.	Pvt.	Co. C.	
Osborn, Earl	Pvt.	Co. B.	Died
Osborn, Millard	Pvt.	Co. C.	
Osborne, Preston E.	Pvt.	Hdqrs. Co.	
Osbourne, Walter G.	Pvt.	Co. D.	Wounded
Osford, William	Pvt.	Co. L.	
Osiier, William Jos.	Sup. Sgt	Supply Co.	
Oslie, Palmer M.	Corp.	Co. M.	Wounded
Oswald, Claude	Pvt.	Co. M.	
Oswald, Frank	Pvt.	Co. E.	
Oswald, Walker	Sgt.	Co. B.	
Ottolino, Pasquale	Pvt.	Hdqrs. Co.	
Overman, Benjamine H.	Pvt.	Hdqrs. Co.	
Owens, Clarence	Pvt.	Co. H.	Gassed
Owens, Dewey	Pvt.	Co. M.	
Owen, James M.	Mechanic	Co. M.	
Owens, Howell	Pvt.	Co. M.	Wounded
Owen, Robert S.	Pvt.	M. G. Co.	Wounded
Owens, William M.	Pvt.	Co. K.	
Oxford, William E.	Corp.	Co. L.	Wounded
Packard, Ernest A.	Wagoner	Supply Co.	
Paden, William C.	Corp.	Co. B.	Wounded
Page, Frank	Wagoner	Supply Co.	
Page, John G.	Bugler	Co. C.	
Page, Russell	Corp.	Co. E.	
Palarpa, Jonas	Pvt.	Supply Co.	
Palladini, Cataldo	Pvt.	Co. D.	Wounded
Palmer, Charles H.	Corp.	Supply Co.	
Pannozzo, Vincenzo	Pvt.	Co. E.	
Papas, Gregory	Pvt.	Co. L.	
Parker, Arthur B.	Pvt.	Co. C.	Wounded
Parker, Claude C.	Pvt.	Co. B.	
Parker, Fred H.	Pvt.	Co. K.	Wounded
Parker, Harold M.	Pvt.	Co. G.	Wounded
Parker, Sherley	Pvt.	Co. F.	
Parker, William A.	Pvt.	Co. B.	
Parkerson, James	Pvt.	Co. I.	
Parres, Ralph A.	Pvt.	Co. E.	
Parrish, Lawrence L.	Musician	Hdqrs. Co.	
Parsley, Tom	Pvt.	Co. G.	
Parson, General F.	Pvt.	Co. M.	
Parson, Jesse E.	Pvt.	Co. K.	
Parsons, Archie L.	Pvt.	Co. F.	
Parsons, Ray W.	Pvt.	Co. L.	
Partee, Raymond	Pvt.	Co. B.	Wounded
Partick, Will L.	Pvt.	Co. L.	
Paschall, Clarence	Pvt.	Co. I.	
Paskrich, John J.	Sgt.	Co. M.	Wounded
Patell, Keke	Pvt.	Co. L.	
Patrick, George W.	Pvt.	Co. M.	
Patrick, Lloyd	Pvt.	Supply Co.	
Patrick, Oary	Pvt.	Co. F.	
Patrick, William R.	Corp.	Co. A.	

THE MEN BEHIND THE GUNS 195

Patten, Ora	Pvt.	Co. B.	Gassed
Patterson, Carl Filmore	Pvt.	Co. M.	
Patterson, John T.	Corp.	Co. A.	
Paul, John B.	Sgt.	Co. E.	
Paxton, Roy I.	Pvt.	Hdqrs. Co.	
Payne, Claud	Pvt.	M. G. Co.	
Payne, Elza C.	Pvt.	San. Det.	
Payne, Frank	Wagoner	Supply Co.	
Payne, Hugh C.	Pvt.	Co. D.	Killed
Payne, John H.	Pvt.	Hdqrs. Co.	
Paysinger, Johnnie	Pvt.	Co. G.	
Peacock, Vernon A.	Pvt.	M. G. Co.	
Pearson, Emil R.	Pvt.	Co. K.	
Peavy, Curtis	Corp.	Co. H.	Wounded
Pederson, Bennie	Pvt.	Co. M.	
Pedigo, Clifford B.	Pvt.	Hdqrs. Co.	
Peebles, Carl T.	Cook	Co. A.	
Peeples, Phillip	Corp.	Co. B.	
Peery, Earl H.	Sgt.	Hdqrs. Co.	
Peery, Thomas R.	Corp.	M. G. Co.	
Peiker, Walter L.	Cook	Hdqrs. Co.	
Pekarek, Otto C.	Bugler	Hdqrs. Co.	
Pelton, Fred N.	Sgt.	Co. G.	Wounded
Pemberton, Tom C.	Corp.	Co. E.	
Penninger, David M.	Pvt.	Hdqrs. Co.	
Pennington, Lee	Pvt.	Co. L.	
Penniston, John E.	Sgt.	Co. F.	
Penrod, Cecil R.	Sgt.	Co. K.	Wounded
Perkins, Abraham	Corp.	Co. I.	Gassed
Perkins, Charley	Corp.	Co. G.	
Perkins, Leo	Pvt.	Co. H.	
Perkinson, James C.	Pvt.	Co. I.	
Perrin, Alfred K.	Pvt.	Co. B.	
Perry, Harry O.	Pvt.	Co. E.	
Perry, Wayne	Pvt.	Co. B.	
Perry, William H.	Pvt.	Co. L.	
Perrydore, Noah F.	Pvt.	Co. G.	
Perterson, Lloyd F.	Pvt.	Co. H.	
Pertl, Lawrence H.	Pvt.	Co. G.	
Peters, Aaron B.	Pvt.	Co. E.	
Peters, John L.	Corp.	Co. E.	Wounded
Peters, William L.	Pvt.	Co. E.	Wounded
Petersen, Peter A.	Pvt.	M. G. Co.	
Peterson, Andrew C.	Sup. Sgt.	Co. E.	Gassed
Peterson, Arthur	Pvt.	Hdqrs. Co.	
Peterson, Carl T.	Pvt.	Hdqrs. Co.	
Peterson, Elmer A.	Pvt.	Co. L.	
Peterson, Gust A.	Cook	Co. H.	
Peterson, Henry	Mechanic	Co. D.	
Peterson, Herman Henry	Pvt.	Co. M.	
Peterson, Oscar B.	Pvt.	Co. C.	
Peterson, Walford G.	Corp.	Co. C.	
Peterson, Wilhelm	Cook	Co. D.	Killed
Petko, Peter J.	Pvt.	Co. F.	
Pettit, Claude C.	Pvt.	Co. H.	
Petty, George W.	Mechanic	Co. A.	
Petty, Roy L.	Pvt.	Co. L.	Wounded
Pfaff, George L.	Pvt.	Co. G.	Wounded
Pfeiffer, David H.	Sgt.	Co. B.	Wounded
Phelps, Edgar	Pvt.	Co. I.	
Phillips, Allenson	Pvt.	Co. H.	Gassed
Phillips, Charley E.	Corp.	Co. B.	
Phillips, George B.	Pvt.	Co. M.	
Phillips, James L.	Sgt.	Co. F.	

Phillips, Roy A.	Pvt.	Hdqrs. Co.	
Phillips, Stone	Pvt.	Co. I.	Wounded
Phillips, William H.	Corp.	Co. D.	
Phillips, Vera	Pvt.	Co. M.	Wounded
Philpott, Paul P.	Corp.	Co. A.	
Piatt, Jilson	Pvt.	Co. M.	Wounded
Picard, Harry L.	Pvt.	Co. G.	Wounded
Pickens, Harry S.	Corp.	Co. E.	
Piel, Frank B.	Pvt.	Co. L.	
Pierce, Albert Z.	Pvt.	Co. C.	
Pierce, Harry	Pvt.	Co. C.	
Pierce, Lonnie F.	Cook	Co. L.	
Pierce, Yancey	Pvt.	Co. K.	
Pierson, Charles G.	Wagoner	Supply Co.	
Piggett, Lynn	Pvt.	Co. I.	
Pinnick, Edward	Pvt.	Co. A.	
Pipes, Charles	Pvt.	Co. B.	
Pipkin, Sidney	Pvt.	Co. M.	
Pippin, Rush T.	Pvt.	Co. L.	
Playford, George I.	Pvt.	Co. K.	Killed
Pleasants, Olin B.	Pvt.	Hdqrs. Co.	
Plummer, Edward B.	Pvt.	Co. F.	
Poage, Russell E.	Pvt.	San. Det.	
Poeschl, Mike	Pvt.	Co. E.	
Poindexter, John K.	Corp.	Supply Co.	
Pointer, Josiah	Pvt.	Co. D.	
Polen, Melvin A.	Pvt.	Co. B.	
Pollack, Henry W.	Pvt.	Co. F.	
Pollard, Claude L.	Stable Sgt.	Supply Co.	
Pond, Ira R. G. A.	Pvt.	Co. G.	
Ponder, Chester H.	Sgt.	Co. E.	
Ponder, William F.	Sgt.	Co. E.	
Pontius, Arthur G.	Sgt.	Co. B.	
Poolini, Joe	Pvt.	Co. H.	
Poorman, Oliver F.	Pvt.	Co. B.	
Pope, William R.	Pvt.	Co. G.	
Popenhagen, George W.	Pvt.	Hdqrs. Co.	
Porter, Clarence R.	Pvt.	Co. C.	Wounded
Porter, Edward C.	Mechanic	Co. B.	Gassed
Porter, Ernest H.	Pvt.	Co. C.	Wounded
Porter, Leo D.	Pvt.	Co. G.	
Portwood, Thomas L.	Corp.	Co. H.	
Posey, Henry E.	Pvt.	Co. F.	
Posh, Phillip H.	Corp.	Co. L.	Wounded
Poteet, Clifford	Sgt.	Co. D.	
Pothetus, George	Pvt.	Co. E.	Wounded
Pottebaum, George S.	Pvt.	Co. E.	
Potter, Clayton E.	Wagoner	Supply Co.	
Potter, Ray L.	Pvt.	Co. H.	
Potter, Robert O.	Pvt.	Co. F.	
Potter, Sidney A.	Pvt.	Co. H.	
Pottle, Ralph R.	Pvt.	San. Det.	
Potts, George W.	Corp.	Co. F.	
Potts, John J.	Wagoner	Supply Co.	
Pouncey, Aubrey H.	Pvt.	Co. H.	
Powell, Charlie G.	Pvt.	Co. K.	
Powell, Don	Pvt.	Co. M.	
Powell, John W.	Pvt.	Co. A.	Wounded
Powers, Ray	Wagoner	Supply Co.	
Prance, Joseph W.	Pvt.	Co. L.	Wounded
Prater, Thomas	Corp.	Co. B.	Gassed
Prather, Clifford	Pvt.	Co. E.	
Prati, Henry	Musician	Hdqrs. Co.	
Pratt, Hiram	Corp.	Co. B.	Gassed

THE MEN BEHIND THE GUNS 197

Presley, Lawrence H.	Pvt.	Co. A.	
Price, Fred G.	Pvt.	Co. A.	Wounded
Price, Roy	Pvt.	Co. G.	
Prickel, Edward A.	Pvt.	Co. C.	
Pride, Jack S.	Sgt.	Co. L.	
Prigge, Arthur J.	Corp.	Co. A.	
Prisley, Lawrence H.	Pvt.	Co. A.	
Prisock, John A.	Pvt.	Co. F.	
Pritchard, Earl J.	Sgt.	Co. G.	
Pritchett, Henry O.	Pvt.	Co. G.	
Pruce, Emil C.	Pvt.	Co. C.	
Pruett, John W.	Pvt.	Co. B.	
Pruitt, Moses S.	Cook	Co. D.	
Prunty, James A.	Pvt.	Co. G.	
Pryor, Alvin L.	Corp.	Co. H.	Wounded
Puchbauer, Arthur	Corp.	Co. L.	Wounded
Pulley, Homer	Corp.	Co. C.	
Pulliam, William Franklin	Pvt.	Co. M.	
Pummell, Theadford W.	Pvt.	Co. D.	
Pummerl, Walter	Corp.	Co. D.	
Purcell, Dewey T.	Sgt.	Co. I.	
Purcell, Gregory E.	Cook	Co. H.	
Purdin, John A.	Corp.	Co. D.	
Purrine, Hallie	Cook	Co. M.	
Pursley, Thomas S.	Bugler	Co. D.	
Puttroff, Archie L.	Corp.	Co. M.	Wounded
Pypes, Delos E.	Sgt.	Co. C.	Wounded
Pytleski, Tony	Pvt.	Co. C.	Wounded
Quathamer, Gerard J.	Pvt.	Co. L.	
Queen, Ralph C.	Pvt.	Co. C.	
Quick, Grover C.	Pvt.	Co. A.	
Quinn, Willie Green	Pvt.	Co. H.	
Rabun, William F.	Pvt.	Co. F.	
Raburn, Henry H.	Pvt.	Co. C.	
Radz, Walter J.	Bugler	Co. G.	Wounded
Rafferty, George F.	Pvt.	Co. M.	
Rains, Virgile L.	Corp.	Co. C.	
Raischel, Blas	Pvt.	Co. I.	
Raker, Charley	Pvt.	Co. F.	
Rakoff, Max	Pvt.	Co. M.	
Raley, James D.	Pvt.	Co. E.	Wounded
Ralph, Earnest	Pvt.	Co. F.	
Ramsey, John	Mechanic	Co. H.	
Ramsey, Leo C.	Pvt.	Co. C.	Gassed
Randall, Perry L.	Pvt.	Co. B.	
Randolph, Robert	Pvt.	Co. I.	
Rasmussen, Arthur C.	Mechanic	Co. K.	
Ratcliffe, Agustus W.	Pvt.	Co. L.	
Rath, Henry	Pvt.	Co. L.	
Raulsten, Noble G.	Pvt.	Co. D.	Wounded
Raulston, Athel A.	Sgt.	Co. M.	Wounded
Ray, Chancey W.	Pvt.	Co. M.	
Ray, Charles P.	Sgt.	Co. A.	
Ray, Guy B.	Corp.	Co. I.	
Ray, Vernon	Pvt.	Co. H.	
Reagan, James B.	Mechanic	Co. H.	
Reasons, James B.	Pvt.	Co. M.	
Rebori, Ralph A.	Pvt.	Co. L	Gassed
Redd, William M.	Pvt.	Hdqrs. Co.	
Redden, William H.	Pvt.	Co. E.	Wounded
Reddy, William E.	Pvt.	Co. A.	
Redmond, Raymond C.	Pvt.	Co. B.	Wounded and Gassed

Name	Rank	Unit	Status
Reed, Cam G.	Pvt.	Co. L.	
Reed, Charles W.	Pvt.	Co. F.	
Reed, Clarence S.	Pvt.	Co. G.	
Reed, John O.	Pvt.	Supply Co.	
Reed, Paul W.	Pvt.	Co. E.	
Reed, Orvil O.	Pvt.	Co. F.	
Reed, Walter	Pvt.	Co. I.	
Reese, Lewis E.	Pvt.	Co. C.	
Reese, Vernon	Corp.	Co. I.	
Reeves, Ernest C.	Corp.	Co. K.	
Reeves, Roscoe	Pvt.	Co. L.	
Reeves, William O.	Pvt.	Co. I.	
Reeves, Walter A.	Pvt.	Co. B.	
Regan, Howard	Pvt.	Co. H.	
Rebori, Ralph	Pvt.	Co. L.	
Reichers, William J.	Pvt.	Hdqrs. Co.	
Reid, William J.	Pvt.	Co. G.	Wounded
Reily, William T.	Pvt.	Hdqrs. Co.	
Reiser, Fred L.	Pvt.	Co. G.	
Remus, Fred E.	Pvt.	Co. A.	Wounded
Reneau, Robert L.	Pvt.	Co. H.	Wounded
Renfro, Dallas T.	Pvt.	Co. D.	
Renfrow, Robert C.	Pvt.	Co. B.	Wounded
Rennekamp, Alfred H.	Pvt.	Go. G.	
Resener, Robert L.	Pvt.	Co. M.	
Reyman, Lee E.	Pvt.	Co. D.	
Reynolds, Otto L.	Pvt.	Co. E.	
Reynolds, Wesley R.	Pvt.	Co. E.	
Rhoades, John F.	Pvt.	Co. C.	
Rhodes, Virgil	Wagoner	Supply Co.	
Rhodes, Walter W.	Pvt.	Co. M.	Wounded
Rice, Coke S.	Sgt.	Co. M.	Wounded
Rice, James N.	Cook	Co. A.	
Rice, Joe L.	Pvt.	Co. H.	
Rice, Orb	Pvt.	Co. M.	
Rice, Roy L.	Pvt.	Co. D.	
Rice, Thomas E.	Pvt.	Co. C.	
Rich, Hosea	Pvt.	Co. G.	
Richards, Homer Crocket	Pvt.	Hdqrs. Co.	Wounded
Richardson, George E.	Pvt.	Co. E.	
Richardson, James M.	Pvt.	Co. F.	
Richardson, Leo	Mechanic	Co. D.	
Richardson, Orvel	Corp.	Co. K.	
Richardson, Oscar E.	Wagoner	Supply Co.	
Richardson, Samuel	Pvt.	Co. G.	
Richmond, Fred C.	Corp.	Co. E.	
Richwine, Ernest	Pvt.	Co. M.	Wounded
Rickert, Otto O.	Pvt.	Co. D.	
Rickman, Poley	Pvt.	Co. M.	
Ricks, Ora R.	Corp.	Co. A.	Wounded
Ricks, Ray A.	Pvt.	Co. A.	Wounded
Rider, Arthur	Pvt.	Co. C.	
Ridgel, Howard L.	Pvt.	Co. C.	
Rieder, Aloysius	Pvt.	Co. A.	
Riegal, Oscar E.	Pvt.	Co. D.	
Rife, Paul	Pvt.	Co. M.	
Rigert, Ignatius J.	Pvt.	Co. A.	
Riggins, Spencer	Wagoner	Supply Co.	
Riggs, Chester A.	Pvt.	Co. B.	
Riggs, Oscar B.	Cook	Co. D.	
Rigley, Floyd H.	Corp.	Co. H.	
Rigley, Harry E.	Sgt.	Co. H.	
Rigsby, Phillip	Pvt.	Co. H.	
Riles, William O.	Pvt.	Co. H.	

THE MEN BEHIND THE GUNS

Riley, Claude	Pvt.	Co. H.	
Riley, Eddie E.	Pvt.	Co. L.	
Riley, John L.	Pvt.	San. Det.	
Riley, John W.	Pvt.	San. Det.	
Riley, Robert J.	Pvt.	Co. A.	
Rippy, Edgar O.	Pvt.	Co. A.	
Risgaard, Narve	Pvt.	Co. G.	
Risinger, Ralph	Corp.	Co. M.	
Rist, Blake L.	Pvt.	Co. E.	
Ritonda, Salvatore	Pvt.	Co. K.	
Rittenhouse, Frank A.	Corp.	Co. F.	
Ritter, Ray W.	Corp.	Co. B.	Missing
Ritter, Roy H.	Pvt.	Co. D.	
Roark, Grover A.	Pvt.	Co. E.	Wounded
Robb, Clifford H.	Pvt.	Co. L.	
Roberson, John G.	Sgt.	Co. H.	
Roberts, Andrew H.	Sgt.	Co. C.	
Roberts, Coin	Pvt.	Co. B.	
Roberts, David E.	Pvt.	Co. C.	
Roberts, Jesse	Pvt.	Co. B.	
Roberts, John R.	Corp.	Co. M.	
Roberts, Marshall B.	Pvt.	Co. L.	
Roberts, Milton J.	Cook	Co. A.	
Robertson, Elmer B.	Pvt.	Co. L.	Wounded
Robertson, Page D.	Pvt.	San. Det.	
Robertson, William F.	Pvt.	Co. M.	Wounded
Robinson, Albert E.	Pvt.	Co. K.	
Robinson, Arthur W.	Pvt.	Hdqrs. Co.	
Robinson, Clarence V.	Pvt.	Co. D.	Wounded
Robinson, Ernest L.	Pvt.	Co. M.	Wounded
Robinson, Guy	Pvt.	Co. C.	
Robinson, Homer D.	Pvt.	Co. D.	Gassed
Robinson, Patrick H.	Sgt.	Co. D.	
Robinson, Phillip	Pvt.	Co. B.	
Robinson, Rush K.	Pvt.	Co. F.	
Robinson, William	Sgt.	Co. I.	
Robinson, William L.	Corp.	Co. D.	
Robison, Wayne H.	Bugler	Co. B.	Gassed
Rodewald, Howard G.	Pvt.	Co. C.	
Rodenberg, Benjamin	Pvt.	Co. B.	
Rodewald, Howard C.	Pvt.	Co. C.	
Rodgers, Hooper H.	Pvt.	Co. L.	
Roe, Williams J.	Wagoner	Supply Co.	
Roebuck, Matthew	Cook	Co. E.	
Rogell, Herman	Pvt.	Co. G.	Wounded
Rogers, Charles G.	Pvt.	Co. C.	
Rogers, George H.	Pvt.	Co. G.	
Rogers, Guy G.	Mess Sgt.	Co. I.	
Rogers, Harry	Pvt.	Co. E.	
Rogers, James M.	Pvt.	Co. D.	
Rogers, Ralph J.	Sgt.	Co. A.	Wounded
Rogers, William	Pvt.	Co. D.	
Rogers, William R.	Pvt.	Co. G.	
Roistacher, Louis	Pvt.	San. Det.	
Roland, Truman	Pvt.	Co. M.	
Rold, Howard C.	Pvt.	Co. G.	
Rolli, Heman O.	Pvt.	Co. H.	
Romick, John Henry	Pvt.	Hdqrs. Co.	Wounded
Rooney, Daniel	Pvt.	M. G. Co.	
Roper, Add	Pvt.	Co. F.	
Roper, Clay M.	Corp.	Co. C.	
Ropp, Chester A.	Corp.	M. G. Co.	
Rorabough, Ralph L.	Pvt.	Co. B.	
Rose, William R.	Pvt.	Co. M.	Wounded

Roseberry, Carl F.	Pvt.	Co. M.	Wounded
Rosech, Oscar C.	Pvt.	Co. G.	
Rosenblum, Rubin	Pvt.	M. G. Co.	
Roseboom, Eugene H.	Pvt.	Co. B.	
Ross, Charles C.	Pvt.	Hdqrs. Co.	Gassed
Rosse, Joel D.	Pvt.	Co. F.	Wounded
Rossetti, Nicholas	Pvt.	Co. G.	
Rossing, Eric	Pvt.	Co. D.	
Rossiter, Floyd	Pvt.	Co. C.	
Rothband, Wolff	Bugler	Co. L.	Wounded
Rothrock, John	Corp.	Co. L.	
Rothrock, James	Corp.	Co. E.	
Rouse, Arvil F.	Pvt.	Co. A.	
Rowe, Dorcy	Pvt.	Co. M.	
Rowe, Ernest C.	Pvt.	Co. B.	
Rowland, Lester	Bugler	Co. H.	
Royle, John L.	Pvt.	San. Det.	Wounded
Rozell, Floyd F.	Pvt.	Co. E.	
Rubenstein, Seeman	Pvt.	Co. M.	
Ruble, Fred E.	Pvt.	Co. B.	
Ruble, Josie	Cook	Co. B.	
Ruby, Erric S.	Pvt.	Co. F.	
Ruby, Frank	Corp.	Co. G.	Wounded
Rudd, Harper O.	Mechanic	Hdqrs. Co.	
Rudy, Benjamin	Pvt.	M. G. Co.	
Ruey, Frank L.	Corp.	Co. D.	
Ruffing, Solomon	Pvt.	Co. B.	
Ruhl, George G.	Pvt.	Co. F.	
Ruiz, Florencio	Pvt.	Co. I.	Gassed
Rundquist, Walter E.	Pvt.	Co. G.	
Runkle, Fred E.	Pvt.	Co. B.	Wounded
Runkle, Olin W.	Pvt.	M. G. Co.	
Runquist, Walter E.	Pvt.	Co. G.	
Rupp, Charles H.	Pvt.	Co. C.	
Rushing, Percy	Pvt.	Co. F.	
Russell, Earl W.	Pvt.	Hdqrs. Co.	
Ruther, Edward H.	Pvt.	Co. B.	
Rutherford, Clarence R.	Wagoner	Supply Co.	
Rutherford, Irving B.	Pvt.	M. G. Co.	
Rutkowski, Alexander	Pvt.	Co. H.	
Rutledge, Dolpher	Pvt.	Co. G.	
Ryan, John P.	Musician	Hdqrs. Co.	
Ryan, Therman	Pvt.	Co. K.	
Ryan, William J.	Pvt.	Co. C.	
Sackman, Leonard	Pvt.	Co. I.	Wounded
Sadie, Joseph	Pvt.	Co. G.	
Sadler, Bennie L.	Pvt.	Co. K.	
Sadler, Monroe C.	Pvt.	Co. H.	
Sailor, Roy	Pvt.	Co. A.	
Sailors, Alvin H.	Pvt.	Co. L.	
Saline, Theodore	Pvt.	Co. E.	
Sallee, Joseph E.	Pvt.	Co. I.	
Sams, Carl P.	Pvt.	Co. K.	
Samuels, Clarence	Corp.	Co. G.	Wounded
Sanders, Burr	Corp.	Co. G.	
Sanders, Henry J.	Corp.	Co. M.	Wounded
Sanders, Homer	Pvt.	Co. L.	
Sanders, Robert L.	Pvt.	Co. F.	
Sandine, Conrad D.	Pvt.	Co. I.	
Sandoval, Nick L.	Pvt.	Co. C.	
Sandy, John W.	Corp.	Co. F.	
Sapp, William W.	Pvt.	Co. L.	
Sarchielli, James	Pvt.	Co. M.	
Sardinsky, Frank	Pvt.	Co. H.	

THE MEN BEHIND THE GUNS 201

Sartain, Albert Henry	Pvt.	Co. M.	
Sarver, Jacob D.	Pvt.	Co. M.	Wounded
Savage, Charley E.	Pvt.	Co. B.	
Savage, Isaac W.	Pvt.	Co. F.	
Saylor, Charles A.	Bugler	Co. A.	
Sayer, George G.	Pvt.	Co. D.	
Scarbrough, Henry Grady	Pvt.	Co. A.	Wounded
Schaefer, Christy	Pvt.	Co. A.	
Schaefer, Raymond J.	Pvt.	Co. D.	
Schappert, Gervase	Pvt.	Co. L.	
Scharr, Frank	Pvt.	Co. H.	
Schauffele, Gust C.	Pvt.	Co. B.	Wounded
Scheinert, Jesse J.	Corp.	Co. B.	
Schick, Martin	Pvt.	San. Det.	
Schiller, Joseph	Corp.	Co. H.	Wounded
Schmid, Charles J.	Pvt.	M. G. Co.	
Schmidt, Henry N.	Pvt.	Co. L.	Gassed
Schnarr, Frank	Pvt.	Co. D.	
Schneider, Lewis J.	Pvt.	Co. M.	
Schoenmann, William E.	Pvt.	Co. L.	
Schreiber, George R.	Pvt.	Co. G.	Wounded
Schrimscher, James P.	Pvt.	Co. C.	
Schuetz, Paul O.	Pvt.	Co. L.	
Schuhmacher, George H. W.	Pvt.	Co. C.	
Schult, Hina C.	Reg. Sgt. Maj.	Hdqrs. Co.	
Schwartz, George	Pvt.	M. G. Co.	
Schwartz, William	Pvt.	Co. B.	
Schweikhart, Erwin F.	Pvt.	Co. B.	
Schwerdt, Louis R.	Pvt.	Co. E.	
Sciabarrasi, Mariano	Pvt.	Co. K.	
Scinto, Fred	Pvt.	Co. H.	
Scott, Allbridge T.	Corp.	Co. E.	
Scott, Enoch	Corp.	Co. M.	Wounded
Scott, Gene	Pvt.	Hdqrs. Co.	
Scott, John E.	Pvt.	M. G. Co.	
Scott, Lionel J.	Corp.	M. G. Co.	
Scott, Ray H.	Pvt.	Co. A.	
Scott, William E.	Pvt.	Co. M.	
Scotten, Hilliard	Pvt.	Co. B.	
Scribner, Frank	Pvt.	Co. G.	
Scully, James H.	Sgt.	Co. F.	
Scurlock, Roscoe	Pvt.	Co. C.	
Sealock, Clyde K.	Pvt.	Hdqrs. Co.	
Searing, William H.	Pvt.	Co. H.	
Sears, Ernest	Pvt.	Co. B.	Gassed
Seaton, Virgil D.	Corp.	Co. G.	Wounded
Seawright, Tom J.	Pvt.	Co. F.	
Sechser, Alfred	Pvt.	Co. L.	
Sedman, Archie	Pvt.	Co. E.	
See, Clarence D.	Pvt.	Co. A.	
Seely, Harrison H.	Pvt.	Co. L.	Wounded
Seitz, Frank J.	Pvt.	Co. L.	
Seller, Floyd	Pvt.	Hdqrs. Co.	
Sellers, Louis M.	Corp.	Co. C.	
Sell, Dee	Pvt.	Co. L.	Gassed
Sells, Edward S.	Pvt.	Co. H.	
Sells, Milton H.	Pvt.	Co. H.	
Semanski, Joseph	Pvt.	Co. G.	
Sewell, Don E.	Pvt.	Co. G.	
Sexton, Charles A.	Corp.	Co. G.	
Seymoure, Robert	Pvt.	Co. I.	
Seymour, Edgar W.	Pvt.	Co. B.	
Shackelford, Harry	Pvt.	Co. L.	Wounded

Shackelford, William	Corp.	Co. L.	
Shadwill, Harold H.	Pvt.	Co. D.	
Shafer, Fred T.	Pvt.	Co. C.	
Shamel, Jennings B.	Sgt.	Co. G.	
Shankle, Green W.	Pvt.	Co. I.	
Shapiro, Archie	Pvt.	Co. G.	
Shapiro, Sam	Pvt.	Co. M.	
Sharp, Buell F.	Pvt.	Co. G.	
Shatto, William	Pvt.	Co. B.	Wounded, Died
Sharp, Claud S.	Musician	Hdqrs. Co.	
Shaw, Paul M.	Pvt.	Co. D.	
Shaw, Ray H.	Corp.	Co. M.	
Chearer, James C.	Pvt.	Co. K.	Wounded
Sheehan, Daniel	Corp.	Co. K.	Wounded
Sheehan, Frank E.	Pvt.	M. G. Co.	
Sheffer, Ernest R.	Pvt.	M. G. Co.	
Sheley, Edward L.	Sgt.	Co. F.	
Shell, Arthur W.	Pvt.	Co. D.	
Shell, James A.	Pvt.	Co. K.	
Shelton, Frank H.	Wagoner	Co. D.	
Shelton, John M.	Pvt.	Co. M.	
Shepherd, Fuller	Pvt.	Co. I.	
Shepherd, Virgil V.	Corp.	Co. M.	Wounded
Sheridan, Arthur J.	Pvt.	M. G. Co.	
Sherman, Clark C.	Pvt.	Co. A.	
Sherman, Harold	Sgt.	Co. L.	
Shetterly, Benjamine	Pvt.	Co. H.	Wounded
Sheward, Harry G.	Pvt.	Co. A.	
Shields, John W.	Pvt.	Co. E.	
Shields, Jesse Alvin	Pvt.	Co. M.	
Shiflet, Judson M.	Pvt.	Co. L.	
Shine, Daniel J.	Corp.	Hdqrs. Co.	
Shine, Michael A.	Horseshoer	Hdqrs. Co.	
Shiplet, Abraham K.	Pvt.	Hdqrs. Co.	
Shipley, Dean	Sgt.	Co. K.	Wounded
Shirel, Thomas E.	Corp.	Hdqrs. Co.	
Shirk, Robert B.	Sgt.	C. A.	
Shivel, Frank B.	Pvt.	Co. L.	
Shoat, Jim C.	Corp.	Co. E.	
Shoemaker, Franklin C.	Pvt.	Co. L.	
Shoemaker, Harry E.	Pvt.	Co. D.	
Shook, Steward W.	Pvt.	Co. E.	
Shorter, George	Pvt.	Co. L.	
Shouse, Charles L.	Pvt.	Co. C.	
Showalter Harry	Pvt.	Co. G.	Wounded
Showers, George W.	Corp.	Hdqrs. Co.	Gassed
Shreffler, Harry F.	Pvt.	Co. G.	
Shreiber, George R.	Pvt.	Co. G.	
Shuert, Floyd C.	Pvt.	Co. B.	Wounded
Shultz, Jesse	Pvt.	Co. L.	
Sibley, Waldo R.	Wagoner	Supply Co.	
Sicking, Edward J.	Wagoner	Supply Co.	
Sickles, Charles L.	Pvt.	Co. M.	
Siebert, Leo M.	Pvt.	Co. D.	
Siegel, Louis	Pvt.	Co. M.	
Siegrist, Warner H.	Corp.	Co. H.	
Sierwernko, Frank	Pvt.	Co. B.	
Sievert, George H.	Pvt.	Co. E.	
Siglow, Angelo	Pvt.	Co. H.	
Silverio, Sabatino	Pvt.	Co. M.	
Simmons, Charles C.	Corp.	Co. B.	Gassed
Simmons, Henry	Pvt.	Co. B.	Wounded
Simmons, James R.	Pvt.	Co. G.	
Simmons, Webster J.	Sgt.	Co. B.	Wounded

THE MEN BEHIND THE GUNS

Simones, John	Pvt.	Co. L.	
Simpson, Earl J.	Pvt.	Co. C.	
Simpson, Ernest	Pvt.	Co. B.	
Simpson, Fred	Pvt.	Co. M.	
Simpson, Hulon E.	Pvt.	Co. K.	
Simpson, William B.	Pvt.	Co. E.	
Sims, Thomas C.	Pvt.	Co. G.	
Singles, Sanford	Pvt.	Co. I.	
Singleton, James S.	Pvt.	Co. H.	
Sires, Clyde H.	Corp.	Co. H.	
Sisco, Claud	Pvt.	Co. M.	
Sisk, William	Pvt.	Co. M.	Wounded
Sitz, Albert R.	Pvt.	Co. I.	
Skaggs, Willard	Pvt.	Co. L.	
Skorbach, George	Pvt.	C. G.	
Slater, Harold C.	Corp.	Co. B.	
Slaughter, Grover F.	Pvt.	Hdqrs. Co.	
Slick, Harry	Corp.	Co. L.	
Smart, Howard A.	Pvt.	Co. B.	Wounded
Smart, John	Pvt.	M. G. Co.	
Smith, Allen B.	Pvt.	Co. F.	
Smith, Arthur E.	Pvt.	Co. D.	
Smith, Austin L.	Pvt.	Co. M.	
Smith, Carl	Corp.	Co. L.	Wounded
Smith, Charles E.	Corp.	Co. H.	
Smith, Charles R.	Pvt.	Co. D.	
Smith, Clarence William	Pvt.	Co. M.	Wounded
Smith, Clarence W.	Pvt.	Co. M.	
Smith, Cleveland J.	Pvt.	Co. M.	
Smith, Clyde	Pvt.	Co. M.	Wounded
Smith, David Lee	Pvt.	Co. E.	
Smith, Ernest C.	Cook	Co. A.	
Smith, Elmer	Pvt.	Supply Co.	
Smith, Edgar	Pvt.	Co. G.	
Smith, Edward	Corp.	M. G. Co.	
Smith, Frank A.	Corp.	Co. D.	
Smith, Fred	Pvt.	Co. I.	Wounded
Smith, George L.	Cook	Supply Co.	
Smith, George L.	Pvt.	Co. M.	
Smith, George N.	Pvt.	Co. L.	
Smith, Harley	Pvt.	Co. K.	
Smith, Harry H.	Pvt.	Co. D.	
Smith, Harry J.	Pvt.	Co. E.	Wounded
Smith, Harry L.	Pvt.	Co. K.	
Smith, Irvin	Pvt.	Co. F.	
Smith, James A.	Pvt.	Co. A.	
Smith, James K.	Pvt.	Co. G.	
Smith, Jesse M.	Pvt.	Co. F.	
Smith, John W.	Pvt.	Co. I.	
Smith, Kelsey	Pvt.	Co. E.	Wounded
Smith, Lemon	Pvt.	Co. I.	
Smith, LeRoy	Sgt.	Supply Co.	
Smith, Lester H.	Pvt.	Hdqrs. Co.	Wounded
Smith, Lloyd L.	Pvt.	Co. F.	
Smith, Louis	Pvt.	Supply Co.	
Smith, Mack J.	Cook	Co. F.	
Smith, Oliver P.	Pvt.	Co. M.	
Smith, Penn	Corp.	Co. G.	
Smith, Robert A.	Pvt.	Co. M.	
Smith, Roy C.	Sgt.	Co. I.	
Smith, Rush D.	Sgt.	Co. A.	Wounded
Smith, Sidney	Pvt.	Co. B.	Wounded
Smith, Sylvester	Pvt.	Co. L.	
Smith, Thane B.	Pvt.	Co. B.	Wounded

Smith, Thomas B.	Corp.	Co. G.	
Smith, William C.	Pvt.	Co. L.	Wounded
Smith, William E.	Pvt.	Co. G.	Gassed
Smith, William F.	Pvt.	Co. D.	
Smith, William W.	Pvt.	Co. A.	Killed
Smoot, Elmer E.	Pvt.	Co. E.	Wounded
Smothers, Elbert H.	Pvt.	Co. E.	
Snapp, Wayne F.	Pvt.	Co. C.	
Snider, Luther E.	Pvt.	Co. M.	
Snodgrass, Earl	Corp.	Co. I.	Gassed
Snorgrass, James F.	Mess Sgt.	Co. A.	
Snorgrass, Joseph	Pvt.	Co. D.	
Snow, Isaac R.	Sgt.	Co. H.	Wounded
Snowden, Henry A.	Corp.	Co. G.	Wounded
Snyder, Clarence C.	Pvt.	Co. L.	
Snyder, Melville	Sgt.	San. Det.	
Soars, Able	Pvt.	Co. H.	
Somers, Raymond	Pvt.	Co. I.	Wounded
Southern, Edward	Corp.	Co. I.	Wounded
Sowell, Roy	Pvt.	Co. L.	
Spaete, Earnest F.	Corp.	Co. B.	
Spagnola, Giobanni	Pvt.	Co. H.	
Spangler, Lawrence	Pvt.	Co. B.	
Sparks, Arlie	Pvt.	Co. B.	Wounded
Sparks, Clifford W.	Sgt.	Co. B.	Wounded
Speed, Wilfred F.	Pvt.	Co. G.	
Speer, Brent	Pvt.	Co. D.	
Spence, George J.	Pvt.	Co. G.	
Spencer, Burton McC.	Pvt.	Co. F.	
Spencer, Jerritt	Pvt.	Co. M.	
Spencer, Joesiah	Pvt.	Co. M.	
Spencer, Rhenix E.	Pvt.	Co. G.	
Spencer, Virgil C.	Pvt.	Co. E.	
Spillers, Dick	Corp.	Co. L.	
Spink, John L.	Pvt.	Co. F.	
Spitzer, Paul O.	Pvt.	Co. C.	
Spoden, Peter	Corp.	Co. C.	
Sprague, Arthur L.	Pvt.	Co. A.	Killed, Exermont
Sprague, Elmer A.	Corp.	Co. A.	Wounded
Spraul, Willie Bee	Pvt.	Co. E.	
Springer, Garnet A.	Pvt.	Co. G.	
Springer, Paul B.	Pvt.	Co. F.	
Springer, William J.	Pvt.	Co. D.	Gassed
Spruce, William	Corp.	Co. B.	
Stack, James S.	Pvt.	Hdqrs. Co.	
Stacy, Cecil	Pvt.	Co. E.	
Staley, Archie L.	Pvt.	Co. H.	
Staley, Samuel	Pvt.	Co. M.	
Stamps, John W.	Pvt.	Co. L.	
Stamps, Lemuel	Corp.	Co. I.	Gassed
Stanaland, Robert M.	Pvt.	Co. G.	
Stapleton, George W.	Corp.	Co. A.	
Stark, Bert	Sgt.	Co. L.	Gassed
Stark, Charles A.	Wagoner	Supply Co.	
Starling, Jay J.	Pvt.	Hdqrs. Co.	
Starr, Fred O.	Sgt. Maj.	Hdqrs. Co.	
Stearns, Henry R.	Pvt.	Co. B.	Wounded
Steed, Bert	Pvt.	Co. D.	
Steele, Earl	Pvt.	Co. A.	
Steele, Harry H.	Pvt.	Co. G.	
Steffen, Albert C.	Pvt.	Co. D.	
Steffens, Leonard H.	Corp.	Co. A.	Wounded
Steffy, Dollas	Pvt.	Co. B.	Gassed
Stegall, John W.	Pvt.	Co. G.	

THE MEN BEHIND THE GUNS

Steinberger, Daniel L.	Pvt.	Co. M.	
Steinbruegge, Frank A.	Pvt.	Co. C.	
Steiner, Walter	Sgt.	Co. L.	
Steinke, Louie F.	Corp.	Co. K.	
Steinmetz, Albert M.	Pvt.	Co. L.	
Stephens, Lee J.	Pvt.	Co. M.	
Stephens, Mckinley	Pvt.	Co. H.	
Stephens, Sherman	Pvt.	Co. F.	
Stephenson, William R.	Bugler	Co. B.	
Stephenson, Hugh	Pvt.	Co. B.	
Stepp, Audley F.	Pvt.	Supply Co.	
Stevens, Charles O.	Pvt.	Co. D.	
Stevens, Floyd E.	Pvt.	Co. D.	
Stevens, Fred	Pvt.	Co. G.	Wounded
Stevenson, Edward	Corp.	Co. C.	
Steward, Clay D.	Pvt.	Co. D.	Wounded
Stewart, Alexander	Pvt.	Hdqrs. Co.	Wounded
Stewart, Elmer O.	Pvt.	Co. F.	
Stewart, James O.	Sgt.	Hdqrs. Co.	Wounded
Stewart, Samuel I.	Pvt.	Co. F.	
Stewart, William H.	Pvt.	Co. F.	
Stigall, Eugene	Pvt.	Co. E.	
Stilwell, Charles G.	Pvt.	Co. C.	
Stillwell, Jesse O.	Pvt.	Co. B.	
Stillwell, John L.	Pvt.	Co. M.	
Stiner, Curtis	Mechanic	Co. B.	Wounded
Stintson, William T.	Pvt.	Co. H.	
Stirewalt, Jacob	Pvt.	Co. M.	
Stith, Frank E.	Pvt.	Hdqrs. Co.	
Stockton, Hugh S.	Corp.	Co. B.	Wounded
Stogsdill, Franklin W.	Sgt.	Co. F.	
Stokes, Ongole L.	Sgt.	M. G. Co.	
Stoll, Walter S.	Corp.	Co. I.	
Stolte, William C.	Pvt.	Co. L.	
Stone, Edward F.	Pvt.	Co. C.	
Stone, Even A.	Corp.	Co. D.	
Stone, Walter	Pvt.	Co. E.	
Stone, William H.	Corp.	Co. H.	
Stone, Wilmer F.	Sgt.	Hdqrs. Co.	
Stoppel, David John	Corp.	Co. L.	
Stout, Orvil V.	Pvt.	Co. B.	
Stout, Oscar L.	Pvt.	Co. H.	
Strable, Albert	Pvt.	Co. A.	
Strange, Nicholas	Pvt.	Co. H.	
Stratten, Truman	Pvt.	Co. I.	
Stratton, Homer	Sgt.	Co. E.	Wounded
Straub, William F.	Pvt.	Co. C.	
Strauss, Karl J.	Pvt.	Co. C.	
Strauss, Phillip J.	Pvt.	Co. B.	
Streator, Floyd D.	Pvt.	Co. L.	
Streeper, Thomas	Corp.	Co. M.	Wounded
Street, Earl	Pvt.	Co. I.	
Street, Thomas Harrison	Pvt.	Co. F.	
Stringer, Francis W.	Pvt.	Co. I.	
Stringer, Nathan E.	Pvt.	Co. A.	Wounded
Strop, Audie J.	Pvt.	Co. H.	Wounded
Stroud, Willie E.	Pvt.	Co. L.	
Stubblefield, Marion	Pvt.	Co. M.	Wounded
Stubblefield, Seth G.	Pvt.	Co. F.	
Stubblefield, Wyatt J.	Pvt.	Co. M.	
Stucker, Walter L.	Corp.	Co. E.	Killed
Stull, Frank M.	Pvt.	Co. I.	
Styers, Robert T.	Pvt.	Co. E.	
Suby, Peter	Pvt.	Co. H.	

Sullivan, Allen O.	Pvt.	Co. K.	
Sumerall, Franklin H.	Pvt.	Co. F.	
Summers, Benjamine H.	Pvt.	Supply Co.	
Summers, George C.	Pvt.	Co. L.	Wounded
Summers, Lon S.	Pvt.	Co. H.	
Summers, Rothie	Corp.	Co. H.	Wounded
Summers, Thomas M.	Sgt.	Co. C.	
Sumpter, Peery E.	Mechanic	M. G. Co.	
Sumrall, William H.	Pvt.	Co. I.	
Suter, Roscoe	Pvt.	Co. A.	
Suttle, Charley P.	Pvt.	Co. E.	
Sutton, Charles	Wagoner	Supply Co.	
Sutton, John F.	Wagoner	Co. L.	
Sutton, Walter B.	Corp.	Co. M.	
Svendsen, Ernest	Pvt.	Co. E.	
Swafford, Albert	Corp.	Co. E.	
Swearingen, Chester B.	Pvt.	Co. L.	
Swearingen, Cuylar H.	Pvt.	Co. G.	
Swearingin, John H.	Pvt.	Co. G.	Wounded
Sweeden, Walter J.	Pvt.	Co. H.	
Sweet, Charlie H.	Pvt.	Co. M.	Wounded
Sykes, Tom	Pvt.	Co. E.	
Sylcox, William M.	Pvt.	Co. H.	
Tabor, Charles Lee	Pvt.	Co. L.	Gassed
Taff, Otis H.	Pvt.	Co. F.	
Taggart, Forest S.	Corp.	Co. F.	
Talbot, Arthur W.	Sgt.	M. G. Co.	
Talcott, Frank	Corp.	Co. K.	
Taney, Henry	Pvt.	Co. A.	Wounded
Tanksley, Thomas	Corp.	Co. B.	
Tann, Ferinand	Pvt.	Co. H.	
Tarbutton, Clyde	Wagoner	Supply Co.	
Tarr, Joseph	Pvt.	Co. L.	
Tate, Thomas T.	Mechanic	Co. C.	
Taubert, Walter W.	Pvt.	Co. C.	
Tayek, Joseph R.	Pvt.	Co. H.	
Taylor, Albert D.	Pvt.	Co. C.	
Taylor, Eugene W.	Sgt.	Co. C.	
Taylor, Geo. E.	Pvt.	Co. H.	
Taylor, George T.	Pvt.	Co. L.	
Taylor, Leslie	Pvt.	M. G. Co.	
Taylor, Lester	Corp.	Co. K.	Wounded
Taylor, Norval	Corp.	Hdqrs. Co.	
Taylor, Okey T.	Pvt.	Co. G.	
Taylor, Richard N.	Pvt.	Co. H.	
Taylor, Robert J.	Sgt.	Co. D.	
Taylor, Roy L.	Pvt.	Co. M.	
Taylor, William	Pvt.	Co. K.	
Teagarden, James M.	Cook	Co. G.	Gassed
Teague, James W.	Pvt.	Co. C.	
Teel, Thomas E.	Wagoner	Co. D.	
Tembusch, William	Pvt.	Co. G.	
Templin, Edward H.	Pvt.	Co. B.	
Teney, John R.	Pvt.	Co. M.	
Tenney, Clement E.	Pvt.	Hdqrs. Co.	
Testa, Salvatore	Pvt.	Co. D.	
Teters, Dorcy A.	Pvt.	Co. E.	
Tetik, Tom	Pvt.	Co. C.	Wounded
Tetrick, John L.	Pvt.	Co. A.	
Teutsch, John M.	Pvt.	Co. G.	
Thacker, Charles	Pvt.	Co. C.	
Thalman, George E.	Corp.	Co. H.	
Thatcher, Stanley	Mechanic	Co. B.	
Thatcher, Wheeler B.	Pvt.	Co. L.	

THE MEN BEHIND THE GUNS 207

Thayer, Lester M.	Sgt.	Co. L.	Wounded
Thayer, Ross M.	Pvt.	Co. D.	
Thiergartner, Matthew	Pvt.	Co. D.	
Thoeni, Simeon, Jr.	Corp.	Co. G.	
Thomas, Ardie R.	Pvt.	Co. E.	
Thomas, Archie I.	Mechanic	Co. F.	Wounded
Thomas, Brack A.	Pvt.	Co. F.	Wounded
Thomas, Charles H.	Pvt.	Hdqrs. Co.	
Thomas, Elmer J.	Pvt.	Co. C.	Wounded
Thomas, George W.	Pvt.	Co. L.	Wounded
Thomas, Grover C.	Pvt.	Co. L.	
Thomas, Jacob	Corp.	M. G. Co.	
Thomas, Meffert R.	Mechanic	Supply Co.	
Thomas, Rothwell H.	Pvt.	Co. B.	Wounded
Thomas, Squire D.	Pvt.	Co. C.	
Thomas, William A.	Pvt.	Co. F.	Gassed
Thomas, William R.	Pvt.	Co. B.	Wounded
Thompson, Benjamine F.	Corp.	Co. C.	Wounded
Thompson, Byron P.	Pvt.	Hdqrs. Co.	
Thompson, Ernest	Pvt.	Co. M.	Wounded
Thompson, Henley	Pvt.	Co. B.	
Thompson, James E.	Pvt.	Co. M.	Wounded
Thompson, James Y.	Pvt.	Co. F.	
Thompson, Marvin E.	Pvt.	Co. H.	
Thompson, Ralph C.	Pvt.	Co. M.	
Thompson, Ralph J.	Pvt.	Co. G.	
Thompson, William G.	Pvt.	Co. C.	
Thorn, Charles H.	Corp.	Co. H.	
Thorne, Lyman	Corp.	Co. B.	
Thornton, Claud	Pvt.	Co. L.	
Thornton, Hershel H.	Corp.	Co. A.	
Thorp, Roy E.	Corp.	Co. I.	
Thorp, William	Pvt.	Co. I.	
Thorsen, Jens T.	Pvt.	Co. H.	Gassed
Thorson, Herbert W.	Sgt.	Co. A.	
Thrasher, Oliver P.	Pvt.	Co. H.	Wounded
Thurmon, William B.	Corp.	Co. A.	
Thurman, William	Pvt.	Co. L.	
Tibbs, Harry	Band Corp.	Hdqrs. Co.	
Tidwell, Elbert B.	Pvt.	Co. K.	Wounded
Tidwell, Jodie Lee	Pvt.	Co. A.	
Tidwell, Oscar Delbert	Pvt.	Co. A.	
Tiesing, Harry W.	Pvt.	Co. E.	
Tillery, Dale J.	Pvt.	Co. C.	
Tilton, Forest	Pvt.	Co. A.	
Timbs, Donnie H.	Pvt.	Hdqrs. Co.	
Tippitt, Jacob M.	Pvt.	Co. M.	Wounded
Tippy, Coy M.	Pvt.	Hdqrs. Co.	
Todd, Carl	Pvt.	Co. M.	
Todd, Joseph T.	Pvt.	Co. M.	Wounded
Todd, Walter E.	Pvt.	Co. M.	Wounded
Tomas, Frank J.	Pvt.	Co. H.	
Tombley, James B.	Pvt.	Co. H.	
Tomlin, Willie A.	Pvt.	Co. H.	
Tompson, Herbert W.	Pvt.	Co. K.	
Tonkinson, Arthur L.	Corp.	Co. D.	
Totten, Ivan R.	Pvt.	Co. B.	
Toughlian, Avedis S.	Pvt.	Co. M.	
Townsend, James	Pvt.	Co. M.	
Townsend, Frank R.	Pvt.	Co. M.	Wounded
Townsend, Leo C.	Pvt.	Co. M.	Wounded
Tracer, Roy S.	Pvt.	Co. H.	
Tracy, Clyde	Pvt.	Co. B.	
Tracy, Louis C.	Cook	Co. B.	

Trant, Philip G.	Pvt.	Co. C.	
Traister, Thomas A.	Pvt.	Co. B.	Wounded
Tratchel, Herman M.	Pvt.	Co. M.	
Travis, Charles L.	Pvt.	Co. E.	
Treadway, William L.	Pvt.	Co. M.	
Trencick, John H.	Corp.	M. G. Co.	
Trevor, Frank S.	Pvt.	Co. D.	
Trigg, Beldon H.	Pvt.	Co. E.	
Trigg, James L.	Pvt.	Co. E.	
Trigg, James C.	Pvt.	Co. D.	
Tripp, Claude E.	Wagoner	Supply Co.	
Tripplett, William F.	Sgt.	Co. D.	Wounded
Trittschler, George	Pvt.	Co. L.	
Trotter, Ray Emerson	Corp.	Co. B.	
Troub, Herbert	Pvt.	Hdqrs. Co.	
Troutt, George W.	Sgt.	Co. I.	Wounded
Troxel, Joe	Sgt.	Co. M.	
Truce, Pery W.	Sgt.	M. G. Co.	
Tucker, Albert J.	Pvt.	Co. F.	
Tucker, Arthur	Mechanic	Co. C.	
Tucker, Aubra L.	Pvt.	Co. A.	
Tucker, Robert C.	Pvt.	Co. H.	
Tucker, Rufus	Pvt.	Co. I.	
Tucker, William	Pvt.	Co. I.	Gassed
Tuckfield, Ralph G.	Corp.	Co. G.	
Tum, Sam	Pvt.	Co. K.	Wounded
Turk, Edward L.	Cook	Co. A.	
Turk, Julius E.	Corp.	Co. A.	
Turner, Albert W.	Pvt.	Co. D.	
Turner, Arthur	Pvt.	Co. F.	Wounded
Turner, Chester Hicks	Pvt.	Co. A.	
Turner, Harry	Pvt.	Co. K.	
Turner, James	Pvt.	Co. M.	Wounded
Turner, Jess	Pvt.	Co. C.	
Turner, Jesse E.	Pvt.	Co. M.	Wounded
Turner, John L.	Pvt.	Co. F.	
Turner, Mon	Pvt.	Co. F.	
Turner, Prentis G.	Pvt.	Co. C.	
Turner, Vere H.	Pvt.	Co. B.	
Tuttle, Clarence W.	Corp.	Co. D.	
Twiton, James	Pvt.	Co. M.	
Tyler, Napoleon	Pvt.	Co. M.	Wounded
Tyner, George W.	Corp.	Co. M.	Wounded
Tyra, Joseph	Pvt.	Co. E.	
Ugowski, Louis E.	Pvt.	Co. D.	
Underwood, Able D.	Pvt.	Co. E.	
Underwood, Robert J.	Pvt.	Co. I.	
Unger, Benjamine	Bugler	Co. H.	
Unroe, Ruben D.	Pvt.	Co. L.	
Upton, Robert	Pvt.	Co. M.	Wounded
Urbanowicz, Stanley	Pvt.	Co. G.	
Urish, Will	Pvt.	Co. B.	Wounded
Utzler, John E.	Pvt.	Co. C.	
Vahrenberg, Otto	Pvt.	Co. E.	
VanBuskirk, Forrest W.	Pvt.	Co. F.	
Vance, Harold P.	Pvt.	Co. G.	
VanCleave, Darwin A.	Pvt.	Co. H.	
Vanderlicht, Allen	Pvt.	Co. C.	
Vanderwurst, William T.	Pvt.	Co. H.	
Vandiver, Joe V.	Sgt.	Co. F.	
VanDiver, Jesse	Mess Sgt.	Co. G.	
VanGilder, Clarence	Cook	Co. F.	Gassed
VanHecke, Eugene Arthur	Corp.	Co. L.	
VanHoozer, Cecil M.	Pvt.	Co. G.	Gassed

THE MEN BEHIND THE GUNS 209

VanHoozier, William R.	Pvt.	Hdqrs. Co.	
Vanhorn, Claude	Pvt.	Co. D.	
Van Horne, Robert G.	Sgt.	Co. G.	
Vanlandingham, Carles	Pvt.	Co. A.	
Vann, Hinton	Pvt.	Co. G.	
Vanschoiack, Charles M.	Pvt.	Co. G.	
Vantassel, Andrew J.	Pvt.	Co. L.	
Varnell, Asher	Pvt.	Co. F.	
Varner, Jesse R.	Pvt.	Co. K.	
Vatstik, Thor	Pvt.	Co. E.	
Vaughn, Harley P.	Corp.	Co. B.	Wounded
Vaughn, William J.	Corp.	Hdqrs. Co.	
Vazquez, Max	Sgt.	Co. A.	
Veith, Arthur B.	Pvt.	Co. A.	
Venturi, Joe	Pvt.	Co. H.	
Vernon, Harley A.	Pvt.	Co. B.	Wounded
Vestal, William E.	Pvt.	Co. H.	
Veteto, Irvin	Pvt.	M. G. Co.	
Vick, Elzie W.	Pvt.	Hdqrs. Co.	Wounded
Vicksell, Robert	Musician	Hdqrs. Co.	
View, Clarence	Corp.	Co. B.	
Vigola, George E.	Pvt.	Co. I.	
Vincent, Delmar F.	Wagoner	Supply Co.	Gassed
Vincent, Jake	Pvt.	Co. D.	
Vinciguerra, Vincenzo	Pvt.	M. G. Co.	
Vineyard, John A. L.	Pvt.	Co. F.	
Vineyard, Lee McK	Pvt.	Co. E.	
Violet, Jesse H.	Pvt.	Co. D.	
Viverett, Lawrence C.	Pvt.	Co. K.	
Voelker, Henry J.	Pvt.	Co. A.	
Vogel, Henry J.	Pvt.	Hdqrs. Co.	
VonBehren, George H.	Pvt.	Co. G.	
Von Oertzen, Robert	Pvt.	Co. B.	
Vos, Albert J.	Pvt.	Co. M.	
Voss, Louis J.	Pvt.	Hdqrs. Co.	
Wacker, Samuel M.	Cook	Co. H.	
Waddle, Alva P.	Pvt.	Co. M.	
Waggener, Edgar F.	Corp.	Co. F.	
Wagner, Charles G.	Musician	Hdqrs. Co.	
Wagner, Roy J.	Pvt.	Co. C.	
Waite, Raymond	Pvt.	Co. D.	Wounded
Wakefield, Thomas J.	Pvt.	Co. E.	
Walker, Guy L.	Corp.	Co. H.	Wounded
Walker, Oswald	Corp.	Co. B.	
Walker, Roscoe	Sgt.	Co. M.	
Walker, Pearl	Pvt.	Co. I.	
Wall, Herbert M.	Pvt.	Hdqrs. Co.	
Wallace, Earl	Cook	Co. K.	Wounded
Wallace, Robert A.	Sgt.	Hdqrs. Co.	
Wallace, Willie B.	Sgt.	Co. E.	
Wallman, Harry A.	Pvt.	M. G. Co.	
Walls, Mark H. .	Corp.	Co. L.	Wounded
Walls, Milton E.	Pvt.	Co. M.	Wounded
Walsh, John R.	Sgt.	Co. F.	Gassed
Walter,Pearl	Pvt.	Co. I.	
Walters, Henry W.	Pvt.	Co. A.	
Walters, Sam	Pvt.	Co. M.	Wounded
Walters, Wilson	Pvt.	Co. K.	
Walton, Carvel H.	Pvt.	Co. L.	
Walton, Malcomb	Pvt.	Co. L.	
Wambeke, Adolf	Pvt.	Co. D.	
Wampler, Clarence E.	Pvt.	Hdqrs. Co.	Wounded
Wamsley, Frank A.	Pvt.	Co. F.	
Wanklyn, Albert Luke	Corp.	Co. M.	Wounded

Ward, Edward	Corp.	Co. G.	Wounded
Ward, Ernest	Mechanic	Co. D.	Wounded
Ward, Flem C.	Cook	Co. G.	Gassed
Wardlow, Dunca R.	Mechanic	Co. E.	
Waring, Bert B.	Corp.	Co. H.	
Waring, George W.	Sgt.	Co. H.	
Warner, Bert W.	Corp.	Co. G.	
Warner, Charles Raymond	Pvt.	Co. M.	
Warner, Claude M.	Pvt.	San. Det.	
Warren, Henry	Pvt.	Co. B.	
Warren, James G.	Pvt.	San. Det.	Wounded
Warren, Kelly	Pvt.	M. G. Co.	Gassed
Warren, Robert V.	Corp.	Co. A.	
Warren, Virgil C.	Pvt.	Co. A.	
Warrington, Herman L.	Pvt.	Co. G.	
Washabaugh, Ralph Virgil	Pvt.	Co. M.	
Waters, Carl K.	Sgt.	Co. G.	
Wathen, Frank V.	Sgt.	Co. E.	
Watkins, Ernest R.	Pvt.	Co. A.	
Watkins, Paul H.	Pvt.	Co. H.	
Watson, Benjamin F.	Pvt.	Co. H.	
Watson, Edgar Ray	Corp.	Co. M.	Wounded
Watson, George D.	Pvt.	Co. M.	Wounded
Watson, George W.	Mechanic	Co. D.	
Watson, Lafe D.	Pvt.	Co. G.	
Watts, James L.	Pvt.	Hdqrs. Co.	
Watts, Paul A.	Pvt.	Co. D.	
Waugh, Warren	Pvt.	Co. B.	
Way, Heber O.	Corp.	Co. A.	
Waymire, Jacob H.	Corp.	Hdqrs. Co.	Wounded
Weathers, Russell O.	Corp.	Co. D.	
Weatherspoon, Bossie	Pvt.	Co. F.	
Weaver, Ralph H.	Musician	Hdqrs. Co.	
Weaver, James	Pvt.	Co. K.	
Weaver, Arley Joseph	Pvt.	Hdqrs. Co.	
Webb, Elma E.	Pvt.	Co. M.	Wounded
Webb, Guy	Pvt.	Co. C.	
Webb, Harry J.	Pvt.	Co. M.	Wounded
Webber, Ivan	Sgt.	Co. G.	Gassed
Weber, Jacob	Pvt.	Co. D.	
Weber, John M.	Pvt.	Co. D.	
Weber, William A.	Pvt.	Hdqrs. Co.	
Weber, William F., Jr.	Pvt.	Co. H.	
Weddle, William E.	Pvt.	Co. A.	
Wedner, Edward	Pvt.	Co. A.	
Weidemann, Walter John	Pvt.	Hdqrs. Co.	
Weidner, Louis E.	Sgt.	Co. C.	
Weiford, Clarence E.	Pvt.	Co. A.	
Weiland, Charles F.	Corp.	Co. A.	
Weimer, Harold E.	Pvt.	Hdqrs. Co.	
Weir, Raymond C.	Sgt.	Hdqrs. Co.	
Weis, Paramore B.	Pvt.	Co. K.	Wounded
Weiser, Benny	Pvt.	Co. M.	
Welbern, John G.	Pvt.	Co. D.	Wounded
Welch, Ernest E.	Pvt.	Co. M.	
Welch, William P.	Pvt.	Co. L.	
Welker, Oscar	Pvt.	Co. H.	
Wells, Dewey	Pvt.	Co. B.	
Wells, Earl H.	Pvt.	Co. A.	Wounded
Wells, Harvey H.	Pvt.	Co. D.	
Wells, Thaddeus R.	Sgt.	Co. C.	
Wener, Alex	Pvt.	Co. A.	

THE MEN BEHIND THE GUNS 211

Wenger, Raymond G.	Sgt.	Co. B.	
Wenk, Milton	Pvt.	M. G. Co.	
Werner, George W.	Pvt.	Co. H.	
Wertich, Francis J.	Pvt.	Co. F.	
West, Frank B.	Pvt.	Co. I.	Wounded
West, Robert D.	Corp.	Co. B.	
West, Virgile	Pvt.	Co. F.	
Wester, John B.	Pvt.	Co. C.	
Westlake, Lloyd E.	Pvt.	Co. H.	
Westmoreland, Bert	Pvt.	Co. M.	
Wetherton, James H.	Pvt.	Co. D.	
Wettstein, Sam	Pvt.	Co. D.	
Whaley, Joseph C.	Pvt.	Co. E.	Wounded
Wheeler, Harry W.	Musician	Hdqrs. Co.	
Wheeler, Ted R.	Musician	Hdqrs. Co.	
Whetstine, Lewis L.	Mess Sgt.	Co. F.	
Whisenhunt, Gilford M.	Pvt.	Co. M.	Wounded
White, Archie L.	Pvt.	Co. H.	
White, Claude V.	Pvt.	Co. C.	
White, Dewey T.	Corp.	Co. I.	Wounded
White, Everett	Pvt.	Co. B.	
White, Herbert F.	Pvt.	Co. D.	
White, Hugh	Pvt.	M. G. Co.	
White, Jack	Pvt.	Co. L.	
White, James L.	Sgt.	Co. B.	
White, Lemuaul	Pvt.	Co. B.	
White, Leo	Pvt.	Co. B.	
White, Lester M.	Pvt.	Co. I.	
White, Meredith H.	Pvt.	Co. C.	
White, Oscar V.	Pvt.	Co. M.	Wounded
White, Robert E.	Pvt.	Co. B.	
White, Roy R.	Pvt.	Co. A.	
Whiteaker, Arthur E.	Pvt.	Co. F.	Wounded
Whiteaker, Oscar	Pvt.	Co. K.	
Whiteside, Leighton B.	Pvt.	Co. L.	
Whithead, Irvin	Pvt.	Co. M.	
Whitlow, John	Wagoner	Co. B.	
Whitlow, Henry	Pvt.	Co. B.	Wounded
Whitney, Alza N.	Pvt.	Co. H.	
Whitsett, Louis R.	Pvt.	Co. F.	
Whittaker, Ray	Pvt.	Supply Co.	
Whittaker, Robert R.	Wagoner	Supply Co.	
Whittington, Jesse	Pvt.	Co. B.	
Whitwell, Herman B.	Pvt.	Co. E.	
Wickizer, Frank F.	Wagoner	Supply Co.	
Widder, Harry E.	Pvt.	Co. C.	
Wieland, Charles Frank	Pvt.	Co. A.	
Wiesemann, Walter A.	Pvt.	Co. D.	Wounded
Wiggins, Ervin J.	Pvt.	Co. I.	
Wilburn, Jim B.	Pvt.	Co. M.	
Wilcox, Jack P.	Wagoner	Supply Co.	
Wilds, Jesse	Pvt.	Co. M.	
Wilhite, James F.	Sgt.	Co. B.	
Wilke, Frederick G.	Pvt.	Co. E.	
Wilkerson, Charlie B.	Pvt.	Co. L.	
Wilkie, Millard F.	Pvt.	Co. H.	Wounded
Wilkie, Wilbur R.	Sgt.	Co. K.	
Wilkins, Charles M.	Mechanic	Hdqrs. Co.	
Wilkins, Jesse W.	Pvt.	Co. H.	
Wilkinson, George A.	Pvt.	Co. D.	
Wilkinson, George A.	Pvt.	Co. B.	
Wilkinson, John L.	Sgt.	Co. G.	Gassed
Wilkinson, Thomas H.	Pvt.	Co. H.	
Willard, Edward T.	Musician	Hdqrs. Co.	

Willard, Paul J.	Pvt.	Co. A.	
Williams, Albert Lee	Wagoner	Supply Co.	
Williams, Alonza C.	Pvt.	M. G. Co.	Wounded
Williams, Baxtor	Pvt.	Co. I.	
Williams, Charles G.	Pvt.	Co. F.	
Williams, Claud W.	Pvt.	Co. M.	
Williams, Clyde B.	Pvt.	Co. L.	
Williams, Edd S.	Pvt.	Co. G.	
Williams, Edward V.	Pvt.	Co. A.	Died, Ger. Hosp.
Williams, George P.	Pvt.	Co. A.	
Williams, Hampton E.	Pvt.	Co. B.	
Williams, James F.	Wagoner	Supply Co.	
Williams, James H.	Pvt.	Co. H.	
Williams, Leslie W.	Pvt.	Co. M.	Wounded
Williams, Lat. M.	Cook	Co. E.	
Williams, Moses	Pvt.	Co. B.	
Williams, Okey W.	Pvt.	Co. H.	
Williams, Paul H.	Pvt.	Co. H.	
Williams, Robert E.	Pvt.	Co. E.	
Williams, Roscoe	Pvt.	Co. F.	
Williams, Seth N.	Pvt.	Co. L.	
Williams, William J.	Sgt.	Hdqrs. Co.	
Williamschen, Diedrich	Pvt.	Co. D.	
Williamson, Maurice	Pvt.	Co. B.	
Williford, Tom	Pvt.	Co. M.	
Willis, John	Pvt.	Co. L.	
Willits, Charles E.	Pvt.	Co. D.	
Wilson, Arthur L.	Pvt.	Co. F.	
Wilson, Albert C.	Corp.	Co. E.	Wounded
Wilson, Clarence J.	Pvt.	Co. H.	
Wilson, Columbus	Pvt.	M. G. Co.	
Wilson, Eugene P.	Mess Sgt.	Hdqrs. Co.	
Wilson, George	Pvt.	Co. M.	
Wilson, Harry	Pvt.	Co. D.	
Wilson, Harry L.	Pvt.	San. Det.	
Wilson, Joe E.	Pvt.	Co. M.	
Wilson, Lynn	Pvt.	Co. I.	
Wilson, Thomas	Pvt.	Co. F.	
Wilson, Will E.	Pvt.	Co. D.	Gassed
Winch, Everett	Pvt.	San. Det.	
Winch, Raymond	Sgt.	Co. F.	Wounded
Winchell, Bud O.	Corp.	Co. F.	
Winchester, Floyd	Wagoner	Supply Co.	
Windheim, Eiles	Pvt.	Co. B.	
Wininger, Homer E.	Pvt.	Co. A.	
Winkelman, August L.	Pvt.	Co. E.	
Winkler, Louis G.	Pvt.	Co. B.	Gassed
Winter, Leonides C.	Pvt.	Co. L.	
Winterbower, John H.	Pvt.	Co. C.	Wounded
Winston, William W.	Corp.	Co. I	
Winston, Hugo A.	Pvt.	Co. M.	Wounded
Wiseman, Basil T.	Pvt.	Hdqrs. Co.	
Witherington, Albert B.	Pvt.	Co. H.	
Withrow, James G.	Pvt.	Co. M.	
Woerther, Walter J.	Pvt.	Co. D.	
Wolf, Clarence A.	Pvt.	Co. H.	
Wolf, Edward Ernest	Pvt.	Co. F.	
Wolfe, Joe	Mechanic	Supply Co.	
Wolfenbarger, Baxter	Cook	Co. A.	
Wolff, Robert H.	Corp.	Co. H.	Gassed
Wolford, George F.	Pvt.	Co. D.	
Womack, Walter H.	Sgt.	Co. H.	
Woods, Carl M.	Pvt.	Co. L.	
Woods, Edd	Pvt.	Co. D.	

THE MEN BEHIND THE GUNS 213

Wood, Frank L.	Pvt.	Co. A.	
Wood, Grady T.	Pvt.	Co. B.	Gassed
Wood, Jessie F.	Pvt.	Hdqrs. Co.	
Woods, Louis	Cook	Co. M.	Wounded
Wood, Oscar C.	Corp.	Co. D.	
Wood, Vick A.	Corp.	Co. C.	
Woods, Willie C.	Pvt.	Co. M.	
Woodson, Otto	Corp.	Co. C.	Wounded
Woodward, William J. B.	Pvt.	Co. C.	
Wooldridge, Earl	Pvt.	Co. H.	
Woolery, Roy	Pvt.	Co. H.	
Workman, Robert R.	Pvt.	Co. K.	
Worley, Cleburne J.	Pvt.	Co. M.	Wounded
Wrangham, Thomas	Pvt.	Co. C.	Gassed
Wren, Lee	Pvt.	Co. H.	
Wright, Andy R.	Corp.	Co. E.	
Wright, Elmo N.	Pvt.	Hdqrs. Co.	
Wright, Frank W.	Pvt.	Co. D.	
Wright, Harry	Corp.	Co. B.	
Wright, Harry D.	Pvt.	Hdqrs. Co.	
Wright, James M.	Pvt.	Co. D.	
Wright, Jesse W.	Mechanic	Co. F.	
Wright, Leonard	Wagoner	Supply Co.	
Wright, Linus D.	Corp.	Co. K.	
Wright, William H.	Pvt.	Co. F.	
Wright, Youles M.	Pvt.	Co. H.	
Wunderle, Paul B.	Pvt.	Co. D.	
Wyant, Warren R.	Sgt.	Co. B.	
Wyrick, Charles E.	Corp.	Co. D.	Wounded
Wyrick, Chester B.	Saddler	Supply Co.	
Yadon, Joseph N.	Pvt.	Hdqrs. Co.	
Yanda, Theodore	Pvt.	Co. C.	
Yates, Vernie W.	Corp.	M. G. Co.	
Yeakle, Estell L.	Pvt.	Co. C.	
Yeakley, Robert	Pvt.	M. G. Co.	
Yeakley, Hobart	Corp.	Co. B.	Wounded
Yoakum, Joe	Corp.	Co. G.	
Yontz, William H.	Sgt.	Co. B.	Gassed
Yore, John O.	Cook	Hdqrs. Co.	
York, Leonard	Wagoner	Co. M.	Wounded
York, Samuel T.	Mechanic	Co. D.	Wounded
York, Walter C.	Corp.	Co. A.	
Young, Charles	Pvt.	Co. C.	
Young, Chester C.	Bugler	Co. E.	
Young, Daniel F.	Pvt.	Co. K.	
Young, William W.	Corp.	Co. A.	Wounded
Youngblood, Dan R.	Pvt.	Co. E.	
Younger, John E.	Pvt.	Supply Co.	
Yowell, Daniel J.	Pvt.	Co. C.	
Zager, Anthony	Pvt.	Co. I.	
Zaiss, Joseph	Reg. Sup. Sgt.	Supply Co.	
Zanarski, Mike J.	Pvt.	Co. D.	
Zanois, Bill (William)	Pvt.	Co. H.	
Zapf, Herman H.	Pvt.	Co. A.	
Zavalney, Vink	Pvt.	Co. E.	Wounded
Zior, Samuel	Pvt.	M. G. Co.	
Zipse, George C.	Pvt.	Co. E.	
Zoeller, Frank S.	Pvt.	M. G. Co.	
Zourdos, Phillip	Pvt.	Hdqrs. Co.	
Zucker, Harry	Pvt.	Co. M.	
Zuk, Karp	Pvt.	Co. H.	

Roster of 140th Infantry
(Alphabetically)

Men Who Were Killed, Wounded, Gassed, or Transferred, and Were Not with the Regiment on April 1, 1919

Abbott, Floyd	Mechanic	Co. I.	Wounded
Abbott, Walter	Pvt.	Hdqrs. Co.	
Adams, Ernest	Pvt.	Co. M.	Killed in Action
Adams, Henry A.	Pvt.	Co. H.	Wounded
Adrian, Charles R.	Pvt.	Co. D.	
Aelem, Everett T.	Wagoner	Supply Co.	Died 2-25-18
Albertson, Levi	Pvt.	Co. A.	Died of Wounds
Albright, Fred L.	Pvt.	Co. H.	Wounded
Aldridge, Phillip E.	Pvt.	Co. H.	
Alger, Henry L.	Pvt.	Co. F.	Wounded
Allen, Elijah J.	Pvt.	Co. H.	
Allen, Manuel F.	Pvt.	Co G.	
Allen, Ollis C.	Pvt.	Co. D.	
Allen, Thomas E.	Cook	Co. E.	Wounded
Allison, Bruce	Bnd. Corp.	Hdqrs. Co.	
Alspaugh, Tyler Brewer	Corp.	Hdqrs. Co.	Wounded
Altenthal, Clarence	Pvt.	M. G. Co.	Killed in Action
Altis, Charles C.	Pvt.	Co. F.	
Amos, William A.	Pvt.	Co. B.	
Anderson, Albert L.	Pvt.	Co. K.	Died B. H. 91
Anderson, Adolph H.	Mechanic	Co. C.	
Anderson, Carl A.	Pvt.	Co. A.	Wounded
Anderson, Roy	Pvt.	Co. H.	Killed in Action
Anderson, Samuel A.	Corp.	Co. C.	Wounded
Andrews, Joe	Pvt.	Co. C.	
Antonio, Appolini	Pvt.	Co. I.	
Appleby, Newton	Pvt.	Co. E.	Wounded
Arnold, John W.	Sgt. Maj.	Hdqrs. Co.	
Arnold, Walter P.	Cook	Co. H.	Wounded
Arnold, William H.	Sgt.	Hdqrs. Co.	
Arnold, George E.	Pvt.	Co. D.	
Arr, Olvie	Pvt.	Co. I.	Wounded
Arthur, Henry	Cook	M. G. Co.	
Ash, William W.	Pvt.	Co. C.	
Asbury, Luther L.	Sgt.	Co. F.	Wounded
Ashby, Floyd B.	Pvt.	Co. H.	Gassed
Ashcraft, Ziba G.	Corp.	Co. H.	Wounded
Askew, Gordon W.	Pvt.	Co. H.	
Ayres, Elbert H.	Cook	Co. I.	
Bacchus, Leslie J.	Corp.	Co. D.	
Bailey, Hoke S.	Pvt.	Co. K.	
Baker, Allen F.	Pvt.	Co. G.	Wounded
Baker, John H.	Pvt.	Co. H.	Killed
Baker, Robert H.	Sgt.	Co. H.	Wounded
Baker, Roy D.	Sgt.	Co. A.	
Baker, William R.	Pvt.	Hdqrs. Co.	
Baldwin, Angus T.	Pvt.	Co. L.	Gassed
Baldwin, Evert W.	Pvt.	Co. F.	
Baldwin, William T.	Pvt.	Co. G.	

THE MEN BEHIND THE GUNS 215

Bales, Cleveland A.	Pvt.	Co. G.	
Ball, Howard S.	Pvt.	Co. B.	Killed
Ball, Ollie	Corp.	Co. I.	Wounded
Bandel, Morris A.	Corp.	Co. G.	Wounded
Barber, Sam	Cook	Co. C.	Killed
Barkley, Ruben G.	Pvt.	Co. D.	
Barmann, John C.	Pvt.	Co. F.	
Barnes, Bartoney	Pvt.	Co. F.	Killed
Barnett, Charles J.	Pvt.	Co. K.	
Barnett, Virgil L.	Pvt.	Co. K.	
Barnett, Merrel J.	Sgt.	Co. B.	
Barnett, John F.	Pvt.	Co. G.	
Barry, Henry J.	Pvt.	Co. B.	
Bateman, William D.	Sgt.	Co. K.	Wounded, Died
Bateman, Walter	Bugler	Co. K.	
Baugh, Wesley	Pvt.	Co. G.	
Baughman, Arthur B.	Corp.	Co. F.	Wounded
Baughman, Dewey G.	Corp.	Co. C.	Killed
Bays, Henry	Pvt.	Co. G.	Wounded
Beal, Eugene	Pvt.	Co. K.	
Beall, Cambridge G.	Pvt.	Co. A.	Wounded
Beard, George T.	Corp.	Co. B.	
Bechtel, Andrew C.	Pvt.	Co. C.	Wounded
Beck, Cecil B.	Pvt.	Hqdrs. Co.	Gassed
Beck, Wilson S.	Pvt.	Co. B.	
Becker, Chris M.	Corp.	M. G. Co.	Wounded
Bedwall, Paul	Corp.	Hdqrs. Co.	
Bedwell, Samuel M.	Corp.	Co. H.	Wounded
Beecher, Alfred	Cook	Co. G.	Wounded
Beer, Samuel S.	Pvt.	Co. K.	Gassed
Beers, Forest H.	Sgt.	Co. K.	Gassed
Begey, Ben F.	Pvt.	M. G. Co.	
Beistll, Tiffin O.	Sgt.	Co. H.	
Beizenhertz, Ewald L.	Pvt.	Co. A.	Wounded, Died
Bell, Elmo J.	Pvt.	Hdqrs. Co.	Wounded
Bender, William	Pvt.	Co. L.	Wounded
Bennett, Chester A.	Corp.	Co. F.	
Bennett, Ellerie L.	Wagoner	Supply Co.	
Benning, Major	Pvt.	Co. A.	
Bensenn, Adolph	Pvt.	Co. G.	
Benson, Vivian K.	Pvt.	Co. H.	
Benson, Hubert	Cook	Co. I.	
Berge, Alfred F.	Pvt.	Co. B.	
Bernstein, Harry	Pvt.	Co. H.	Wounded
Biggs, Rufus	Corp.	Co. A.	
Binz, Fred H.	Corp.	Co. G.	Gassed
Birdwell, Jesse W.	Pvt.	Co. G.	Wounded
Bishop, George B.	Corp.	Co. K.	Wounded
Bishop, Warner J.	Sgt.	Co. A.	
Black, Jos. H.	Pvt.	Co. B.	Dead
Black, William P.	Pvt.	Co. D.	Killed
Blackburn, David E.	Corp.	Co. A.	
Blackford, Calvin	Bugler	Co. C.	Wounded
Blackwell, Charles L.	Cook	Co. F.	Gassed
Blackwell, Dick	Corp.	Co. B.	Gassed
Blackwell, Thomas Martin	Pvt.	Co. A.	Wounded
Blann, Lawrence R.	Pvt.	Co. G.	Killed
Blanton, Emmett E.	Pvt.	Co. C.	
Blattner, Charles	Pvt.	Co. L.	
Blaylock, Hervy L.	Pvt.	Co. D.	
Blaylock, Will	Pvt.	Co. K.	Wounded
Bledsoe, Carl Allen	Pvt.	Co. F.	Gassed
Blegen, Paul O.	Pvt.	Co. A.	
Blessing, Joseph W.	Pvt.	Co. A.	Wounded

Bliss, Frank J.	Sgt.	Co. A.	
Blocher, Joseph S.	Sgt.	Co. L.	
Block, Joseph	Corp.	Co. B.	Killed
Blyze, Joseph H.	Pvt.	Co. E.	
Boatwright, Ed	Pvt.	Co. C.	Wounded
Bodwell, George F.	Pvt.	Co. C.	Wounded
Bolin, Bennie E.	Pvt.	Co. E.	
Bollinger, Jesse M.	Pvt.	Co. H.	Wounded
Bond, Fred A.	Pvt.	Co. D.	
Bonner, Henry Jake	Pvt.	Co. A.	Wounded
Boon, Willis L.	Pvt.	Co. D.	Wounded
Borchardt, Albert	Pvt.	Co. I.	Wounded
Borchert, Leo L.	Pvt.	Hdqrs. Co.	
Borckman, Gilbert G.	Pvt.	Co. G.	
Boswell, Merrith H.	Pvt.	Co. G.	Killed
Bottoms, Rolla T.	Corp.	Co. B.	
Boulton, Ray	Sgt.	Co. E.	
Bourne, Edgar J.	Sgt.	M. G. Co.	
Bowen, Leroy F. C.	Pvt.	San. Det.	
Bowman, Lester L.	Pvt.	Co. A.	
Boyce, Oliver	Pvt.	Co. I.	Wounded
Boyd, Milton	Pvt.	Co. A.	Wounded
Boyer, Otis L.	Pvt.	Co. F.	Wounded
Boylau, Bernard F.	Pvt.	Co. C.	
Boyle, Frank J.	Pvt.	Co. C.	Wounded
Boysel, Albert M.	Pvt.	Co. C.	
Brabeck, Joseph	Corp.	Co. K.	Wounded
Bradley, Roy M.	Pvt.	Co. H.	
Bradshaw, Clarence A.	Sgt.	Co. K.	
Brainard, Earl A.	Sgt.	Co. E.	Wounded
Breazier, Earl B.	Pvt.	Co. E.	
Breckenridge, John C.	Sgt.	Co. K.	
Breckenridge, Eddie	Pvt.	Co. H.	
Breedlove, Elza	Pvt.	Co. G.	Killed, Sniper
Breedlove, Everet	Pvt.	Co. G.	Wounded
Brendel, John F. C.	Pvt.	Co. C.	
Brewsaugh, Eaden O.	Pvt.	Co. I.	Gassed
Bridges, Thomas W.	Pvt.	Co. D.	Killed
Brockman, Carl	Sgt.	Co. L.	
Brogberg, Edward A.	Pvt.	Co. H.	Killed
Brooks, Charles H.	Pvt.	Co. K.	
Brothers, Edward	Pvt.	Co. L.	Wounded
Brothers, Edgar	Pvt.	Co. I.	
Brown, Albert A.	Corp.	Co. E.	Wounded
Brown, Andy A.	Pvt.	Co. F.	
Brown, Ernest	Corp.	Co. H.	
Brown, Frank A.	Sgt.	Hdqrs. Co.	
Brown, George C.	Pvt.	Co. H.	Gassed
Brown, Gordon M.	Corp.	Co. K.	Killed
Brown, Henry	Pvt.	Co. I.	
Brown, Lewis S.	Corp.	Co. H.	Wounded
Brown, Willie E.	Pvt.	Co. F.	
Browne, William A.	Pvt.	San. Det.	
Broyles, Jesse R.	Pvt.	Co. H.	
Bruffey, Raymond T.	Pvt.	Hdqrs. Co.	Wounded
Brumfield, Roger T.	Pvt.	Co. A.	Wounded, Died
Brundage, Charles H.	Pvt.	Co. C.	Wounded
Bryant, Jonathan O.	Pvt.	Co. H.	
Bryant, Ray H.	Pvt.	Co. G.	Killed
Buchanan, Harold E.	Pvt.	Co. K.	
Buchan, James N.	Wagoner	Supply Co.	
Buchman, Ralph E.	Corp.	Co. E.	
Buck, Clarence R.	Pvt.	Hdqrs. Co.	Wounded
Buckman, Julius M.	Pvt.	Co. C.	Wounded

THE MEN BEHIND THE GUNS   217

Buckner, Carl J.	Corp.	Co. H.	Wounded
Buehre, Ernest H.	Pvt.	Co. K.	Wounded
Buetler, Frank A.	Pvt.	Co. F.	
Bumgardner, Jacob E.	Pvt.	Co. E.	
Bundy, James	Pvt.	Co. E.	
Burchett, Thomas M.	Pvt.	Co. I.	
Burke, Edmund M.	Sgt.	Co. G.	
Burk, John C.	Corp.	Co. D.	
Burnett, Oscar P.	Pvt.	Co. G.	Wounded
Butler, Joseph C.	Pvt.	Co. D.	
Butterfield, Charles E.	Sgt.	Co. K.	
Button, Flynn F.	Pvt.	Co. C.	Killed
Byard, Ernest L.	Pvt.	Co. G.	
Byrd, Robert H.	Corp.	Supply Co.	
Caldwell, Elmer	Pvt.	Co. K.	
Caldwell, Frank	Pvt.	Co. M.	Wounded
Caldwell, Lon S.	Pvt.	M. G. Co.	Killed
Callery, Ralph E.	Sgt.	Co. F.	Wounded
Calvert, Thomas R.	Pvt.	Co. F.	
Calvin, Paul C.	Pvt.	Co. F.	
Camden, Oscar F.	Pvt.	Co. K.	
Camp, Joseph	Cook	Co. E.	
Campbell, Arthur L.	Sgt.	Co. B.	
Campbell, Earl H.	Pvt.	Co. M.	Killed
Campbell, Eugene O.	Pvt.	Co. H.	Killed
Canaday, Charles M.	Pvt.	Co. D.	Gassed
Carroll, Hubert W.	Corp.	Co. G.	Wounded
Carroll, James W.	Pvt.	Co. M.	
Carroll, Philip M.	Pvt.	M. G. Co.	Died of Wounds
Carter, Arch A.	Pvt.	Hdqrs. Co.	Wounded
Carter, George	Pvt.	Co. E.	
Case, Elmer L.	Pvt.	Co. D.	Wounded
Casteel, Harvey	Corp.	Co. E.	Killed
Caton, H. P.	Pvt.	Co. B.	Killed
Caughenbaugh, John C.	Pvt.	M. G. Co.	
Caylor, Leonard C.	Sgt.	Co. F.	
Chandler, Ira B.	Pvt.	Co. C.	Wounded
Chaney, Walter J.	Pvt.	Co. F.	
Chestnut, Kirby	Sgt.	Co. B.	
Christy, Lester B.	Pvt.	Co. G.	Wounded
Claborn, Walter H.	Pvt.	Co. A.	
Clark, Virgil	Pvt.	Co. I.	Wounded
Clark, William L.	Pvt.	Co. A.	
Clasby, Earl D.	Pvt.	Co. A.	
Clebenstine, Elk	Pvt.	Co. L.	
Clement, Darius	Pvt.	Co. G.	
Clevenger, Everett	Pvt.	Co. H.	
Cluckey, Charles	Wagoner	Co. G.	
Cobb, Lawrence L.	Corp.	Co. G.	
Cobb, Willie	Pvt.	Co. L.	Wounded
Coberly, John A.	Pvt.	Co. K.	
Coffey, Chester M.	Pvt.	Hdqrs. Co.	
Coffin, Charles	Pvt.	Co. L.	Wounded
Coleman, James M.	Pvt.	Co. L.	Wounded, Died
Coleman, John E.	Pvt.	Co. C.	
Coll, Harry	Pvt.	Co. F.	
Coller, Thomas C.	Pvt.	Co. K.	Wounded
Collier, Henry	Pvt.	M. G. Co.	Killed
Collins, Ben C.	Pvt.	Co. F.	Wounded
Collins, Emil Z.	Pvt.	Co. F.	
Collins, Otis F.	Sgt.	Co. M.	
Collins, William A.	Pvt.	San. Det.	
Collum, Ralph B.	Pvt.	Hdqrs. Co.	Wounded
Colyar, Irving M.	Pvt.	Co. K.	Wounded

Conley, Mike	Pvt.	Co. M.	
Connelly, Patrick K.	Wagoner	Supply Co.	
Cons, Clarence F.	Sgt.	Co. F.	
Cook, Edgar B.	Pvt.	Co. A.	Killed
Cook, Fred	Pvt.	Co. M.	
Cook, Teddie	Pvt.	Co. L.	Wounded
Cooley, William A.	Pvt.	M. G. Co.	Killed
Coons, Daniel F.	Cook	Co. G.	
Cooper, Henry R.	Pvt.	Co. D.	Wounded
Cooper, Ohla M.	Pvt.	Co. C.	Wounded
Cooper, Silas W.	Pvt.	Co. F.	
Cooper, Victor J.	Pvt.	Co. G.	Wounded
Cora, Claiborn	Pvt.	Co. K.	
Corbett, Fred H.	Pvt.	Co. H.	
Cordell, Amos	Pvt.	Co. E.	
Cordell, William B.	Pvt.	Co. E.	
Cordill, Russell M.	Pvt.	Co. E.	Wounded
Corlberg, John Edwin	Pvt.	Co. M.	Killed
Cornett, Charles	Pvt.	Co. B.	Killed
Corporon, Harold	Pvt.	Hdqrs. Co.	
Cosgriff, Earl J.	Corp.	Co. C.	Killed
Couch, Robert P.	Pvt.	Co. G.	Wounded
Coughlin, Harry W.	Sgt.	Co. E.	
Cover, William P.	Pvt.	Hdqrs. Co.	Killed
Cowgill, Walter	Corp.	Co. L.	Killed
Cowick, Mike	Pvt.	Co. C.	
Cox, Lloyd J.	Sgt.	Co. K.	Wounded
Cozine, Alva	Corp.	Co. B.	
Crain, Jerry N.	Pvt.	Co. G.	Killed
Crambert, William E.	Sgt.	Co. E.	
Crawford, Joseph	Pvt.	Co. D.	Died of Wounds
Crawford, William R.	Sgt.	Co. K.	Wounded
Crews, Arthur E.	Pvt.	Co. C.	
Crews, Lester	Musician	Cas. Band	
Crittenden, Thomas R.	Pvt.	Co. A.	Killed
Crook, Oron B.	Pvt.	Co. H.	Died of Wounds
Crook, Thomas C.	Cook	M. G. Co.	Died B. H.
Cross, Charles C.	Sgt.	Co. A.	
Crouch, Edward	Pvt.	Co. C.	
Crow, Ed. A.	Corp.	Co. E.	
Crowley, Willard	Pvt.	Co. F.	
Crown, Solomon L.	Pvt.	Co. L.	Wounded
Cuberly, Fred R.	Corp.	Co. K.	
Culbertson, Marion	Pvt.	Co. I.	
Culley, Charles S.	Pvt.	Co. A.	Wounded
Cullom, George T.	Corp.	Co. A.	Killed
Curtis, Leonard	Pvt.	Co. C.	
Curtin, James T.	Pvt.	Hdqrs. Co.	
Dagley, Scott	Corp.	Co. H.	Wounded
Dahl, Harry O.	Corp.	Co. E.	
Dailey, Charles O.	Pvt.	Co. E.	
Dailey, Elton N.	Corp.	Co. E.	
Daily, Francis V.	Pvt.	Co. K.	
Dancey, Paul	Corp.	Co. I.	Killed
Danford, Charles O.	Pvt.	Co. E.	
Dannenberg, Herman H.	Color Sgt.	Hdqrs. Co.	
Darcy, John M.	Pvt.	Co. L.	Wounded
Darlington, William	Pvt.	Co. I.	
Darnell, Wm. H.	Pvt.	Co. F.	
Darrah, Lee	Mechanic	Co. F.	
Darrah, Loyd E.	Cook	M. G. Co.	
Daugherty, Harvey N.	Pvt.	Hdqrs. Co.	Killed
Daul, John F.	Pvt.	San. Det.	
Davidson, Robert C.	Pvt.	Co. C.	Wounded

THE MEN BEHIND THE GUNS 219

Name	Rank	Unit	Status
Davidson, Wilton W.	Pvt.	Supply Co.	
Davison, Bert	Pvt.	Hdqrs. Co.	
Davis, David D.	Pvt.	Co. G.	Wounded
Davis, Earl H.	Pvt.	Co. D.	
Davis, Elbert A.	Pvt.	Co. C.	
Davis, Guy Carl	Pvt.	Hdqrs. Co.	Wounded
Davis, Harry S.	Sgt.	San. Det.	Wounded
Davis, Jewell	Pvt.	Co. E.	
Davis, Jobe	Pvt.	Co. C.	
Davis, Leslie	Pvt.	Co. K.	Wounded, Died
Davis, Milo	Pvt.	Co. C.	
Davis, William H.	Pvt.	Co. L.	
Dawson, Francis M.	Pvt.	Co. E.	
Dawson, Henry	Pvt.	Co. E.	
Deatherage, Virgil P.	Corp.	Co. H.	Wounded
Decker, Daniel	Ptg.	Co. B.	
Decker, George E.	Pvt.	Co. B.	
Dédo, Charles G.	Sgt.	Co. C.	
DeGroat, Fred	Mess Sgt.	Co. C.	
Deis, James F.	Sgt.	Co. K.	Killed
Denhardt, Lucian O.	Pvt.	Co. A.	
Dennis, Otto	Corp.	Co. I.	
Dennis, Ruby	Pvt.	Co. H.	
Dent, Lee W.	Pvt.	Co. I.	Wounded
Denton, Raymond C.	Pvt.	Hdqrs. Co.	Wounded
Detrich, William A.	Pvt.	San. Det.	
Detrie, Ambros	Pvt.	Co. I.	Wounded
Devaney, Michael E.	Pvt.	Co. E.	
DeWitt, Ralph E.	Sgt.	Co. A.	
Dickerson, Jesse L.	Pvt.	Co. H.	
Dickerson, William J.	Pvt.	Co. D.	
Diemer, Frank	Pvt.	Co. F.	
Dignan, Emmett J.	Sgt.	Hdqrs. Co.	
Dillon, David A.	Pvt.	Co. C.	
Dillon, Joseph	Sgt.	San. Det.	Killed
Dingey, George D.	Pvt.	Co. F.	
Dirk, Henry E.	Corp.	Co. F.	
Divine, James R.	Pvt.	Co. C.	
Dixon, Charley M.	Pvt.	Co. K.	
Dodd, Frank	Pvt.	Co. H.	
Dodson, George B.	Pvt.	Co. G.	Gassed
Donna, Peter	Pvt.	Co. C.	
Donovan, John	Pvt.	Hdqrs Co.	Wounded
Dorrell, Otto	Pvt.	Co. C.	
Dosch, Charles A.	Pvt.	Co. L.	
Doty, William E.	Pvt.	Hdqrs. Co.	
Dougherty, Stephen E.	Sgt.	M. G. Co.	
Douglas, James A.	Pvt.	Co. H.	
Douglass, Leonard	Pvt.	Co. C.	
Dover, Peter	Pvt.	Co. K.	
Dowell, Roy E.	Pvt.	Co. C.	
Dowey, John	Sgt.	Co. C.	Died of Wounds
Dowling, John F.	Pvt.	Co. D.	
Drake, William N.	Pvt.	Supply Co.	
Dreasler, Clarence O.	Pvt.	Co. K.	Wounded
Drovetta, John H.	Corp.	Co. A.	Died B. H.
Drury, Archie J.	Pvt.	Co. A.	
Dry, Clarence C.	Sgt.	Co. I.	Killed
Dugger, Ross	Pvt.	Co. B.	Wounded
Dumas, Hugh L.	Pvt.	Co. L.	Killed
Duncan, Gilbert R.	Corp.	Co. C.	Wounded
Dunn, Harry	Sgt.	Co. H.	
Durham, Henry F.	Pvt.	Hdqrs. Co.	
Eaden, Herbert	Pvt.	Co. I.	

Eades, Floyd A.	Sgt.	Co. E.	
Eagan, Emmette A.	Pvt.	Co. A.	
Earp, Cleave	Pvt.	Co. K.	Wounded
Easley, Buford	Pvt.	Co. G.	Killed
Easter, Joe T.	Pvt.	Co. E.	Killed
Ecton, Frank C.	Sgt.	Co. B.	
Edes, Merold L.	Pvt.	Co. C.	
Edwards, Arlie	Pvt.	Co. K.	Gassed
Edwards, John C.	Corp.	Co. B.	
Egner, Charles J.	Corp.	Co. C.	Wounded
Einig, Walter J.	Machinist	Co. C.	Wounded
Elliott, Don	Sgt.	Co. D.	
Elliott, Graham	Pvt.	Co. H.	Wounded
Elliott, William L.	Pvt.	Co. K.	
Ellis, Charles H.	Pvt.	Co. M.	
Ely, Sims	Sup. Sgt.	Co. G.	
Embrey, Guy	Pvt.	Co. K.	Wounded
Engberg, Raymond O.	Corp.	Co. G.	Wounded
Engler, Marshall H.	Corp.	Co. D.	Wounded
Ennis, George	Pvt.	Co. K.	Wounded
Epperson, Joseph	Pvt.	Co. C.	
Erickson, Charlie	Pvt.	Co. C.	
Erickson, John H.	Pvt.	Hdqrs. Co.	
Esaw, Peter D.	Corp.	Co. D.	
Ettinger, William L.	Pvt.	Co. M.	Wounded
Evans, Claude O.	Pvt.	Co. C.	Wounded
Evans, Elmer E.	Pvt.	Co. G.	
Evans, Floyd A.	Pvt.	Co. K.	
Evans, Harry P.	Pvt.	Hdqrs. Co.	
Evans, Thomas F.	Pvt.	Co. K.	
Evans, Thomas I.	Corp.	Co. A.	
Everett, Noah H.	Cook	Co. H.	Gassed
Farmer, Arlo J.	Pvt.	Co. A.	Wounded
Farmer, McKinley	Corp.	Co. G.	Wounded
Felkins, Earl E.	Pvt.	Co. M.	
Fenster, Joseph	Pvt.	Co. H.	
Fenton, William	Pvt.	Co. M.	Wounded
Ferguson, Sam G.	Pvt.	Co. G.	
Fisher, Alfred E.	Pvt.	Co. H.	Wounded
Fisher, Ernest	Pvt.	San. Det.	
Fisher, William H.	Pvt.	Co. F.	Killed
Fite, Marion C.	Pvt.	Co. K.	Wounded
Fitzgerald, Walter	Pvt.	Co. E.	
Fitzpatrick, Glen	Pvt.	Co. C.	Killed
Fitzpatrick, Raymond R.	Pvt.	Co. K.	Wounded
Fixico, Sonny	Pvt.	Co. L.	Killed
Fizer, Bennie C.	Sgt.	Co. A.	
Flaherty, Joseph F.	Pvt.	Co. H.	
Fleek, Lawrence E.	Pvt.	Co. M.	
Fletcher, George E.	Wagoner	Supply Co.	
Floyd, Henry O.	Pvt.	San. Det.	
Floyd, Samuel D.	Pvt.	Co. F.	Wounded
Foley, Samuel R.	Cook	Co. H.	
Foltz, Lester L.	Corp.	Co. K.	
Ford, James C.	Pvt.	Co. H.	
Ford, Louis E.	Pvt.	Co. K.	Killed
Forester, James A.	Pvt.	Co. E.	
Forsythe, Walter	Corp.	Co. I.	Wounded
Foster, Oscar R.	Pvt.	Co. K.	
Fowler, Samuel C.	Sgt.	Co. M.	Gassed
Fox, Charles	Corp.	Co. L.	Killed
Fox, Mott L.	Corp.	Co. E.	Wounded
Fox, Roy O.	Pvt.	Co. K.	
Franklin, William	Cook	Co. E.	Wounded

THE MEN BEHIND THE GUNS 221

Franks, Elbert W.	Pvt.	Co. I.	
Franzie, Francisco	Pvt.	Co. H.	Died of Wounds
Frazier, Willie L.	Pvt.	Co. A.	
Frederick, Charles	Sgt.	Co. C.	
Frederick, Samuel L.	Pvt.	Co. K.	Killed
Frederick, Samuel R.	Pvt.	Co. I.	Died of Wounds
Fredman, Royal J.	Sgt.	M. G. Co.	
French, Lawrence L.	Pvt.	Co. D.	
Frerichs, Edward A.	Pvt.	Co. A.	
Friend, Elmer	Pvt.	Co. K.	Wounded
Frost, Chauncey B.	Pvt.	Co. B.	Gassed
Fuller, Oda B.	Corp.	Co. F.	
Fullerton, Forest T.	Sgt.	Co. D.	
Fuqua, Edgar	Corp.	Co. M.	Killed
Gaddy, Monte	Corp.	Co. K.	
Gaines, Benjamine L.	Pvt.	Co. H.	Wounded
Gaines, Norman I.	Sgt.	Co. L.	
Galvin, William M.	Pvt.	Supply Co.	
Garner, Charles C.	Pvt.	Co. D.	
Garnett, Hervy	Pvt.	Co. E.	Killed
Garrett, Solomon N.	Corp.	Co. E.	Wounded
Garrett, Walter C.	Pvt.	Co. D.	
Garrison, John	Pvt.	Co. H.	
Gartin, Alva	Mechanic	Co. F.	Wounded
Gaupp, Gus O.	Pvt.	Co. K.	Wounded
Geist, Edwin J.	Pvt.	Co. A.	Wounded
Gentry, Wayne	Pvt.	Co. B.	Died of Wounds
Geyer, George D.	Sgt.	Co. C.	Died
Giager, Fred	Pvt.	Co. L.	Wounded
Gibbons, Calvert V.	Mechanic	Co. B.	
Gibson, Phil S.	Sgt.	Co. G.	
Giles, Henry	Pvt.	Co. I.	Wounded
Giles, Leslie F.	Pvt.	Co. D.	
Gill, Glover	Corp.	Co. K.	Wounded
Ginger, Virgil	Pvt.	Co. K.	
Givens, Lloyd B.	Pvt.	Co. I.	
Glastetter, Martin	Pvt.	Hdqrs. Co.	
Glover, Ale	Pvt.	Co. K.	
Godat, James E.	Sgt.	Co. C.	
Goddard, Nathan J.	Pvt.	Co. F.	
Godt, Henry W.	Pvt.	Co. C.	Wounded
Goff, Samuel L.	Pvt.	Co. K.	Wounded
Goodwin, Bill	Pvt.	Co. K.	Wounded
Goodman, Maurice W.	Pvt.	Hdqrs. Co.	
Gordon, Winfred D.	Pvt.	Hdqrs. Co.	Gassed
Gosoroski, Frank M.	Pvt.	Co. A.	
Gossard, Hampton D.	Sgt.	Co. L.	Wounded
Gottschalk, Otto	Pvt.	Co. L.	Wounded
Gower, William C.	Pvt.	Co. M.	
Graen, Eldon	Color Sgt.	Hdqrs. Co.	
Gragg, Lora G.	Pvt.	Co. K.	
Graham, Charles N.	Cook	Co. E.	
Graham, Ray	Corp.	Co. E.	
Grant, John H.	Sgt.	Hdqrs. Co.	
Grant, Joseph W.	Pvt.	Co. D.	
Graves, Harold F.	Sgt.	Co. G.	
Gray, Arthur B.	Pvt.	Co. E.	
Gray, Charles A.	Pvt.	Hdqrs. Co.	
Gray, Robert H.	Sgt.	Co. F.	
Green, Buford	Pvt.	Co. I.	
Green, Charles M.	Wagoner	Supply Co.	
Greene, Francis W.	Corp.	M. G. Co.	Killed
Green, John W.	Pvt.	Co. C.	
Greer, Leslie E.	Pvt.	Co. C.	Wounded

Green, Merel C.	Corp.	Co. L.	Wounded
Greenwell, Alvie R.	Sgt.	Co. K.	Died of Wounds
Greer, Al	Pvt.	Co. A.	
Greer, Alfred J.	Pvt.	Co. K.	Wounded
Greer, Noah	Corp.	Co. I.	Wounded
Greer, Raymond S.	Pvt.	Co. K.	Killed
Greer, Robert	Pvt.	Co. K.	
Gregg, Walter H.	Pvt.	Co. H.	
Gregory, Robt. L.	Corp.	Co. F.	Gassed
Gresham, Floyd A.	Sgt.	Co. M.	
Griffith, Fred	Pvt.	Co. G.	Killed
Griggsby, William A.	Pvt.	Co. L.	
Grote, Sherman	Pvt.	Co. I.	Killed
Grovenburgh, Norman H.	Pvt.	Co. L.	
Guinn, Roy C.	Pvt.	Co. K.	Wounded
Gunderson, Glenn	Corp.	Co. A.	
Haberstroh, Ray E.	Sgt.	Co. I.	
Hackney, Harry	Pvt.	Co. B.	Gassed
Hager, Carl	Pvt.	Co. I.	Killed
Hageman, Ralph L.	Pvt.	Co. D.	Died of Wounds
Hagle, James T.	Pvt.	Co. G.	
Hahn, Charles	Sgt.	Co. H.	Gassed
Hahn, Joseph F.	Pvt.	Co. A.	Wounded
Haist, George	Corp.	Co. I.	Wounded
Haist, Sterling	Pvt.	Co. I.	Wounded
Hale, Carrel P.	Pvt.	Co. L.	Killed
Hale, Frank L.	Corp.	Co. B.	
Haley, Roy P.	Pvt.	Co. B.	
Halin, George W.	Corp.	Hdqrs. Co.	Wounded, Died
Hall, George R.	Pvt.	Co. G.	
Hallett, Charles M.	Pvt.	M. G. Co.	Wounded
Halverson, Iver	Pvt.	Co. E.	Wounded
Hammer, Oscar J.	Sgt.	Co. A.	Wounded
Hammontree, Virgil I.	Corp.	Co. K.	Wounded, Died Died B. H.
Hampton, Grant	Pvt.	Co. C.	Gassed
Hampy, Ernest E.	Sgt.	Co. D.	
Hamstra, Klaas	Pvt.	Co. B.	Wounded
Hanby, Elmer	Pvt.	Hdqrs. Co.	Wounded
Hancock, Paul F.	Sgt.	Co. G.	
Haney, William H.	Pvt.	Co. B.	
Hanks, Claude	Pvt.	Co. H.	Killed
Hanks, Jacob	Pvt.	Co. I.	
Hanson, Alfred	Pvt.	Co. C.	Wounded, Died
Harlan, James E.	Sgt.	M. G. Co.	Wounded
Harper, Ralph P.	Sgt.	Co. B.	Died of Wounds
Harrington, Phillip	Corp.	Co. I.	Wounded
Harris, Fred B.	Pvt.	Co. H.	
Harris, Jack	Corp.	Co. C.	Wounded
Harris, Lester L.	Corp.	Co. C.	Killed
Harris, Marion L.	Corp.	Co. H.	
Harris, Robert L.	Mechanic	Co. M.	
Harris, Roy D.	Pvt.	Co. I.	
Harris, Walter H.	Cook	Co. E.	
Harris, William J.	Corp.	Co. D.	Wounded
Harrison, Robert D.	Sgt. Mjr.	Hdqrs. Co.	Wounded
Hartman, Lee H.	Pvt.	Co. C.	Wounded
Hartness, George W.	Pvt.	Co. D.	
Harvey, Frederick O.	Pvt.	Co. E.	
Hauber, John M.	Pvt.	Hdqrs. Co.	
Haydon, Robert D.	Corp.	Hdqrs. Co.	Wounded
Hayes, Guy	Pvt.	Co. I.	
Hays, John W.	Pvt.	Co. M.	
Hazlett, Harold H.	Pvt.	Hdqrs. Co.	

THE MEN BEHIND THE GUNS 223

Head, William R.	Pvt.	Co. A.	
Healey, Harry W.	Pvt.	Co. B.	Died of Wounds
Heferkamp, Harry A. H.	Pvt.	Hdqrs. Co.	Killed
Heineman, Arthur	Pvt.	Co. I.	
Heisserer, Vincent	Pvt.	Co. L.	
Heisterberg, Edward J.	Corp.	Co. D.	Wounded
Helvey, Willie B.	Pvt.	Co. E.	Wounded
Hemmen, Arthur W.	Sup. Sgt.	Co. I.	Wounded
Henderson, Eugene	Pvt.	M. G. Co.	Wounded
Henderson, John	Corp.	Co. I.	
Hendricks, Henry A.	Pvt.	Co. G.	
Hendricks, Lee R.	Sgt.	Co. E.	
Hendrix, Arthur W.	Pvt.	Co. H.	Wounded
Hendrix, Johnston A.	Pvt.	Co. K.	Killed
Henkel, Anthony	Pvt.	Co. I.	Killed
Henley, Otis	Pvt.	Co. K.	
Henry, James Harrison	Pvt.	Co. L.	
Henry, James N.	Sgt.	Co. F.	
Hensley, James	Pvt.	Co. L.	
Hensen, Ernest E.	Pvt.	Co. E.	
Herink, Albert	Pvt.	Co. L.	
Herman, Edward	Pvt.	Co. L.	Wounded
Herron, Arthur O. D.	Pvt.	Co. I.	Gassed
Hessenflow, Jesse	Corp.	Co. H.	
Heureux, Onseimel	Pvt.	Co. I.	
Hiam, Bennie	Pvt.	Co. I.	
Hiatt, George E.	Pvt.	Co. K.	Wounded and Gassed
Hiatt, Russell S.	Sgt.	Co. D.	Wounded
Hickerson, Temple	Corp.	Co. I.	Gassed
Hicklin, Elmer	Corp.	Co. I.	
Hickman, Harry E.	Pvt.	Co. M.	
Hight, Floyd	Sgt.	Co. I.	
Hill, Cecil H.	Sgt.	Co. I.	Wounded
Hill, Clinton V.	Sgt.	Co. K.	
Hill, Roscoe C.	Pvt.	Co. G.	
Hill, Warren	Pvt.	Supply Co.	
Hilliard, Doniphan	Mechanic	Co. E.	Killed
Hilton, Theodore E.	Pvt.	Co. H.	
Hinderson, John F.	Corp.	Co. I.	
Hindman, Justus	Pvt.	Hdqrs. Co.	
Hines, Sheridan	Pvt.	Co. E.	
Hinrichs, John S.	Sgt.	Co. D.	
Hitt, Lawrence	Shoemaker	Co. L.	
Hobbs, Joe B.	Pvt.	Co. I.	Wounded
Hobbs, Roy C.	Pvt.	Co. D.	Wounded
Hoffman, Harry L.	Pvt.	Co. I.	
Hogan, Carl W.	Sorp.	Co. E.	
Hogan, Sidney M.	Pvt.	Hdqrs. Co.	
Hogie, Hans	Pvt.	Co. I.	
Hohler, William	Pvt.	Co. L.	Wounded
Holbert, Leonard M.	Corp.	Co. K.	
Hollis, James A.	Pvt.	Co. E.	
Holloway, Clyde	Pvt.	Co. F.	
Holloway, Guy M.	Pvt.	Co F.	Killed
Holm, Harry E.	Pvt.	Co. I.	Wounded
Holmes, Harry	Pvt.	Co. B.	
Holot, Dan	Pvt.	Co. E.	Wounded
Holt, Delbert E.	Corp.	Co. F.	
Holt, Willie E.	Pvt.	Co. F.	Gassed
Holterman, Anthony J.	Pvt.	Co. D.	Captured, Alsace
Hooker, Robert J.	Pvt.	Co. I.	
Hooper, Herbert	Pvt.	Co. H.	

Hoover, Earl F.	Sgt.	Co. H.	Wounded
Hoover, Henry J.	Sgt.	Co. L.	
Hornady, Thomas R.	Pvt.	Hdqrs. Co.	Wounded
Horner, Omer	Pvt.	Supply Co.	
Hosford, Guy F.	Pvt.	Supply Co.	
Hosterman, Roland R.	Pvt.	Co. M.	Killed
Hotsenpiler, James T.	Sgt.	Co. D.	
Howard, Harry W.	Corp.	Hdqrs. Co.	
Howard, James	Pvt.	Co. I.	Wounded
Howe, Clyde E.	Pvt.	Co. K.	Wounded
Howe, Joseph R.	Sgt.	Co. A.	
Howey, Paul H.	Pvt.	San. Det.	
Huelskamp, Henry G.	Pvt.	Hdqrs. Co.	
Huerter, Francis E.	Pvt.	Co. G.	Wounded
Huey, Frank L.	Pvt.	Co. D.	Wounded
Huff, George L.	Sgt.	Hdqrs. Co.	Wounded
Huffman, Charles E.	Pvt.	Co. K.	Wounded
Huft, Fred	Pvt.	Co. I.	Killed
Hughes, Charles L.	Pvt.	Co. K.	Wounded
Hughes, Harry R.	Sgt.	Co. G.	
Hulett, Earl	Pvt.	Co. H.	
Hunt, Albert	Pvt.	Co. K.	Wounded
Hunt, Irvin	Pvt.	Co. K.	
Hunt, John C.	Sgt.	Co. A.	
Hunt, William	Corp.	Co. C.	
Hunter, George L.	Pvt.	Co. I.	
Huppert, Elwin	Pvt.	Co. K.	
Hurley, Ray H.	Pvt.	Co. L.	Gassed
Hursh, Guy C.	Corp.	Hdqrs. Co.	
Husted, Charles E.	Sgt.	Co. D.	Wounded
Hutchins, Roy	Pvt.	Co. L.	
Hutchinson, Wylie	Pvt.	Hdqrs. Co.	
Hutson, Harry	Pvt.	Co. H.	
Inman, Louis F.	Pvt.	Co. E.	
Isaacson, Albert C.	Pvt.	Co. L.	Wounded
Jacklitch, Ernest	Pvt.	Co. I.	Wounded
Jackson, Harvey	Sgt.	M. G. Co.	
Jackson, Leonard W.	Corp.	Co. I.	Wounded
Jackson, Paul	Pvt.	Co. C.	
Jacobs, Forest L.	Pvt.	Hdqrs. Co.	
James, Charles C.	Wagoner	Supply Co.	
James, Lawrence E.	Corp.	Co. D.	
James, Walter H.	Pvt.	Co. H.	Wounded
Jarrett, Herman	Pvt.	Hdqrs. Co.	
Jay, Samuel	Pvt.	Co. K.	Killed
Jenkins, Clarence A.	Pvt	Co. A.	
Jenson, John J.	Corp	Co. I.	
Jobe, Joseph C.	Pvt.	Co. F.	Wounded
Joernes, Clark	Pvt.	Co. L.	Killed
Johnson, Albert J.	Pvt.	Co. F.	Wounded
Johnson, Claud A.	Pvt.	Co. I.	Wounded
Johnson, Earl P.	Corp.	Co. D.	
Johnson, Eilert Martin	Corp.	Co. I.	
Johnson, Ernest O.	Pvt.	Co. A.	
Johnson, Harley W.	Pvt.	Co. I.	
Johnson, Homer P.	Pvt.	Co. I.	
Johnson, Marion F.	Wagoner	Supply Co.	
Johnson, Walter P.	Pvt.	Co. I.	Wounded
Johnson, William C.	Mechanic	Co. L.	
Johnston, Eugene E.	Pvt.	Hdqrs. Co.	
Jones, Dephonia	Pvt.	Co. L.	Wounded
Jones, Lee	Pvt.	Co. D.	
Jones, Riley V.	Corp.	Co. L.	Wounded
Jones, Robert	Pvt.	Co. I.	

Jones, Robert C.	Pvt.	Co. B.	Killed
Jones, Thomas A.	Pvt.	Co. H.	Killed
Jordan, Charles	Pvt.	Co. L.	Killed
Jordan, Ned	Pvt.	Co. E.	
Jorgensen, Peter G.	Cook	Co. L.	
Joste, Fred S.	Asst. Bnd. Ldr.	Hdqrs. Co.	
Junken, William H.	Sgt.	Co. B.	
Kagle, William M.	Pvt.	Co. H.	
Kaiser, William	Bugler	Co. I.	
Kane, Louis W.	Sgt.	Hdqrs. Co.	
Kane, Robert E.	Sup. Sgt.	Co. K.	Wounded
Keaton, Thomas F.	Cook	Co. C.	Killed
Kee, Arthur	Pvt.	Co. I.	
Keefner, Edward W.	Sgt.	Co. G.	
Keefover, Charles C.	Pvt.	Co. B.	Died, B. H. 91
Keeton, Hugh	Pvt.	Co. K.	
Keith, Benjamine	Corp.	Co. M.	Wounded
Keith, Glenn A.	Pvt.	Co. G.	
Keller, Alvin C.	Pvt.	Co. D.	Wounded
Kelley, Henry James	Pvt.	Co. F	Wounded
Kennedy, Harry F.	Pvt.	Hdqrs. Co.	Killed
Kennedy, James M.	Pvt.	Co. K.	Wounded
Kennedy, John W.	Saddler	Supply Co.	
Kennedy, Roy A.	Sgt.	Co. D.	Wounded
Kennedy, Russell E.	Pvt.	Co. I.	
Kerr, John H.	Pvt.	Co. A.	Killed
Kersey, Vernon	Corp.	Co. I.	
Kersley, George E.	Pvt.	Co. K.	Wounded
Killian, Gilbert	Pvt.	Co. M.	Killed
Kimmich, Robert	Bugler	Co. L.	
King, Clarence	Pvt.	Hdqrs. Co.	Wounded
King, Henry W.	Pvt.	Hdqrs. Co.	
King, Lewis A.	Sgt.	Co. E.	
Kingsley, Ralph W.	Sgt.	Co. F.	
Kirby, William T.	Corp.	Co. D.	Wounded
Kirtley, Willard	Pvt.	Hdqrs. Co.	Wounded
Kiso, Hugh J.	Corp.	Co. I.	
Kitterman, Walter E.	Pvt.	Co. K.	Killed
Kittle, James W.	Pvt.	Co. I.	Wounded
Klebenstein, Elk	Pvt.	Co. L.	Wounded
Kloster, James	Pvt.	Co. C.	Wounded
Klosski, Stanley	Pvt.	Co. M.	
Knight, Guy E.	Pvt.	Co. K.	
Knittel, David	Pvt.	Co. K.	
Knoch, Luther B.	Pvt.	Co. M.	
Knoor, Paul	Pvt.	Co. D.	Wounded
Knupp, Charles W.	Pvt.	Hdqrs. Co.	
Koch, Fred A.	Sup. Sgt.	Co. F.	
Koch, Joseph F.	Pvt.	Co. L.	Wounded Died B. H.
Koerner, Henry	Corp.	Co. L.	Wounded
Koester, William J.	Pvt.	Co. G.	Wounded
Koontz, Carl J.	Pvt.	Co. D.	
Kraft, Moses	Corp.	Co. G.	
Kramer, George L.	Pvt.	Co. K.	
Kreeger, George W.	Corp.	Co. B.	Captured
Kuehl, Frederick C.	Sgt. Maj.	Co. E.	
Kunze, Joseph G.	Pvt.	Co. D.	Wounded
Lacy, William C.	Pvt.	Co. K.	Killed
Laffon, Milerd F.	Pvt.	Co. I.	Wounded
Laflask, Denver	Pvt.	Co. E.	
Lamar, Robert L.	Pvt.	Co. F.	
Lance, Anthony C.	Pvt.	Co. I.	Wounded
Lane, Edward J.	Pvt.	Co. H.	Gassed

Lane, Thomas E.	Sgt.	Co. F.	
Lane, Burnam	Cook	Co. L.	
Lang, Albert W.	Pvt.	Co. C.	Wounded
Langan, Harry W.	Wagoner	Supply Co.	Wounded
Langton, Leo D.	Corp.	Co. D.	
Lannoye, William	Pvt.	Co. K.	Wounded
Laswell, Gustave	Musician	Cas. Band	
LaVelle, Grover J.	Pvt.	Co. L.	
Lawhon, Edward	Pvt.	Co. B.	Wounded
Lawrence, Roy A.	Wagoner	Co. E.	
Lawson, Andrew	Sgt.	Co. D.	
Lawson, Harry E.	Pvt.	Co K.	
Layher, Clarence F.	Pvt.	Hdqrs. Co.	Killed
Layman, Ray	Musician	Co. M.	Killed
Layman, Roy	Pvt.	Co. A.	Killed
Leahy, Dan J.	Pvt.	Co. A.	Killed
Lease, Martin L.	Pvt.	Co. F.	
Leavitt, Dewey V.	Pvt.	Co. Co.	Wounded
Leavitt, Jacob W.	Mechanic	Co. I.	Killed
Lee, Arnold M.	Pvt.	Co. D.	
LeFrance, Albert A.	Pvt.	Co. K.	
Lehman, Elmer J.	Sgt.	M. G. Co.	
Leininger, George	Pvt.	Co. B.	Wounded
Lemanski, True J.	Pvt.	Co. H.	Wounded
Lemonds, Luther A.	Pvt.	Co. I.	Killed
Leniton, Errol D.	Sgt.	Co. E.	
Lesem, Rurie L.	Musician	Cas. Band	
Leslie, Luther Claude	Pvt.	Co. F.	
Lessley, Charlie C.	Pvt.	Co. D.	Wounded
Lewis, Aubrey S.	Pvt.	M. G. Co.	Wounded
Lewis, Homer N.	Cook	San. Det.	
Lewis, Merton E.	Pvt.	Co. G.	
Lewis, Milton O.	Pvt.	Co. G.	Killed
Lewis, William M.	Corp.	Co. G.	Wounded
Lieskie, Joseph	Corp.	Co. L.	Wounded
Lindsey, Mont. O.	Pvt	Co. H.	Died of Wounds
Linrud, Ole	Pvt.	Co. K.	
Linton, John	Pvt.	Co. E.	Killed
Lipper, Walter S.	Pvt.	Co. B.	Killed
Lipscomb, Arthur E.	Pvt.	Co. D.	Wounded
Little, Andrew J.	Pvt.	Co. H.	
Little, Louis L.	Corp.	Co. K.	
Litzinger, Martin T.	Pvt.	Co. K.	Wounded
Livingston, George C.	Pvt.	Co. K.	Wounded
Lloyd, Samuel G.	Pvt.	Hdqrs. Co.	Wounded
Lokey, William	Pvt.	Co. E.	
Long, Eligah R.	Corp.	Co. E.	
Long, Henry J.	Pvt.	Hdqrs. Co.	Killed
Long, John	Pvt.	Co. I.	Killed
Long, Maxwell F.	Pvt.	Co. F.	
Long, Milton O.	Pvt.	Co. G.	Killed
Longan, Layton L.	Pvt.	Co. D.	Killed
Looney, Joseph	Pvt.	Co. A.	
Loschen, John	Pvt.	Hdqrs. Co.	Gassed
Louis, Loomis	Pvt.	Co. I.	
Lovless, Merrel	Corp.	Co. I.	Wounded
Lowe, Benjamine F.	Pvt.	Hdqrs. Co.	
Lower, Earl G.	Pvt.	M. G. Co.	
Loyd, James I.	Pvt.	Co. G.	
Lucas, Wesley C.	Pvt.	Co. K.	Wounded
Lucas, William E.	Pvt.	Hdqrs. Co.	
Lucic, Steve	Corp.	Co. E.	Wounded
Luetkemeyer, John F.	Pvt.	Co. G.	Wounded
Lunak, Frank	Pvt.	Co. E.	

THE MEN BEHIND THE GUNS 227

Lunbeck, Herbert T.	Corp.	Co. K.	Wounded
Lupton, Clifford L.	Sgt.	Co. I.	
Lusk, Thomas C.	Sgt.	Co. K.	Wounded
Lust, John C.	Pvt.	Co. L.	
Lydeen, Verner	Pvt.	Co. K.	Wounded
McBaine, Leo C.	Pvt.	Co. A.	Wounded
McBee, Lawrence G.	Pvt.	Hdqrs. Co.	
McBride, Earl R.	Musician	Cas. Band	
McCaferty, Ewing A.	Pvt.	Co. H.	
McCall, Thomas N.	Wagoner	Supply Co.	
McCann, John L.	Pvt.	Co. E.	
McClanahan, Tobe	Pvt.	Co. F.	
McCleary, Roy A.	Corp.	Hdqrs. Co.	
McClintock, Lloyd H.	Corp.	Co. B.	
McClure, Burl	Corp.	Co. F.	Wounded
McConnell, Edward J.	Pvt.	Co. E.	Wounded
McCorkendale, James O.	Pvt.	Co. E.	
McCormick, Daniel Patrick	Pvt.	Hdqrs. Co.	Wounded
McCormick, Edward	Pvt.	Co. L.	Wounded
McCourt, John W.	Corp.	Co. M.	
McCoy, Jonathan S.	Pvt.	Co. G.	Died of Wounds
McCracken, Dent	Bugler	Co. L.	
McCracken, James	Pvt.	Co. I.	
McCracken, James B.	Pvt.	Co. I.	
McDaniels, James A.	Pvt.	Co. A.	
McDill, John R.	Sgt.	Co. C.	
McDonald, Alexander	Pvt.	Co. K.	Wounded
McDonald, Howard	Sgt.	Co. E.	
McDonald, Roy L.	Pvt.	Co. E.	
McDonald, Richard P.	Corp.	Co. B.	
McDonough, Michael Joseph	Pvt.	Co. L.	
McDowell, Richard L.	Pvt.	Co. C.	Killed
McFall, Harry E.	Sgt.	Co. I.	
McFarland, John B.	Pvt.	Co. D.	
McGaugh, Maurice R.	Pvt.	Hdqrs. Co.	Wounded
McGee, Lee L.	Corp.	Co. E.	Killed
McGee, Samuel D.	Corp.	Co. E.	
McGehee, Ira E.	Pvt.	Co. D.	Wounded
McGuinn, William F.	Pvt.	M. G. Co.	Wounded
McGuinnis, Joseph	Mess Sgt.	Co. I.	Wounded
McGuire, Charles V.	Pvt.	Co. H.	
McGranahan, Theodore L.	Pvt.	Co. K.	
McGraw, Aubrey O.	Pvt.	Co. A.	
McKernan, John G.	Pvt.	Hdqrs. Co.	
McKinney, Frank	Pvt.	Co. E.	Killed
McKinney, Orisen A.	Pvt.	Co. E.	
McLain, Walter F.	Corp.	Co. D.	Gassed
McLain, William G.	Pvt.	Co. A.	
McLean, Duncan	Pvt.	Co. L.	
McLean, Horace H.	Musician	Hdqrs. Co.	
McMilin, Edgar	Pvt.	Co. F.	Wounded
McMillian, Walter L.	Pvt.	Co. L.	Wounded
McMillen, Luther V.	Cook	Co. H.	
McMullen, Dent M.	Pvt.	Co. M.	
McNatt, Virgil E.	Pvt.	Co. K.	Wounded
McNaughton, Leslie L.	Pvt.	Co. L.	
McQuire, Albert	Sgt.	Co. I.	
McQueen, Frank T.	Sgt.	Hdqrs. Co.	
Mack, Peter F.	Pvt.	Co. K.	Wounded
MacDonald, Alexander	Pvt.	Co. K.	
Mackey, Caleb M.	Wagoner	Supply Co.	
Maddock, Earl	Corp.	Co. I.	Wounded

Magmuson, Gustave W.	Pvt.	Co. L.	Wounded
Mahoney, Clarence J.	Pvt.	Co. A.	
Mainard, Charles A.	Pvt.	Co. K.	Wounded
Mainard, Nood	Pvt.	Co. K.	
Malicky, Charles	Pvt.	Co. M.	
Maloney, Luke G.	Corp.	Co. A.	Wounded
Mankin, Dewey J.	Pvt.	Hdqrs. Co.	
Manley, Edgar R.	Pvt.	M. G. Co.	
Mariner, Walter J.	Corp.	Co. E.	
Markham, Clarence I.	Corp.	Co. H.	
Marking, Frank H.	Pvt.	Co. C.	Wounded
Markland, Elvis H.	Pvt.	Co. G.	Wounded
Marksbury, Joseph H.	Pvt.	Co. A.	
Marley, Perry	Pvt.	Co. H.	
Marrs, John H.	Pvt.	Co. C.	Wounded
Marteau, Vivian	Sgt.	Co. K.	
Martin, Avery E.	Pvt.	Co. K.	
Martin, John P.	Pvt.	San. Det.	
Martin, Thomas J.	Corp.	Hdqrs. Co.	Wounded
Marsh, Homer	Pvt.	Co. L.	
Marshall, Arthur	Corp.	Co. K.	Wounded
Marshall, Harold	Pvt.	San. Det.	
Martin, Marshal	Pvt.	Co. I.	Wounded
Martin, William	Pvt.	Co. F.	Wounded
Marts, Lindon E.	Wagoner	Sopply Co.	
Massey, Pinkey F.	Pvt.	Co. I.	
Masteller, Harvey E.	Pvt.	Co. B.	
Masterson, Walter N.	Pvt.	Co. F.	Gassed
Mathews, William J.	Corp.	Co. K.	Wounded
Matkin, John T.	Sgt.	Hdqrs. Co.	
Mayer, Charles M.	Pvt.	Co. G.	
Mayfield, Andrew L.	Pvt.	Co. B.	Gassed
Mayne, William J.	Cook	Co. E.	Gassed
Mays, Frank P.	Pvt.	Co. K.	
Meade, Vernon	Sgt.	Co. L.	
Mechlin, Clarence H.	Pvt.	Co. D.	Wounded
Meek, Albert L.	Pvt.	M. G. Co.	Wounded
Meharg, John	Pvt.	Co. K.	
Mehl, Fred	Sup. Sgt.	Co. L.	
Meily, Guy Ora	Pvt.	Co. L.	Wounded, Died
Mellini, Giuseppe	Pvt.	Co. D.	Wounded
Mellor, George T.	Cook	Co. G.	
Merritt, Jerre B.	Pvt.	Co. C.	
Meyer, Frank J.	Pvt.	Co. H.	
Michael, Garrie E.	Corp.	Co. G.	Wounded
Michaels, Mike	Pvt.	Co. I.	
Michal, John	Wagoner	Supply Co.	Dead
Micklich, Anthony	Pvt.	Co. D.	
Mikkila, Thorstone E.	Pvt.	Co. D.	
Milhorn, Ed.	Pvt.	Co. K.	
Miller, Arthur W.	Corp.	Co. K.	Wounded
Miller, Edward S.	Bugler	Co. E.	
Miller, Franz A.	Pvt.	Co. D.	
Miller, James M.	Pvt.	Hdqrs. Co.	Wounded
Miller, Jesse L.	Pvt.	Co. A.	
Miller, Leonard R.	Pvt.	Co. G.	Killed
Miller, Ray J.	Pvt.	Co. M.	
Miller, Richard W.	Pvt.	Co. L.	
Miller, Roy B.	Corp.	Hdqrs. Co.	Wounded
Miller, William F.	Pvt.	Co. F.	Wounded
Milloy, John P.	Pvt.	Co. L.	Wounded
Ming, Theodore	Pvt.	Co. D.	Wounded
Minnis, Arthur	Pvt.	Co. K.	Wounded
Minnix, Samuel R.	Pvt.	Co. G.	

THE MEN BEHIND THE GUNS 229

Miotti, Casimiro	Corp.	Co. F.	
Mitchell, Earl	Wagoner	Supply Co.	Killed
Mitchell, John F.	Pvt.	Hdqrs. Co.	
Mitchell, Leslie L.	Pvt.	Co. D.	Killed
Mizell, Emerson	Pvt.	Co. I.	
Mock, Samuel A.	Sgt.	Co. B.	
Mohs, Otto	Pvt.	Co. L.	
Montgomery, Clarence	Pvt.	Co. H.	
Montgomery, Frank V.	Pvt.	Co. L.	Wounded
Montgomery, Gilbert F.	Pvt.	Co. K.	Killed
Mooney, George	Pvt.	Co. G.	
Moore, Day D.	Pvt.	Co. L.	Killed
Moore, Richard D.	Pvt.	Co. F.	Wounded
Moore, Robert W.	Pvt.	Co. I.	Gassed
Moore, Russell L.	Pvt.	Co. L.	
Moore, Wm. P.	Pvt.	Co. —.	Died B. H.
Mootz, Melvin	Pvt.	Co. L.	Wounded
Morgan, Charles W.	Pvt.	Co. H.	Wounded
Morlin, Victor G.	Pvt.	Co. F.	
Morlock, Orinza	Wagoner	Supply Co.	
Morris, Frank P.	Pvt.	Co. M.	Killed
Morris, Thomas H.	Pvt.	Co. K.	Wounded
Morrison, George L.	Pvt.	Co. E.	
Morrow, Arthur A.	Pvt.	Co. D.	
Morrow, Willie E.	Pvt.	Co. K.	Wounded
Morse, William	Pvt.	Co. L.	
Mort, Leo M.	Pvt.	Co. F.	Gassed
Moses, Frank E.	Sgt.	Hdqrs. Co.	
Mounts, Roy E.	Pvt.	Co. E.	Wounded
Mueller, John M.	Pvt.	Co. A.	Wounded
Munger, Earl L.	Sgt.	Co. G.	
Munger, Paul M.	Sgt.	Co. H.	Wounded
Munyen, Lee I.	Pvt.	Co. I.	Wounded
Murphy, Charles L.	Pvt.	M. G. Co.	Wounded
Myers, Burnard J.	Pvt.	Co. D.	
Myers, Sherman H.	Cook	Co. A.	
Napier, Charles L.	Pvt.	Hdqrs. Co.	
Nave, Frederick W.	Cook	Co. C.	
Needles, Charles H.	Pvt.	Hdqrs. Co.	Wounded
Neely, Arthur D.	Bugler	Co. K.	Gassed
Neher, Fred	Pvt.	Co. M.	Killed
Neighbours, Ray	Pvt.	Co. B.	
Neill, John A.	Pvt.	Co. I.	
Neill, Oran	Pvt.	Co. B.	
Nelms, Artie M.	Pvt.	Co. G.	Wounded
Nelson, Herman P.	Pvt.	Co. H.	Wounded
Nesselhof, William	Sgt.	Co. E.	
Nevins, Lynn W.	Corp.	Co. L.	
Newberry, George W.	Pvt.	M. C. Co.	
Nichols, Arvell	Pvt.	Co. I.	
Nickelson, John T.	Pvt.	Co. E.	
Nickols, John E.	Pvt.	M. G. Co.	Wounded
Nierstheiner, John	Sgt.	Co. I.	Wounded
Nikkila, Thorsten D	Pvt.	Co.	Died B. H.
Nitcher, John	Pvt.	Co. L.	Wounded
Nix, William T.	Sgt.	Co. G.	
Nolan, Roy	Pvt.	Co. L.	Gassed
Norcross, Roy G.	Wagoner	Supply Co.	
Noland, James T.	Bnd. Sgt.	Hdqrs. Co.	
Northcott, James T.	Pvt.	Co. C.	Killed
Norton, Leo R.	Mechanic	Supply Co.	
Noski, Levi	Pvt.	Co. E.	Wounded
Oberhaus, Walter J.	Pvt.	Co. C.	Killed
OBryan, James	Pvt.	Co. I.	

ODell, Jack	Pvt.	Co. G.	
O'Hara, Howard P.	Pvt.	Co. M.	
Oglevie, Jess M.	Sgt.	Co. D.	
Oldfather, William J.	Wagoner	Supply Co.	
Oldham, Charles W.	Sgt.	Co. C.	
Oliver, Elzia Lee	Pvt.	Co. C.	Killed
Oliver, Gabe	Pvt.	Co. C.	Killed
Oliver, John H.	Pvt.	Co. F.	
Oller, John	Pvt.	M. G. Co.	
Olson, Matt	Pvt.	Co. M.	
ONeill, Clinton	Pvt.	Co. E.	
O'Riley, Frank	Corp.	Co. E.	
Ormsby, Richard C.	Sgt.	Co. M.	
Ortell, Earl	Sgt.	Co. M.	
Osterhaut, William B.	Pvt.	Co. G.	
O'Sullivan, Allen	Corp.	Co. K.	Wounded
Oswald, Frank	Pvt.	Co. E.	Killed
Oswald, Oliver	Pvt.	Co. I.	
Otey, Basil R.	Col. Sgt.	Hdqrs. Co.	
Overton, Charles	Pvt.	Co. M.	Wounded
Overton, Leotis C.	Pvt.	Co. C.	Killed
Owens, Clarence	Pvt.	Co. K.	
Owens, Earl	Pvt.	Hdqrs. Co.	Died B. H.
Owens, James Lee	Pvt.	Co. H.	Wounded
Owens, Thomas F.	Pvt.	Co. G.	
Oxford, James N.	Pvt.	Co. C.	
Pack, Herbert	Pvt.	Co. K.	
Paden, Frank G.	Pvt.	Co. K.	
Padgett, Ivel V.	Pvt.	Co. C.	Wounded
Page, Verr L.	Corp.	Co. C.	
Painter, Orval C.	Sgt.	Co. M.	
Palmer, John R.	Pvt.	Hdqrs. Co.	
Palmer, Wylie S.	Pvt.	Co. D.	
Pape, Walter H.	Pvt.	Co. E.	
Parker, Gurney B.	Pvt.	Co. F.	Killed
Parker, Harold W.	Corp.	Co. K.	Gassed
Parker, Harvey W.	Corp.	Co. M.	
Parker, William B.	Pvt.	Hdqrs. Co.	
Parsons, Charles A.	Wagoner	Supply Co.	
Patterson, Homer	Sgt.	Co. F.	
Patterson, Ted R.	Pvt.	Co. G.	
Patton, Wade K.	Pvt.	San. Det.	
Pattrick, Earnest	Pvt.	Co. E.	
Peace, Dale I.	Pvt.	Co. C.	
Pearson, Basil L.	Pvt.	Co. A.	Gassed
Pearson, George W. C.	Pvt.	Hdqrs. Co.	Killed
Pearson, Lorenzo B.	Pvt.	Co. G.	
Pearson, Walter E.	Pvt.	Co. E.	
Peel, John R.	Corp.	Co. I.	
Peerson, James H.	Pvt.	Co. C.	Wounded
Peine, Tony W.	Pvt.	Co. D.	Gassed
Pennington, Orrin A.	Pvt.	Co. G.	
Pennington, William O.	Pvt.	Co. M.	Wounded
Perkins, James E.	Corp.	Co. K.	Wounded
Perry, Albert C.	Pvt.	Hdqrs. Co.	Wounded
Perry, Earl M.	Pvt.	Co. G.	
Peterson, Delmar R.	Corp.	Co. C.	
Petit, George W.	Pvt.	Co. G.	
Phaling, Edward S.	Pvt.	Co. L.	
Phelps, George H.	Pvt.	Co. G.	Killed
Phenix, Carl M.	Pvt.	Co. M.	
Phillips, Andrew J.	Pvt.	Co. C.	Gassed
Phillips, Armour W.	Pvt.	Co. I.	
Phillips, Jesse	Pvt.	Co. I.	

Phillips, Sidney B.	Corp.	M. G. Co.	
Phoenix, Oscar	Pvt.	Co. F.	
Pickett, Lin	Pvt.	M. G. Co.	
Piechowiak, Clarence E.	Pvt.	Hdqrs. Co.	Wounded
Pifer, Ray L.	Sgt.	Co. G.	Wounded
Pike, Fred J.	Cook	Co. A.	Wounded
Pilgrim, Walter	Pvt.	Co. L.	
Pim, Myron D.	Corp.	Co. G.	Wounded
Pinoskogee, Joe	Pvt.	Co. E.	
Pipes, Eugene F.	Sgt.	Co. C.	Wounded
Pipkin, Porter J.	Pvt.	Co. E.	
Pippitt, Elmer S.	Corp.	Co. A.	
Pitman, Roe E.	Pvt.	Co. E.	
Plante, Joseph	Corp.	Co. C.	Gassed
Planteen, Ralph R.	Pvt.	Co. G.	Wounded
Plemmons, Charles E.	Pvt.	Co. F.	
Plumley, Alex	Horseshoer	M. G. Co.	
Plummer, Roy Earl	Pvt.	Co. C.	
Pocost, Harry B.	Corp.	Co. K.	Wounded
Poe, Raymond	Pvt.	Co. A.	
Poertner, Otto E.	Pvt.	M. G. Co.	Killed
Ponder, Hubert L.	Pvt.	Co. E.	Killed
Pope, Alexander	Pvt.	Co. A.	
Post, Mark H.	Cook	Supply Co.	
Pott, Clarence E.	Musician	Cas. Band	
Potter, George	Pvt.	Co. B.	
Potter, Wilfred J.	Sgt.	Co A.	
Pralle, Albert	Pvt.	Hdqrs. Co.	
Prater, Floyd R.	Pvt.	San. Det.	Wounded
Pratt, John F.	Pvt.	Co D.	
Presnell, Avery	Pvt.	Co. I.	
Preston, George W.	Sgt.	Co. G.	Wounded
Prey, Arthur C.	Pvt.	Co. F.	Wounded
Price, Thomas C.	Pvt.	Co. G.	
Priddy, Charles A.	Pvt.	Co. M.	
Primrose, Archie D.	Pvt.	Co. G.	
Procell, William U.	Cook	Supply Co.	
Pullen, Frank	Pvt.	Co. K.	Wounded
Quick, Everett L.	Pvt.	Co. D.	Wounded
Quigley, Robert C.	Corp.	Co. G.	
Rackley, Mack	Pvt.	Co. E.	Killed
Rader, John H.	Corp.	Co. F.	
Rader, Lee	Pvt.	Co. F.	
Rafferty, Geo. F.	Corp	Co. M.	
Ragan, Walter F.	Pvt.	Supply Co.	
Railsback, Thomas S.	Pvt.	Co. K.	
Rankin, Hugh B.	Pvt.	M. G. Co.	
Rasico, Paul E.	Pvt.	Co. L.	Wounded
Rath, Walter W.	Pvt.	Co. C.	Gassed
Ray, Russell D.	Pvt.	Co. H.	
Rayhill, Finis E.	Bugler	Co. D.	Wounded
Rayner, Matt E.	Pvt.	Co. C.	Wounded
Rayner, William	Pvt.	Supply Co.	
Raynor, Rolf	Sgt.	Co. K.	Wounded
Redman, Jim H.	Pvt.	Co. G.	Wounded
Reed, Robert H.	Sgt.	Co. C.	
Reed, William F.	Pvt.	Co. D.	Wounded
Reese, Stavous B.	Pvt.	Co. C.	
Reeve, Ralph J.	Corp.	M. G. Co.	Wounded
Rehkugler, John G.	Sgt.	Co. C.	Wounded
Reid, Glen B.	Pvt.	Co. C.	Wounded
Reineke, Joseph E.	Pvt.	Co. G.	Wounded
Reynolds, Earl C.	Corp.	Co. E.	
Reynolds, Fred J.	Pvt.	Co. D.	

Reynolds, Lester	Pvt.	Co. K.	Wounded
Reynolds, Otta G.	Pvt.	Co. E.	Wounded
Rice, Sidney	Corp.	Co. L.	
Richards, Floyd E.	Sgt.	Co. L.	
Richards, Henry E.	Pvt.	Hdqrs. Co.	Wounded
Richardson, Albert	Cook	Co. K.	Wounded
Richardson, Roy R.	Sgt.	Co. A.	
Richardson, Thomas	Pvt.	Co. G.	Wounded
Richter, Julius J.	Sgt.	Co. D.	
Riley, Andrew W.	Pvt.	Co. F.	
Riley, John W.	Corp.	Co. A.	Wounded
Riley, Claud C.	Pvt.	M. G. Co.	Killed
Risebig, Phillip R.	Mechanic	Co. A.	Wounded
Rissler, Charles G.	Sgt.	Co. D.	
Ritchie, John D.	Pvt.	Co. C.	
Rives, Arthur B.	Pvt.	Co. L.	Wounded
Roark, Cap	Pvt.	Co. E.	Wounded
Roberts, Boyd	Pvt.	Co. I.	
Roberts, Earl P.	Corp.	Co. H.	Wounded
Roberts, Earnest L.	Mechanic	Co. B.	Killed
Roberts, Emmett S.	Pvt.	Co. G.	Wounded
Roberts, Phillip B.	Sgt.	Co. E.	Wounded
Roberts, Roy E.	Corp.	Co. H.	Wounded, Died
Robertson, Fred R.	Pvt.	Co. K.	Wounded
Robertson, Irvin E.	Pvt.	Co. D.	Wounded
Robertson, Will	Pvt.	Co. K.	
Robinson, Albert E.	Sgt.	Co. L.	Wounded
Robinson, Carter A.	Pvt.	Co. D.	Wounded
Robinson, Edwin B.	Sgt.	Co. B.	
Roche, Joseph V.	Sgt.	Co. L.	Wounded
Rockwell, Herbert R.	Pvt.	Hdqrs. Co.	Wounded
Rodgers, Cleveland G.	Corp.	Hdqrs. Co.	Wounded
Rodman, Richard F.	Bugler	Co. G.	Gassed
Roettger, Christ	Pvt.	Co. A.	Wounded
Rogers, Edward L.	Sgt.	Hdqrs. Co.	
Rogers, Harry B.	Sgt.	Co. K.	Wounded
Rogers, James F.	Sgt.	Hdqrs. Co.	
Rogers, Wallace J.	Pvt.	M. G. Co.	Wounded
Rogers, William A.	Pvt.	Co. L.	Wounded
Rogozinski, Stefan	Mechanic	Co. I.	
Rohrer, Lee R.	Pvt.	Co. G.	Gassed
Rolighed, Ole B.	Pvt.	Co. G.	Wounded
Roper, Henry E.	Sgt.	Co. H.	
Rosenfield, Milton S.	Sgt.	Co. M.	
Roseveld, Will	Pvt.	Co. C.	Killed
Ross, George A.	Pvt.	Co. M.	
Ross, James	Pvt.	Co. B.	Wounded, Died
Rouse, George S.	Corp.	Co. A.	Wounded
Rugh, Elmer O.	Sgt.	Co. E.	
Runnie, Clarence	Pvt.	Co. G.	Killed
Rush, Frank	Pvt.	Co. I.	
Rush, John T.	Corp.	Co. A.	
Russell, Harry Edwin	Pvt.	Co. F.	Died B. H.
Russell, Howard Lee	Pvt.	Co. F.	Gassed
Russell, Oscar L.	Pvt.	Co. C.	Killed
Rust, Arch F.	Pvt.	Co. F.	
Rustad, Julius O.	Pvt.	Co. E.	Wounded
Rutheaford, Charles C.	Mechanic	Co. C.	Wounded
Sadewhite, John C.	Pvt.	Co. F.	
Sadler, Arthur W.	Pvt.	Co. H.	
Samide, Rudolph J.	Pvt.	Co. M.	
Sampson, Harold A.	Pvt.	Co. G.	Died B. H.
Sampson, Thomas Curtis	Pvt.	Co. L.	Wounded
Sanders, James L.	Pvt.	Co. E.	Wounded

Sanders, Lou W.	Pvt.	Co. F.	
Sandman, Frank	Pvt.	Co. H.	
Sands, Henry C.	Pvt.	Co. D.	Wounded
Saunders, Arthur E.	Wagoner	Supply Co.	
Sawyer, Dudley W.	Corp.	Co. A.	Killed
Sayre, Roswell B.	Sgt. Maj.	Hdqrs. Co.	Killed
Schaich, Robert H.	Pvt.	Co. I.	
Schroeder, Hugo C.	Pvt.	Co. C.	Wounded
Schwerdt, Louis R.	Pvt.	Co. E.	
Scott, Claude	Corp.	Co. I.	
Scott, Edward J.	Sgt.	Co. M.	
Scott, John W.	Pvt.	Co. D.	
Seeley, Bert W.	Pvt.	Co. D.	Killed
Segelcke, Rudolph J.	Pvt.	San. Det.	
Sehorn, Clifford	Pvt.	Co. L.	Died of Wounds
Seiler, William	Sgt.	Co. K.	Wounded
Seip, Martin	Pvt.	Hdqrs. Co.	Wounded
Sexton, Levi S.	Corp.	Co. K.	
Shaeffer, Ross N.	Pvt.	Co. D.	Killed
Sharpe, Emory J.	Pvt.		
Shaw, Guy W.	Pvt.	Co. D.	Wounded
Shaw, Wilson B.	Cook	Co. M.	
Shawhan, Spencer S.	Sgt.	Co. A.	
Shea, John E.	Pvt.	Hdqrs. Co.	
Sheeley, Virgil P.	Corp.	Co. L.	Wounded
Shelton, Ernest A.	Pvt.	Hdqrs. Co.	
Shelby, Homer T.	Pvt.	Co. H.	
Shimkus, Charles S.	Pvt.	Co. H.	Gassed
Shipler, Clarence H.	Pvt.	Co. I.	Wounded
Shoemaker, James T.	Pvt.	Co. H.	Wounded
Shooll, Paul W.	Pvt.	Co. F.	Gassed
Showalter, Frank James	Pvt.	Hdqrs. Co.	Wounded
Shropshire, John H.	Sgt.	Co. E.	Gassed
Sidener, Henry F.	Pvt.	Co. G.	
Siegman, Roy E.	Corp.	Co. C.	
Sigman, Don	Pvt.	Co. M.	
Simmons, Rodney	Pvt.	Co. B.	
Simms, Rudy S.	Bugler	M. G. Co.	Wounded
Simpson, William B.	Pvt.	Co. E.	
Simpson, William F.	Pvt.	Co. K.	
Singleton, Russell	Pvt.	Co. C.	
Sisk, Alba H.	Pvt.	Co. D.	Wounded
Sisk, Forest O.	Sgt.	Co. G.	
Skiffington, Frank P.	Pvt.	M. G. Co.	
Skiles, James W.	Pvt.	Co. F.	Killed
Skinner, Ethel M.	Corp.	Co. E.	Wounded
Skyles, George W.	Pvt.	Co. F.	
Slack, Carroll L.	Pvt.	Co. A.	Wounded
Slemmons, William G.	Pvt.	Co. M.	Wounded
Slick, Bennie	Pvt.	Co. L.	
Sloan, Elmer N.	Pvt.	Hdqrs. Co.	
Smalley, Horace	Pvt.	Co. D.	Wounded
Smith, Albert O.	Mechanic	Co. C.	Wounded
Smith, Alva	Cook	Co. B.	Died B. H.
Smith, Earl B.	Sgt.	Co. H.	
Smith, Frank	Pvt.	Co. A.	
Smith, Fred G.	Pvt.	Co. H.	Killed
Smith, George W.	Sgt.	Co. M.	
Smith, Hearl E.	Sgt.	Co. F.	Wounded
Smith, Hugh E.	Pvt.	Co. L.	
Smith, Irving R.	Sgt.	Co. D.	Captured
Smith, James G.	Sgt.	Hdqrs. Co.	
Smith, John P.	Pvt.	M. G. Co.	
Smith, Norman R.	Sgt.	Co. L.	Wounded

Smith, Oscar	Pvt.	Co. L.	Wounded
Smith, Russel D.	Pvt.	Co. H.	Wounded
Smith, Upton B.	Pvt.	Co. A.	Wounded
Smith, William W.	Pvt.	Co. G.	Killed
Snipes, Talbot	Pvt.	Co. I.	Killed
Snorgrass, Joseph	Pvt.	Co. D.	
Snyder, Buel C.	Sgt.	Co. F.	Wounded
Snyder, Guymon	Pvt.	Co. G.	Killed
Snyder, Harvey L.	Pvt.	Hdqrs. Co.	
Sovern, Claude L.	Pvt.	Co. M.	
Spano, Gus	Pvt.	Co. I.	
Sparks, Grover J.	Pvt.	Co. L.	Wounded
Sparks, Hanley F.	Pvt.	Co. L.	
Sparks, James	Pvt.	Co. I.	Killed
Sparks, John W.	Pvt.	Hdqrs. Co.	
Sparman, William R.	Corp.	Co. M.	
Speers, James H.	Corp.	Co. A.	Wounded
Spencer, Adolphus B.	Pvt.	Co. C.	
Spencer, James	Pvt.	Co. M.	Wounded
Spero, Joe C.	Pvt.	Co. D.	
Spielman, Clements L.	Pvt.	Co. A.	
Sprick, George W.	Pvt.	Co. E.	Wounded
Spry, Walker	Corp.	Co. B.	Wounded
Spurlock, John E.	Cook	Supply Co.	
Stacey, Alexander P.	Pvt.	Co. E.	Wounded
Stacy, William S.	Pvt.	Co. L.	Wounded
Staebler, Anton B.	Mechanic	Co. M.	Wounded
Stand, Leander F.	Corp.	Co. M.	Wounded
Stapelton, Frank H.	Sgt.	Co. K.	Wounded
Stapleton, Walter	Pvt.	Co. A.	Wounded
Stark, Charles O.	Pvt.	Co. B.	
Starks, Nathenial	Wagoner	Supply Co.	
Stearns, Harry L.	Corp.	Supply Co.	
Steck, George W.	Pvt.	Hdqrs. Co.	Wounded
Steele, Harry B.	Corp.	Co. D.	
Stein, Claud N.	Sgt.	Co. I.	Killed
Stephens, Joseph L.	Pvt.	Co. K.	
Stephens, Raymond A.	Sgt.	Co. C.	
Stephens, Robert	Corp.	Co. B.	Wounded
Stephens, Roy A.	Corp.	M. G. Co.	Gassed
Stephenson, Eaaton H.	Pvt.	Hdqrs. Co.	Wounded
Stevenson, Rowland H.	Corp.	M. G. Co.	Died of Wounds
Stewart, Cleo H.	Sgt.	Co. G.	Wounded
Stewart, Owen B.	Pvt.	Co. E.	
Stewart, William J.	Mechanic	Co. I.	
Stidham, William H.	Cook	Hdqrs. Co.	
Stigall, John W.	Pvt.	Co. G.	Killed
Still, William	Pvt.	Co. H.	
Stinson, Julian T.	Sgt.	Co. F.	
Stocker, Robert C.	Cook	Co. F.	Gassed
Stockton, Roy	Pvt.	Co. L.	
Stone, Dudley	Sup. Sgt.	Co. H.	
Stone, George B.	Pvt.	Hdqrs. Co.	Killed
Storhaug, John	Corp.	Co. D.	
Strange, Roy C.	Pvt.	Co. C.	Wounded
Stranger, Arthur	Pvt.	Co. C.	
Stroble, Albert	Pvt.	Co. A.	Died Ger. Hosp.
Strole, Walfred	Corp.	Co. K.	
Stuart, Harry J.	Pvt.	Co. A.	Wounded
Sullivan, Marion	Pvt.	Co. L.	Wounded
Sullivan, Troy J.	Pvt.	Co. D.	Wounded
Summers, Walter	Mechanic	Co. L.	Wounded
Surratt, Oscar	Pvt.	Co. I.	Wounded
Swain, John O.	Pvt.	Hdqrs. Co.	Died B. H.

THE MEN BEHIND THE GUNS 235

Name	Rank	Unit	Status
Swain, William J.	Sgt.	Co. K.	
Swanson, Frank A.	Pvt.	Co. A.	
Swanson, Walter	Pvt.	Co. I.	
Swearingin, Leonard L.	Corp.	Co. G.	Wounded
Swoboda, Leo A.	Corp.	M. G. Co.	Gassed
Szramkowski, Joseph	Pvt.	Co. C.	
Szramkowski, Leo T.	Pvt.	Co. C.	
Talbot, Arthur W.	Sgt.	M. G. Co.	
Talbott, William N.	Pvt.	Hdqrs. Co.	Gassed
Talcott, Floyd C.	Corp.	Co. D.	Wounded
Taney, Daniel	Pvt.	Co. A.	Wounded
Tanner, Ralph P.	Sgt.	Co. K.	Killed
Tarnce, James	Pvt.	Co. I.	Wounded
Tate, Clarence T.	Pvt.	Co. M.	
Tatum, George	Pvt.	Co. H.	
Taulbert, Earl P.	Pvt.	Hdqrs. Co.	
Taylor, Daniel W.	Mechanic	Co. H.	Gassed
Taylor, Donald G.	Pvt.	Co. A.	
Taylor, Warren W.	Corp.	Co. F.	Gassed
Teal, Walter	Pvt.	Co. G.	Wounded
Thackston, Curtis	Pvt.	Co. H.	Killed
Thayer, Luther	Pvt.	Co. K.	
Thibeault, Wilfred	Pvt.	Co. L.	Killed
Thomas, Chalmer N.	Pvt.	Co. E.	Died
Thomas, Cleo L.	Pvt.	Co. G.	
Thomas, John W.	Pvt.	Co. G.	Wounded
Thomas, Zack	Pvt.	Co. M.	Killed
Thompson, Jesse A.	Pvt.	Co. H.	
Thomason, John	Sgt.	Co. H.	Wounded
Thrower, Arthur C.	Musician	Cas. Band	
Tilly, Orvill C.	Sgt.	Co. I.	Gassed
Timmons, Jess	Pvt.	Co. K.	
Tippen, Roy E.	Corp.	Co. H.	Killed
Todd, Horace E.	Cook	Co. D.	
Torp, Dewey M.	Pvt.	San. Det.	
Totzauer, William	Mechanic	Co. K.	Wounded acc.
Tower, Ranson E.	Pvt.	Hdqrs. Co.	
Tracy, Edward	Pvt.	Co. B.	Died of Wounds
Tracy, Ralph E.	Pvt.	Co. C.	Wounded
Trigas, Lewis G.	Pvt.	Co. H.	
Trigg, Steven	Pvt.	Co. F.	Wounded
Trissell, Archie L.	Pvt.	Co. C.	Killed
Troub, Ernest E.	Pvt.	Co. E.	
Truesdale, Ross R.	Corp.	Co. I.	
Truesdell, Enos L.	Pvt.	Co. F.	Wounded
Tucker, Elmer	Pvt.	Hdqrs. Co.	Killed
Tucker, James I.	Corp.	Co. K.	Wounded
Tuel, George L.	Sgt.	Co. A.	
Tuggle, Herbert	Pvt.	Co. C.	Wounded
Tunks, Emory D.	Pvt.	Co. G.	
Turner, Charles	Pvt.	Co. K.	Wounded
Turney, Charles W.	Corp.	Hdqrs. Co.	
Tuttle, Cecil L.	Pvt.	Co. D.	Wounded
Ulrickson, Frank L.	Pvt.	Co. L.	
Underwood, Richard	Pvt.	Co. L.	
VanBriggle, Walter	Cook	Co. L.	Killed
VanBrunt, Odo	Corp.	Co. I.	Wounded
Vanvacter, Vernie	Pvt.	M. G. Co.	Wounded
VanWinkle, Floyd	Corp.	Co. F.	Gassed
Vaughn, Homer J.	Pvt.	Co. C.	Wounded
Vaughn, Lawrence T.	Pvt.	Co. D.	Captured
Vickers, Ralph W.	Pvt.	Co. A.	
Viles, Alson Leon	Pvt.	Co. L.	Wounded
Vollmar, John M.	Sgt.	Co. F.	Killed

Name	Rank	Unit	Status
Wadtke, Henry W.	Pvt.	Co. B.	
Wagner, Ray D.	Pvt.	Co. C.	Killed
Waldron, Charles	Pvt.	Co. L.	
Walford, George	Pvt.	Co. H.	
Walker, Lincoln	Pvt.	Co. G.	Wounded
Walker, Morris A.	Pvt.	Co. D.	Wounded
Walker, Orlan	Corp.	Co. K.	Wounded
Walker, Robinson C.	Pvt.	Co. E.	Killed
Wallace, Henry	Corp.	Co. H.	
Walling, Russell	Pvt.	Co. G.	
Walsh, John	Pvt.	Co. B.	
Waltman, Chester A.	Sgt.	Co. L.	
Walton, Robert	Pvt.	Co. M.	
Walton, Thomas	Corp.	Co. A.	
Warder, John M.	Pvt.	Co. A.	
Warren, Jessie Bert	Pvt.	Co. K.	Wounded
Washburn, Seth W.	Pvt.	Co. D.	Wounded
Washington, George S.	Pvt.	San. Det.	Wounded
Watkins, Harry H.	Pvt.	Co. B.	Killed
Watson, George A.	Corp.	Co. K.	Wounded
Watson, John W.	Corp.	Co. K.	Wounded
Weaver, Frank T.	Sgt.	Co. A.	
Weaver, James	Pvt.	Co. K.	
Webb, Lester J.	Pvt.	Co. A.	Wounded
Weeks, Jacob	Pvt.	Co. L.	
Wees, Herbert R.	Pvt.	Hdqrs. Co.	
Weil, Marshall W.	Pvt.	Hdqrs. Co.	
Weiser, Mark F.	Corp.	Hdqrs. Co.	Gassed
Welch, Arthur	Pvt.	Co. D.	
Wells, Ernest F.	Musician	Cas. Band	
West, Herman R.	Pvt.	Co. E.	Wounded
West, James L.	Pvt.	Co. E.	Killed
West, Lionel M.	Pvt.	Co. E.	
Wheeler, Will	Pvt.	Co. L.	
White, Floyd	Pvt.	Co. M.	Wounded
White, Frank T.	Pvt.	San. Det.	
White, Joseph C.	Sgt.	Co. B.	
White, Marshall Z.	Pvt.	Co. H.	
White, Roger E.	Sgt.	Co. B.	Killed
Whitney, Luther P.	Sgt.	Hdqrs. Co.	Wounded
Whitworth, Andrew G.	Pvt.	Co. K.	Wounded
Wiles, Claude E.	Pvt.	Co. F.	
Wiley, Otis L.	Pvt.	Co. A.	
Wilkerson, Frank S.	Pvt.	Co. H.	
Williams, Carvin	Pvt.	Co. A.	
Williams, Chester C.	Pvt.	Co. C.	Wounded
Williams, Claude V.	Pvt.	Co. G.	Wounded
Williams, Claude E.	Mechanic	Co. F.	Wounded
Williams, Courtis	Pvt.	Co. L.	Wounded
Williams, Harry	Corp.	Co. B.	
Williams, Ivy	Corp.	Co. I.	
Williams, Rogers	Pvt.	Hdqrs. Co.	Wounded
Willoughby, Thomas B.	Pvt.	Co. F.	
Wilmott, Robert P.	Sgt.	Co. E.	Gassed
Wilson, Archie A.	Corp.	Co. E.	
Wilson, Arthur C.	Pvt.	Co. D.	Gassed
Wilson, Dolph	Corp.	Hdqrs. Co.	
Wilson, John	Pvt.	Co. K.	Killed
Wilson, Landon	Cook	Co. L.	
Wilson, Ralph H.	Pvt.	Co. C.	Killed
Wilson, Verne R.	Sgt.	Hdqrs. Co.	
Windsor, Richard N.	Sgt.	Co. B.	
Winfrey, Ray B.	Corp.	Co. D.	Wounded
Wingate, John R.	Sgt.	Co. G.	Later Killed

THE MEN BEHIND THE GUNS

Winslow, Joseph	Sgt.	Co. C.	Gassed
Winton, Robert L.	Pvt.	Co. M.	
Wirth, Charles C.	Pvt.	M. G. Co.	Killed
Wiseman, Charles F.	Pvt.	Co. B.	Died B. H. 91
Wiseman, Erle L.	Corp.	Co. L.	Killed
Wittmer, Robert A.	Pvt.	Co. D.	Wounded
Witty, Clifford C.	Pvt.	Co. M.	Wounded
Wolfe, Charles A.	Pvt.	M. G. Co.	
Wood, Charles B.	Pvt.	M. G. Co.	Died of Wounds
Woods, Karl	Pvt.	Co. L.	
Woolard, Earl J.	Pvt.	Co. H.	
Woolery, Walter F.	Pvt.	Co. G.	Died of Wounds
Woolley, Runie	Corp.	Co. I.	Wounded
Wooten, Sibert	Corp.	Co. H.	
Wright, Claude F.	Pvt.	Co. L.	
Wvobleski, Alec	Pvt.	Co. D.	Wounded
Wyatt, Clarence V.	Pvt.	Co. G.	Killed
Yager, Ira N.	Pvt.	M. G. Co.	Wounded
Yates, George W.	Corp.	Co. H.	Gassed
Yates, Herbert P.	Pvt.	Co. G.	Wounded
Youngberg, Chester	Sgt.	Co. L.	Gassed
Young, Ferol J.	Pvt.	M. G. Co.	Wounded
Young, Frank	Pvt.	Co. K.	
Young, Lemar	Sgt.	Co. I.	
Zawacki, Joseph J.	Pvt.	Co. G.	Wounded
Zeiger, Charles L.	Stable Sgt.	M. G. Co.	
Zavalney, Mark	Pvt.	Co. E.	Wounded
Zeller, Charles L.	Corp.	M. G. Co.	Gassed
Zents, Leo J.	Corp.	M. G. Co.	Wounded
Zimmerman, Wesley	Corp.	Co. F.	
Zuber, George	Pvt.	Co. L.	

Third Missouri Infantry
As of August 4, 1917

FIELD AND STAFF
Kansas City

Colonel
  Philip J. Kealy,
                Commanding
Major,
  Claude H. Congdon
Major,
  John F. Constable

Major,
  Francis D. Ross
1st Lieut. & Bn. Adt.
  John P. Griebel
1st Lieut. & Bn. Adjt.
  Willard L. Coe
1st Lieut. &Bn. Adjt.
  Jerry F. Duggan

HEADQUARTERS COMPANY
Kansas City

Captain,
  James F. Imes
Reg. Sergeant Major,
  Page, Russell
Battalion Sgt. Major,
  Arnold, John W.

Battalion Sgt. Major
  Everhart, Charles T.
Battalion Sgt. Major,
  Sayre, Roswell B.
1st Sergeant,
  Lott, Frank K.

Color Sergeant,
  Dannenberg, Herman A.
Color Sergeant,
  Otey, Basil R.
Supply Sergeant,
  Stewart, James O.
Mess Sergeant,
  Wilson, Eugene P.
Stable Sergeant,
  Lamb, Charles R.
Sergeant,
  Quinton, Telesphore P.
Cooks:
  Chandler, Earl M.
  Delahunt, John L.
Horseshoer,
  Shine, Michael A.
Band Leader,
  Kendrick, Benpamin H.
Assistant Band Leader,
  Joste, Fred S.
Sergeant Bugler,
  Kammann, Bodo A.
Band Sergeant,
  Dedrick, Daniel D.
Band Corporals:
  Allison, Silas Bruce
  Dean, Marquess
  Hartge, Paul
  Sharp, Claude S.
1st Class Musicians:
  Crockett, John
  McLain, Horace G.
2d Class Musicians:
  Bowne, Charles G.
  Noland, James J.,

Prati, Henry
3rd Class Musicians:
  Bower, Ralph M.
  Burnell, Frank J.
  Davis, Fred Lauren
  Frost, Sam H.
  Hall, Charley
  Johnston, Herbert
  Keilback, Charles J.
  Knake, Herman H.
  Lackey, Boyce
  Lenge, Roscoe E.
  Metz, Carl S.
  Parrish, Lawrence L.
  Vicksell, Robert
  Wheeler, Harry W.
  Wheeler, Ted R.
1st Class Privates:
  Jacobs, Hawley
  Peery, Earl H.
  Whitney, Luther P.
Privates:
  Brewster, Willie E.
  Ferguson, Joseph B.
  Halin, George W.
  Hursh, Guy C.
  Kennedy, Harry F.
  Lucas, William Everett
  Merriweather, George E.
  Phillips, Roy A.
  Shine, Daniel J.
  Tippy, Coy M.
  Weir, Raymond C.
  Weiser, Mark F.
  Williamson, Frank A.

SUPPLY COMPANY
Kansas City

Captain,
  Frank G. Ward
2d Lieutenant,
  William F. Ward
1st Sergeant
  Briody, George W.
Rgt. Supply Sergeants:
  Damico, Edward O.
  Osiier, William J.
  Zaiss, Joseph
Stable Sergeant,
  Hughey, Edward Leo
Mess Sergeant,
  McKeehan, John M.
Corporal:
  Kuhns, Ivan C.

Cook,
  Procell, William
Horseshoer,
  Hamm, George C.
Saddlers:
  Kennedy, John W.
  Lonsdale, William E.
  Norton, Leo R.
Wagoners:
  Bennett, Elleria Lee
  Brogdon, Nathan T.
  Buchan, James Emory
  Byrd, Robert
  Connelly, Patrick
  Daniels, Charlie A.
  Galvin, William M.

THE MEN BEHIND THE GUNS 239

Haxton, Ellis
Haywood, Archa R.
Henderson, George H.
Johnson, James A.
Johnson, Marion F.
Jones, William B.
Ligon, Millard
Lindsay, Roy
Lowe, Oscar
Malone, Thomas
Oldham, Earon T.
Olsen, Benjamin

Parsons, Charles A.
Payne, Frank
Pierson, Charles G.
Pollard, Claude A.
Russ, Fred K.
Saunders, Arthur
Sibley, Waldo R.
Speaker, Fred
Stearns, Harry L.
Wickizer, Frank F.
Wilcox, Jack P.
Wright, Leonard A.

MACHINE GUN COMPANY
Kansas City

Captain,
　Warren L. Osgood
1st Lieutenant,
　William C. Gordon
2d Lieutenants:
　Ralph E. Truman,
　Richard W. Hocker
1st Sergeant,
　McGuire, Arnold R.
Stable Sergeant,
　Gill, Harold J.
Mess Sergeant,
　Akers, John D.
Sergeants:
　Bogard, Eugene D.
　Dougherty, Stephen E.
　Fredman, Royal J.
　Harvey, Frederick E.
　Hatfield, Robert A.
　Jackson, Harvey
　Keene, Leon
　Talbott, Arthur W.
Corporals:
　Greene, Francis W.
　Keefer, Clarence A.
　Lehman, Elmer J.
　Matkin, John F.
　Meagher, Vincent M.
　Moses, Frank E.
　Phillips, Sidney B.
　Zents, Lee J.
Horseshoer:
　Burnell, Thomas C.
Mechanics:
　Mills, Walter
　Nicholson, Ernest
Cooks:
　Halstead, Carl B.
　Lower, James W.

Buglers:
　Beaumont, Howard B.
　Blaylock, Charles W.
1st Class Privates:
　Bruening, Winfield H.
　Carfrae, Robert W.
　Carroll, Phillip M.
　Dana, Herbert C.
　David, Cecil R.
　Flanner, Edgar H.
　Newberry, George W. Jr.
　Prollock, John G.
　Rankin, Hugh B.
　Reeve, Ralph J.
　Swoboda, Lee A.
　Zeigler, Charles L.
Privates:
　Barnes, Romie M.
　Becker, Chris M.
　Caputo, James
　Cooley, McCabe
　Cunningham, George W.
　Donnelly, Ray V.
　Dunham, Cecil R.
　Evans, John M.
　Flinn, Ernest J.
　Frost, Harry L.
　Fulton, John C.
　Gardner, Richard O.
　Henry, Edgar H.
　Hickman, John L.
　Hinzman, Harry
　Hoard, Edgar F.
　Imes, George D.
　Kendrick, James M.
　Laurant, Joseph
　Lower, Earl C.
　Lyon, Lewis B.
　Major, Duncan A.

Martgan, Tad L.
Martin, Lee W.
Meek, Albert L.
Meyer, Abraham
Miller, Jesse T.
Neves, Albert L.
Owen, Robert S.
Peery, Thomas R.
Pollucca, Guiseppi

Runkle, Olin W.
Shimmer, John
Slater, Richard V.
Stevenson, Rowland H.
Sumpter, Perry E.
White, Hugh
Wolfe, Charles A.
Yager, Ira M.

COMPANY A
Kansas City

Captain,
  John W. Armour
1st Lieutenant,
  Lloyd V. Wise
2nd Lieutenant,
  William E. Scott
1st Sergeant,
  Ray, Charles P.
Mess Sergeant,
  Cunningham, Clyde C.
Supply Sergeant,
  Kane, Lewis W.
Sergeants:
  Richardson, Roy R.
  DeWitt, Ralph Emerson
  Olney, Howard R.
  Hunt, John C.
  Weaver, Frank F.
  Bliss, Frank J.
Corporals:
  McKernan, John G.
  Morse, Ira L.
  Sharpe, Emory J.
  Carey, Dady M. Jr.
  Shawhan, Spencer S.
  Cousins, Sydney A.
  Clark, Jesse C.
  McDonald, William J.
  McDonald, Richard P.
  Baker, Louis C.
Cooks:
  Aumann, George
  Egbert, Asa N.
  Hufstedler, Roy D.
Bugler:
  Livingston, Gurnest W.
Mechanics,
  Yager, Frank Ralph
  O'Rourke, Walter R.
1st Class Privates:
  Cook, Edgar B.
  Frerichs, Edward A.

Gunderson, Glenn
Hardy, Harold
Hunter, H. Ward
Lerche, John M.
Pippitt, Elmer S.
Rush, John T.
Sawyer, Dudley W.
Sprague, Elmer A.
Privates:
  Arnold, Harry P.
  Baker, Hugh C.
  Ballard, W. Calvin
  Barber, Hugh M.
  Barnett, Joseph
  Billington, Fred W.
  Blackburn, David F.
  Blackburn, Marshall L.
  Brekey, John E.
  Brown, John
  Buchanan, Everet G.
  Buhr, Edward P.
  Campbell, James W.
  Carroll, George W.
  Chambers, Dan J.
  Clemings, Claude F.
  Clemmons, Ralph L.
  Cox, Willie G.
  Denhardt, Lucian O.
  Dimmitt, Cecil E.
  Dover, Peter
  Drake, Harvey H.
  Drury, Archie J.
  Evans, Frank J.
  Evans, Harry
  Farmer, Arlo J.
  Fowler, Edwin B.
  Freed, Joe I.
  Garfield, William
  Gaynor, Michael
  Green, Thomas
  Grist, James
  Hall, Lester C.

THE MEN BEHIND THE GUNS 241

Hatton, Ralph
Jenkins, Clarence A.
Johns, Benjamin P.
Keyton, Clarence E.
Leahy, Don J.
Long, Maxwell F.
Marksbury, Joseph H.
Milam, Milton R.
Moxom, Theo. R.
Myers, Sherman H.
Neale, Virgil C.
Niles, LeRoy
Oliver, Henry K.
Patterson, John T.
Peyton, Marion L.
Pike, Fred J.
Pope, Alexander
Pressley, Lawrence H.
Quirk, Joe
Rice, James N.
Risebig, Philip R.
Roardink, Hendrius C.
Roberts, J. Milton
Rogers, Ralph J.
Ross, Charles Cleveland
Saunders, Ernest L.
Saylor, Charles A.
Schick, Martin

Schroeder, Frank W.
Sheward, Harry G.
Shirk, Robert B.
Smith, Albert
Smith, James Arthur
Snodgrass, James F.
Snyder, Harvy L.
Speers, James W.
Spielman, Clemens L.
Sprague, Arthur L.
Stark, Charles A.
Steele, Earl
Stewart, Chauncey L.
Stokes, George A.
Stuart, Harry J.
Taylor, Donald G.
Tetrick, John L.
Tilton, Forest F.
Troub, Ernest
Turk, Edward L.
Vicker, Ralph W.
Way, Heber O.
Webb, Lester J.
Welford, Clarence E.
Wells, Earl H.
White, Roy R.
Winchester, Floyd

COMPANY B
Boonville

Captain,
  Carl F. Scheibner
1st Lieutenant,
  Warren T. Davis
2nd Lieutenant,
  William F. Short
1st Sergeant,
  Barnert, Merl Joseph
Mess Sergeant,
  Dovis, J. Clemens
Supply Sergeant,
  Miller, Carl A.
Sergeants:
  Wilhite, James Frank
  Haley, Roy P.
  Potter, George
  Campbell, Arthur L.
  White, Joseph C.
  Huber, Charles H.
  McRoberts, Emmett F.
Corporals:
  Lachner, William G.
  Lohse, Edgar C.

  Mock, Samuel A.
  White, Roger E.
  Yountz, William H.
  Bottom, Rollo T.
  Pfeiffer, David H.
  Windsor, Richard N.
  Stillwell, Jesse O.
  Simms, Fred
  Logan, John Parker Jr.
  Simmons, Webster J.
  Stephens, Robert H.
Cooks:
  Langhans, George
  Cauthon, John
Mechanic,
  Jenkins, Cecil
1st Class Privates:
  Coulter, Monte Christo
  Haley, James Junius
  Holmes, Harry R.
  Kohn, William P.
  Mayfield, Andrew L.
  Peeples, Philip

Renfro, Robert C.
Shea, John Jr.
Spaete, Ernest F.
Von Oertzen, Robert
Willard, Edward Truston
Privates:
Bagby, Stephen Y.
Beard, George T. Jr.
Becker, Daniel R.
Berry, Wayne R.
Biltz, Rolla L.
Bridges, Edwin
Brown, Clarence W.
Cash, Frank W.
Cornett, Charles
Cramer, Wyatt
Crum, Oscar
Cullumber, William R.
Davis, Harry H.
Davis, Jesse H.
Dichion, Percie
Doehne, Alonzo S.
Donohew, James M.
Dorflinger, John M.
Edwards, John C.
Fenical, Jewel
Fowler, Ira O.
Gentry, Ben C.
Gibbons, Calvert V.
Groves, Edward F.
Groves, Irvin L.
Hayes, George E.
Hayes, Rutherford B.
Hichcox, Tom A.
Huelskamp, Henry J.
Hurt, Ewing R.
Johnston, Eugene E.
Kane, John D.
Kennedy, James M.
Kimlin, Fred A.
Kleasner, Eugene F.
Klein, George
Klein, Tony
Kreeger, George H.
Kreeger, James L.
LaVonette, Prince A.

Leininger, George W.
McMellon, John H.
Malott, Sylvanus
Mock, Carl W.
Moore, Kemper S.
Muncy, Claud Lee
Murphy, Riley W.
Neighbors, Ray E.
Oswald, Walker
Partee, Raymond R.
Phillips, Charley E.
Poertner, Otto E.
Robinson, Phillip M.
Robinson, Robert E.
Ross, James Alfred
Russell, Earl W.
Schell, Albert R.
Scotten, William
Sears, Ernest
Simmond, Charles Christopher
Simmons, Henry
Simmons, Rodney E.
Simmons, Roy Elmer
Simpson, Ernest N.
Slein, Louis
Spry, Walker Allen
Stephenson, Hew
Stiner, Curtis
Stockbell, Silas R.
Thatcher, Stanley M.
Thomas, Neffert E.
Thomas, Rothwell H.
Thomas, William R.
Thorne, Lyman
Tuckley, Ralph A.
Vaughan, Harley P.
Warren, Henry W.
Wells, Dewey F.
Weyland, Lon H.
White, James
Whitlow, Henry
Whitlow, John
Williams, Hampton E.
Wood, Grady T.
Wyrick, Chester B.
Zoeller, Frank S.

COMPANY C
Kansas City

Captain,
  Hunter C. Crist
1st Lieutenant,
  Thomas J. Wilson,

2d Lieutenant,
  Joseph Lieberman,
1st Sergeant,
  Brown, Frank A.

THE MEN BEHIND THE GUNS

Supply Sergeant,
  Widener, Louis E.
Mess Sergeant,
  Johnson, Harry Henry
Sergeants:
  Dedo, Charles G.
  Crockett, William A.
  Frederick, Charles
  Winslow, Joseph
  Sicking, Edward J.
Corporals:
  Greathouse, Ivory
  Douthat, Richard H.
  Oldham, Charles W.
  Pipes, Eugene F.
  Allen, Ernest
  Roberts, Andrew H.
  Hinkefent, Julius C.
  McDill, John R.
  Gertscher, John
  Matson, Joe F.
Cooks:
  Peiker, Walter L.
  Parrish, Joseph S.
Buglers:
  Taulbert, Earl R.
  Phillips, Arlie
Mechanics:
  McCaulla, Willis B.
1st Class Privates:
  Brant, Gilp
  Carlson, Edgar G.
  Chilson, Clifford C.
  Corporan, Harold
  Cover, William P.
  Divine, James R.
  Duncan, Gilbert R.
  Eckland, George A.
  Graham, Albert H.
  Hampton, Grant
  Harris, Jack
  Hoxsey, Russell T.
  Inger, Earl L.
  Johns, Clarence L.
  Norberg, Gerald
  Post, Mark Henry
  Powers, L. Ray
  Pypes, Delos E.
  Reece, Orville J.
  Rehkugler, John G.
  Robinson, Willis G.
  Rogers, Charles G.
  Singleton, Russell
  Taylor, Eugene W.
  Wood, Vic A.
  Woolery, Elmer L.
Privates:
  Abbott, Walter
  Adams, John R.
  Alberts, Frank
  Ash, William W.
  Ashworth, William
  Bechtel, Andrew
  Carey, James
  Carr, Louis T.
  Coffey, Chester
  Coleman, John E.
  Cooley, William A.
  Cowiak, Mike
  Craig, Henry J.
  Cullivan, Thomas J.
  Davis, Elbert A.
  Dillon, David A.
  Dodson, Cris E.
  Edes, Merold L.
  Egner, Charles J.
  Eing, Walter T.
  Epperson, Joseph
  Evans, Frank A.
  Fetters, Theodore R.
  Gay, George W.
  Gentry, Ed.
  Greene, John W.
  Griffitts, Wilbur E.
  Harness, Earl
  Hendrix, Clyde C.
  Howell, George W.
  Jackson, Paul
  James, Jesse F.
  Johnson, Carl
  Jones, Everett N.
  Lang, Albert William
  Lowe, Benjamin F.
  Lynch Thomas N.
  McCullough, Robert V.
  Mann, Howard H.
  Martin, Edward
  Mitchell, John K.
  Monroe, Harold
  Montorano, Frank
  Mount, Eugene V.
  Neff, Roland S.
  Noak, Oscar
  O'Connor, Richard J.
  Queen, Ralph C.
  Ramey, Frank D.
  Ramsey, Leo C.
  Rice, Orien D.
  Roe, John H.
  Rutherford, Charles C.

Sellers, Louis M.
Siegmund, Roy E.
Smith, Albert O.
Snapp, Wayne F.
Sorrels, Homer W.
Steele, Beverly M.
Stone, Edward P.
Stranger, Arthur

Strauss, Karl E. J.
Summers, Thomas M.
Tilley, Dale J.
Turney, Charley W.
Webb, James L.
Weinzerl, Franz
Young, Arleigh T.

COMPANY D
Kansas City

Captain,
  Thomas D. Ross
1st Lieutenant
  Roy E. Stafford
2nd Lieutenant,
  Benton F. Munday,
1st Sergeant,
  Ross, Francis R.
Supply Sergeant,
  Kennedy, Roy A.
Mess Sergeant
  Amen, Nicholas C.
Sergeants:
  Ward, Ernest
  Lawson, Andrew
  Smith, Irving R.
  Hinrichs, John F.
  Stout, Jay E.
  Starkey, Charles G.
Corporals:
  Reed, Robert H.
  Kiper, Richard, G.
  York, Samuel T.
  Huff, George L.
  Elliott, Don
  Bacchus, Leslie J.
  Rogers, James A.
  Warren, Kelley
  Wetherton, James H.
  Richards, William A.
Cooks:
  Hite, Robert D.
  Bogue, Charles A.
  Dixon, Elmer
Mechanics,
  Shelton, Frank H.
Buglers:
  Talcott, Floyd C.
  Redford, Joseph N.
1st Class Privates:
  Dabney, Frank W.
  Dale, Low Z.
  Decamp, James W.

Deskin, William A.
Ellfeldt, Ralph J.
Grant, Joseph W.
Greenberg, Benjamin
Gregg, Walter S. Jr.
Koontz, Carl J.
Langton, Leo D.
Mason, Jeptha H.
Monahan, George E.
Murphy, John
Reynolds, Fred J.
Robinson, Patrick H.
Trevor, Frank L.
Privates:
  Adrian, Charles R.
  Allen, Howard E.
  Allen, Ollie C.
  Arnold, George E.
  Ashmore, Artie L.
  Aubley, Clifford F.
  Ballard, Leroy G.
  Boulware, Sidney F.
  Boyle, George W.
  Brooks, Chester Claude
  Brown, Edwin
  Butler, Joseph C.
  Bruffey, Raymond
  Brummett, Elvis
  Butler, Joseph C.
  Carpenter, Oliver F.
  Cason, Orval L.
  Colville, James M.
  Colville, Tecumseh P.
  Conlon, Luke J.
  Curtin, James F.
  Curto, Armando
  Darddea, Pasquale
  Desebeo, Mike
  Dimon, Jesse
  Dimon, Lewis
  Downing, Richard B.
  Esaw, Peter D.
  Gartman, Robert Henry

THE MEN BEHIND THE GUNS 245

Gordon, Winfred D.
Gormly, Charles E.
Gormly, Willlian W.
Grant, John H.
Haines, Roy C.
Hall, Lonzie V.
Harmon, Ernest P.
Hiatt, Russell A.
Holbert(Leonard M.
Holterman, Anthony J.
Howard, George C.
Howk, Howard B.
Huey, Frank L.
Husted, Charles E.
Hyatt, John B.
James, Charles C.
Jenkins, Herbert J.
Johnson, Erroll P.
Kensinger, James Hartwell
Kirk, Harry M.
Kohler, Bion
Lane, Richard T.
Lyon, Paul
McCleary, Roy A.
McGaugh, Maurice
McHarness, David C.
McKeon, Thomas A.
McKinley, Noah F.
McLain, Walter F.
Madsen, John C.
Martin, William E.

Micklich, Anthony
Miller, Steve
Moberly, William
Moorman, Russell S.
O'Connell, Dennis M.
Oglevie, Jesse N.
Paxton, Jesse N.
Paxton, Roy
Payne, Hugh
Peterson, Wilhelm
Poindexter, John K.
Poteet, Clifford
Pruitt, Moses Simmons
Pummell, Theadford W.
Reynolds, Fred J.
Roy, Pierce M.
Rudd, Harper O.
Smalley, Horace
Smith, Chester
Smith, William F.
Sedo, Joe C.,
Steele, Harry B.
Taylor, Hobert J.
Todd, Horace E.
Walte, Raymond
Ware, Noble O.
Welborn, John G.
Welch, Arthur
Wright, James Marion
Wrobleski, Aleck
Wyrick, Charles E.

COMPANY F
Kansas City

Captain,
 William A. Smith
1st Lieutenant,
 J. Pierce Kane
2nd Lieutenant,
 John H. Pleasants
1st Sergeant,
 Nesselhof, William
Supply Sergeant,
 Roberts, Phillip B.
Mess Sergeant,
 Peterson, Andrew C.
Sergeants:
 Shropshire, John Henry
 Leniton, Errol D.
 Rugh, Elmer O.
 Eades, Floyd A.
 Crambert, William
 Coughlin, Harry
 Searles, Jack
Corporals:
 McDonnell, Edward M.
 Swain, Wilhelm W.
 Lozier, Adrian C.
 Brainard, Earl A.
 Stratton, Homer.
 Curtis, Clark
 Cordill, William B.
 Dawson, Herold L.
 Borchert, Leo

Forrester, James A.
Pemberton, Tom Cutis
Marchant, Clifford
Cooks:
 Moon, Willard W.
 Hatcher, Fred C.
Mechanic,
 Buell, Ralph B.
Bugler,
 Miller, Edward S.
1st Class Privates:
 Caulk, Ross R.
 Cordill, Amos F.
 Dahl, Harry
 Everett, Halley L.
 Fox, Mott L.
 German, Walter
 Glover, Edward E.
 Goodman, Morris
 Breves, Leo
 Hollis, James Arthur
 Kitchell, Ralph J.
 Kubicki, Felix C.
 Leaf, Murvel J.
 Lucic, Stva
 McGee, Lee L.
 Mayne, William J.
 O'Reily, Frank
 Potheles, George
 Tower, Ransom E.
Privates:
 Allen, Thomas E.

Anderson, James K.
Appleby, Neuton
Bell, James V.
Bennett, Joseph
Boulton, Ray
Bresneham, James J.
Brumbaugh, John William
Bubhe, Steve
Buchman, Ralph E.
Carter, George W.
Cisneros, Felix
Cisneros, Louis
Cordill, Russell M.
Cundiff, Chester
Curren, William
Dailey, Charles O.
Dailey, Elton, M.
Danford, Charley O.
Davis, Jewell
Davis, Robert W.
Dean, Albert Rollins
Durel, Caron A.
Fain, Tom
Ferry, Harrison H.
Fleming, Frank
Foster, William
Franklin, William H.
Frizzell, Byron
Goetting, Philip O.
Green, Charles M.
Hendricks, Lee R.

Hill, Oscar E.
Hunt, Philip
Harris, Walter H.
Husken, Carl Edward
Ingles, Robert G.
Linton, John
Long, Harry C.
McDarmon, Thomas G.
McDonald, Howard
McDonald, Roy L.
Mariner, Walter J.
Matney, George W.
Milner, Leo R.
Moore, James A.
Mount, Harry E.
Mounts, Roy E.
Mouritson, Anton
Owens, James
Peterman, William P.
Pryor, Charles Shelby
Ray, Harlan J.
Richardson, Arthur Harold
Ruvolos, Joseph
Shankester, Claude G.
Skinner, Ethell W.
Slein, Abe
Smith, Harry J.
Smoot, Elmer E.
Steere, Glen H.
Stoward, Owen B.
Travis, Charles L.
Trigg, James L.
Troube, Herbert
Turner, Ruby L.
Vineyard, Lee McK
Walthan, Frank V.
Williams, Roger
Wilmot, Robert P.
Young, John

COMPANY F
Kansas City

Captain,
  Jefferson M. Dunlap
1st Lieutenant,
  Rhodes F. Arnold
2nd Lieutenant,
  Frank H. Grigg
1st Sergeant,
  Lancy, Thomas E.
Supply Sergeant,
  Koch, Fred A.
Mess Sergeant,
  Chamblin, Robert L.
Sergeants:
  Asbury, Luther L., Jr.
  Kingsley, Ralph W.
  Graen, Eldon P.
  Henry, James N.
  Hagen, Fendell A.
Corporals:
  Vitt, Albert M.
  Calfee, John Clark
  Callery, Ralph E.
  Walsh, John R.
  Baughman, Arthur B.
  Hallett, Charles M.
  Cons, Clarence F.
  Stinson, Julian T.
  Gray, Robert H.
  Snyder, Buel C.
  Belt, Alfred E.
Cooks:
  Manning, William H.
  Zimmerman, Wesley
  Ham, William W.
Buglers:
  Bennett, Chester A.
  Bell, Guy
Mechanic,
  McGerr, Joseph W.
1st Class Privates:
  Anderson, Chamblin
Beckman, Ralph P.
Brantner, Claude L.
Breckenridge, Dewey
Brown, Andy A.
Chamblin, Lee F.
Charlton, Rowland H.
Deggett, William H.
DeWitt, Arnand A.
Dye, Raymond E.
Gray, Herbert C.
Hughes, Phillip H.
Lembeck, William H.
Needles, Charles H.
Niess, Herman
O'Connor, William D.
Peniston, John E.
Richter, Roy A.
Rickets, Carl V.
Sadewhite, John C.
Sandy, John W.
Sheley, Edward L.
Stocker, Robert C.
Taggart, Forest S.
Torp, M. Dewey
VanGilder, Clarence
Van Winkle, Floyd
Wallace, Robert A.
Williams, Claude E.
Privates:
Alak, Ed.
Ball, Sneed
Barrett, William F.
Black, Herbert
Blackwell, Charles T.
Booker, William H.
Boyer, Otis L.
Bright, Joseph J.
Briscoe, Delo M.
Calvin, Paul C.
Claypole, William
Coll, Harry
Collins, Emil Z.
Crist, George N.
Darrah, Lee
Diemer, Frank
Dingey, George
Dodd, Carl W.
Etzler, Richard J.
Fitzpatrick, Clifford E.
Fletcher, Edward S.
Gibson, Albert G.
Gleason, Leo F.
Gurney, Frank S.
Haley, William J.
Hannon, Noel D.
Hanyon, William A.
Hart, Sam B.
Hornaday, Thomas R.
Lane, Jack A.
Lindsey, Ben B.
Linenberger, Anton P.
McClure, Burl
McMahon, Joseph B.
Martin, John P.
Marts, Lindon, E.
Michal John
Miller, Clyde E.
Mort, Leo M.
Needles, Clifford C.
Pickett, Griffith H.
Rhodes, Virgil
Rittenhouse, Frank A.
Rupp, Leonard W.
Russell, Harry E.
Scully, James H.
Shool, Paul W.
Trigg, Steven
Vandiver, Joe V.
Vineyard, John A. L.
Warren, James C.
Williamson, Allen E.
Wilson, Arthur L.
Wilson, John W.
Wood, Jesse F.
Wright, Harry D.
Yadon, Joseph M.

COMPANY G
Kansas City

Captain,
  Henry E. Lewis
1st Lieutenant,
  Fred C. Wilhelm
2nd Lieutenant,
  Harry A. Pilcher
1st Sergeant,
  Wingate, John R.
Supply Sergeant,
  Keffner, Edward W.
Mess Sergeant,
  Nix, William T.
Sergeants:
  Mineah, Harold J.
  Hutchinson, William S.
  Burke, Edmund M.
  Graves, Harold F.
  Holcomb, John A.
  Stewart, Cleo H.
Munger, Earl L.
Leeper, Charles L.
Corporals:
  Tuckfield, Ralph G.
  Needles, Ralph E.
  Rogers, Edward L.
  Brockman, Gilbert G.
  Byard, Ernest L.
  Ely, Sims
  Pelton, Fred N.
  Quigley, Robert C.
  Best, John L.
  Buck, Clarence R.
  Jackson, William S.
  Smith, Penn.
  Johnson, Charles L.
  Beckett, Paul B.
  Hogan, Sidney M.
Cooks:
  Hogan, Lineas G.
  Gabbert, Aubrey
  Beacher, Alfred
Artificer,
  Baker, William C.
1st Class Privates:
  Bandel, Morris A.
  Bierman, Joseph W.
  Binz, Fred H.
  Dignam, Emmet J.
  Dollar, David B.
  Engerg, Raymond O.
  Forkner, Artie
  Friess, Charles R.
  Gault, John M.
  Hancock, Paul F.
  Huerter, Francis E.
  Huerter, Victor J.

THE MEN BEHIND THE GUNS

Jones, Rodney P.
Lemon, Roy
Lewis, William M.
McPherson, James H.
Pierson, Lorenzo B.
Perry, Earl
Pritchard, Earl J.
Ruby, Frank
Sanders, Burr
Sloan, Elmer M.
Smith, Thomas B.
Walling, Russell
Waters, Carl
Privates:
Beasley, Everett C.
Benham, George S.
Boatman, Clarence D.
Bryant, Ray H.
Carroll, Hubert W.
Cashman, John J.
Clement, Darius
Clucky, Charles
Coberly, Leonard
Connor, Blaine
Coons, Daniels E.
Cooper, Victor
Copeland, Ross
Daniels, Charlie

Dobrela, George J.
Dyer, Pat.
Eads, Dow L.
Elliott, Harry E.
Evans, Elmer E.
Flack, Roy E.
Gilbert, Wilbert
Glenn, Don
Gray, Ralph
Hall, Lester C.
Hatch, George C.
Heisey, Ivan A.
Hirschfield, Harry C.
Hogan, Willis W.
Hukill, Earl
Kenney, Charles A.
Larrabee Vernice
Leutkemeyer, John F.
Lewis, Merton E.
Lewis, Milton O.
Low, Earl R.
McCarty, John H. E.
McNabb, Leon
Marshall, Edward
Meyer, Charles M.
Mellor, George I.
Michael, James
Miller, Jacob J.

Morehead, Charles A.
Murphy, Thomas
Myers, Worthy C.
Osterhaut, William B.
Otott, Edward
Patterson, Ted R.
Payne, Frank
Pim, Myron D.
Porstman, Walter E.
Preston, George W.
Radz, Walter J.
Richardson, Samuel
Roberts, Emmet S.
Roberts, Herbert
Rodman, Richard F.
Rogell, Herman
Samuels, Clarence
Sewell, Don E.
Shearer, Paul C.
Sowers, Floyd E.
Steele, Harry H.
Trent, Tony
Walker, Lincoln
Walls, William
Wees, Herbert R.
Wich, Christ
Wilkins, Charles M.

COMPANY H
Liberty

Captain,
　William R. Hardin
1st Lieutenant,
　John R. Smiley
2nd Lieutenant,
　Frank P. Farrar
1st Sergeant,
　Farrar, Robert M.
Supply Sergeant,
　Stone, Dudley S.
Mess Sergeant,
　Taylor, George B.
Sergeants:
　Mace, John H.
　Beistle, Tiffin, O.
　Swinney, John J.
　Thomason, John
　Baker, Robert H.
Corporals:
　Watts, James L.
　Baker, William N.
　Richardson, George
　Owens, James E.
　Martin, Thomas J.
　Eidson, Robert V.
　Hoover, Earl F.
　Yingling, Oda M.
　Unger, Benjamin
　Freeman, Tanner H.
　Summers, Rothie
　DeYoung, John
Cooks:
　Smith, Fred G.
　Warren, Ollie
Mechanic,
　Kennedy, Frank R.
Bugler,
　Rowland, Lester
1st Class Privates:
　Berry, Orion
　Bratcher, Lee Roy
　Deatherage, Virgil P.
　Ray, Russell D.
　Robertson, John G.
　Schiller, Joseph
　Snow, Isaac R.
　Tatham, Arthur R.
Privates:
　Arnold, Walter P.
　Ashby, Floyd B.
　Ball, Harry

Barclay, John
Beck, Cecil
Beery, Wilkerson C.
Benson, Vivian K.
Bowers, Joseph M.
Bradley, Roy M.
Breachinridge Eddie
Broderick, Waldo O.
Campbell, Eugene O.
Campbell, George A.
Carey, Ira N.
Columbia, Harmon
Corum, Alonzo
Cummins Raymond W.
Dagley, Scott
Davis, Chester
Davis, Everett
Davis, Fred J.
Davis, William J.
Deen, Cleo C.
Dennis, Ruby
Douglas, James
Elliott, Graham
Evans, Cecil D.
Fairchild, Milon
Fields, Rufus A.
Fisher, Alfred E.
Flaherty, Joseph F.
Foley, Luther B.
Foley, John P.
Foley, Samuel R.
Gawluk, Joe
Giles, Ben R.
Gouris, Efthemeous
Harris, Lester C.
Harris, Marion L.
Heavenhill, Clint G.
Heinzman, Merle
Hendrix, Arthur W.
Hessenflow, Jesse
Hess, Ernest
Hill, Harry
Johnson, Albert J.
Jones, Fred H.
Kehew, George H.
Kelly, Roy P.
Kennedy, Joseph L.
Kirtley, Willard
Kollar, Joe S.

Larkin, Charles J.
Lemanski, True J.
McClintock, Hurley J.
McMillen, Luther V.
Maloney, Robert E.
Markham, Clarence I.
Mayers, John D.
Moore, Harry L.
Mores, George
Morris, Preston P.
Meyer, Charles C.
Nelson, Charles
Nelson, Herman P.
Nickolich, Fred
Overman, Benjamin
Owen, Clarence
Owens, James Lee
Palmer, John R.
Paradise, William
Parker, Lee
Patrick, William L.
Perkins, Leo
Portwood, Tom
Potter, Clayton E.
Potter, Ray L.
Purcell, Gregory E.
Reel, Charles
Rigley, Floyd H.
Rigley, Harry E.
Roberts, Roy E.
Sires, Clyde
Sloan, James E.
Smith, LeRoy
Smith, Roy
Smith, Russell D.
Still, William
Stone, George B.
Talbott, William N.
Taylor, Daniel W.
Thomas, Brack A.
Tritt, John
Walker, Guian L.
Waring, George
Weaver, Ralph E.
Williams, Albert L.
Wills, Hilary J.
Willyard, Rufus L.
Windsor, John L.
Yates, Lewis D.
Zagar, Frank

COMPANY I
Kansas City

Captain,
  Walter H. Williams
1st Lieutenant,
  Rolla B. Holt
2nd Lieutenant,
  John V. Starks
1st Sergeant,
  Hanes Samuel M.
Supply Sergeant,
  Cooperider, Noel L.
Mess Sergeant,
  Rogers, Guy G.
Sergeants:
  Boehler, Adolpr
  Haberstroh, Ray
  Hight, Floyd
  Hynes, George I
  Lupton, Clifford L.
  Tilley, Orval C.
Corporals:
  Brown, Clyde M.
  Dry, Clarence C.
  Downing, Elmer C.
  Hammen, Arthur W.
  Hill, Cecil
  Kiso, Hugh J.
  Loveless, Merrill
  McFall, Harry E.
  Scott, Claude J.
  Stein, Claude N.
  William, Frank W.
Cooks:
  Brown, Henry
  Truesdale, Ross R.
Buglers:
  Kaiser, William
  Keys, Burson T.
Artificer,
  Leavitt, Jacob W.
1st Class Privates:
  Clark, Virgil
  Dennis, Otto
  Flora, Norman
  Heineman, Alfred D.
  Jarrell, Sandford
  Jensen, John J.
  Southern, Edward
  Young, Lamar
Privates:
  Abbott, Floyd H.
  Anes, William R.
  Bernhard, Fred G.
  Bradley, George
  Brothers, Edgar
  Brummitt, Carl
  Conroy, John
  Coe, Bennie H.
  Dancy, Paul
  Davis, Paris
  Don Carlos, Robert
  Farley, Clarence E.
  Ferguson, Joe E.
  Gail, Augustus, O.
  Garthwait, Roy
  Gibbons, Austin
  Goodridge, David
  Graves, Russell D.
  Graves, Wesley
  Greer, Noah
  Gregg, Gaylord F.
  Haist, George
  Harrington, Phillip
  Hays, Guy
  Henderson, John F.
  Henkel, Anthony
  Herron, Arthur O. D.
  Hickerson, Temple R.
  Holl, Steven E.
  Jacks, John W.
  Jester, Albert
  Jhnston, Harvey T.
  Jones, Frederick A.
  Kelly, John F.
  Kennedy, Miller R.
  Kreditch, Michael
  Laird, Edward
  Langan, Harry W.
  Lanternier, Joseph
  Lisenbee, Clifford
  McCarthy, Louis E.
  McClure, Moody
  McGinniss, Joseph
  McKee, Samuel
  Martin, Alva C.
  Maddox, Earl J.
  Micles, Mike
  Moriarty, Will T.
  Morse, Harry C.
  Page, Frank
  Parish, Lee R.
  Pence, Robert E.
  Perkinson, James C.
  Perry, Albert C.
  Petty, Owen J.
  Pittenger, George W.
  Pursel, Dewey
  Ragan, Arthur F.
  Raischei, Blas
  Roberts, Boyd H.
  Robinson, William
  Rogocinski, Stefan
  Ross, Charles W.
  Ruiz, Florencio
  Rush, Frank
  Sanoff, Sam
  Saymore, Robert
  Sharkey, Jack H.
  Snodgrass, Earl M.
  Spano, Gus
  Spender, James E.
  Swanson, Walter
  Van Brunt, Ode F.
  Van Kirk, Albert
  West, Frank B.
  Wilson, Lin
  Winston, William W.
  Wolley, Runie
  Zagar, Anthony

COMPANY K
Kansas City

Captain,
  Walter R. Barnes
1st Lietenant,
  Samuel W. Henderson, Jr.
2nd Lieutenant,
  Orville S. Bowman, Jr.
1st Sergeant,
  Raynor, Rolf
Mess Sergeant,
  Penrod, Cecil R.
Sergeants:
  Hill, Clinton V.
  Bateman, William D.
  Saunders, Fred
  Rogers, Harry B.
  Breckenridge, John C.
  Ortell, Earl
  Rassmusen, Anton
Corporals:
  Seiler, William
  Cuberly, Fred R.
  Kane, Robert E.
  McKenzie, Albert
  Dover, Robert
  Shipley, Dean
  Bodwell, Paul
  Eubanks, Hale B.
  Railsback, Bryan
  Beers, Forrest H.
  Swain, William J.
Cooks:
  Jones, George W.
  Robinson, Albert E.
Buglers:
  Bateman, Walter
  Mercer, Wesley
Mechanic,
  Barnes, Homer J.
1st Class Privates:
  Boyce, Herbert
  Butterfield, Charles E.
  Cornell, Frank
  Evans, Floyd A.
  Fitzpatrick, Lee
  Fowler, Samuel C.
  Hammontree, Virgil I.
  Hunter, Alec
  Little, Louis L.
  Miller, Roy B.
  Penrod, Harry
  Stapleton, Frank H.
  Starling, Jay J.
  Tanner, Ralph
  Tompson, Herbert W.
  Totzauer, William
  Turley, Jacob
  Turley, Robert M.
  Wolfe, Joe
Privates:
  Armstrong, George R.
  Arnett, Harold J.
  Ashbaugh, Arthur A.
  Baker, Joseph
  Baker, William R.
  Battles, Robert D.
  Begey, Ben F.
  Bishop, George B.
  Bokis, Charley
  Brents, Henry D.
  Burns, Neil
  Buslovitz, Adam
  Byrne, George T.
  Coberly, John A.
  Cook, Edward
  Cox, J. Lloyd
  Craven, Herman
  Cronhardt, Frank
  Davis, Judson
  Day, Edward
  Fitzpatrick, Raymond R.
  Funck, Paul
  Gaddy, Monte
  Gaupp, Gus O.
  Golledge, Frank T.
  Hadley, Walter D.
  Hampton, Leon V.
  Hill, Virgil H.
  Homburg, William
  Hughes, Charles L.
  Huppert, Elwin
  Johnson, Harrison
  Kinney, John
  Lindlow, Charles O.
  Lucas, Wesley C.
  Lunbeck, Herbert F.
  Lusk, Thomas
  Lynch, Thomas
  McBee, Lawrence G.
  McConnell, Edward J.

THE MEN BEHIND THE GUNS

McNatt, Virgil E.
Magula, Frank
Marshall, Gilbert E.
Mathews, William J.
Mode, William J.
Neely, Arthur D.
Owens, William M.
Parker, Harold, W.
Perkins, Harold W.
Pierce, Yancy

Pocost, Harry B.
Reeves, Ernest C.
Rode, Albert
Sciabarrasi, Mariano
Sexton, Levi S.
Sheehan, Daniel
Sheehan, Phillip
Smith, Harley
Starbeck, Hugh A.
Stockwell, Elmer

Strole, Walfred
Taylor, Lester G.
Tucker, James
Tum, Sam
Ulshoefer, Anthony
Vanetten, James E.
Vickrey, Sidney L.
Young, Frank

COMPANY L
Kansas City

Captain,
  Murry Davis
1st Lieutenant,
  Russell C. Throckmorton
2nd Lieutenant,
  Stephen O. Slaughter
1st Sergeant,
  Waltman, Chester A.
Supply Sergeant,
  Lake, Arthur W.
Mess Sergeant,
  Richards, Floyd E.
Sergeants,
  Smith, James G.
  Blocher, Joseph S.
  Dreeben, Harry
  Elbs, George J.
  Smith, Norman R.
Corporals:
  Adkins, Melville H.
  Robinson, Albert E.
  Allee, Moses
  Brockman, Carl
  Collins, Milo R.
  Waymire, Jacob H.
  Degraffenreid, Joe
  Stark, Bert
  Roche, Joseph V.
  Newman, Charles
  Gossard, Hampton D.
  Hoover, Henry
Mechanic,
  Summers, Walter D.
Cooks:
  Lane, Burnam
  Posh, Phillip
Buglers:
  Mitchell, John F.
  Rothland, Wolff
  Coakley, William

Coffin, Charles W.
Frisbie, Leland
1st Class Privates:
  Hellums, Lawrence
  Helmick, Andrew J.
  Higby, Clarence P.
  Kelly, Thomas B.
  LaVelle, Grover J.
  Leonard, John P.
  Lewis, Aubrey S.
  Lieskie, Joseph
  Marshall, Harold
  Mehl, Fred C.
  Nevins, William J.
  Slick, Bennie R.
  Sparks, John W.
  Stadler, Charles E.
  Steiner, Walter S.
  Stone, Wilmer
  Thayer, Lester M.
  Youngberg, Chester
Privates:
  Ahern, Daniel
  Bender, William
  Bledsoe, Russell
  Brothers, Edward
  Carr, Noflet B.
  Cook, Teddie R.
  Corbin, Dean
  Coughlan, John M.
  Cowgill, Walter W.
  Dumas, Hugh L.
  Fox, Charles E.
  French, Michael
  Gregory, William S.
  Grenrood, Joseph F.
  Hancock, Leonides
  Hamby, Elmer
  Harmon, Martin
  Hassler, James
  Hay, Thomas G.

Herman, Edward
Harvey, Edward
Huff, Alonzo C.
Hulbert, Ralph D.
Jacobson, Ruben
Johnson, Rufus P.
Jones, Earl
Jordan, Charles L.
Lee William R.
Lloyd, Samuel G.
Lossone, Frank
McCracken, Dent
Maderick, George
Marsh, Homer
Maule, Harold
Meily, Guy Ora
Menardi, George
Meyer, Henry
Moore, Day D.
Mott, Marvin
Nall, Roly R.
Newby, Milton
Oliver, Kamp I
Paulsen, Marimus
Pennell, William
Phaling, Edward S.
Powell, Dewey M.
Rayner, William
Rees, William A.
Rice, Sidney
Rogers, William A.
Sherman, Harold H.
Slick, Harry
Thatcher, Wheeler B.
Trigg, Beldon H.
Van Briggle, Walter
Van Hecke, Arthur
Wiseman, Erle L.
Woods, Karl M.
Zuber, George Andrew

COMPANY M
Kansas City

Captain,
  George T. Pfeiffer
2nd Lieutenant,
  William J. Baxter
1st Sergeant,
  Arnold, William H.
Supply Sergeant
  Culberson, Stacy
Mess Sergeant,
  Winfrey, Ray D.
Sergeants:
  Erwin, William E.
  Woodbury, Frank B.
  Odom, Walter E.
  Ritter, George F.
  King, Lee
  Streeper, Thomas
Corporals:
  Donohoe, James W.
  Samide, Rudolph, J.
  Scott, Edward J.
  Moon, Charles L.
  Ormsby, Richard C.
  Shaw, Ray H.

Bird, Arthur C.
Paskrich, John J.
Liebst, Kasper M.
Cooks:
  Gresham, Floyd A.
  Granzella Viver
Musicians:
  Layman, Ray
  Heinold, Proctor L.
Mechanic,
  Staebler, Anton B.
1st Class Privates:
  Arnold, William L.
  Bryan, Harry M.
  Chamberlain, Herry
  Chandler, Robert B.
  Collins, Otis F.
  Frith, Roy N.
  Fuqua, Edgar
  Harris, Robert L.
  Hays, John W.
  Hickenlooper, Thomas W.
  Hopkins, Paul F.

Kratville, Milo
Overstreet, Walter L.
Painter, Orval C.
Patchin, Levey Gould
Roberts, John R.
Schriver, Joseph M.
Shaw, Wilson B.
Slemmons, Williams G.
Tate, Clarence E.
Troxel, Joe
Waddle, Alva P.
Privates:
  Arbuthnot, George W.
  Bailey, Floyd F.
  Barnes, Walter
  Blevins, Ernest V.
  Bockhahn, Alfred
  Bryant, Richard S.
  Buford, Ted L.
  Buford, William
  Calvert, James W.
  Cleeton, Linzie V.
  Clevy, Clarence T.
  Cole, William A.

Collum, Ralph B.
Daugherty, Lewis B.
Deis, James F.
Dennis, Waldo C.
Ellis, Charles H.
Fitzmaurice, Robert E.
Foulks, Walter O.
Fuqua, Samuel O.
Gaffney, William P.
Gildea, Francis
Green, John
Hatcher, Charlie L.
Henkel, William J.
Hosford, Guy T.
Hosterman, Roland R.
Johnson, John H.
Keith, Benjamin
Kindig, Frank R.
Klouski, Stanly

Knoch, Joseph
Knoch, Luther B.
Korpnick, John L.
Layman, Roy
Lee Charles E.
Lewis, Ira Everett
McMullin, Dent M.
Mathews, Clarence J.
Miller, Ray J.
Mossman, Eugene L.
O'Hare, Howard P.
Owen, James M.
Owens, Dewey
Phillips, Vera
Puttroff, Archie L.
Ray, Chauncey W.
Rice, Coke S.
Roseberry, Carl F.

Rosenfield, Milton B.
Sarver, Jacob D.
Shepherd, Virgil V.
Smith, George W.
Severn, Claude L.
Stefanski, Franz J.
Stone, Allen J.
Sullivan, William J.
Swain, John O.
Taylor, Alonza C.
Thatcher, Garrett M.
Thompson, James E.
Turner, James
Watson, George D.
White, Floyd
White, Frank T.
Winston, Hugo A.
Woods, Louis A.

SANITARY DETACHMENT
Kansas City

Major,
  Ernest W. Slusher
Captain,
  Archie W. Johnson
1st Lieutenant,
  Glen H. Broyles
1st Lieutenant,
  Edwin C. White, Jr.
1st Class Sergeant,
  Johnson Sidney J.
Sergeants:
  Dillon, Joseph
  Haus, Frank

Liebst, Charles A. Jr.
1st Class Privates:
  Burchett, William F.
  George, Hollis A.
  Howey, Paul H.
  Kirchodd, Charles
  Krenzer, William W.
  Lewis, Homer M.
  McDonald, Theodore
  Meuller, Ralph H.
  Reynolds, Harold J.
  Smith, Norman R.
  Snyder, Melville

Warren, Claude M.
Williams, Ernest W.
Wilson, Harry L.
Privates:
  Carr, Charles L.
  Carroll, Jack
  Darby, Wells
  Davis, Harry S.
  Jeans, Chester D.
  Lane, Clark
  McGaugh, Homer
  O'Meara, Tom J.
  Patton, Wade K.

Sixth Missouri Infantry
As of August 4, 1917

FIELD AND STAFF
Jefferson City

Colonel,
  Albert Linxwiler
  Commanding
Lieutenant Colonel,
  Bennett C. Clark

Major,
  Carl L. Ristine
Major,
  Warren L. Mabrey
Major,
  William T. Morgan

1st Lieut. & Bn. Adjt.,
  Albert S. Gardner
1st Lieut. & Bn. Adjt.,
  Rufus C. Kemper
1st Lieut. & Bn. Adjt.,
  Alexander S. Oliver

HEADQUARTERS COMPANY
Cape Girardeau

Captain,
  Ray E. Seitz
Rgt. Sgt. Maj.,
  Jennings, Edward A.
Bn. Sgt. Maj.,
  Harrison, Robert D.
Bn. Sgt. Maj.,
  Rogers, James F.
Bt. Sgt. Maj.,
  McQueen, Frank T.
1st Sergeant,
  Harrison, Arthur W.
Color Sergeant,
  Howard, Harry W.
Sergeant,
  Schultz, Hina C., Jr.
Cook,
  Stack, Sylvester
Privates:
  Bell, Elmo J.
  Davison, Bert
  Esken, Orvil P.
  Goodin, William

Harris, James R.
Haydon, Robert D.
Henson, Wm. A.
Hicks, William A.
Hipsher, Otto
Hutchinson, Wylie
King, Clarence
Melton, Ira
Miller, Jesse Lee
Myers, Fred C.
Sellers, Floyd
Shirel, Thomas E.
Welch, Dean W.
Band Leader,
  Schuchert, Clarence E.
Asst. Band Leader,
  Lesem, Rurie L.
Sergeants:
  Danks, Thomas A.
  Foster, Ernest P.
Corporals:
  Hunter, Walter F.
  Kassel, Elmore W.

King, James E.
Patton, Leslie E.
1st Class Musicians:
  Danks, Harry E.
  Thrower, Arthur C.
2nd Class Musicians:
  Crews, Lester
  Foster, Moses F.
  Kempe, Walter F.
3d Class Musicians:
  Bentley, Albert E.
  Bledsoe, Carl P.
  Clayton, Ethelbert A., Jr.
  Danks, William H.
  Heyle, James R.
  Kaiser, Oscar C.
  Kassel, Clarence W.
  Laswell, Gustavus
  McBride, Earl R.
  Pott, Clarence E.
  Tibbs, Harry
  Wells, Ernest F.
  Wilson, William

THE MEN BEHIND THE GUNS

SUPPLY COMPANY
Seymore

Captain,
  Oliver Guy Jones
Rgt. Sup. Sgt.,
  Wilson, Vern R.
Rgt. Sup. Sgt.,
  Hamilton, David
Rgt. Sup. Sgt.,
  Dickison, William A.
1st Sergeant,
  Mankin, Dewey J.
Mess Sergeant,
  Coday, Walter C.
Stable Sergeant,
  Hoover, Frank D.
Corporal,
  Felin, Henry E.
Horseshoer,
  Carter, John A.

Saddler,
  Fyan, William H.
Cook,
  Mackey, Caleb M.
Wagoners:
  Aelem, Everett H.
  Briggs, Franklin O.
  Carrick, Raymond
  Carter, Garrett W.
  Claxton, Howard N.
  Cloud, Austin W.
  Craig, William C.
  Davis, Levis A.
  Denney, William W.
  Dougan, Ivy A.
  Dyche, Clarence M.
  Fisher, Roy A.
  Fletcher, George E.

George, Pleamon A.
Hailey, Joseph T.
Handy, Roy
Hicks, James H.
Humbyrd, Wm. C.
Kennedy, Geo. W.
Manning, Charley F.
Mingus, Ephraim L.
Morris, Roscoe E.
Norcross, Roy G.
Packard, Ernest A.
Potts, John J.
Richardson, Oscar E.
Roe, William J.
Spurlock, John E.
Tarbutton, Clyde
Tripp, Claude E.
Viles, Robert C.
Whittaker, Robert R.

MACHINE GUN COMPANY
Carterville

Captain,
  Vance R. Thralls
1st Lieutenant,
  Arch M. Baird
2d Lieutenant,
  Orie S. Imes
1st Sergeant,
  Newell, Harvey E.
Mess Sergeant,
  Steward, Louis G.
Supply Sergeant,
  Leathers, Robert W.
Stable Sergeant,
  Goldsberry, William O.
Sergeants:
  Bourne, Edgar J.
  Harlan, James E.
  Hutchinson, Jesse A.
  McCollum J. Bert
  Nelson, Frank C.
  True, Percy W.
  Wood, Charles B.
Corporals:
  Blanton, Henry H.
  DeClure, Archie F.
  Hill, Leonard E.
  Hill, Ray
  Pierce, Forest
  Smith, Edward
  Stokes, Ongole L.
  Wirth, Charles C.

Horseshoer,
  Plumley, Alexander
Mechanics:
  Smith, John Phillip
  Young, Ferol J.
Cooks:
  Darrah, Loyd E.
  Dixon, Arlan K.
Buglers:
  Horine, Sidney F.
  Sims, Rudy S.
Privates:
  Andrew, Hadaley J.
  Arthur, Henry
  Barnett, Lee D.
  Binning, Charles L.
  Bishop, Earl N.
  Bly, Joe D.
  Brown, Ralph L.
  Caughenbaugh, John C.
  Cobb, Luther W.
  Collier, Henry
  Cook, Al J.
  Crook, Thomas C.
  Daugherty, Jessie C.
  DeWitt, Lawrence
  Edgar, Sam H.
  Fultner, Philip
  Gabriel, Clarence O.
  Gordon, George H.
  Grigg, Otto H.

Griner, John H.
Harbin, John W.
Hawks, Leslie W.
Hayward, Orville C.
Killian, Maynard
Klein, Harold H.
McCloud, Claude D.
McCoy, Guy
McCoy, Jesse
McGuinn, William Francis
Manley, Edgar Bill
Mead, Harvey
Miller, Herbert F.
Montgomery, Clarence
Moore, Robert A.
Mote, Guy C.
Murphy, Charles L.
Nichols, John E.
Payne, Claud
Peacock, Vernon A.
Points, Frank E.
Price, John D.
Ropp, Chester Allen
Stephens, Roy A.
Whitley, Jack
Williams, Alonzo C.
Williams, Rolla B.
Wilson, Columbus
Yates, Vernie W.
Zeller, Charles L.

COMPANY A
Lexington

Captain,
  Ralph W. Campbell
1st Lieutenant,
  Harry W. Boardman
2nd Lieutenant,
  William Stonestreet
1st Sergeant,
  Nove, Willie M.
Supply Sergeant,
  Baker, Roy D.
Mess Sergeant,
  Howard, Robert J.
Sergeants:
  Haekker, Karl P.
  Bishop, Warner F.
  Erickson, John H.
  Mussatto, Joseph A.
  Amos, James R.
  Bear, James E.
Corporals:
  Frazier, J. Wilson
  Culley, Charles S.

Hawkins, William
Cross, Charles C.
Hammer, Oscar J.
Hammer, Karl F.
Howe, Joseph R.
Cullon, George T.
Galladay, Roscoe H.
Beisenherz, Edward L.
Fizer, Bennie C.
Mechanics:
  Petty, George W.
Cooks:
  Greer, Al
  Biggs, Rufus
Privates:
  Anderson, John P.
  Atteberry, Cecil H.
  Aytes, Elex L.
  Bailey, Hobart W.
  Benning, Major
  Benoist, Frank L.
  Bezing, Fritz

Book, Charles
Bowman, James
Brumfield, Roger
Clark, William L.
Collins, Edward H.
Cunningham, John C.
Darrah, Forest O.
Daugherty, Harvey M.
Douglas, John H.
Eagan, Emmett A.
Eaton, Clyde
Emery, Ormy
Fieldcamp, Dick C.
Foster, Arthur B.
Frazier, Willie L.
Geraughty, James
Gillibert, Louis C.
Gosoraski, Frank M.
Hall, Lee
Harney, Joseph F.
Head, William R.
Hill, Warren

FROM DONIPHAN TO VERDUN

Hollingsworth, Jay G.
Horn, Jesse
Huddleston, Joseph F.
Iles, Cecil R.
Jamison, James R.
Johnson, Ernest O.
Kincheloe, James P.
Kroencke, Emil L.
Legg, Arthur P.
Looney, Joseph
McClure, Clyde E.
McCormick, Myron,
McFadden, Clarence
McGraw, Aubrey
McLain, William G.
Masoni, John
Martin, Theodore
Morvel, Louis E. H.
Myers, Charles H.

Nelson, Dewey
O'Dell, Lee
Poe, Raymond
Potter, Wilfred, J.
Redd, William M.
Rider, Gilbert J.
Riley, John W.
Ross, Orvill
Rouse, Arvil F.
Rouse, George S.
Sec, Clarence D.
Smith, Ernest C.
Smith, Louis G.
Smith, Upton, B.
Smith, William L.
Stapleton, George W.
Stapleton, Walter,
Steffens, Leonard H.
Stephens, Frank T.

Taney, Daniel
Taney, Henry
Thomas, Charley H.
Thorson, Herbert W.
Tucker, Aubra L.
Vasques, Max
Verwork, Julius
Walton, Thomas
Wansing, Traut B.
Warder, John M.
Warren, Robert V.
Wiley, Otis L.
Willard, Andy J.
Willard, Paul J.
Williams, Carvin
Williams, Edward V.
Wolfenberger, Baxter
Wood, Elba
Young, Wm. W.

COMPANY B
St. Joseph

Captain,
  James E. Weis
1st Lieutenant,
  Oscar L. Harper
2nd Lieutenant,
  Edward S. Garner, Jr.
1st Sergeant,
  Weir, Will J.
Supply, Sergeant,
  White, Robert E.
Mess Sergeant,
  Leighty, Harold H.
Sergeants:
  Abbott, James B.
  Charlesworth, Earl A.
  Masteller, Emory L.
  Robinson, Edwin B.
  Miles, Ivel E.
  Junken, William H.
  Wilson, Dolph
  Messenger, Webb
Corporals:
  White, Lee
  Farkas, Adam
  Tracy, Edward
  Prater, Thomas
  Sparks, Clifford W.
  Harper, Ralph
  Chestnut, Kirby
  Lollis, Oscar
  Wyant, Warren R.
  Jones, Oscar
  Williams, Harry
  McLean, Earl
  Brunswig, Philip H.
  Lacy, George T.
  Waugh, Oren
  Paden, William C.
  Masteller, Harvey E.
  Porter, Edward C.
  Yeakley, Grover E.
Buglers:
  Malotte, John
  Robinson, Wayne H.
Cooks:
  Pratt, Hiram
  Tracy, William
  Culver, Fordys
Mechanics,
  Hovey, James A.
  Williams, Harry
Privates:
  Alberts, Samuel
  Aldrich, Charles M.
  Ball, Howard S.

Banister, Earl F.
Blackwell, Dick
Blotz, Thomas
Bowen, Alvin
Bowen, Charles D.
Brown, Bert
Brown, Gene M.
Caton, H. P.
Chilton, Paul J.
Clark, Ray
Cook, Walter
Cozine, Alvin
Cozine, Roy
Cramer, Clarence E.
Crandall, Earl
Crose, Albert
Dean, John B.
Decker, Daniel K.
Decker, George E.
Dennis, Bert
Devine, William H.
Dittemore, Aubrey C.
Downs, Roner
Dugger, Ross
Durkin, Joseph W.
Ecton, Frank C.
Ellis, Charles E.
Fixek, John
Fouts, Fred
Fry, Francis W.
Fuhrer, Roy
Gallagher, John P.
Gentzell, Robert
German, Earl
Gibson, Jake
Griffith, Earl N.
Griffiths, Lester
Gore, Ilda
Groves, Edward
Hackney, Perry S.
Haeberle, Harry G.
Hale, Frank L.
Haney, William H.
Hardman, Charles H.
Harrison, Robert
Hinkle, Lyman J.
Hallowell, Frank
Huston, Richard
Hubbard, Robert E.
Jenkins, Henry
Jones, Charles A.
King, William T.
Kirtley, Arthur
Lacy, George T.
Lawhon, Edward F.

Lear, Albert O.
Leighty, Edward L.
LeRoy, Frank
Lewis, Fred
Lewis, Marvin
McClintock, Lloyd H.
McKee, Phillip C.
McLean, Earl
Miles, George T.
Miller, Clinton
Miller, Joseph W.
Miller, Robert
Moore, LeRoy
Morlock, Orenza
Morris, Garlin J.
Munden, Lewis E.
Myers, Fred W.
Neff, Louis J.
Osborn, Earl
Parker, William A.
Patrick, Lloyd
Patton, Ora
Phillbrick, Lawrence W.
Pontius, Arthur C.
Reeves, Walter A.
Roberts, Coin
Roberts, Ernest K.
Ross, James
Scheinert Jesse J.
Shatto, William
Smart, Howard A.
Smith, Alba
Smith, Thane B.
Sparks, Arley
Stark, Charley O.
Stephenson, William
Stockton, Hugh S.
Stout, Orval V.
Tanksley, Thomas
Thompson, Henley D.
Thompson, John
Totten, Ivan R.
Tracy, Clyde
Tracy, Louis C.
View, Clarence
Walsh, John E.
White, Lemuel
Whittington, Jesse
Wright, Elmo N.
Wright, Harry
Yeakley, Hobart
Yeakley, Robert H.

THE MEN BEHIND THE GUNS

COMPANY C
St. Joseph

Captain,
 William P. St. John
1st Lieutenant,
 Guido, L. Schaff
2nd Lieutenant,
 Frank F. Tracy
1st Sergeant,
 Kuehl, Frederick C.
Supply Seargeant,
 DeGrost, Fred E.
Mess Sergeant,
 Schmille, Henry F.
Sergeants:
 Bruegger, Emil G.
 Compton, Cecil C.
 Dovey, John
 Funson, Harry J.
 Hindman, Justus
 Gillespie, William R.
 Showers, George W.
 Stephens, Raymond A.
Corporals:
 Bell, Earl T.
 Compton, Morris G.
 Cooley, William W.
 Courtney, Frank E.
 Flynn, Richard T.
 Geyer, George D.
 Guthrie, William W.
 Harris, James A.
 Marstella, Fred S.
 Morgan, Eddie A.
 Morris, Glen B.
 Schatzman, Aubrey M.
 Steele, Paul
 Wagner, Frank F.
 Weaver, Ralph P.
Cooks:
 Dolan, Joseph P.
 Sparks, Louis J.
 Thomas, Robert
Buglers:
 Blackford, Galvin
 Reid, Glen B.
Mechanic:
 Hertzel, Peter
Privates:
 Alvis, Reuben A.
 Amend, Bryan
 Anderson, Samuel A.

Arnett, Wilson H.
Arnold, Earl
Barkley, Sidney J.
Baubits, Ross
Bauman, Dewey
Blackford, Louis S.
Blaga, Joseph
Boyle, Frank J.
Brigham, Robert
Cain, Clarence L.
Calhoon, Charles B.
Conner, Roy
Courtney, Wilbert M.
Craig, James R.
Curtin, Tom John
Cuzzort, Harry D.
Davis, Jobe
Davis, Louis B.
Davis, Milo
Davis, William Bohn
Dawson, William E.
Detweiler, Ira
Dowell, Roy B.
Dowell, Sanford. J.
Drake, William N.
Dukes, Le Roy A.
Durham, Henry P.
Ellis, Harry E.
Elson, Fred R.
Evans, Claude C.
Fitzpatrick, Glen
Fleshman, Samuel F.
Flowers, Grover
 Cleveland
Fritz, Mike
Fuson, John O.
Gay, Murril, K.
Gibson, Benjamin
Gomel, Frank
Goodman, Frank C.
Gossin, George D.
Green, Albert
Green, Frank
Hainline, Wallace
Hall, Cecil J.
Harris, Lester L.
Hartman, Lee H.
Hartnett, James L.
Haynes, Oscar
Hinkle, Ray S.

Howard, Fred
 McKinley
Hunt, William
Imus, Wayman H.
Jensen, William P.
Jones, George E.
Julian, Wesley H.
Katon, Thomas F.
Kelley, Earl H.
Kelley, James A.
Kendrick, Timothy P.
Keyser, Edward A.
Kienzel, John W.
King, F. Cecil
King, Roy E.
Kneer, Clark W.
Kuhn, Alvin L.
Larson, Harry E.
Leavitt, Dewey V.
Leffler, Perry C.
Lowrie, William
McBrayer, Arthur O.
McCall, Thomas M.
McCoy, Gilbert G.
Mallory, Lee
Marrs, John H.
Merritt, Jere E.
Miles, James A.
Miller, James M.
Nave, Fred W.
Nowland, George
Padgett, Ivel V.
Palmer, Elmer H.
Payne, John H.
Peterson, Delmar Ray
Rader, George
Riordan, Michael
Seip, Martin L.
Sheffer, Charles
Smith, Elmer
Sollars, Thomas
Stephenson, Edward
Strange, Roy C.
Tracy, Ralph E.
Trant, Philip G.
Tucker, Arthur
Walker, Vessie
Wampler, Clarence E.
Whitten, James J.
Wilson, Rolph H.
Wiseman, Basie F.

COMPANY D
Sedalia

Captain,
 Harry B. Scott
1st Lieutenant,
 Harry O. Berry
2nd Lieutenant
 Joseph H. Sallisbury
1st Sergeant,
 Dunnica, John Leon
Mess Sergeant,
 Martin, Oran Alonzo
Supply Sergeant,
 Scott, Lionel J.
Sergeants:
 Triplet, William S.
 Richter, Julius J.
 Rissler, Charles
  Gordon
 Herndon, George B.
 Baldwin, William V.
 Knox, Lloyd V.
Corporals:
 Porter, John C.
 Dowd, Lee Mack
 Lowrey, William H.

Lamm, Gordon
Maness, Henry M.
Hampy, Ernest E.
Adair, Rabon
Holsenpiller, James F.
Burke, John C.
Heisterberg Edward J.
Barnett, Robert L.
Rendleman, Benjamin
 L.
Mechanic,
 Durham, Henry F.
Cook,
 Meager, Leo James
Bugler,
 Rayhill, Finis Edward
Privates
Anderson, Luther C.
Anderson, William H.
Bass, Alva
Bond Fred Arthur
Bryant, Ellis C.
Canaday, Charles Max
Carlock, LeRoy

Cooper, Henry Ray
Croy, Harold B.
Cunningham, Henry D.
Davis, Earl H.
Dickerson, William
 Joseph
Douglas, Norman H.
Duyett, John R.
Engler, Marshall H.
Enos, Don M.
Enos, Loran D.
Falknor, Carl C.
Fletcher, William H.
Franklin, Joseph D.
Friend, Frank W.
Fullerton, Forrest T.
Garner, Charles C.
Garrett, Walter C.
Glass, James W.
Glazebrook, James G.
Gupton, Carl W.
Hamm, William M.
Harris Jacob Jefferson
Harris, William J.

Hayes, William Allen
Henderson, John Samuel
Heuitt, Calep
Hunt, Lester E.
Jackson, John
Jocoy, Charles William
Johnston, Herbert E.
Lane, John H.
Lawson, Ace Levi
Lawson, Edmon Russell
Leftwich, James W.
Lewis, Frank E.
Lewis, William O.
Lipscomb, Arthur E.
Longan, Layton L.
McCullough, James T.
Manley, James M.
March, Thomas B.
Marcum, Willie
Mathews, Walter I.
Meagher, Leo J.

Miller, Clyde James
Mills, John Wesley
Monroe, Emmett, H.
Moore, Zacharias
Mullineaux, Joseph A.
Mullins, Harry R.
Mullins, Hayden G.
Myrick, John H.
Owen, James F.
Palmer, Charles H.
Palmer, Wiley S.
Penland, William A.
Phillips, William H.
Pursley, Thomas S.
Quick, Eve.ett Litton
Riggs, Oscar B.
Robinson, Carter A.
Robinson, Clarence V.
Robinson, George A.
Robinson, Homer D.
Robinson, William L.
Rofle, Sidney R.

Sands, Henry C.
Scott, Alva
Scott, Genne
Scott, Walter
Siebert, Leo M.
Simmers, Henry N.
Simmers, Robert E.
Sisk, Albo H.
Speer, Brent
Speer, Ezra E.
Stephens, Charles Oliver
Tuttle, Cecil L.
Washburn, Seth W.
Weathers, Russell Olive
Welch, George W.
Weston, Harry B.
Wilson, Arthur C.
Witte, Gus E.
Wilford, George F.
Wood, DeWitt

COMPANY E
Doniphan

Captain,
  Henry E. Braschler
1st Lieutenant,
  David M. Robertson
2nd Lieutenant,
  Howard C. Lane
1st Sergeant,
  Lewis, Samuel A.
Supply Sergeant,
  Odom, Edley R.
Mess Sergeant,
  Milliams, Lat M.
Sergeants:
  Pope, Robert D.
  Paul, John B.
  King, Lewis A.
  Keith, Hudson A.
  Dunn, Michael
  Hope, Anderson M.
Corporals,
  Boster, Chester A.
  Bond, Edgar
  Corckran, Joe
  Casteel, Harve
  Easter, Joe T.
  Hancock, John M.
  Hope, Charlie
  McKinney, Frank
  Napier, Charles L.
  Ponder, Arthur R.
  Sanders, James L.
  Wall, Herbert M.
Cooks:
  Camp, Joseph
  Blyze, Joseph H.
Buglers:
  Richmond, Fred C.
  Ponder, Arno L.
Privates:
  Ashhcroft, Robert L.
  Belcher, Ebenezer E
  Bevans, George R.
  Bolin, Bennie E.

Boxx, Walter W.
Brakefield, Lee
Brown, Albert A.
Bryant, James W.
Bumbardner, Jacob
Cavens, Herman L.
Coleman, Ralph L.
Crowe, Ed A.
Davis, Claude A.
Davis, Harry
Dawson, Francis M.
Desich, Emery
Dixon, Kenneth S.
Dixon, Leonard L.
Dizmang, Roy L.
Donley, Monroe L.
Duncan, James M.
Dunigan, Lee R.
Dunigan, McKinley
Few, Walter E.
Garrett, Solomon M.
Gibson, Charles R.
Gibson, Homer
Gray, Arthur B.
Greer, Leonard D.
Hancock, Aaron S.
Harder, Claude A.
Harris, James A.
Helvey, Frank
Hill, Elmer, E.
Hillard, Doniphan
Hines, Sheridan
Holt, Orbra V.
Hopkins, James S.
Inman, Lewis F.
Lawhon, Cal. M.
Lawhon, Frank
Leraux, John N.
Logan, John W.
Lokey, William M.
Long, Elijah R.
Lorey, James M.
McDowell, William J.
McGee, Samuel D.
McKinney, Noah

McKinney, Orason A.
McQuay, Aldris, D.
McWilliams, Lewis M.
Maberry, Olvert
Martin, Thomas J.
Mesaros, Frank
Miller, Lewis
Mills, Jesse R.
Mounce, Charlie S.
Naesa, Louis
Naylor, Raymond C.
Novock, Earl
Nowak, Adam
Perry, Harry O.
Peters, William Lawrence
Pitman, Roe E.
Ponder, Chester H.
Ponder, Hubert L.
Ponder, William F.
Rackley, Mack
Reed, Oscar
Shoat, James C.
Smelser, Clarence S.
Starkey, Sidney M.
Stucker, Walter L.
Sullivan, Silvester
Swofford, Albert
Taylor, William E.
Thomas, Jacob
Towner, William A.
Trotter, Elias Wier
Tyra, Joseph R.
Wakefield, Thomas G.
Wardlow, Dauca Roy
West, Herman R.
West, Jim L.
West, Lionel M.
Whitehead, Frank W.
Whitewell, Herman B.
Williams, Robert E.
Wilson, Archie A.
Wright, Andy R.
Young, Chester A.

COMPANY F
Willow Springs

Captain,
  We'ter W. Durnell
1st Lieutenant
  Jo. C. Ferguson
2nd Lieutenant,
  Richard H. Stogsdill
Sergeants:
  Fleming, Harry H.

Gray, Charles A.
Oldfather, William J.
Holloway, Guy M.
Haycraft, Philip E.
German, Harold F.
Brauner, Clark E.
Caylor, Leonard C.
Vollmar, John L.

Corporals:
Smith, Heard C.
Patterson, Homer
Holloway, Clyde
Thomas, Archie I.
Drymon, Floyd
Phillips, James L.
Marcellus, Mahlon G.

THE MEN BEHIND THE GUNS   255

Hengel, Frederick B.
Bradshaw, Walter
Winch, Raymond
James Elum O.
Mechanic,
 Gartin, Alva
Cooks:
 Whetistine, Lewis L.
 Anderson Thomas A.
Buglers:
 Lane, Thomas H.
 Ruby, Eric S.
Privates:
Abbott, Ollie E.
Anderson, Chester
Anglin, Ernest L.
Baldwin, Everett W.
Beck, Clyde O.
Belshe, Lawrence L.
Booher, Benjamin F.
Bradford, George T.
Bridge, Louis R.
Brown, Willie H.
Browning, Merl R.
Caulder, John H.
Chaney, Walter J.
Crisco, Herbert P.
Collins, Ben C.
Cooper, Silas, W.
Cox, John M.
Cox, Noah E.
Crain, William J.
Cunningham, Hugh R.
Dermon, John M.
Dirk, Henry E.

Dove, Fred E.
Duckworth, Joseph W.
Ferrell, Clifford E.
Findley, Benjamin C.
Floyd, Samuel D.
Frank, Napoleon R.
Gentry, John M.
Goddard, Nathan J.
Hall, Weaver
Hengel, Carl J.
Herndon, Joseph F.
Higginbotham, Herman H.
Hill, Bob
Holden, George F.
Holt, Delbert, E.
Holt, Willie E.
Johnson, Frank W.
Laws, Orval G.
Lease, Martin L.
Lewis, Clive A.
Linderer, Charley
Lingle, Walter S.
Loch, William A.
McClanahan, Tobe
McClellan, Ralph K.
McGowan, Jasper C.
Means, John C.
Miller, William F.
Moody, Harry L.
Murrell, McF.
Muxlow, Glenn D.
Myers, Roy J.
Noblitt, Thomas E.
Norris, Cecil L.

Oliver, John H.
Orr, James R.
Pennington, Wm. A.
Pennington, Wm. D.
Plemmons, Charles E.
Rader, John H.
Rader, Lee
Reed, John O.
Reed, Orval O.
Rogers, Wallace J.
Rothgeb, Leland S.
Rust, Arch F.
Sanders, Lou W.
Shannon, William E.
Shelton, Charley
Skyles, George W.
Smith, Irvin,
Smith, Lloyd L.
Smith, Mack J.
Stewart, Jasper L.
Stewart, William H.
Stogsdill, Franklin W.
Taff, Odis H.
Taylor, Ira B.
Taylor, Warren, W.
Thomas William A.
Waggoner, Edgar F.
Weatherman, Elmer B.
West, Virgle
Whittaker, Ray
Wiles, Claudie E.
Willoughby, Thomas B.
Winch, Everett

COMPANY G
Richmond

Captain,
 Jacob L. Milligan
1st Lieutenant,
 Robert Kirk Brady
2nd Lieutenant
 Cecil M. Farris
1st Sergeant.
 Littman, Arthur
Mess Sergeant,
 Tarwater, Roy E.
Supply Sergeant,
 Wilkinson, John L.
Sergeants:
 Davis, Gerald H.
 Sisk, Forest O.
 Hughes, Howard Roy
 Weber, Ivan
 Saunders, Wade H.
Corporals:
 Pifer, Ray L.
 Ward, Edward
 Brown, Gerald B.
 Farmer, McKinley
 Sexton, Charles A.
 Kraft, Moses,
 Hutchinson, Robert L.
 Bryce, James
 Rogers, Ernest
 Roark, Harry E.
 Brown, William E.
Cooks:
 Ward, Flem C.
 Vandiver, Jesse
Mechanic,
 Cates, Jesse L.
Buglers:
 Cook, Myrel J.
 Van Horn, Robert G.

Privates:
Abbott, Albert W.
Anderson, Charlie
Baker, Claytin
Bales, Cleveland A.
Belle, George
Blann, Lawrence R.
Bowman, Roscoe
Brady, Elvie W.
Brockman, Guthrie
Burnett, Clyde
Burnett, Oscar P.
Cheek, Middleton. A.
Coleman, Virgil
Cook, Ralph H.
Couch, Robert T.
Covey, Clyde E.
Craven, Carl V.
Dale, Ernest
Dennis, Charles J.
Dickey, Ward S.
Dixon, John
Elliott, Ast D.
Everett, Noah H.
Foster, Frank H.
Gardner, Lloyd G.
Gibson, Phil S.
Gorman, Sanford B.
Griffith, Fred
Hamil, William F.
Hannah, Charley
Henderson, Floyd H.
Hicks, Tillman
Highwater, Raymond
Hill, Roscoe C.
Jones, Harry S.
Keith, Glenn. A.
Liles, Oscar P.
Lochard, Ernest M.

Loyd, James I.
Luellen, William W.
Maples, John F.
Mayabb, Orba M.
Michael, Garrie E.
Middleton, Charles L.
Miller, Leonard R.
Mooney, George
Moyer, Allen B.
Mulliken, Elmer
Odell, Jack
O'Neal, William A.
Phelps, George H., Jr.
Price, Thomas C.
Prunty, James A.
Reed, Clarence S.
Richards, Henry E.
Richardson, Thomas
Rider, Earl
Sampson, Harold A.
Seaton, Virgil D.
Sidener, Henry F.
Slaughter, Grover F.
Snowden, Henry A.
Spence, George J.
Stevens, Fred
Stevens, Walter
Stigall, John W.
Swearingen, John H.
Swearengen, Leonard L.
Teal, Walter
Teagarden, James M.
Thompson, Noah K. T.
Thompson, Ralph J.
Thompson, Richard
Vanhoozer, Cecil N.
Yoakum, Claud
Yoakum, Joseph

COMPANY H
Dexter

Captain,
  James C. Kenady
1st Lieutenant,
  Claude M. Skelton
2nd Lieutenant,
  Clarence G. Smith
1st Sergeant,
  Ellis, James D.
Mess Sergeant,
  Dunn, Harry
Supply Sergeant,
  Smith, Earl B.
Sergeants:
  Dunn, Joel E.
  Julian, John T.
  Munger, Paul M.
  Roper, Henry E.
Corporals:
  Brown, Ernest
  Buchannan, Glyn
  Burrow, Arthur P.
  Cox, Meredith
  Day, Cecil L.
  Fowler, John H.
  Harris, Jesse T.
  Hicks, Herbert
  Lane, James T.
  Lasater, Thomas J.
  McGehee, Theodore
  Oliver, Clarence P.
  Singleton, James S.
  Wallace, Henry
  Wantland, R. Orley
  Womack, Walter M.
Cooks:
  Driskell, Robert H.
  Kilmer, Elvin E.
Buglers:
  Brooks, Earl C.
  Hooker, Henry Otis
Mechanics:
  Teel, John F.
  Turner, James R.
Privates
  Adams, Henry A.
  Allen, Lewdorth E.
  Anderson, Roy
  Ashcraft, Zibo G.
  Ashworth, Ben L.
  Bailey, Ralph D.
  Bedwell, Samuel M.
  Blocker, James M.
  Bolin, John A.
  Bollinger, Jesse M.
  Brannock, Bert
  Brown, Floyd P.
  Brown, Lewis S.
  Caldwell, Lou S.
  Caldwell, Luther R.
  Carlton, Ora
  Carwile, James C.
  Chasteen, Otto
  Charman, Richard C.
  Clevenger, Evert
  Davis, Amos
  Davis, John O.
  Dickerson, Arthur L.
  Dickerson, Jesse L.
  Dillion, R. Thomas
  Dodd, Frank
  Doyle, Thomas C.
  Dunning, James M.
  Edwards, Herrel
  Elliott, Edgar G.
  Ford, James C.
  Foreman, Glenn J.
  Gaines, Benjamin L.
  Garrison, John
  Gray, Bub
  Hahn, Charlie
  Hanks, Claude
  Harper, William E.
  Harris, Fred B.
  Harris, George W.
  Hartley, Clinton N.
  Hezlip, Robert A.
  Hefner, Fred
  Hill, Lawrence E.
  Hisan, Elmer
  Holland, John J.
  Hopkins, Ezra
  Horton, Jackson
  Howell, Homer
  Hurst, Floyd J.
  Hurst, William A.
  Hutson, Harry
  Irons, Jack
  James, Charles L.
  Jett, Everett.
  Jones, James A.
  Jones, John R.
  Jones, Stanley
  Jones, Thomas A.
  Joseph, Oliver
  Julian, Elbert A.
  Kagle, William W.
  Keaton, Charles H.
  Keaton, James S.
  Keen, Charles G.
  King, Henry W.
  King, James A.
  Kirby, Charles D.
  Lindsey, Mont O.
  Little, Andrew J.
  McAllister, Harry
  McDowell, Benjamin
  McFarlan, Walter
  McGehee, Gilbert
  McGhee, Cecil
  McGuire, Charles V.
  Marley, Perry
  Martin, Jesse
  Mathney, Gardiner
  Mayberry, Robert
  Meeks, Cletis W.
  Miller, Rufus
  Milner, Bernice
  Montgomery, Clarence L.
  Oglevie, George
  Peavey, Curtis
  Pryor, Alvin L.
  Ramsey, John
  Reagan, James B.
  Riley, Claude
  Roberts, Earl P.
  Sadler, Arthur Wm.
  Sadler, Monroe C.
  Shelby, Homer T.
  Shetterly, Benjamin E.
  Shoemaker, James T.
  Stalion, Marcus
  Strop, Audi J.
  Sylcox, William M.
  Tatum, George
  Thackston, Curtis
  Thorn, Charles H.
  Tippen, Roy E.
  Tracer, Roy
  Turner, Claude B.
  Walker, Oscar
  White, Marshall
  Whitney, Alza N.
  Wilkie, Millard F.
  Wolff, Robert H.
  Woolard, Earl
  Yates, George W.

COMPANY I
Kennett

Captain,
  Fred Ordway Wickham
1st Lieutenant,
  Samuel T. Adams
2nd Lieutenant,
  Ernest A. Shirley
1st Sergeant,
  Lowe, James H.
Supply Sergeant,
  Niersheimer, John E.
Sergeants:
  Trout, George W.
  Smith, Roy C.
  Kersey, Bronie
  Hall, Robert S.
  Mead, Charles
Corporals:
  McGuire, Albert
  Benson, Hilbert E.
  Evans, Fred S.
  Sparks, James Ralph
  Husband, Lesley
  Hollis, Ivy D.
  Eatman, John
  Webb, Dock T.
  Snipes, Joseph Talbert
  Riley, Earl
  Pierce, Arch F.
Buglers:
  Lewis, Loomis
  Pool, James A.
Mechanic,
  Stewart, William J.
Cooks:
  Presnell, Avery
  Ayers, Elbert H.
  McAnally, John F.
Privates:
  Adams, Andrew Jackson
  Ball, Ira
  Ball, Ollie
  Beck, James W.
  Best, Will
  Bishop, Odie F.
  Black, Ermur
  Boner, Edward
  Boner, Edward
  Brewsbaugh, Edwin O.
  Browser, Fred
  Burris, Orvil
  Cagle, James C.
  Carlile, Franklin Joseph
  Clubb, Grover
  Clubb, John
  Crim, Arthur Mack
  Culberton, Marion V.
  Darlington, Willie L.
  Denam, Harvey E.
  Dudley, Jesse
  Dunnivan, Cecil
  Eadon, Herbert
  Elliott, Dolph G.
  Forsythe, Walter
  Frederick, David C.
  Frederick, Samuel R.
  Gabriel William Elmer
  Green, Beauford
  Hall, John F.
  Hanks, Ackland, Jr.

THE MEN BEHIND THE GUNS

Hanks, Jacob
Hartsoe, Otho
Hatcher, William Howard
Hicklin, Lee E.
Holbrooks, Henry H.
Jackson, Isaac
Jackson, Watson
Jones, Albert C.
Kersey, Vernon
Killian, Charles H.
King, Albert F.
King, Ed
Knight, Cecil Andrew
Lemonds, Luther A.

Mangold, Thomas O.
Masters, Jacob C.
Mead, Alva L.
Mizzell, Emerson
Mullins, Clarence
Neill, John A.
Nichols, Orvill
Noe, Erie
O'Bryant, James
Oller, John W.
Owens, John W.
Peel, John R.
Perkins, Abraham
Pickett, Lin
Ray, Guy B.

Reese, Verhan
Sackman, Leonard
Shelton, Ernest A.
Smith, Leamon
Somer, Raymond
Stamps, Samuel S.
Starns, Alfred
Suratt, Oscar
Taruce, James
Tharp, Roy E.
Tharp, William
Walker, Pearl
Walker, Prentice Nuten
White, Dewey F.
Williams, Baxter

COMPANY K
Sikeston

Captain,
  Charles L. Malone
1st Lieutenant
  Seth T. Reeder
2nd Lieutenant,
  William R. Malone
1st Sergeant,
  Richardson, Albert
Mess Sergeant,
  Malone, John R.
Sergeants,
  Bryant, Ray
  Ginger, Virgil
  Greenwell, Alva R.
  Caldwell, Elmo
  Milhorn, Ed
  Gill, Glover
  Lawson, Harry E.
Corporals:
  Wilkey, Wilburn R.
  Norris, Wallace
  Payne, Eli
  Blyalock, Will
  Byan, Therman
  Fowler, Edgar T.
  McCormick, Jim H.
  Marshall, Arthur
  Simpson, William F.
Cooks:
  Marteau, Vivian
  Venerable, Luther James
Privates:
  Armstrong, Will
  Arnold Herbert
  Arnold, Louis
  Bacon, William

Bailey, Van
Barnett, Charles J.
Beal, Eugene
Blake, Ray
Branch, Arthur
Brooks, Charles H.
Browning, Claude
Bruner, James
Cooley, Harry
Cora, Claiborn
Crosby, Mason
Davis, John B.
Dillard, Johnson H.
Dillon, Clarence
Dobbs, Albert
Dobbs, Henry
Duncan, Frank C.
Edwards, Arlie
English, Thomas J.
Etheridge, Harry
Gill, Elmer
Glover, Ale
Goodwin, Bill
Greer, Alfred
Greer, Robert
Haggard, William C.
Hampton, Homer
Harbison, Everett
Harbison, Norman
Harp, Alber
Henly, Otis,
Hobbs, Ules
Hogan, Sam
Hoover, Frank
Howard, Earl
Hummel, John H.
Hunt, Albert R.

Hunt, Irwin R.
James, Farris
Jones, Ira
Knupp, Charles W.
Laster, James
Lenon, Otto
Lofton, Boyd
Loucks, Ben
Lowry, George
McCormick, Marshall
McLard, Laurence E.
Mainard, Charles A.
Mainard, Nood
Modglin, Lyndolph W.
Monroe, Herschel
Nicols, Dewey
Odell, Raymond
O'Sullivan, Allen
Pack, Herbert M.
Potter, Curtis,
Potts, William
Pullman, Franklie L. L.
Reynolds, Lester
Robertson, Fred R.
Roper, Joseph
Stephens, Joseph L.
Talcott, Frank
Tidwell, Elbert B.
Timmons, Jesse
Toler, Claud T.
Vick, Eliza
Vivrett, Lawrence
Walker, Orion
Wallace, Earl
Walters, Wilson
Watson, John W.
Weaver, James
Wilson, John

COMPANY L
Cape Girardeau

Captain,
  Wilson C. Bain
1st Lieutenant,
  Howard N. Frissell
2nd Lieutenant,
  Harry W. Gaines
1st Sergeant,
  Godart, James E.
Supply Sergeant,
  Rodgers, Cleveland G.
Mess Sergeant,
  Williams, William J.
Sergeants:
  Behymer, Benjamin F.
  Gibbs, Claibourne, R. Jr.
  Husserrer, Vincent
  Pride, Jack S.
  Stack, George W.
Corporals:
  Beckman, Robert L.
  Blattner, Charles F., Jr.

Gaines, Norman I.
Halter, Albert L.
Hayes, John E.
Hensley, George C.
Killough, Josephus J.
Nichol, Arthur P.
Summers, George C.
Wilson, Landon R.
Cooks:
  Henley, Charles F.
  Smith, Sylvester V.
Buglers:
  Kimmich, Robert
  Nevins, Lynn W.
Mechanics:
  Estes, Roland
  Althenthal, Clarence G.
Privates:
  Baldwin, Angus F.
  Baum, George D.
  Bell, King
  Boon, Lemmie

Bowman, James T.
Brown John L.
Campbell, William
Caraker, Horace
Chappius, Pierre L.
Clifford, Courtney
Cobb, Willie R.
Coleman, James M.
Copen, Lum
David, Moritz
Davidson, Wilton W.
Davis, John
Davis, Otto J.
Demon, Roy M.
Dillingham, James M.
Eades, Fred
Endicott, Roma
Fornes, Benjamin B.
Funk, Walter C.
Geisner, Leo G.
Gerecke, Alvin W.
Glass, Walter
Glastetter, Martin

Hager, Frank
Hager, Harry H.
Henley, Archie
Hensley, James R.
Hitt, Lawrence A.
Hohler, Otto
Hohrer, William H.
Hopper, Raymond A.
Howard, George D.
Howard, Jesse
Hutchins, Roy L.
Hutchinson, Charles F.
Jackson, Lawrence C.
Joernes, Clark A.
Jones, Dephonie
Jones, James P.
Jordan, Raymond
King, Roy
Koch, Joseph F.

Koch, Raymond
Long, James H.
McClellan, Jesse
McCormack, Thomas
McCormick, Edd
McCormick, Walter
Messmer, Albert
Meyers, Clarence R.
Morse, William
Newlin, Lyles E.
Nolan, Roy S.
Oxford, William E.
Prance, Joseph W.
Puchbauer, Arthur
Rasico, Paul E.
Revelle, James
Rodgers, Harper H.
Rothrock, John C.
Smith, Arthur

Smith, George M.
Smith, Henry C.
Smith, Oscar
Smith, Shelby C.
Stedham, William H.
Sullivan, Marion
Sullivan, Samuel E.
Sutton, Charles D.
Sutton, John F.
Tarr, Joseph F.
Waldron, Charles
Walker, Birdie R.
Wallace, Guy E.
Walton, Carvel, H.
Walton, Malcomb R.
Weimer, Harold
Williams, Curtis
Witzed, Herman

COMPANY M
Poplar Bluff

Captain,
  Grant Davidson
1st Lieutenant,
  Henry E. Black
2nd Lieutenant,
  Frank M. Cox
1st Sergeant,
  Rafferty, George F.
Supply Sergeant,
  Sutton, Walter Baird
Mess Sergeant,
  Moore, Arthur W.
Sergeants:
  Adams, Roscoe G.
  Branch, Richard E.
  Ferguson, Harry
  Meadows, John T.
  Prestage, Norman A.
  Raulston, Athel A.
  Tyner, George
Corporals:
  Campbell, Earle
  Carpenter, David
  Clark, Columbus R.
  Gunzel, Otto C.
  Harrison, Harry C.
  Kearby, Robert
  Kern, O. Oscar
  Malone, Charles
  Maynard, Dewey
  Miller, Charles
  Oswald, Claude
  Overton, Charles
  Parce, Oscar, L.
  Shaw, Lee
  Taylor, Roy L.
  Worley, Cleburn J.
  Yocum, Alan
Cooks:
  Angelo, Liverain
  Purrine, Hallie O.
Buglers:
  Henderson, Joseph M.
  Neff, Leol M.
Mechanic,
  Ettinger, William L.
Privates:
  Alexander, Barnie
  Allsman, Jerry
  Beard, Grover T.
  Black, Ellsworth
  Blazier, Clarence J.

Board, Curtis
Brantley, Felix J.
Britts, Ed J.
Burgin, Walter E.
Byrd, Alva
Carrol, James W.
Cates, James L.
Clark, Myrtle
Collier, Pearcey
Conley, Mike
Coonce, Lee Roy
Cown, Roy
Cudd, Willie
Darby, Fred W.
Davis, Earl
Davis, Golden
Dodson, Harvey E.
Dunning, Wayne G.
Eads, Lee
Edwards, Theo. R.
Erwin, Sherman W.
Ewing, William F.
Felkins, Earl
Fisher, Roy
Fowler, Jesse
Fowler, Roy E.
Gibbs, Edward
Gillin, Miles
Gillispie, Ola W.
Givens, Allen
Gower, William C.
Greer, Herbert
Guard, Hays
Harrington, Charles
Hays, James
Higginbotham Earl
Hixon, Edward
Hobbs, William J.
Howell, Charlie
Ivey, Albert H.
Ivey, Allen D.
Ivey, John L.
Ivey, Richard F.
Irvin, George
Jennings, Corwin B.
Jett, Delpha
Jones, John F.
Kell, James Owen
Kellums, John
Kellums, Nottley
Killian, Gilbert
Killian, Theodore R.

Lampston, John
Lankley, Charles J.
Lee, John
Lee, Richard F.
Loyd, Claude O.
McClintock, Claude
McIver, Lawrence
Macon, Clarence
Mast, John
Mauk, Claud
Mauk, Hiram
Mayberry, Claude
Melton, Charles
Melton, Jesse
Mitchell, Earl
Murry, Walter
Owens, Howell
Parker, Arthur
Parker, Harvey W.
Phenix, Carl E.
Piatt, Jilson S.
Pipkin, Sidney
Reasons, James Britton
Redwine, Thomas
Rice, Orb
Rickman, Foley
Riggens, Spencer
Riggs, Dude
Risinger, Ralph
Roark, Jesse
Rolland, Thurman
Rose, William R.
Ross, George A.
Scaggs, Lee Henry
Schnider, Lewis J.
Scott, Enoch
Sisk, William V.
Smith, Oliver P.
Sparman, William R,
Spencer, James
Summers, Ben H.
Thompson, Roy G.
Todd, Carl
Townsend, Jim
Walker, Roscoe
Waller, James E.
Webb, Henry
Wilburn, Oscar
Worley, Sam
York, Lenard

SANITARY DETACHMENT
West Plains

Major,
  Albert H. Thornburgh
1st Lieutenant,
  George W. Phipps

1st Lieutenant,
  Francis G. Bond
1st Lieutenant,
  Ford A. Barnes

1st Sergeant,
  Bohrer, Charles R.
Sergeants:
  Harlin, Amos R.

THE MEN BEHIND THE GUNS 259

Dowler, Harold C.
Woods, Wilson Otto
Privates:
Bacon, Amiel E.
Bates, Don Arthur
Cagle, Lewis B.
Claxton, Henry C.
Crider, Albert F.
Edwards, Harry O.
Edwards, Roy B.
Floyd, Henry Oglesby

Galloway, Clark S.
Grimmett, Alfred Benton
Groce, Dallas
Groce, Lawrence
Horniday, George E.
Howell, Joe R.
Ingold, Marion T.
Krause, J. Martin
Ludwig, Carl W.
Males, Earl

Messara, Thomas W.
Morse, J. Alpha
Payne, Elza
Pottle, Ralph L.
Prater, Floyd R.
Reed, Orr, M.
Robertson, Page D.
Boyle, John Leemon
Sinclair, Edward P.
Turner, Jessie L.
Washington, George S.
Williams, Webster W.

HONORS

DISTINGUISHED SERVICE CROSS

Major Murray Davis
Major Ernest W. Slusher
Lt. Samuel T. Adams
Pvt. Pearl D. Chartier Co. H.
Sgt. Clarence C. Dry Co. I

Pvt. Wayne R. Berry Co. B.
Capt. Harry S. Whitthorne C. L
Sgt. John L. Wilkinson Co. G
Sgt. John H. Mace Co. H
Lt. Col. Fred L. Lemmon

Pvt. Herld Smith Co. F

BELGIAN CROIX DE GUERRE

Pvt. Walter Teal Co. G

CITED IN ORDERS

Corp. Edward S. Fletcher Co. F
Corp. Paul Dancy Co. I
Sgt. Robert M. Farrar
Sgt. Herbert C. Gray Reg. Int.
Capt. George H. Simpson
Pvt. Monte Coulter Co. B
Corp. John G. Rehkugler Co. C
Pvt. Glen Fitzpatrick Co. C
Cgt. John Dowey
Corp. Julius C. Hinkefent
Pvt. Chris E. Dodson
Sgt. Albert E. Robinson Co. L
Sgt. John W. Keys Reg. Int.
Joe E. Hanna Co. I
Odra B. Haggard Co. I
Wm. J. Haley, Co. F
Corp. Victor J. Huerter Reg. Int.
Pvt. E. A. McCaferty Co. H
Capt. J. L. Milligan Co. G
Mess. Sgt. Guy C. .Rogers
Capt. Henry L. Rothman M. C.
Thomas B. Kelly Co. L
Capt. Harry W. Gaines
Lt. Wm. E. Scott.

Sgt. Claud N. Stein
Joseph M. Yadon
Pvt. Elza Hopkins Co. H
Pvt. Wilfred Speed Co. G
Pvt. Merritt M. Boswell Co. G
Pvt. Oliver Joseph Co. H
Capt. John W. Armour Co. A
Capt. Rolla B. Holt Co. I
Capt. .Ralph W. Campbell Co. D
Capt. R. K. Brady
Lt. C. M. Farris
Chaplain Evan A. Edwards
Chaplain J. Oliver Buswell
Chaplain William L. Hart (Knights of Columbus Chaplain)
Major Julius A. Redman
Corp. Fred C. Bernard

Lt. Wm. K. Nottingham, and Deis, Edgar and Samuel Fuqua, Killian, Walters, Williams, Barnes, Fenton, Morris, Streeper, Tippitt, Todd, Townsend, Turner, Vick, Waddle and Worley of Co. M.

www.ingramcontent.com/pod-product-compliance
Lightning Source LLC
Chambersburg PA
CBHW031346230426
43670CB00006B/454